CADOGAN
guides

Dana Facaros & Michael Pauls

LOMBARDY
MILAN & THE ITALIAN
LAKES

Introduction and Guide to the Guide	vii
The Best of Lombardy	xi
Travel	1
Practical A–Z	15
History	43
Art & Architecture, & Where to Find it	57
Topics	63
Milan	71
The Lombard Plain	107
The Italian Lakes	131
Architectural, Artistic and Historical Terms	223
Language	226
Chronology	243
Index	247

D1018647

Cadogan Books plc

London House, Parkgate Road, London SW11 4NQ, UK

Distributed in North America by The Globe Pequot Press
6 Business Park Road, PO Box 833, Old Saybrook,
Connecticut 06475–0833

Reprinted 1995

Design by Animage
Cover illustration by Povl Webb
Maps © Cadogan Guides, drawn by Thames Cartographic Ltd

Editing: Linda McQueen
Series Editors: Rachel Fielding and Vicki Ingle

Proofreading: Stephanie Maury and Linda McQueen
Indexing: Dorothy Frame
Production: Book Production Services

A catalogue record for this book is available from the British Library
Library of Congress Cataloguing and Publication data available
ISBN 0–94–7754–76–8

Output by Cooling Brown Ltd.
Printed and bound in Great Britain by Redwood Books on Jordan Opaque supplied by McNaughton Publishing Papers Ltd.

About the Authors

Dana Facaros and Michael Pauls have written 11 Cadogan Guides to Italy. For 3 years they and their two children lived in a tiny Umbrian village; now they have moved to an equally remote French village in the Lot. From here, the Cadogan France series is evolving.

Acknowledgements

The publishers would like to thank Horatio Monteverde for the illustrations, Horatio Monteverde and Kicca Tommasi at Animage for the design, Lindsay Hunt for her work on the practical information sections, the Italian State Tourist Board in London, Dorothy Frame for the index and Mike Adams, Maureen Dewick, Paul Hopgood and Donald Paton at Thames Cartographic for the maps.

Please help us to keep this guide up to date

We have done our best to ensure that the information in this guide is correct at the time of going to press. But places and facilities are constantly changing, and standards and prices in hotels and restaurants fluctuate. We would be delighted to receive any comments concerning existing entries or omissions.

All contributors will be acknowledged in the next edition, and will receive a copy of the Cadogan Guide of their choice.

Contents

| Introduction | vii | The Best of Lombardy | xii |
| Guide to the Guide | xii | | |

Travel 1–14

Getting There	2	Getting Around	8
By Air from the UK and Ireland	2	By Boat	9
By Air from the USA and Canada	3	By Train	9
By Rail	3	By Coach and Bus	11
By Road	4	By Car	11
Entry Formalities	5	Hiring a Car	13
Passports and Visas	5	By Taxi	14
Customs	5	Hitchhiking	14
Currency	5	By Motorcycle or Bicycle	14
Tour Operators and Special-interest Holidays	6		

Practical A–Z 15–42

Buying a House	16	Packing	28
Children	16	Photography	29
Climate and When to Go	17	Post Offices	29
Crime and Police Business	18	Shopping	30
Disabled Travellers	18	Sports and Activities	33
Embassies and Consulates	19	Telephones	35
Festivals	19	Time	36
Food and Drink	21	Toilets	36
Health and Emergencies	25	Tourist Offices	36
Maps and Publications	26	Weights and Measures	37
Money	26	Where to Stay	37
Opening Hours and National Holidays	27	Women Travellers	41

History

Quarrelsome Celts,
Imperialistic Romans 44
Height and Depths of Empire 44
Fairly Good Goths and
Really Nasty Lombards 45
Threshold of the Middle Ages 46
The Rise of the *Comune* 48
Guelphs and Ghibellines, and
the Renaissance 49
Three Grim Centuries of
Foreign Rule 50
From Napoleon to Italian
Unification 52
Lombardy Takes Off 53
Finally in the Driver's Seat:
Lombardy and Milan Today 54

Art & Architecture, &Where to Find it

Prehistoric and Roman 58
Early Middle Ages 58
Romanesque and
Late Medieval 58
Renaissance 59
Baroque 61
Neoclassicism and
Romanticism 62
20th Century 62

Topics

The Caffè of Italian
Enlightenment 64
Guelphs, Ghibellines and
Old Red Beard 65
The Best Fiddles in the World 66
Romans of the Lake 67
The Immortal Fool 68

Milan

History 74
Getting to and from Milan 78
Getting Around 80
Tourist Information 81
Piazza del Duomo 81
Brera and its Accademia 88
West of the Duomo 91
South of the Duomo 95
The Ticinese Quarter 96
The Navigli District 96
Sports and Activities 97
Where to Stay 97
Eating Out 100
Entertainment and Nightlife 102
Short Excursions from Milan 105

The Lombard Plain

107–30

Pavia	108	Around Cremona:	
Around Pavia:		Soncino and Crema	118
Lomello and Vigévano	113	Mantua	119
Cremona	113	Around Mantua	128

The Italian Lakes

131–222

Lake Orta and Domodossola	133	La Brianza	172
Lake Maggiore	141	Beyond Como:	
Stresa	143	the Valleys of Sondrio	173
Between Lakes Maggiore and Lugano	150	Bergamo	180
Lake Lugano	153	Lake Iseo and the Val Camonica	188
Lake Como	157	Brescia	195
The City of Como	159	Lake Garda	203
Lecco and its Lake	169	Sirmione	207

Architectural, Artistic and Historical Terms

223–5

Language

226–42

Chronology

243–6

Index

247–270

Maps

The Best of Lombardy and the Lakes	*inside front cover*
Lombardy and the Lakes	viii–ix
Milan	72–3
Mantua	121
Lakes Maggiore and Orta	134–5
Lakes Como and Lugano	154–5
Brescia	196
Lake Garda	204–5

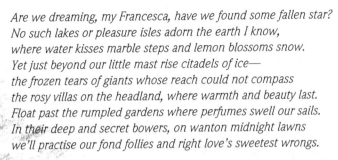

Are we dreaming, my Francesca, have we found some fallen star?
No such lakes or pleasure isles adorn the earth I know,
where water kisses marble steps and lemon blossoms snow.
Yet just beyond our little mast rise citadels of ice—
the frozen tears of giants whose reach could not compass
the rosy villas on the headland, where warmth and beauty last.
Float past the rumpled gardens where perfumes swell our sails.
In their deep and secret bowers, on wanton midnight lawns
we'll practise our fond follies and right love's sweetest wrongs.

Felix Binkley

Introduction

The Italian Lakes and the old art towns of Lombardy invite all kinds of indulgences. Linger on a lakeshore terrace in the evening, over a saffron risotto and a glass of Bardolino or Franciacorta, as landscapes that inspired the backgrounds of Leonardo's greatest paintings dissolve and the scents of jasmine and night flowers fill the air. Golden lights come to life along the shore as if fastening a fairy necklace around the water; little islands seem to hover in the twilight over the glassy surface before melting into the total silhouette of night.

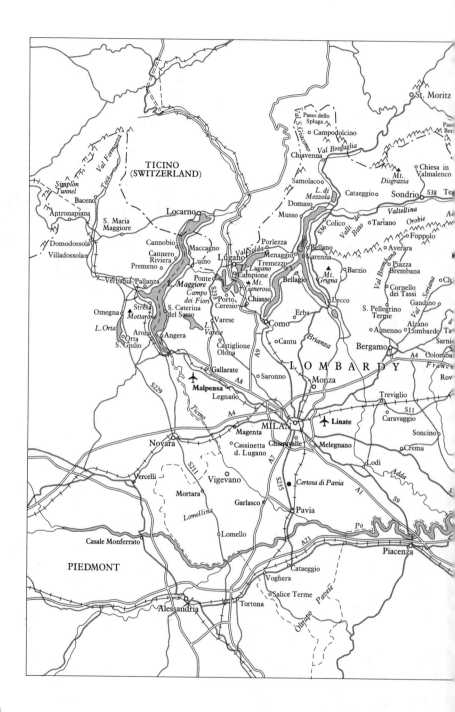

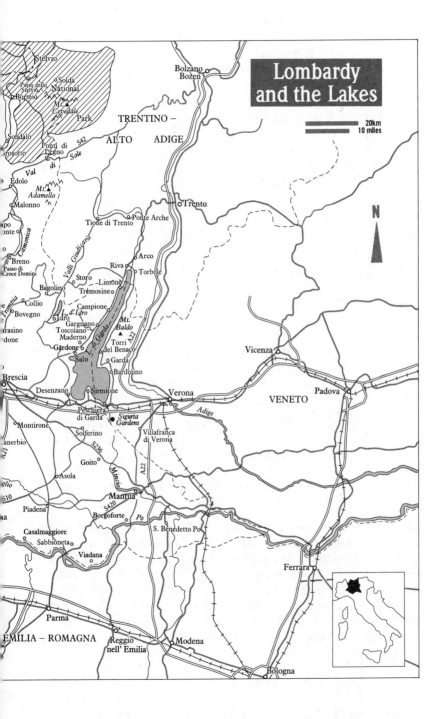

Lombardy and the Lakes

20km
10 miles

N

Throughout history, the millions of frostbitten travellers, pilgrims, conquering armies and future popes and pushy emperors who lumbered over the treacherous passes of the Alps would be stopped in their tracks by a vision as powerful and terrible and beautiful as an epiphany: at their feet, wedged into the flanks of the snowcapped mountains, lay the Garden of Eden itself. Elegant, long lakes were its centrepiece, warmed by a glowing sun that had nothing in common with that old cheese in the sky they knew back home; on their chiselled shores lemons, figs, roses, pomegranates and palms grew in luxuriant abundance. And beyond these magical Mediterranean fjords the fertile Lombard plain spread its charms back to the edge of the horizon, dangling some of the richest art cities of Italy like diamonds across its bosom.

The finished product, the Lombardy and Lakes we see today, is the result of primordial blasts of ice. In the last glacial, huge masses of ice rolled down from the Alps, ironing flat the Lombard plain. On the way they gouged out deep welts in the rock, far deeper than the level of the Adriatic sea, sculpting (there's no other word for it) some of the most sublime lakes, anywhere. Lombardy's character was similarly formed by violence. Countless gangsters coveted this earthly Eden (not the least of whom were the Lombards themselves, who liked the odd swig of mead from the skulls of their enemies). Many invaders settled down to stay and turn their energy to farming and especially to trade, the natural occupation for people living at the crossroads between Italy, France, Switzerland, and Austria and the Tyrrhenian and Adriatic seas.

Early in the Middle Ages, mercantile Lombardy invented the idea of the *comune*, a kind of independent city-state, the antithesis of feudalism. The *comuni*'s new outlook on the world, freedom of action, wealth, and their increasingly sophisticated ruling families, keen on embellishing their palaces and cities with art, were leading factors in ushering in the Renaissance, which has left some of its greatest treasures behind in Milan, Mantua, Bergamo, Como and Brescia.

Lombardy has been making some big noises recently, adding more than its share to the contradictions and confusions besetting modern Italy. Pilgrims of old, descending from the Alps on this Garden of Eden, trod softly so as not to disturb God's angel with the fiery sword. Nowadays you can rest assured that he's run off to join the circus. Nevertheless, the advent of Berlusconi and the substitution of vague, soft-touch commercial mumbo-jumbo for the honest politics Italy needs suggests that the Tree of Knowledge remains untouched, still defended by a viper—the symbol of Milan itself.

Guide to the Guide

This book begins with the great cities of Lombardy, the largest and most populated region in Italy. We start with **Milan**, the republic's greatest metropolis with nearly four million inhabitants, the adopted home of Leonardo da Vinci, mecca of finance and fashion, a city of action mutability and modernity, and most Italians' favourite vision of what the new Italy is all about. Milan has the most art, the biggest cathedral, La Scala opera, the best football teams, and an attitude that encompasses all the above.

The next section covers southern Lombardy, including the three jewels of Lombardy's Po plain: **Pavia**, capital of Italy in the Dark Ages; violin-making **Cremona**; and the Renaissance art city of **Mantua**.

Northern Lombardy, and a piece of eastern Piedmont and western Veneto, all form part of the **Italian Lakes**, that lovely and legendary district beloved of poets since Roman times. Westernmost is little **Lake Orta** and the famous Simplon tunnel near Domodossola; nearby **Lake Maggiore** has its Borromean isles and the world-famous resort of Stresa. Then comes zigzagging **Lake Lugano**, which Italy shares with Switzerland, and lovely **Lake Como**, with resorts deeply engraved on the English traveller's Romantic memory— Bellagio, Cernobbio, Tremezzo and Menaggio. From the northeast bank of Como extends the Valtellina, surrounded by Lombardy's rugged Alps, stretching all the way to Bormio and the western confines of Stelvio National Park. To the south of the Valtellina are more lakes—Iseo and tiny Idro—and two excellent art cities, **Bergamo** and **Brescia**, and to the east the national park of the Val Camonica. Easternmost is **Lake Garda**, nicknamed the 'Riviera of the Dolomites' for its dramatic surroundings. Sirmione, Gardone, Limone and Riva are its most famous resorts; good wines grow between its eastern shore and Verona.

The Best of Lombardy

The following highly selective list, illustrated by the colour map inside the front cover of this book, may help you decide where to spend your time.

Art and Architecture

Milan is an art city in its own right; works by the greatest artists of Italy and beyond are in the Brera, Ambrosiana and the Galleria Poldi-Pezzoli, and you could easily spend three days here, taking in nearby **Pavia** and its famous Certosa in a day trip. **Bergamo** and **Mantua** are also top-notch, the former for its medieval Città Alta and the Carrara Academy, the latter for the renaissance palaces of the Gonzaga dukes.

Gardens and Villas

The climate of the larger lakes allows a remarkable diversity of plant life, ranging from alpine varieties to cacti. Some of Italy's most famous gardens are to be found around Lake Como (**Villa Carlotta** and the villas at **Bellagio**) and Lake Maggiore (**Isola Bella, Isola Madre**, and the **Villa Taranto**); there's also **Le Torbiere**, water lily garden by Lake Iseo, and Mantua's **Valletta Belfiore** is famous for its lotus blossoms in July and August.

Castles

Castello Sforza at **Soncino**; Rocca di Angera, on Lake Maggiore, with frescoes; Malpaga, the Renaissance castle of the great condottiere Bartolomeo Colleoni, with more interesting frescoes, near **Bergamo**; romantically beautiful Scaliger castles at **Sirmione** and **Malcésine**, on Lake Garda. Also at **Sirmione** don't miss the romantic Grotte di Catullo.

Cathedrals and Churches

Como, Cremona, Brescia, Monza (with the treasure of the 6th-century Lombard queen Theodolinda), **Lodi Vecchio**.

Opera

La Scala, of course, in **Milan**, with its accompanying opera museum; also the Donizetti Museum and Theatre in **Bergamo** and the spurious but appropriately sombre 'Casa di Rigoletto' in **Mantua**.

Man-made Wonders

The Colossus of Charles Borromeo, at **Arona** on Lake Maggiore; **Santa Caterina del Sasso**, also on Lake Maggiore, a convent built on a cliff-face; Il Vittoriale, the home of Gabriele D'Annunzio, with its tomb, at **Gardone Riviera**; the covered bridge at **Pavia**.

Natural Wonders

Two spectacular waterfalls: the grand 300m Cascata della Frua, north of **Domodossola**, and Acqua Fraggia, near **Borgonuova** in Valchiavenna.

Small Towns and Villages

Charming villages are scattered all over Lombardy. Look for **Orta San Giulio** on Lake Orta and Renaissance **Castiglione Olona**, near Varese, with the lovely frescoes of Masolino da Panicale; **Sabbioneta**, an ideal Renaissance town near Mantua; **Bellagio**, high on the headland where Lake Como forks, with its amazing views and 12th-century church of San Giocomo; **Clusone**, with its frescoes and 16th-century astronomical clock on the town hall; and **Sirmione** and **Malcésine** on Lake Garda.

Shopping Specialities

Cremona for violins, **Como** for silk—and, of course **Milan** for fashion!

Winter Sports

Bormio, at the top of the Valtellina, is one of Italy's top winter sports centres and the gateway to the glacier-encrusted **Stelvio National Park**.

Hotels and Restaurants

The area is littered with top hostelries—restaurants like Vecchia Lugana at **Sirmione**, L'Albereta in **Erbusco**, the Trattoria Guada il Canal in **Crema**, Il Cigno in **Mantua** and *nuova cucina* specialist, Emiliano, at **Stresa**. Special hotels include the former 17th-century monastery San Rocco at **Orta San Giulio**, the Belle Epoque, sumptuous Des Isles Borromées in **Stresa**, the palatial Villa d'Este at **Cernobbio** and, for an oasis of tranquillity, the Villa Cortine in **Sirmione**—plus many more.

Travel

Getting There	2
By Air from the UK and Ireland	2
By Air from the USA and Canada	3
By Rail	3
By Road	4
Entry Formalities	5
Passports and Visas	5
Customs	5
Currency	5
Tour Operators and	
Special-interest Holidays	6
Getting Around	8
By Boat	9
By Train	9
By Coach and Bus	11
By Car	11
Hiring a Car	13
By Taxi	14
Hitchhiking	14
By Motorcycle or Cycle	14

By Air from the UK and Ireland

Flying is the quickest and easiest way of getting to Italy from the UK, and the gateway for Lombardy is **Milan**. International flights use **Malpensa Airport**, about 50km northwest of the city. Domestic and European flights use **Linate Airport** about 7km east. Direct scheduled flights to Milan are operated by **Alitalia**, ✆ (071) 602 7111, and **British Airways**, ✆ (081) 897 4000. Besides London, you can also fly from Birmingham or Manchester in the summer. The real challenge is not so much finding a flight, but finding a bargain, especially in the high season (mid-May to mid-September); the trick is to start hunting well in advance, or, if you're a gambler, at the last moment. The advantages of shelling out for a full **scheduled** fare are that few restrictions are imposed on when you travel or how long you stay. To sweeten the deal, promotional perks like rental cars, discounts on domestic flights and accommodation, tours et cetera may also be included. **Children** travel for greatly reduced fares (£20 for the under-twos on an adult's lap; 20% discount for children aged 2–11). *Bona fide* **students** with suitable ID also receive handsome discounts . Special fares booked in advance, however (PEX, APEXand so on) may save you as much as 50% of the cost. Typical fares to Milan on British Airways or Alitalia are currently around £250 return in high season. Booking restrictions apply; you have to book at least 7 days ahead, and stay a Saturday night abroad. Ticket changes involve high penalties.

There are no direct flights from **Ireland** to Italy. The best bet is to travel to London and fly from there. Cheapest Dublin–London flights are operated by **Ryan Air** (landing at Stansted or Luton), though **Aer Lingus** and **British Midland** take you directly into Heathrow, which is more convenient and will probably save time and money in the end. From Belfast, both British Airways and British Midland operate to Heathrow. If you're a student, substantial discounts may be available: contact **USIT** at 12–21 Aston Quay, O'Connell Bridge, Dublin 2, ✆ (01) 679 8833, or Fountain Centre, College St, Belfast, ✆ (0232) 324073.

discounts and special deals

London is a great centre for discounted flights, and you should be able to find a good deal if you allow enough time. Seat-only charters to Milan may cost as little as £160 off-peak; contact a reputable agent such as **Trailfinders**, **STA**, or **Campus Travel** (ABTA-registered, who won't bunk off with your cash and leave you stranded). Alternatively you can book directly through a charter or holiday operator. The Italian specialist **Air Travel Group**, at 227 Shepherd's Bush Road, Hammersmith, London W6 7AS, ✆ (081) 748 7575, incorporates Pilgrim Air, Magic of Italy and Italian Escapades, *see* pp.6–8.

Classified sections of weekend newspapers also advertise discounted fares (in London, get *Time Out* or other listings magazines, and the *Evening Standard* or the free newspapers like *TNT* or *Trailfinder* from near tube stations). Peak season is Easter and summer, when there are generally a couple of flights a day from London (book well ahead). The major charter agencies are Italy Sky Shuttle (operated by Pilgrim Air), ℂ (081) 563 7194 (information), ℂ (081) 748 1333 (reservations), Skybus, ℂ (071) 373 6055, and LAI, ℂ (071) 837 8492. Rock-bottom fares are generally subject to restrictions, and departure or arrival times may be inconvenient or uncertain. STA and Campus Travel offer exceptionally good deals for students.

By Air from the USA and Canada

Transatlantic airlines **Delta, TWA, United Airlines** and **Air Canada** all have direct flights to Rome or Milan from a number of cities, including New York, Boston, Miami, Chicago, Los Angeles, Toronto or Montreal, but **Alitalia** has the most options. Summer round-trip fares from New York to Italy cost around $1000, from Montreal or Toronto about $1300 Canadian.

Alternatively, you may prefer to take a flight to London or some other European city (Paris or Amsterdam, for example) and change there, a reasonably economical option. Apex or SuperApex deals are better value than scheduled fares, though you may prefer to pay extra for security, flexibility and convenience on such a long jouney (9–15 hours' flying time). Beware the restrictions imposed on special fares, and plan well in advance. Obviously, low-season flights (between November and March) tend to be a great deal cheaper than peak-season ones, and mid-week fares are generally lower than at weekends.

As in Britain, a host of cheap deals are advertised in the travel sections of major newspapers like the *New York Times, LA Times* or *Toronto Star.* If you are prepared to take pot luck, try for a stand-by or consolidated fare, or consider a courier flight (remember you can only take hand luggage with you on these deals). **Now Voyager**, ℂ (212) 431 1616, is one of the main US courier flight companies (annual membership fee), based at Suite 307, 74 Varrick St New York NY 10013. **Board Courier Services** operates in Canada, ℂ (514) 633 0740 in Toronto or Montreal; ℂ (604) 338 1366 in Vancouver. Both **STA** and **Council Travel** are well worth contacting for cheaper charter flights and budget student travel. Both agencies have branches in several major US cities. In Canada, **Travel Cuts**, ℂ (416) 979 2406, specializes in discounted student fares. Numerous travel clubs and agencies also specialize in discount fares (you may have to pay a membership fee).

By Rail

Lombardy is easily accessible by rail from the UK. From London the journey time to Milan takes about 22 hours, via Lille and Basel; services run daily in summer. Return fares range from about £160 to £240. Once you've added the cost of a couchette (£12 or so), rail travel is scarcely cheaper than flying unless you are able to take advantage of student or youth fares. Discounts are available for families, and young children. **Interail** (UK) or **Eurail** (USA/Canada) passes give unlimited travel for under-26s throughout Europe for one or two months. Various other cheap youth fares (BIJ tickets etc.) are also available; organize these before you leave home. Useful addresses for rail travel include **Eurotrain**, 52 Grosvenor Gardens, London SW1, ℂ (071) 730 8518; **Wasteels Travel** 121 Wilton Rd, London SW1, ℂ (071) 834 7066; **Transalpino** (at most main rail stations), any branch of **Thomas Cook**, or **CIT** (*see* addresses below). In the USA or Canada, contact **Rail Europe**, central office at 226–230 Westchester Avenue, White Plains, NY 10604, © 914 682 2999 or 800 438 7245. **Wasteels** also have a US office at 5728 Major Boulevard, Suite 308, Orlando, 32819 Florida, © (407) 351 2537.

If you are just planning to see Italy, these passes may not be worthwhile (*see* 'Getting Around', below, for more detail on rail passes). A month's full Interail pass costs £249, though you can now buy cheaper zonal passes covering three or four countries only. CIT offices, which act as agents for Italian State Railways, are based as follows:

CIT Offices

UK: Marco Polo House, 3–5 Lansdowne Rd, Croydon, Surrey, © (081) 686 0677.

US: 342 Madison Ave, Suite 3297, New York, NY 10173, © (212) 697 2100. There's also an 800 number you can call from anywhere: © (800) 223 0230.

Canada: 1450 City Councillors St. Suite 750, Montreal H3A 2E6, © (514) 845 910.

In Italy, a good bet for discounted train tickets, flights etc. is **CTS**, Corso P. Ticinese 83, Milan, © (02) 837 2674.

A convenient pocket-sized **timetable** detailing all the main and secondary Italian railway lines, is now available in the UK, costing £6 (plus 50p postage). Contact Accommodation Line Ltd, 11–12 Hanover Square, London W1; Y Knot Travel, Morley House, 1st Floor, 314/320 Regent St, London W1; or Italwings, Travel & Accommodation, 87 Brewer St, London W1. If you wait until you arrive in Italy, however, you can pick up the Northern Italy timetable at any station for about L4500.

By Road

Eurolines is the main international **bus** operator in Europe, with representatives in Italy and many other countries. In the UK, they can be found at 52 Grosvenor Gardens, Victoria, London SW1, © (071) 730 0202, and are booked through National Express. Regular services run to many northern Italian cities, including Milan, where they will generally arrive at the Piazza Castello. Needless to say, the journey is long and the relatively small saving in price (a return ticket from London to Milan costs about £119) makes it a masochistic choice in comparison with a discounted air fare, or even rail travel. However, if it isn't pitch-dark, you'll catch a fleeting glimpse of Mont Blanc and Turin on the way.

To bring a GB-registered **car** into Italy, you need a vehicle registration document, full driving licence, and insurance papers. Non-EC citizens should preferably have an international driving licence which has an Italian translation incorporated. Your vehicle should display a nationality plate indicating its country of registration.

It's the best part of 24 hours' driving time even if you stick to fast toll roads. The most scenic and hassle-free route is via the Alps, avoiding crowded Riviera roads in summer, but if you take a route through Switzerland, expect to pay for the privilege (£14 or SF30 for motorway use). In winter the passes may be closed and you will have to stick to those expensive tunnels (one-way tolls range from about L22,000 for a small car). You can avoid some of the driving by putting your car on the train, though this is scarcely a cheap option. Express Sleeper Cars run to Milan from Paris or Boulogne (infrequently in winter). Milan is a major junction of Italy's motorways, and many smaller national roads. Fog and snow can make it a hazardous winter destination. Foreign-plated cars are currently entitled to free breakdown assistance from the **ACI** (Italian Touring Club).

For information on driving in Italy, contact the motoring organisations **AA**, ✆ (0256) 20123, or **RAC**, ✆ (081) 686 0088, in the UK, and **AAA**, ✆ (407) 444 4000, in the USA.

Entry Formalities

Passports and Visas

EU nationals with a valid passport can enter and stay in Italy as long as they like, or they may stay a year with a British Visitor's Passport, available from the post office. Citizens of the USA, Canada, Australia and New Zealand need only a valid passport to stay up to three months in Italy, unless they get a special visa in advance from an Italian embassy or consulate (*see* **Practical A–Z** p.19).

By law you should register with the police within eight days of your arrival in Italy. In practice this is done automatically for most visitors when they check in at their first hotel. Don't be alarmed if the owner of your self-catering property proposes to 'denounce' you to the police when you arrive—it's just a formality.

Customs

EU nationals over the age of 17 can now import a limitless amount of goods for personal use, provided duty has already been paid. Non-EU nationals have to pass through the Italian Customs. How the frontier police manage to recruit such ugly, mean-looking characters to hold the submachine guns and drug-sniffing dogs from such a good-looking population is a mystery, but they'll let you be if you don't look suspicious and haven't brought along more than 200 cigarettes or 100 cigars, or more than a litre of hard drink or three bottles of wine, a couple of cameras, a movie camera, 10 rolls of film for each, a tape-recorder, radio, record-player, one canoe less than 5.5m, sports equipment for personal use, and one TV (though you'll have to pay for a licence for it at Customs). Pets must be accompanied by a bilingual Certificate of Health from your local veterinary inspector. You can take the same items listed above home with you without hassle— except of course your British pet. US citizens may return with $400 worth of merchandise—keep your receipts.

Currency

There are no limits to how much money you bring into Italy: legally you may not export more than L20,000 000 in Italian banknotes, a sum unlikely to trouble many of us, though officials rarely check.

UK operators mostly offer holidays in the Lakes area, including many tours of gardens and villas, and painting courses. City and opera visits to Milan can also be arranged. Not all those operators listed below are necesssarily ABTA-bonded; we recommend you check before booking.

in the UK

Abercrombie & Kent (Milan in all seasons; gardens of the Veneto and Lombardy), Sloane Square House, Holbein Place, London SW1W 8NS.   (071) 730 9600 ℂ

ACE Study Tours (Italian Lakes, villas and gardens), Babraham, Cambridge CB2 4AP.
(0223) 835055 ℂ

Aria (Milan opera), 69 Cranbrook Road, London W14 2LT.   (081) 994 0977 ℂ

Arvonia (coach tours), The Square, Llanrug, Caernarfon, Gwynedd LL55 4AA.
(0286) 675175 ℂ

Brompton Travel (gardens and opera), Brompton House, 64 Richmond Road, Kingston-upon-Thames, Surrey KT2 5EH.   (081) 549 3334 ℂ

Campus Travel, 52 Grosvenor Gardens, SW1, or 174 Kensington High St, London W8.
(071) 730 3402 ℂ

Citalia, Marco Polo House, 3–5 Lansdowne Road, Croydon CR9 1LL. (081) 686 5533 ℂ

Cityjet (Milan city breaks), Cityjet House, 65 Judd Street, London WC1H 9QT.
(071) 383 0322 ℂ

Cosmos (Lakes guided tours), Tourama House, 17 Holmesdale Road, Bromley, Kent BR2 9LX.   (081) 464 3444 ℂ

Cox & Kings (garden and villa tours), St James Court, 45 Buckingham Gate, London SW1E 6AF.   (071) 873 5002 ℂ

Cresta Italy (Milan city and opera; Como), Holiday House, Victoria Street, Altrincham, Cheshire WA14 1ET.   (0345) 125333 ℂ

Crystal Premier (Lakes and gardens), Crystal House, The Courtyard, Arlington Road, Surbiton, Surrey KT6 6BW.   (081) 399 5144 ℂ

DA Tours (coach tours), Willaimton House, Low Causeway, Culross, Fife KY12 8HL.
(0383) 881700 ℂ

Eddie Brown Tours (coach tours), 8 Tower Street, York YO1 1SA.   (0904) 640706 ℂ

Enterprise, Groundstar House, London Road, Crawley, West Sussex RH10 2TB.
(0293) 560777 ℂ

Eurobreak (Milan city), 10–18 Putney Hill, London SW15 6AX.   (081) 780 0909 ℂ

Facet Travel (coach tours), Buxted House, Framfield Road, Buxted, Nr Uckfield, East Sussex TN22 4PG.   (0825) 732266 ℂ

Gordon Overland (painting by Lake Iseo), 76 Croft Rd, Carlisle, Cumbria CA3 9AG.
(0228) 26795 ℂ

Greenways (walking tours), 88 Little Glen Road, Glen Parva, Leicester LE2 9TS.
(0533) 774687 ℭ

Inghams, 10–18 Putney Hill, London SW15 6AX. (081) 786777 ℭ

Insight (coach tours), Insight International Building, 26/28 Paradise Road, Richmond, Surrey TW9 1SE. (081) 332 2900 ℭ

Italian Escapades (Milan), 227 Shepherds Bush Rd, London W6 7AS. (081) 748 2661 ℭ

Italian Interlude (Milan), Triumph House, 1889 Regent Street, London W1R 7WD.
(071) 494 2031 ℭ

Italiatours (Milan opera), 205 Holland Park Ave, London W11 4XB. (071) 371 1114

JMB (opera and gardens), Rushwick, Worcester WR2 5SN. (0905) 425628 ℭ

Kirker (Milan city breaks), 3 New Concordia Wharf, Mill Street, London SE1 2BB.
(071) 231 3333 ℭ

Leahys Travel (pilgrimages, Verona & Lake Garda), 116 Harpenden Road, St Albans, Herts AL3 6BZ. (0727) 852394 ℭ

Magic of Italy, 227 Shepherds Bush Road, London W6 7AS. (081) 748 7575 ℭ

Martin Randall Travel (Duchy of Milan—guest lecturers), 10 Barley Mow Passage, Chiswick, London W4 4PH. (081) 742 3355 ℭ

Martin Rooks, Astral Towers, Betts Way, Crawley, W. Sussex RH10 2GX. (0293) 554455 ℭ

Newmarket, McMillan House, Worcester Park, Surrey KT4 8RH. (081) 335 3030 ℭ

Noble Caledonia (Gardens of the Lakes), 11 Charles Street, Mayfair, London W1X 7HB.
(071) 491 4752 ℭ

Page & Moy (Gardens of the Lakes), 136–140 London Road, Leicester LE2 1EN.
(0533) 524433 ℭ

Pilgrim Air, 227 Shepherd's Bush Road, London W6 7AS. (071) 748 1333 ℭ

Prospect Music & Art (opera; villas and gardens), 454/458 Chiswick High Road, London W4 5TT. (081) 995 2151 ℭ

Raffaello Holidays, Cityjet House, 65 Judd St, London WC1H 9QT. (071) 383 0322 ℭ

Saga (Majesty of the Lakes), The Saga Building, Middelburg Square, Folkestone, Kent CT20 1AZ. (0303) 857000 ℭ

Shearings (Lakes—accompanied tours), Miry Lane, Wigan, Greater Manchester WN3 4AG. (0942) 824824 ℭ

Solos (singles holidays), 41 Watford Way, London NW4 3JH. (081) 202 0855 ℭ

Sovereign, Astral Towers, Betts Way, Crawley, W. Sussex RH10 2GX. (0293) 599900 ℭ

Special Tours (Italian Lakes and villas—escorted tours), 81a Elizabeth Street, London SW1W 9PG. (071) 730 2297 ℭ

STA, 74 & 86 Old Brompton Road, London SW7, or 117 Euston Road, London NW1.
(071) 937 9921 ℭ

Sunvil, Sunvil House, 7 & 8 Upper Sq., Old Isleworth, Middx TW7 7BJ. (081) 568 4499 ℭ

Tappins, Station Road, Didcot, Oxon OX11 7LZ. (0235) 819393 ℭ

Thomson, Greater London House, Hampstead Rd, London NW1 7SD. (081) 200 8733 ©

Tjaereborg, Astral Towers, Betts Way, Crawley, W. Sussex RH10 2GB. (0293) 554444 ©

Trafalgar, 5 Bressenden Road, London SW1E 5DF. (071) 235 7090 ©

Trailfinders, 194 Kensington High Street, London W8. (071) 937 5400 ©

The Travel Club of Upminster (painting holidays—Lake Orta; gardens tours), Station Road, Upminster, Essex RM14 2TT. (0708) 225000 ©

Travel for the Arts (Milan opera holidays), 117 Regent's Park Road, London NW1 8UR. (071) 483 4466 ©

Travelsphere (coach tours), Compass House, Rockingham Road, Market Harborough, Leicestershire LE16 7QD. (0858) 464818 ©

Venice Simplon-Orient Express, Sea Containers House, 20 Upper Ground, London SE1 9PF. (071) 928 6000 ©

Voyages Jules Verne (garden and villa tours—Lakes Como, Maggiore), 21 Dorset Square, London NW1 6QG. (071) 723 5066 ©

Wallace Arnold (Italian Lakes—coach tours), Gelderd Rd, Leeds, LS12 6DH. (0532) 310739 ©

in the USA

CIT Tours, 342 Madison Ave, Suite 3297, New York, NY 10173. (212) 697 2100 ©
6033 West Century Blvd, Suite 980, Los Angeles, CA 90045. (310) 338 8615 ©

Dailey-Thorp Travel (Milan opera), 330 West 58th Street, New York, NY 10019. (212) 307 1555 ©

Italiatour, 666 5th Avenue, New York, NY 10103. (212) 765 2183 ©

Maupintour, 1515 St Andrew's Drive, Lawrence, Kansas 66047 (913) 843 1211 ©

Olson Travelworld, 970 West 190th Street, Suite 425, Torrance, California 90502. (310) 354 2600 ©

Trafalgar Tours, 11 East 26th Street, New York, NY 10010. (212) 689 8977 ©

Travel Concepts (wine/food), 62 Commonwealth Ave, Suite 3, Boston, MA 02116. (617) 266 8450 ©

For self-catering and camping specialists *see* **Practical A–Z**, 'Where to Stay', pp.39–41.

Getting Around

Italy has an excellent network of airports, railways, highways and byways and you'll find getting around fairly easy—until one union or another takes it into its head to go on strike (to be fair, they rarely do it during the high holiday season). There's plenty of talk about passing a law to regulate strikes, but it won't happen soon, if ever. Instead, learn to recognize the word in Italian: *sciopero* (*sho*-per-o), and do as the Romans do—quiver with resignation. There's always a day or two's notice, and strikes usually last only a day, just long enough to throw a spanner in the works if you have to catch a plane. Keep your ears open and watch for notices posted in the stations.

All the major lakes are crisscrossed by a complex network of *battelli* (boats) and *aliscafi* (hydrofoils), some of which are regular ferries, others cruise or excursion boats either available for hire, or operating to set schedules. All services are seasonal, and massively reduced during the winter. Day or longer passes allowing unlimited travel on any particular lake are available. Some services transcend frontiers and pass into Swiss waters. Ask for timetables at tourist offices, or if you're in Milan call in at the *Gestione Navigazione Laghi,* Via L Ariosto 21, ✆ (02) 481 2086. The main companies are listed below.

Como: *Navigazione Lago di Como* , Piazza Cavour, Como, ✆ 30 40 60
Maggiore: *Navigazione Lago Maggiore,* Via Principe Tomaso 70, Stresa,✆ 0323 30393
Garda: *Navigazione sul Lago di Garda,* Piazza Matteotti, Desenzano, ✆ 030 914 1321
Iseo: *Navigazione sul Lago d'Iseo,* Via Nazionale 16, Bergamo, ✆ 035 971 482

Italy's national railway, the **FS** (*Ferrovie dello Stato*) is well run, inexpensive (despite recent price rises) and often a pleasure to ride. There are also several private rail lines around cities and in country districts. Some, you may find, won't accept Interrail or Eurail passes. On the FS, some of the trains are sleek and high-tech, but much of the rolling stock hasn't been changed for fifty years. Possible FS unpleasantnesses you may encounter, besides a strike, are delays, crowding (especially at weekends and in the summer), and crime on overnight trains, where someone rifles your bags while you sleep. The crowding, at least, becomes much less of a problem if you reserve a seat in advance at the *Prenotazione* counter. The fee is small and can save you hours standing in some train corridor. On the upper-echelon trains, **reservations** are mandatory. Do check when you purchase your ticket in advance that the date is correct; unlike in some countries, tickets are only valid the day they're purchased unless you specify otherwise. A number on your reservation slip will indicate in which car your seat is—find it before you board rather than after. The same goes for sleepers and couchettes on overnight trains, which must also be reserved in advance.

Tickets may be purchased not only in the stations, but at many travel agents in the city centres. Fares are strictly determined by the kilometres travelled. The system is computerized and runs smoothly, at least until you try to get a reimbursement for an unused ticket (usually not worth the trouble). Be sure you ask which platform (*binario*) your train arrives at; the big boards posted in the stations are not always correct. If you get on a train without a ticket you can buy one from the conductor, with an added 20% penalty. You can also pay a conductor to move up to first class or get a couchette, if there are any places available.

There is a fairly straightforward **hierarchy of trains**. At the bottom of the pyramid is the humble *Locale* (euphemistically known sometimes as an *Accelerato*) which often stops even where there's no station in sight; it can be excruciatingly slow. When you're checking the schedules, beware of what may look like the first train to your destination—if it's a *Locale*, it will be the last to arrive. A *Diretto* stops far less, an *Expresso* just at the main towns. *Intercity* trains whoosh between the big cities and rarely deign to stop. *Eurocity* trains link Italian cities with major European centres. Both of these services require a supplement, some 30% more than a regular fare. Reservations are free, but must be made at least five hours before the trip, and on some trains there are only first-class coaches. Trains serving the most important routes have names such as the *Vesuvio* (Milan, Bologna, Florence, Rome, Naples), the *Adriatico* (Milan, Rimini, Pesaro, Ancona, Pescara, Foggia, Bari), or the *Colosseo/Ambrosiano* (Milan, Bologna, Florence, Rome). The real lords of the rails are the *ETR 450 Pendolino* trains, kilometre-eaters that will speed you to your destination as fast as trains can go (in Italy!). For these there is a more costly supplement and on some only first-class luxury cars.

The FS offers several **passes**. One which you should ideally arrange at a CIT or Italian rail agent office (e.g. Wasteels) before arriving in Italy is the 'Travel-at-Will' ticket (*Biglietto Turistico Libera Circolazione*), available only to foreigners. This is a good deal only if you mean to do some very serious train-riding on consecutive days; it does, however, allow you to ride the *Intercity/Eurocity* without paying a supplement. Tickets are sold for 8, 15, 21, or 30-day periods, first or second class, with 50% reductions for children under 12. At the time of writing an 8-day second-class ticket is around £88 and the 30-day ticket is £152. A more flexible option is the 'Flexi Card' which allows unlimited travel for either four days within a nine-day period (second class £66, first class £98), 8 days within 12 (second class £94, first class around £140), 12 days within 30 (second class £120, first class £190), and you don't have to pay any supplements. Another ticket, the *Kilometrico*, gives you 3000 kilometres of travel, made on a maximum of 20 journeys, and is valid for two months; one advantage is that it can be used by up to five people at the same time. However, supplements are payable on *Intercity* trains. Second-class tickets are currently £90, first-class £152. Other discounts, available only once you're in Italy, are 15% on same-day return tickets and 3-day returns (depending on the distance involved), and discounts for families of at least four travelling together. Senior citizens (men 65 and over, women 60) can also get a *Carta d'Argento* ('silver card') for L40,000 entitling them to a 20% reduction in fares. A *Carta Verde* bestows a 20% discount on people under 26 and also costs L40,000.

Refreshments on routes of any great distance are provided by bar cars or trolleys; you can usually get sandwiches and coffee from vendors along the tracks at intermediary stops. Station bars often have a good variety of takeaway travellers' fare; consider at least investing in a plastic bottle of mineral water, since there's no drinking water on the trains.

Besides trains and bars, Italy's stations offer **other facilities**. All have a *Deposito*, where you can leave your bags for hours or days for a small fee. The larger ones have porters (who charge L1000–L1500 per piece) and some even have luggage trolleys; major stations have an *Albergo Diurno* ('Day Hotel', where you take a shower, get a shave and have a haircut), information offices, currency exchanges open at weekends (not at the most advantageous rates, however), hotel-finding and reservation services, kiosks with foreign papers, restaurants, etc. You can also arrange to have a rental car awaiting you at your destination—Avis, Hertz, Aurotrans and Maggiore are the firms most widespread in Italy.

Beyond that, some words need to be said about riding the rails on the most serendipitous national line in Europe. The FS may have its strikes and delays, its petty crime and bureaucratic inconveniences, but when you catch it on its better side it will treat you to a dose of the real Italy before you even reach your destination. If there's a choice, try for one of the older cars, depressingly grey outside but fitted with comfortably upholstered seats, Art Deco lamps and old pictures of the towns and villages of the country. The washrooms are invariably clean and pleasant. Best of all, the FS is relatively reliable, and even if there has been some delay you'll have an amenable station full of clocks to wait in; some of the station bars have astonishingly good food (some do not), but at any of them you may accept a well-brewed cappuccino and look blasé until the train comes in. Try to avoid travel on Friday evenings, when the major lines out of the big cities are packed. The FS is an honest crap shoot; you may find a train uncomfortably full of Italians (in which case stand by the doors, or impose on the salesmen in first class, where the conductor will be happy to change your ticket). Now and then, you may just have a beautiful 1920s compartment all to yourself for the night—even better if you're travelling with your beloved—and be serenaded on the platform.

By Coach and Bus

Inter-city coach travel is sometimes quicker than train travel, but also a bit more expensive. The Italians aren't dumb; you will find regular coach connections only where there is no train to offer competition. Coaches almost always depart from the vicinity of the train station, and tickets usually need to be purchased before you get on. In many regions they are the only means of public transport and well used, with frequent schedules. If you can't get a ticket before the coach leaves, get on anyway and pretend you can't speak a word of Italian; the worst that can happen is that someone will make you pay for a ticket. The base for all **country bus** lines will be the provincial capitals.

City buses are the traveller's friend. Most northern cities label routes well; all charge flat fees, at the time of writing around L1200, for rides within the city limits and immediate suburbs. Bus tickets must always be purchased before you get on, either at a tobacconist's, a newspaper kiosk, in bars, or from ticket machines near the main stops. Once you get on, you must 'obliterate' your ticket in the machines in the front or back of the bus; controllers stage random checks to make sure you've punched your ticket. Fines for cheaters are about L50,000, and the odds are about 12 to 1 against a check, so many passengers take a chance. If you're good-hearted, you'll buy a ticket and help some overburdened municipal transit line meet its annual deficit.

By Car

A car is certainly the best and most convenient way to get to the more remote parts of Lombardy, but quite unnecessary in Milan, where public transport is extremely efficient and parking is hell on wheels. If you must bring a car into the centre, look for ATM car parks on the outskirts (marked with a white P on a blue background), or dump your car in one of the large parking lots at the termini of the underground (Ⓜ) lines. Unauthorized cars with Italian plates are barred from the centre during the daytime, all week. Other large tourist towns, like Bergamo, can also be a major headache with a car.

Third-party insurance is a minimum requirement in Italy (and you should be a lot more than minimally insured, as many of the locals have none whatever!). Obtain a Green Card from your insurer, which gives automatic proof that you are fully covered. Also get hold of a **European Accident Statement** form, which may simplify things if you are unlucky enough to have an accident. Always insist on a full translation of any statement you are asked to sign.

Breakdown assistance insurance is obviously a sensible investment (e.g. AA's Five Star or RAC's Eurocover Motoring Assistance). Don't give the local police any excuse to fine you on the spot for minor infringements like worn tyres or burnt-out sidelights (such infringements could cost you L150,000 or more on a bad day). A **red triangular hazard sign** is obligatory; also recommended are a spare set of bulbs, a first-aid kit and a fire extinguisher. Spare parts may be tricky to find for non-Italian cars.

Petrol (*benzina*; unleaded is *benzina senza piombo*, and diesel *gasolio*) is still very expensive in Italy despite price changes in 1992 (around L1500 per litre; fill up before you cross the border). Many petrol stations close for lunch in the afternoon, and few stay open late at night, though you may find a 'self-service' where you feed a machine nice smooth L10,000 notes.

Motorway (*autostrada*) tolls are quite high; the journey from Milan to Rome on the A1 will cost you around L60,000 at the time of writing. Rest-stops and petrol stations along the motorways stay open 24 hours. Other roads—*superstrade* on down through the Italian grading system—are free of charge.

Italians are famously anarchic behind a wheel, though perhaps less so in the northwest than elsewhere in Italy, where the temperament of the careful Swiss seems to have seeped slightly over national boundaries. Nonetheless you will find places where all warnings, signals and generally recognized rules of the road are ignored. The only way to beat the locals is to join them by adopting an assertive and constantly alert driving style. Bear in mind the ancient maxim that he/she who hesitates is lost (especially at traffic lights, where the danger is less great of crashing into someone at the front than of being rammed from behind). All drivers from boy racers to elderly nuns seem to tempt Providence by overtaking at the most dangerous bend, and no matter how fast you are hammering along the *autostrada* (toll motorway), plenty will whizz past at apparently supersonic rates. North Americans used to leisurely speed limits and gentler road manners will find the Italian interpretation of the highway code especially stressful.

Speed limits (generally ignored) are officially 130kph on motorways (110kph for cars under 1100cc or motorcycles), 110kph on main highways, 90kph on secondary roads, and 50kph in built-up areas. Speeding fines may be as much as L500,000, or L100,000 for jumping a red light (a popular Italian sport).

If you are undeterred by these caveats, you may actually enjoy driving in Italy, at least away from the congested tourist centres. Signposting is generally good, and roads are usually excellently maintained. Some of the roads are feats of engineering that the Romans themselves would have admired—bravura projects suspended on cliffs, crossing valleys on vast stilts, winding up hairpins. Milan is a major motorway junction, and access to the rest of Italy (and indeed the rest of Europe) is possible from the city (all roads lead to Milan). The A4 (Milan–Turin) is very busy and an accident blackspot.

Buy a good road map (the Italian Touring Club series is excellent). The **Automobile Club of Italy** (ACI) is a good friend to the foreign motorist. Besides having bushels of useful information and tips, they offer a free breakdown service, and can be reached from anywhere by dialling **116**—also use this number if you have to find the nearest service station. If you need major repairs, the ACI can make sure the prices charged are according to their guidelines.

ACI Offices in Lombardy

Bergamo:	Via A Maj 16, ✆ (035) 247 621
Brescia:	Via XXV Aprile 16, ✆ (030) 40 561
Como:	Viale Masia 79, ✆ (031) 556 755
Cremona:	Via XX Settembre 19, ✆ (0372) 29 601
Domodossola:	Via A de Gasperi 12, ✆ (0324) 42 008
Mantua:	Piazza 80 Fanteria 13, ✆ (0376) 325 691
Milan:	Corso Venezia 43, ✆ (02) 7745
Pavia:	Piazza Guicciardi 5, ✆ (0382) 301 381
Sondrio:	Via Milano 12, ✆ (0342) 212 213
Varese:	Viale Milano 25, ✆ (0332) 285 150
Vigévano:	Viale Mazzini 40, ✆ (0381) 85 129

hiring a car

Hiring a car or camper van is simple but not particularly cheap. In Italian it's called *autonoleggio*. There are both large international firms through which you can reserve a car in advance, and local agencies, which often have lower prices. Air or train travellers should check out possible discount packages. Most companies will require a deposit amounting to the estimated cost of the hire. VAT of 19% is applied to car hire, so make sure you take this into account when checking prices. Most companies have a minimum age limit of 21 (23 in some cases). A credit card makes life easier, and you will need to produce your licence and a passport. Current 1994 rates are around L90,000 per day for a small car (Fiat Panda, for instance) with unlimited mileage and collision damage waiver, including tax (hire for three days or longer is somewhat less pro rata). Most major rental companies have offices in Milan, most at the airports or the Stazione Centrale (Hertz, Avis, Maggiore and Europcar). If you need a car for longer than three weeks, leasing may be a more economic alternative. The National Tourist Office has a list of firms in Italy that hire caravans (trailers) or camper vans. Non-residents are not allowed to buy cars in Italy.

By Taxi

Taxis are fairly expensive, so don't take too many of them if you're on a tight budget. The average meter starts at L6400, and adds L300 per kilometre. There are extra charges for luggage, trips to the airport; rates go up after 10pm and on Sundays and holidays. They don't stop if hailed on the streets; head for a taxi-rank (marked with a yellow line on the road). Radio-taxi services operate in Milan.

Hitchhiking

It is illegal to hitch on the *autostrade*, though you may pick up a lift near one of the toll booths. Don't hitch from city centres, head for suburban exit routes. For the best chances of getting a lift, travel light, look respectable and take your shades off. Hold a sign indicating your destination if you can. Never hitch at points which may cause an accident or obstruction; Italian traffic conditions are bad enough already! Risks for women are lower in northern Italy than in the more macho south, but it is not advisable to hitch alone. Two or more men may encounter some reluctance.

By Motorcycle or Bicycle

The means of transport of choice for many Italians; motorbikes, mopeds and Vespas can be a delightful way to see the country. You should only consider it, however, if you've ridden them before—Italy's hills and alarming traffic make it no place to learn. You must be at least 14 for a *motorino* (scooter) and 16 for anything more powerful. Helmets are compulsory. Costs for a *motorino* range from about L20,000 to L35,000 per day, scooters somewhat more (up to L50,000). Italians are keen cyclists as well; racing drivers up the steepest hills; if you're not training for the Tour de France, consider the region's topography well before planning a bicycling tour, especially in the hot summer months. You can hire a bike in most Italian towns. Prices are about L10,000–L20,000 per day, which may make buying one interesting if you plan to spend much time in the saddle (L190,000–L300,000), either in a bike shop or through the classified ad papers put out in nearly every city and region. Alternatively, if you bring your own bike, do check the airlines to see what their policies are on transporting them. Bikes can be transported by train in Italy, either with you or within a couple of days—apply at the baggage office (*ufficio bagagli*).

Buying a House   16
Children   16
Climate and When to Go   17
Crime and Police Business   18
Disabled Travellers   18
Embassies and Consulates   19

Practical A–Z

Festivals   19
Food and Drink   21
Health and Emergencies   25
Maps and Publications   26
Money   26
Opening Hours   27
Packing   28
Photography   29
Post Offices   29
Shopping   30
Sports and Activities   33
Telephones   35
Time   36
Toilets   36
Tourist Offices   36
Weights and Measures   37
Where to Stay   37
Women Travellers   41

Buying a House

Ritzy lakeshore villas command awesome prices, but rural real estate is still one of Italy's great bargains. Even in today's saturated marketplace, you can achieve a lifetime's dream by buying a run-down property and restoring it lovingly to your own tastes and needs. But beware the pitfalls. One estate agent is amazed that his English clients invariably express two major concerns about a property: drainage and the presence of a bidet, as if it were an instrument of the devil! What they should be asking are questions about water supply, electricity, and road access—often big problems for that isolated, romantic farmhouse that has caught their eye. Another thing to remember before purchasing a home or land is that you need permission from the local *comune* to make any changes or improvements, and it's no good buying anything unless you're pretty sure the *comune* will consent (for a size-able fee, of course) to let you convert the old cellar or stable into a spare bedroom. Another thing to remember is that though there are no annual rates (property tax) to pay, there's a 10% IVA (VAT) to be paid on the purchase price for a house and 17% on land, as well as a hefty Capital Gains Tax on selling price and profit to be paid by the seller. Italians tend to get round this by selling at one price and writing down another on the contract. But remember if you sell you'll be in the same bind.

Once you've agreed to buy, you pay a deposit (usually 25–30%) and sign a *compromesso*, a document that states that if you back out you lose your deposit, and if the seller changes his mind he forfeits double the deposit to you (be sure your *compromesso* includes this feature, called *caparra confirmatoria*). Always transfer payment from home through a bank, taking care to get and save a certificate of the transaction so you can take the sum back out of Italy when you sell. After the *compromesso*, your affairs will be handled by a *notaio*, the public servant in charge of registering documents and taxes who works for both buyer and seller. If you want to make sure your interests are not overlooked, you can hire a *commercialista* (lawyer-accountant) who will handle your affairs with the *notaio*, including the final transfer deed (*rogito*), which completes the purchase at the local Land Registry. Upon signing, the balance of the purchase price generally becomes payable within a year. The next stage for most buyers—restoration—can be a nightmare. Make sure the crew you hire are experienced and that you're pleased with their work else-where—don't hesitate to ask as many other people in your area as possible for advice. One book that offers some clues on the ins and outs of taxes, inheritance law, residency, gardening, etc. is *Living in Italy*, published by Robert Hale, London 1991.

Children

Even though a declining birthrate and the legalization of abortion may hint otherwise, chil-dren are still the royalty of Italy, and are pampered, often obscenely spoiled, probably more fashionably dressed than you are, and never allowed to get dirty. Surprisingly, most of them somehow manage to be well-mannered little charmers. If you're bringing your own *bambini* to Italy, they'll receive a warm welcome everywhere. Many hotels offer advanta-geous rates for children and have play areas, and most of the larger cities have permanent

Luna Parks, or funfairs. Other activities young children enjoy (besides endless quantities of pizza, spaghetti and ice cream) are a day at Lake Garda's **Gardaland** at Castelnuovo (Italy's closest approximation to Disneyland), the **Parco Minitalia** at Capriate S. Gervasio, or the **Parco della Preistoria** (dinosaurs) at Rivolta d'Adda. **Pastrengo**, east of Lake Garda, has another leisure park with still more dinosaurs (alas, concrete ones) and more lively-looking creatures like Tibetan oxen, tigers and hippos in its autosafari park. The **Villa Pallavicino** in Stresa has a children's zoo with sealions and zebras. **Lake cruises**, of course, are for children of all ages (the younger sort travel half-price). If a **circus** visits town, you're in for a treat; it will either be a sparkling showcase of daredevil skill or a poignant, family-run, modern version of Fellini's *La Strada*. The big cities can be fun for kids, too. **Milan**'s Natural History Museum not only has stuffed rhinos, but a good playground in the gardens nearby. Other good bets are canal tours, a trip to the top of the Duomo, and a visit to the Museum of Science and Technology (though there are hardly enough buttons to push and hands-on activities for kids under 10).

Climate and When to Go

As Italian temperature charts go, the northwest has the most thrilling; the weather here is much more fun that it is in most places. The Alpine climate meets the Mediterranean head-on, and on the whole the latter wins, making Lombardy both a summer and a winter destination. Mantua and the other cities along the Po are chilly and fog-bound in winter, and steam baskets in August. The Italian Lakes, shielded by the Alps from the worst extremes of winter, are large enough to maintain a Mediterranean climate at alpine altitudes, and their shores are decorated with some of Italy's most beautiful gardens.

Winter is a good time for seeing Milan at its cultural liveliest, when you can meet more natives and find the sights blissfully uncrowded (if sometimes closed!). The Lakes themselves, however, may well be shrouded in mist for weeks on end. **Spring** is delightful with warmer temperatures, blossoming trees and flowers—still uncrowded apart from Easter. A few days of intermittent rain is about the worst that can happen. During the **summer** the shores of the Lakes are very crowded, and there are scores of festivals and special events, though the cities are more or less abandoned to tourists from August to September 15. It rarely rains (though isolated, dramatic thunderstorms may occur), and outside the plains the temperatures are usually remarkably pleasant. **Autumn** is another ideal time to go for the magnificent colours, the grape harvests, and blue balmy days (though rain may intrude during October and November).

Average Temperatures in °C (°F)

	Jan	April	July	October
Milan	1.9 (35)	13.2 (55)	24.8 (76)	13.7 (56)
Lake Como	6.0 (43)	13.3 (55)	23.7 (74)	9.8 (50)
Lake Maggiore	5.2 (41)	12.9 (54)	23.9 (74)	10.1 (50)
Lake Garda	4.0 (39)	13.2 (55)	24.5 (76)	14.7 (58)

Average Monthly Rainfall in mm (in)

	Jan	April	July	Oct
Milan	62 (3)	82 (3)	47 (2)	75 (3)
Lake Como	74 (3)	47 (2)	12 (0.5)	20 (1)
Lake Maggiore	90 (4)	61 (3)	20 (1)	22 (1)
Lake Garda	31 (1)	62 (3)	72 (3)	89 (4)

Crime and Police Business

Police, ℰ 113

Northern Italians tend to look down on what they perceive as the corruption and inefficiency of the south, in particular the central government in Rome. But Milan, Italy's second city, is itself by no means devoid of corruption, and many riveting political scandals have occurred in the last few years. There is a fair amount of petty crime all over Italy—purse snatchings, pickpocketing, minor thievery of the white-collar kind (always check your change) and car break-ins and theft—but violent crime is rare. Scooter-borne purse-snatchers can be foiled if you stay on the inside of the pavement and keep a firm hold on your property (sling your bag-strap across your body, not dangling from one shoulder); pickpockets strike in crowded street cars and gatherings; don't carry too much cash, and split it so you won't lose the lot at once. In cities and popular tourist sights, beware groups of scruffy-looking women or children with placards, apparently begging for money. They use distraction techniques to perfection.. The smallest and most innocent-looking child is generally the most skilful pickpocket. If you are targeted, the best technique is to grab sharply hold of any vulnerable possessions or pockets and shout furiously. (Italian passers-by or plain-clothes police will often come to your assistance if they realize what is happening.) Be extra careful in train stations, don't leave valuables in hotel tooms, and always park your car in guarded lots or on well-lit streets, with temptations well out of sight. Purchasing small quantities of soft drugs for personal consumption is technically legal in Italy, though what constitutes a small quantity is unspecified, and, if the police don't like you to begin with, it will probably be enough to get you into big trouble.

Political terrorism, once the scourge of Italy, has declined greatly in recent years, mainly thanks to special quasi-military squads of black-uniformed national police, the *Carabinieri*. Local matters are usually in the hands of the *Polizia Urbana*; the nattily dressed *Vigili Urbani* concern themselves with directing traffic, and handing out parking fines. If you need to summon any of them, dial ℰ 113.

Disabled Travellers

Italy has been relatively slow off the mark in its provision for disabled visitors. Uneven or non-existent pavements, the appalling traffic conditions, crowded public transport, and endless flights of steps in many public places are all disincentives. Progress is gradually being made, however. A national support organization in your own country may well have specific information on facilities in Italy, or will at least be able to provide general advice. The Italian tourist office or CIT (travel agency) can also advise on hotels, museums with ramps etc. If you book your rail travel through CIT, you can request assistance if you are wheelchair-bound.

In the UK, contact the **Royal Association for Disability & Rehabilitation** (RADAR), 25 Mortimer St, London W1N 8AB, ✆ (071) 637 5400, and ask for their guide *Holidays & Travel Abroad: A Guide for Disabled People* (£3.50). Americans should contact **SATH** (Society for the Advancement of Travel for the Handicapped), 347 Fifth Avenue, Suite 610, New York 10016, ✆ (212) 447 7284. Another useful organisation is **Mobility International**, at 228 Borough High Street, London SE1, ✆ (071) 403 5688, or PO Box 3551, Eugene, Oregon 97403, USA, ✆ (503) 343 1284. If you need help while you are in Milan or around the Lakes, contact the local tourist offices, who can be very helpful and have even been known to find wheelchair-pushers on the spot.

Embassies and Consulates

Italian embassies abroad

UK:	38 Eaton Place, London SW1X, ✆ (071) 235 9371; 32 Melville Street, Edinburgh 3, ✆ (031) 226 3631; 2111 Piccadilly, Manchester, ✆ (061) 236 3024.
Ireland:	63–65 Northumberland Road, Dublin, ✆ (01) 601 744; 7 Richmond Park, Belfast, ✆ (0232) 668 854
USA:	690 Park Avenue, New York, NY, ✆ (212) 737 9100; 12400 Wilshire Blvd, Suite 300, Los Angeles CA, ✆ (213) 8200 622
Canada:	136 Beverley St. Toronto, ✆ (416) 977 1566
Australia:	61–69 Macquarie St, Sydney 2000, NSW ✆ (02) 2478 442
New Zealand:	34 Grant Rd, Thorndon, Wellington, ✆ (04) 7473 5339

embassies in Italy

UK:	Milan: Via San Paulo 7, Milan, ✆ (02) 723 001
Republic of Ireland:	Largo Nazareno 3, Rome, ✆ (06) 678 2541
USA:	Via Principe Amedeo 2–10, Milan, ✆ (02) 290 351
Canada:	Via Vittorio Pisani 19, Milan, ✆ (02) 669 7451
Australia:	Via Turati 40, Milan, ✆ (02) 659 8727

Festivals

Festivals in Italy are often more show than spirit (there are several exceptions to this rule), but they can add a note of colour and culture to your holiday. Some are great costume affairs dating back to the Middle Ages or Renaissance; others recall ancient pre-Christian religious practices; and there are a fair number of music festivals, antique fairs,and, most of all, festivals devoted to the favourite national pastime—food. Note that many dates are liable to slide into the nearest weekend.

Jan–July	Opera and ballet at La Scala, **Milan.**
Jan 6	Three Kings Procession, **Milan.**
Mid-Jan–May	Musical afternoons (*I pomeriggi musicali*), **Milan.**
Jan 26	Bonfire of the Giubiana, **Cantù** (Como), with fireworks.
Jan 31	San Giulio, boat procession, **Lake Orta.**
Feb	Shrovetide carnivals at **Schignano** (Como) with a parade of *bei* or elegant figures and *brutt* (ragged ones), ending with a bonfire; **Bagolino** (Brescia); **Milan** (processions, floats, children's events etc.).
Ash Wednesday	Bigolada celebrations at Castel d'Ario, **Mantua** (communal feasting on spaghetti with anchovies in main piazza).
Feb 11–12	San Bello at **Berbenno** (Sondrio), folk festival in honour of Fra' Benigno, a handsome local friar.
Lent, 1st Sun	**Grosio** (Sondrio) traditional carnival with floats and food.
Feb 15	San Faustino (**Brescia**) patron saint fair and festival.
March	Fashion collections, **Milan.**
Mid-March	Sant'Ambroggio carnival, **Milan.**
Easter	**Bormio**, parade of Easter floats.
Mar–April	Concerts at San Maurizio church in Monastero Maggiore, **Milan.**
April 9–10	**Bergamo**, re-enactment of the Oath of the Lombard League (historical costumes and pageantry.
End April/ 1st week May	**Orta San Giulio**, Ortafiori flower festival.
April–May	**Milan**, Jazz festival Citta di Milano.
May	Piano competition, **Bergamo** and **Brescia.** **Legnano** (Milan), Palio del Carroccio, celebrating defeat of Barbarossa by the Lombard League in 1176 (medieval parade and horse-race).
Corpus Christi	**Premana** (Como) and **Grosio** (Sondrio), processions with decorated streets
June	Festival Cusiano di Musica Antica, **Orta San Giulio.**
June 4	Navigli Festival, **Milan**
	Pizzighettone (Cremona), historical pageant and flag-tossing to commemorate imprisonment of François Ier.
June 6	Festa of San Gerardo, **Monza** (feast of patron saint who once rescued the sick during a flood by turning his cloak into a raft).

June 23–24	**Ossuccio** (Como), 300-year-old festival with illuminations in snail shells on Comacina, boat procession, flat throwing and folk music.
July 2	Festa della Madonna della Foppa, **Gerosa** (Bergamo), marking an apparition of the Virgin.
July 29–30	Melon Festival at **Casteldidone** (Cremona).
July, last Sun	Pizzoccheri festival, woodland feasting on grey noodles, **Teglio** (Sondrio).
August	Vacanze a Milano, **Milan**, theatre and musical events.
Aug 15	Ferragosto holiday, marked by the exhibition of the *madonnari*, pavement artists, at **Curtatone** (Mantua).
Aug, last wk	San Vito, with big fireworks, at **Omegna** (Lake Orta).
End Aug–Sept	*Settimane Musicali*, musical weeks at **Stresa** on Lake Maggiore.
September	Italian Grand Prix, **Monza**.
Sept, 2nd Sun	Horse palio with Renaissance costumes at **Isola Dovarese** (Cremona).
Sept, 3rd Sun	Crotti festival at **Chiavenna** (Sondrio) with songs, dances, food and wine.
October	Spring–summer fashion collections, **Milan**.
Oct–Nov	Organ concerts at San Maurizio in Monastero Maggiore, **Milan**.
Oct, 1st Sun	Festa della Madonna del Rosario, **Montodine** (Cremona), with illuminated procession of boats down the River Serio and fireworks.
December 7	La Scala opera season opens; Feast of Sant'Ambroggio and 'O Bei O Bei' antique market, **Milan**.
Christmas Eve	Torchlight procession of the shepherds at **Canneto dell'Oglio** (Mantua); underwater Christmas crib at **Laveno** (Varese) until Epiphany.
Dec–April	Stagione di Prosa, **Brescia** (theatrical performances).

Food and Drink

There are those who eat to live and those who live to eat, and then there are the Italians, for whom food has an almost religious significance, unfathomably linked with love, *La Mamma*, and tradition. In this singular country, where millions of otherwise sane people spend much of their waking hours worrying about their digestion, standards both at home and in the restaurants are understandably high. Few Italians are gluttons, but all are experts on what is what in the kitchen; to serve a meal that is not properly prepared and more than a little complex is tantamount to an insult.

For the visitor this national culinary obsession comes as an extra bonus to the senses—along with Italy's remarkable sights, music, and the warm sun on your back, you can enjoy some of the best tastes and smells the world can offer, prepared daily in Italy's kitchens and fermented in its countless wine cellars.

This applies all over the country, despite the well-known gibe of southerners that Lombardy's cooking is designed for people so anxious to get to work that they don't have time to waste on eating. While it is true that lunch for many office workers in Milan consists of a rapid snack, those with more leisure can eat extremely well, and (if you avoid obvious expense-account places) inexpensively. If you are ever bored poring over a menu in northwest Italy, you've been nipped in the tastebuds. Many Italian dishes need no introduction—pizza, spaghetti, lasagne and minestrone are familiar to all. What is perhaps less well known is the tremendous regional diversity at the table. Milan, of course, offers a chance to eat many regional and foreign dishes in a host of restaurants (some may be interested to know that Italy's first specifically vegetarian restaurants appeared here), but a strong local style of cuisine also exists, based on **polenta** (a yellowish cornmeal flour a bit like American 'grits') and **rice**. Butter, rather than oil, is often used as a cooking medium. **Gorgonzola** and **Bel Paese** are the region's most famous cheeses. Soft, creamy **mascarpone**, now achieving cult status in UK supermarkets, is also a Lombard product.

As Europe's major producer of rice, Lombardy is predominantly the land of the **risotto**, ranging from the traditional saffron-tinted *risotto alla milanese* to seasonal concoctions with porcini mushrooms or asparagus, or even fruit and raisins in some *cucina nuova* restaurants; also try homemade **pasta** with gorgonzola, or imaginatively stuffed with squash, meat or spinach. A local pasta speciality is *pizzocheri* (a buckwheat noodle from the Valtellina). Italy's speciality dried meats (*carpaccio, prosciutto* and *Bresaola della Valtellina*) make popular starters. A wide variety of **fish**, fresh or sun-dried, comes from the Lakes, especially trout and pike, or smaller silvery creatures displayed in large tanks (*pesce misto*) often served *in carpione* (marinated with herbs and fried); and admirers of slippery dishes like eels, frogs or snails will find happiness in the lowlands of the Po. **Donkey** meat appears with alarming frequency on menus from Lake Orta to Mantua; even King Kong would balk before *stu'a'd'asnin cünt la pulenta* (stewed donkey with polenta). But don't despair—more appetising main courses include *ossobuco, cotoletta alla milanese* (Lombard wiener schitzel), duckling, and the hearty regional pork and cabbage stew, *cazzoela* or *cassuoela* (two of 25 different spellings). *Bistecca milanese* is a veal fillet fried in breadcrumbs. Polenta is even made into desserts, but *torta di tagliatelle* (a cake with egg pasta and almonds) is perhaps more appealing. *Panettone*, a light fruit cake with raisins and candied fruit, is another Milanese speciality, as are *biscotti* (handmade biscuits flavoured with nuts, vanilla and lemon).

Breakfast (*colazione*) in Italy is no lingering affair, but an early morning wake-up shot to the brain: a **cappuccino** (espresso with hot foamy milk, often sprinkled with chocolate— incidentally first thing in the morning is the only time of day at which any self-respecting Italian will touch the stuff), a *caffè latte* (white coffee) or a *caffè lungo* (a generous portion of espresso), accompanied by a croissant-type roll, called a *cornetto* or *briosce*, or a fancy pastry. This repast can be consumed in any bar and repeated during the morning as often as necessary. Breakfast in most Italian hotels seldom represents great value.

Lunch (*pranzo*), generally served around 1pm, is the most important meal of the day for the Italians, with a minimum of a first course (*primo piatto*—any kind of pasta dish, broth or soup, or rice dish or pizza), a second course (*secondo piatto*—a meat dish, accompanied by a *contorno* or side dish—a vegetable, salad, or potatoes usually), followed by fruit or dessert and coffee. You can, however, begin with a platter of *antipasti*—the appetizers Italians do so brilliantly, ranging from warm seafood delicacies to raw ham (*prosciutto crudo*), salami in a hundred varieties, lovely vegetables, savoury toasts, olives, pâté and many many more. There are restaurants that specialize in *antipasti*, and they usually don't take it amiss if you decide to forget the pasta and meat and just nibble on these scrumptious *hors-d'œuvres* (though in the end it will probably cost more than a full meal). Most Italians accompany their meal with wine and mineral water—*acqua minerale*, with or without bubbles (*con* or *senza gas*), which supposedly aids digestion—concluding their meals with a *digestivo* liqueur.

Cena, the **evening meal**, is usually eaten around 8pm. This is much the same as *pranzo* although lighter, without the pasta: a pizza and beer, eggs or a fish dish. In restaurants, however, they offer all the courses, so if you have only a sandwich for lunch you can have a full meal in the evening.

In Italy the various terms for types of **restaurants**—*ristorante*, *trattoria*, or *osteria*—have been confused. A *trattoria* or *osteria* can be just as elaborate as a restaurant, though rarely is a *ristorante* as informal as a traditional *trattoria*. Unfortunately the old habit of posting menus and prices in the windows has fallen from fashion, so it's often difficult to judge variety or prices. Invariably the least expensive restaurant-type place is the *vino e cucina*, simple places serving simple cuisine for simple everyday prices. It is essential to remember that the fancier the fittings, the fancier the bill, though neither of these points has anything at all to do with the quality of the food. If you're uncertain, do as you would at home—look for lots of locals. When you eat out, mentally add to the bill (*conto*) the bread and cover charge (*pane e coperto*, between L2000–3000), and a 15% service charge. This is often included in the bill (*servizio compreso*); if not, it will say *servizio non compreso*, and you'll have to do your own arithmetic. Additional tipping is at your own discretion, but never do it in family-owned and -run places.

People who haven't visited Italy for years and have fond memories of eating full meals for under a pound will be amazed at how much **prices** have risen; though in some respects eating out in Italy is still a bargain, especially when you figure out how much all that wine would have cost you at home. In many places you'll often find restaurants offering a *menu turistico*—full, set meals of usually meagre inspiration for L18,000–25,000. More imaginative chefs often offer a *menu degustazione*—a set-price gourmet meal that allows you to taste their daily specialities and seasonal dishes. Both of these are cheaper than if you had ordered the same food à la carte. When you leave a restaurant you will be given a receipt (*scontrino* or *ricevuto fiscale*) which according to Italian law you must take with you out of the door and carry for at least 60 metres. If you aren't given one, it means the restaurant is probably fudging on its taxes and thus offering you lower prices. There is a slim chance that the tax police (*Guardia di Fianza*) may have their eye on you and the restaurant, and if you don't have a receipt they could slap you with a heavy fine (L30,000).

We have divided restaurants into the following price categories:

very expensive	over L80,000
expensive	L50,000–80,000
moderate	L30,000–50,000
inexpensive	below L30,000

There are several alternatives to sit-down meals. The '**hot table**' (*tavola calda*) is a stand-up buffet, where you can choose a simple prepared dish or a whole meal, depending on your appetite. The food in these can be truly impressive; many offer only a few hot dishes, pizza and sandwiches, though in every fair-sized town there will be at least one *tavola calda* with seats where you can contrive a complete dinner outside the usual hours. Little shops that sell pizza by the slice are common in city centres. At any grocer's (*alimentari*) or market (*mercato*) you can buy the materials for countryside or hotel-room **picnics**; some places in the smaller towns will make the sandwiches for you. For really elegant picnics, have a *tavola calda* pack up something nice for you. And if everywhere else is closed, there's always the railway station—bars will at least have sandwiches and drinks, and perhaps some surprisingly good snacks you've never heard of before. Some of the station bars also prepare *cestini di viaggio*, full-course meals in a basket to help you through long train trips. Common snacks you'll encounter include *panini* of prosciutto, cheese and tomatoes, or other meats; *tramezzini*, little sandwiches on plain, square white bread that are always much better than they look; and pizza, of course.

Wine

Italy is a country where everyday wine is cheaper than Coca-Cola or milk, and where nearly every family owns some vineyards or has some relatives who supply most of their daily needs—which are not great. Even though they live in one of the world's largest wine-growing countries, Italians imbibe relatively little, and only at meals.

If Italy has an infinite variety of regional dishes, there is an equally bewildering array of regional wines, many of which are rarely exported because they are best drunk young. Unless you're dining at a restaurant with an exceptional cellar, do as the Italians do and order a carafe of the local wine (*vino locale* or *vino della casa*). You won't often be wrong. Most Italian wines are named after the grape and the district they come from. If the label says **DOC** (*Denominazione di Origine Controllata*) it means that the wine comes from a specially defined area and was produced according to a certain traditional method. **DOCG** (*Denominazione d'Origine Controllata e Garantia*) is allegedly a more rigorous classification, indicating that the wines not only conform to DOC standards, but are tested by government-appointed inspectors. At present few wines have been granted this status, and those mainly from Italy's more prestigious Tuscan vineyards, but the number is planned to increase steadily.

The well-known **Valpolicella**, **Bardolino** and **Soave** are produced on the shores of Lake Garda, and plenty filters through into local restaurants, though technically these wines hail from the Veneto region. Lombardy itself produces many commendable country wines which are comparable with those of Piedmont (and often cheaper), though its residents often snobbily prefer to drink wine from other regions, and it is the enterprising Swiss (many of whom own local vineyards) who snap up the most interesting vintages and whistle them over the border in their Mercedes car-boots. Lombardy's best wines come from the sunny hillsides of the Valtellina near the Swiss border (**Grumello, Sassella**, or **Inferno**). Here the vines are grown on immensely steep walled terraces, and cables are used to transfer the grapes to the valleys below at harvest-time. Light sparkling white wines and mellow reds hail from the **Franciacorta** region, and are often found in restaurant carafes around the Lakes. The Po valley produces a large quantity of wine, much through cooperatives. **Sangue di Giuda, Barbacarlo** and **Buttafuoco** are some of the best, typically *frizzante* reds.

Other drinks Italians are fond of post-prandial **brandies** (to aid digestion)—the famous Stock or Vecchia Romagna labels are always good. **Grappa** (*acquavitae*) is usually tougher, and often drunk in black coffee after a meal (a *caffè corretto*). Other items in any Italian bar include **Campari** , the famous red bitter, drunk on its own or in cocktails; **Vermouth, Fernet Branca, Cynar** and **Averno,** popular aperitif/digestives; and liqueurs like **Strega**, the witch potion from Benevento, apricot-flavoured **Amaretto,** cherry **Maraschino**, aniseed **Sambuca,** as well as any number of locally brewed elixirs, often made by monks.

Health and Emergencies

Fire, © 115
Ambulance, © 113

You can insure yourself for almost any possible mishap—cancelled flights, stolen or lost baggage and health. While national health coverage in the UK and Canada takes care of their citizens while travelling, the US doesn't. Check your current policies to see if they cover you while abroad, and under what circumstances, and judge whether you need a special **traveller's insurance** policy. Travel agencies sell them, as well as insurance companies; they are not cheap.

Citizens of EU countries are entitled to **reciprocal health care** in Italy's National Health Service and a 90% discount on prescriptions (bring **Form E111** with you). The E111 does not cover all medical expenses (e.g. no repatriation costs, and no private treatment), and it is advisable to take out separate travel insurance for full cover. Citizens of non-EU countries should check carefully that they have adequate insurance for any medical expenses, and the cost of returning home. Australia has a reciprocal health care scheme with Italy, but New Zealand, Canada and the USA do not. If you already have health insurance, a student card, or a credit card, you may be entitled to some medical cover abroad.

In an **emergency,** dial © 115 for fire and © 113 for an ambulance in Italy (*ambulanza*) or to find the nearest hospital (*ospedale*). Less serious problems can be treated at a *Pronto Soccorso* (casualty/first aid department) at any hospital clinic (*ambulatorio*), or at a local health unit (*Unita Sanitarial Locale*—USL). Airports and main railway stations also have

first-aid posts. If you have to pay for any health treatment, make sure you get a receipt, so that you can make any claims for reimbursement later.

Dispensing **chemists** (*farmacia*) are generally open 8.30am–1pm and 4–8pm. Pharmacists are trained to give advice for minor ills. Any large town will have a *farmacia* that stays open 24 hours (in **Milan** there is Carlo Erba, Piazza del Duomo 21); others take turns to stay open (the address rota is posted in the window).

No specific **vaccinations** are required or advised for citizens of most countries before visiting Italy; the main health risks are the usual travellers' woes of upset stomachs or the effects of too much sun. Take a supply of useful **medicaments** with you (e.g. insect repellent, anti-diarrhoeal medicine, antiseptic cream), and any drugs you need regularly.

Most Italian doctors speak at least rudimentary English, but, if you can't find one, contact your embassy or consulate for a list of English-speaking doctors. Standards of health care in Milan and Lombardy in general are higher than in some parts of Italy.

Maps and Publications

The maps in this guide are for orientation only, and to explore in any detail invest in a good, up-to-date regional map before you arrive. For an excellent range of maps in the UK, try **Stanford's**, 12–14 Long Acre, London WC2 9LP, © (071) 836 1321, or the **Travel Bookshop**. In the USA, try **The Complete Traveller**, 199 Madison Avenue, New York, NY 10016, © (212) 685 9007. Excellent maps are produced by the **Touring Club Italiano**, **Michelin**, and the **Istituto Geografico de Agostini**. They are available at all major bookshops in Italy (e.g. Feltrinelli) or sometimes on newsstands. Italian tourist offices are helpful and can often supply good area maps and town plans. Those around the Lakes can provide good walking maps. Try also the **Club Alpino Italiano**, Via Volta 56, Como, © (031) 264177.

Books are more expensive in Italy than in the UK, but some excellent shops stock English-language books. In **Milan**, try the **American Bookstore**, Via Camperio 16 (at Largo Cairoli), or the **English Bookshop**, Via Mascheroni 12. Milan's local newspaper is the *Corriere della Sera*, which virtually rivals Rome's *La Reppublica*. All major English-language newspapers can be found in Milan, perhaps a day or two old. *Time, Newsweek* and *The Economist* are also readily available. For local information, look out for *Milan is Milano, What's On in Milan* and *Milano Mese*, all available at the main tourist office. There's a **Reuters** news service at the SIP telephone office in Galleria V Emanuele II. The *Milano Design Guide* helps you find your way round the world's design capital.

Money

It's a good idea to order a wad of *lire* from your home bank to have on hand when you arrive in Italy, the land of strikes, unforeseen delays and quirky banking hours (*see* below), though take care how you carry it. Obtaining money is often a frustrating business involving much queueing and form-filling. The major banks and exchange bureaux licensed by the Bank of Italy give the best exchange rates for currency or traveller's cheques. Hotels, private exchanges in resorts and FS-run exchanges at railway stations usually have less advantageous rates, but are open outside normal banking hours. There are several weekend exchange offices in Milan, e.g. **Banca Ponti**, Piazza del Duomo 19 (Sat am only); **Banca delle Comunicazioni**, Stazione Centrale; **American Express**, Via Brera 3. In addition there are exchange offices at both airports. Remember that Italians indicate decimals with commas and thousands with full points.

Besides traveller's cheques, most banks will give you cash on a recognized credit card or Eurocheque with a Eurocheque card (taking little or no commission), and in big cities such as Milan you can find automatic tellers (ATMs) to spout cash on a Visa, American Express or Eurocheque card. You need a PIN number to use these. Make sure you read the instructions carefully, or your card may be retained by the machine. MasterCard (Access) is much less widely acceptable in Italy. Large hotels, resort area restaurants, shops and car hire firms will accept plastic as well; many smaller places will not. From sad experience, Italians are wary of plastic—you can't even use it at motorway petrol stops.

You can have money transferred to you through an Italian bank but this process may take over a week, even if it's sent urgent *espressissimo.* You will need your passport as identification when you collect it. Sending cheques by post is inadvisable.

Opening Hours

Although it varies from region to region, with Lombardy bearing more resemblance to northern Europe than the Mediterranean south, most of Italy closes down at 1pm until 3 or 4pm to eat and properly digest the main meal of the day. Afternoon hours are from 4 to 7, often from 5 to 8 in the hot summer months. Bars are often the only places open during the early afternoon. Most of Milan closes down completely during August, when locals flee from the polluted frying pan to the hills, lakes or coast.

Banks: Banking hours vary, but core times in Milan and major towns of Lombardy are usually Monday to Friday 8.30am–1.00pm and 3–4pm, closed weekends and on local and national holidays (*see* below). Outside normal hours though, you will usually be able to find somewhere to change money (albeit at disadvantageous rates), with the greatest choice in Milan.

Shops: Shops in northern Italy are usually open Monday–Saturday from 8am to 1pm and 3.30pm to 7.30pm, though hours vary according to season and are shorter in smaller centres. In Milan, shopping capital of Italy (if not the universe), hours are longer. Some supermarkets and department stores stay open throughout the day.

Churches: Italy's churches have always been a prime target for art thieves and as a consequence are usually locked when there isn't a sacristan or caretaker to keep an eye on things. All churches, except for the really important cathedrals and basilicas, close in the afternoon at the same hours as the shops, and the little ones tend to stay closed. Always have a pocketful of coins for the light machines in churches, or whatever work of art you came to inspect will remain shrouded in ecclesiastical gloom. Don't do your visiting during services, and don't come to see paintings and statues in churches the week preceding Easter—you will probably find them covered with mourning shrouds.

Museums and Galleries: Many of Italy's museums are magnificent, many are run with shameful neglect, and many have been closed for years for 'restoration', with slim prospects of reopening in the foreseeable future. With two works of art per inhabitant, Italy has a hard time financing the preservation of its national heritage; it's as well to inquire at the tourist office to find out exactly what is open and what is 'temporarily' closed before setting off on a wild goose chase.

In general, Sunday afternoons and Mondays are dead periods for the sightseer—you may want to make them your travelling days. Places without specified opening hours can usually be visited on request—but it is best to go before 1pm. We have listed the hours of important sights and museums, and specified which ones charge admission. **Entrance charges** to Lombardy's star museums are quite steep but others are fairly low, and some sights are completely free. For museums and galleries the average is L5000 to L6000, for churches or cathedrals about L4000, and for castles, palaces, villas and their gardens around L6000. Prices that substantially exceed these amounts will be marked *adm exp*. EC citizens under 18 and over 65 get free admission to state museums, at least in theory.

Tourist Offices: Known under various initials as EPT, APT or AAST, Italian tourist offices usually stay open from 8am to 12.30 or 1pm, and from 3 to 7pm, possibly longer in summer. Few open on Saturday afternoons or Sundays. Information booths can also be found at major railway stations and can provide hotel lists, town plans and terse information on local sights and transport. Queues can be maddeningly long. English is spoken in the main centres. If you're stuck, you may get more sense out of a friendly travel agency than an official tourist office.

National Holidays

Most museums, as well as banks and shops, are closed on the following national holidays:

1 January (New Year's Day), **6 January** (Epiphany), **Easter Monday**, **25 April** (Liberation Day), **1 May** (Labour Day), **15 August** (Assumption, also known as *Ferragosto*, the official start of the Italian holiday season), **1 November** (All Saints' Day), **8 December** (Immaculate Conception), **25 December** (Christmas Day), **26 December** (*Santo Stefano*, St Stephen's Day).

The feast day of Saint Ambrose (*Sant'Ambroggio*) on **7 December** is the closest the hard-working Milanese have to a civic holiday.

Packing

You simply cannot overdress in Italy; whatever grand strides Italian designers have made on the international fashion merry-go-round, most of their clothes are purchased domestically, prices be damned. Now whether or not you want to try to keep up is your own affair and your own heavy suitcase. It's not that the Italians are very formal; they simply like to dress up with a gorgeousness that adorns their cities just as much as those old Renaissance churches and palaces. The few places with dress codes are the major churches and basilicas (no shorts, sleeveless shirts or strappy sundresses—women should tuck a light silk scarf in a bag to throw over the shoulders), casinos, and a few posh restaurants.

After agonizing over fashion, remember to pack small and light: trans-Atlantic airlines limit baggage by size (two pieces are free up to 1.5m in height and width; in second claass you're allowed one of 1.5m and another up to 110cm). Within Europe limits are by weight; 20 kg (44lbs) in second class, 30 kg (66lbs) in first. You may well be penalized for anything larger. If you're travelling mainly by train, you'll want to keep bags to a minimum: jamming big suitcases in overhead racks in a crowded compartment isn't much fun for anyone. Never take more than you can carry, but do bring the following: any prescription medicine you need, an extra pair of glasses or contact lenses if you wear them; a pocket knife and corkscrew (for picnics), a flashlight (for dark frescoed churches, caves and crypts), a travel alarm (for those early trains) and a pocket Italian-English dictionary (for flirting and other emergencies; outside the main tourist centres you may well have trouble finding someone who speaks English). If you're a light sleeper, you may want to invest in earplugs. Your electric appliances will work in Italy if you adapt and convert them to run on 220 AC with two round prongs on the plug. Beyond that, what you bring depends on when and where you go (*see* 'Climate' above).

Photography

Film and **developing** are much more expensive than they are in either the UK or the USA, though there are plenty of outlets where you can obtain them. For example, a roll of film or *pellicola* (36 exposures, 100 ASA) costs around L8500, and L23,000 for developing. The equivalent slide film costs about L6,000 (L10,000 to develop). You are not allowed to take pictures in most museums and in some churches. Most cities now offer one-hour processing if you need your pics in a hurry. Lombardy's light is less dazzling than in the vivid south, and clarity may be affected by Milanese air pollution or local mists, but allow for extra brightness reflected off the water if you're by the Lakes.

Post Offices

Dealing with *la posta italiana* has always been a risky, frustrating, time-consuming affair. One of the scandals that mesmerized Italy in recent years involved the minister of the post office, who disposed of literally tons of backlog mail by tossing it in the Tiber. When the news broke, he was replaced—the new minister, having learned his lesson, burned all the mail the post office was incapable of delivering. Not surprisingly, fed-up Italians view the invention of the fax machine as a gift from the Madonna.

If you want to take your chances, post offices are usually open from 8am until 1pm (Monday to Saturday), or until 6 or 7pm in a large city. The main post office in **Milan** is at Piazza Cordusio. To have your mail sent poste restante (general delivery), have it addressed to the central post office (*Fermo Posta*) and expect three to four weeks for it to arrive. Make sure your surname is very clearly written in block capitals. To pick up your mail you must present your passport and pay a nominal charge. Stamps (*francoboli*) may be purchased in post offices or at tobacconists (*tabacchi*, identified by their blue signs with a white T). Prices fluctuate. The rates for letters and postcards (depending how many words you write!) vary according to the whim of the tobacconist or postal clerk.

You can also have money telegraphed to you through the post office; if all goes well, this can happen in a mere three days, but expect a fair proportion of it to go into commission.

Shopping

'Made in Italy' has become a byword for style and quality, especially in fashion and leather, but also in home design, ceramics, kitchenware, jewellery, lace and linens, glassware and crystal, chocolates, bells, Christmas decorations, hats, straw work, art books, engravings, handmade stationery, gold and silverware, bicycles, sports cars, woodworking, a hundred kinds of liqueurs, aperitifs, coffee machines, gastronomic specialities, and antiques (both reproductions, and the real thing). Where more so than in design-conscious Milan, Italy's major shopping centre and a cynosure of innovative style and fashion throughout the world? Shops and galleries are sprinkled throughout the city, and many products are made for export. Trade fairs and exhibitions abound, and much glossy, multi-lingual literature is available in design shops. Surprisingly in this Aladdin's cave, big-city competition keeps prices lower than most Italian cities and usually much lower than you'll find in posh resort boutiques. Elsewhere in Lombardy, Como is famous for silks, Cremona (Stradivarius' home-town) for musical instruments and nougat (*torrone*), and Castiglione Olona holds a large antiques market on the first Sunday of each month.

If you are looking for antiques, be sure to demand a certificate of authenticity—reproductions can be very, very good. To get your antique or modern art purchases home, you will have to apply to the Export Department of the Italian Ministry of Education—a possible hassle. You will have to pay an export tax as well; your seller should know the details. Be sure to save receipts for Customs on the way home. Italians don't much like department stores, but there are a few chains (*see* below). The main attraction of Italian shopping, however, is to buy luxury items. Prices for clothes are generally very high, and sizes are tailored for slim Italian builds. Shoes, in particular, tend to be narrower than in most western countries.

Shopping in Milan

Most shops are closed all day Sunday and Monday morning.
Food stores close on Monday afternoons.

Many of the big names in designer apparel and jewellery have their boutique 'headquarters' in what is known as the **Quadrilatero**, defined by Via Montenapoleone, Via della Spiga, Via S. Andrea and Via Borgospesso. Nearly all the shops here have branch offices eslewhere in Milan and in other cities; some of the better established, like Gucci, Armani, and Krizia, are glorified international chain stores. You may just find the latest of the latest pret-à-porter designs on Montenapoleone, but be assured they'll soon show up elsewhere, expensive enough, but without the high snob surcharges.

The aura and status created around the Italian garment industry is as much due to quality as to a certain wizardry with words and images, a language of glamour that could provide the subject for a doctoral thesis for an anthropologist from New Guinea. But then again, Italians have always liked to put on the dog, *la bella figura*; it's in their blood. The hype machine has turned this traditional trait into a national obsession—there are countless Italian fashion magazines (most of them emanating from Milan, naturally), and a weekly television programme devoted to *La Moda*. After an hour of window-shopping, however, only a die-hard fashion slave would disagree with Walter Benjamin's 'Monotony is nourished by the new'.

the Quadrilateral

The **jewellers** were here first, in the 1930s; since then, to have an address on Via Montenapoleone has meant status and quality. Among the most interesting on the street are **Buccellati** (No.4), considered by many the best jewellery designer in Italy, featuring exquisitely delicate gold work and jewels, each piece individually crafted. **Calderoni** (No.8) is fun for lavishly kitsch creations, while for something more traditional, try **Maboussin**, at No.29.

The artsy displays of clothing and, increasingly, shoes (in 1987 the Milanese staged a demonstration in protest at the takeover of their sacrosanct Montenapo by such 'Millipedes') are a window shopper's paradise. **Missoni's** ravishing knits for women and men are at Montenapoleone 1; **Valentino** and his classics are at Via Santo Spirito 3; **Krizia** sells her famous knits, evening dresses, and children's wear at Via della Spiga 23, and there's more designer children's wear at **Gio Moretti**, Via della Spiga 29. **Armani's** chief Milanese outlet is at Via Sant'Andrea 9, featuring his famous 'unstructured' jackets for men and women, while **Mila Schön** sells both her women's and her men's styles at Montenapoleone 2, and her men's at No.6. For quiet sophistication from a designer who has an 'architectural' approach, visit **Gianfranco Ferré**, who was the first Italian in years to branch out from pret-à-porter into individualist haute couture (women's clothes, Via della Spiga 11; men's next door). **Gianni Versace** displays his innovations on Via della Spiga 4 and at Montenapoleone 11, **Adriana** at Via della Spiga 22, and **Yves Saint Laurent** at Via Sant'Andrea 10. Three classics of couture are on Via Sant'Andrea: **Hermès** at 21, **Fendi** at 16 and **Chanel** at 12. The two bad boys of fashion are also represented: **Gaultier** at Via della Spiga 20 and **Moschino** at Via Sant'Andrea 14 and Via Durini 14 (near, also, to **Emporio Armani**).

Lace and leather are also well represented. Italian leather goods are known in most parts of the world simply through the name **Gucci**, which has a shop at Montenapoleone 5. **Ferragamo** sells his famous designs and shoes for men and women at Montenapoleone 3. **Beltrami**, at Montenapoleone 16 and in the Galleria San Babila, has the most outrageous and colourful women's shoes in Italy. Interesting shoes can also be found on Montenapoleone at **Sergio Rossi**, and **Della Vane**, at numbers 15 and 20, respectively.

Amongst the profusion of jewels, clothes, leathers and shoes there are also some antique dealers and furriers. **Lorenzi**, Montenapoleone 9, is the city's most refined pipe and male accessories shop. The **Salumaio di Montenapoleone**, at No.12, has an infinite array of hams, salamis, pasta, and cheeses, and nearly every gourmet item imaginable. If you need a break from shopping, **Café Cova** at Via Montenapoleone 8, or **Baretto**, Via Sant'Andrea 3, will keep you caffeinated while floating in the ozone of chic.

the city centre

Besides the great Galleria Vittorio Emanuele, several minor gallerias branch off the Corso Vittorio Emanuele, each a shopping arcade lined with good quality and reasonably priced shops. In Piazza del Duomo a monument almost as well known as the cathedral itself is Milan's biggest and oldest department store, **La Rinascente**; it's also the only one to have been christened by Gabriele D'Annunzio. La Rinascente has six floors of merchandise, with especially good clothing and domestic sections, offering a wide array of kitchen appliances dear to the heart of an Italian cook. There's a cafeteria on the top floor with great views over the cathedral. Other central shops include those of **Fiorucci**, who has his main headquarters in the Galleria Passerella; **Mandarina Duck**, in Galleria San Carlo, with a vast variety of bags and travelling cases; **Fratelli Prada**, Galleria Vittorio Emanuele, with classic, beautifully crafted leather goods; and **Guenzati**, Via Mercanti 1, which will make a velvet lover's heart flutter; they also do made-to-order clothes. Cheeses, from the most exotic to the most everyday, have been sold since 1894 at the **Casa del Formaggio**, Via Speronari 3, near the Duomo. **Rizzoli**, in the Galleria Vittorio Emanuele, is one of the city's best-stocked bookshops (with many English titles), owned by the family that founded the Corriere della Sera. Also in the Galleria, **Messaggerie Musicali** is one of the best in town for musical scores. On Sunday morning, a **Stamp and Coin Market** is held in Via Armorari, behind the Central Post Office.

The shops on busy Via Torino have some of Milan's more affordable prices, especially in clothes and footwear. **Frette**, at No.43, has an excellent section of moderately priced household linens, while **La Bottega del Tutù**, No.48, has everything for your favourite ballerina; at **Vergelio**, No.23, you can find reasonably priced shoes, and a bit further down **Foot Locker** is handy for sports shoes and accessories.

the Brera district

As well as a Monday market in the Piazza Mirabello and the **Antiques Fair** (every last Sunday of the month, along Naviglio Grande), Brera offers some of Milan's most original shops. Unusual and bizarre antiques are the mainstay of **L'Oro dei Farlocchi**, Via Madonnina 5; **Naj Oleari**, Via Brera 5, has unusual children's clothes and household items; **Piero Fornasetti**, Via Brera 16, has rather eccentric home decorations; exotic handmade papers can be found at the **Legatoria Artistica**, Via Palermo 5; and **Surplus**, Corso Garibaldi 7, has a marvellous array of second-hand garments. The latest Italian fashions are also reasonably priced at the big **COIN** department store, Corso Garibaldi 72.

On **Corso Buenos Aires** (ⓂLima), one of Milan's longest and densest shopping thoroughfares, you can find something of every variety and hue; one unusual shop is **Le Mani d'Oro**, Via Gaffurio 5 (near Piazzale Loreto), which specializes in *trompe l'œil* objects and decorations, while **Guerciotti**, Via Tamagno 55 (parallel to Corso Buenos Aires), makes bicycles to order. Another shopping street with excellent merchandise and reasonable prices is **Via Paolo Sarpi** (ⓂMoscova), formerly the city's Chinatown. Other interesting shops: **Sardinia Shop**, Largo Cairoli 2, with carpets and baskets from the island of the *nuraghi*; **Faenze di Faenza**, Via Stoppani 10, with faience ware; **Franco Leoni**, Via Urbano III 1 (just off Corso Porto Ticinese), has antique Italian dolls; and **Il Discanto**, Via Turati 7, with exotic instruments and jewellery from Asia and Africa. For an excellent selection of books in English, try either **The English Bookshop**, Via Mascheroni 12 (ⓂConciliazione) or **The American Bookstore**, Largo Cairoli, near the castle. If you're interested in the latest designs in all kinds of furniture, Milan has a major concentration of showrooms and stores near the centre: well worth a look are **Artemide**, Corso Monforte 19; **De Padova**, Corso Venezia 14; **Dilmos**, Piazza San Marco 1; and **Alias**, Via Fiori Chiari 3.

Perhaps the best place to hunt for designer bargains in Milan is the Saturday market in **Viale Papiniano**, in the Navigli. On December 7 (St Ambrose's Day), there's a fine antiques market, the **O Bei, O Bei**, in the Piazza Sant'Ambrogio.

Sports and Activities

Beaches: The beaches around the Lakes are mostly shingly strips—useful platforms for sunbathing or landing boats, but little more. Many of them shelve steeply and the water is never very warm. And however sparkling the water may seem from a distance, some areas suffer pollution and are not recommended for bathing (Garda is said to be the cleanest). At least, though, Lake beaches aren't plagued by that peculiarly Italian phenomenon, the *concessionaire*, who parks ugly lines of sunbeds and brollies all the way along the best stretches of coast, and charges all comers handsomely for the privilege. Sirmione, on Lake Garda, has a number of small swimming beaches on its eastern flank, while on the western shore Toscolano-Maderno has one of the best of all Garda beaches. Nearby Limone sul Garda has a beach over 3km long.

Casinos: Italy retains a curious outpost in the centre of Lake Lugano, surrounded by the Italian-speaking but resolutely Swiss canton of Ticino. Campione d'Italia's *raison d'être* is a prosperous casino where the Swiss get a chance to throw caution and any spare francs at the croupiers. Other nationalities with money to burn are also welcome (take your passport, and a jacket and tie).

Fishing: Lombardy's rivers are renowned for good fishing. Many freshwater lakes and streams are stocked, and, if you're more interested in fresh fish than the sport of it, there are innumerable trout farms. To fish in fresh water you need to purchase a year's membership card (currently L189,000) from the *Federazione Italiana della Pesca Sportiva*, which has an office in every province; they will inform you about local conditions and restrictions. Bait and equipment are readily available.

Football: Soccer (*il calcio*) is a national obsession. For many Italians its importance far outweighs tedious issues like the state of the nation, the government, or any momentous international event—not least because of the weekly chance (slim but real) of becoming an instant *lira* billionaire in the *Lotteria Sportiva*. The sport was actually introduced by the English, but a Renaissance game, like a cross between football and rugby, has existed in Italy for centuries. Modern Italian teams are known for their grace, precision and teamwork; rivalries are intense, scandals rife. The tempting rewards offered by such big-time entertainment attract all manner of corrupt practices, yet crowd violence is minimal compared with the havoc wreaked by Britain's lamentable fans. Serie A is the equivalent of the first division, comprising 18 teams, and **Milan**, triumphant from its recent success in the European Cup, is at the top of the tree. Milan's two teams, **Inter** and **AC Milan**, play on alternate Sundays during the season, at San Siro Stadium on Piazza Meazza. To reach it, take tram 24 or buses 95, 49 or 72. Tickets are available from the stadium, or from Milan Point, © 78 27 68, Largo Corsia dei Servi 11. For Inter matches, you can get tickets at branches of Banca Popolare di Milano.

Golf: These northwestern zones are the best region in Italy to practise inexpert swings on a wide variety of beautifully set courses, particularly around Lake Como. Write or ring beforehand to check details before turning up. Most take guests and hire equipment (a selection of these is given below, but there are many others).

> **Barlassina** (18 holes): 22030 Birago di Camnago, © (0362) 560621
> **Bergamo** (27 holes): 24030 Almenno S. Bartolomeo, © (035) 640 028
> **Carimate** (18 holes): 22060 Carimate, © (031) 790 226
> **La Pinetina** (18 holes): 22070 Appiano Gentile, © (031) 933 202
> **Menaggio e Cadenabbia** (18 holes): 22010 Grandola e Uniti, © (0344) 32103
> **Milan** (27 holes): 20052 Parco di Monza, © (039) 303 081
> **Molinetto** (18 holes): 20063 Cernusco sul Naviglio, © (02) 921 05128
> **Monticello** (36 holes): 22070 Cassina Rizzardi, © (031) 928 055
> **Varese** (18 holes): 21020 Luvinate, © (0332) 229 302
> **Villa d'Este** (18 holes): 22030 Montorfano, © (031) 200 200

Hiking and Mountaineering: These sports become steadily more popular among native Italians every year, and Lombardy now has a good system of marked trails and Alpine refuges run by the **Italian Alpine Club** (CAI) located in every province (even the flat ones, where they organize excursions into the hills). If you're taking some of the most popular trails in summer (especially in the Stelvio National Park or around the Lakes), you would do well to write beforehand to reserve beds in refuges. Walking in the Alps is generally practicable between May and October, after most of the snow has melted; all the necessary gear—boots, packs, tents—are available in Italy but for more money than you'd pay at home. The CAI can put you in touch with Alpine guides or climbing groups if you're up to some real adventure, or write to the Italian national tourist board for a list of operators offering mountaineering holidays. Some Alpine resorts have taken to offering *Settimane Verdi* (Green Weeks)—accommodation and activity packages for summer visitors similar to skiers' White Weeks. Trails around Lakes Como and Iseo are particularly interesting. Other areas to head for are the **Parco Nazionale dell' Stelvio** and the **Val Malanca**. For more arduous climbing, the northern province of Valtellina is best.

Motor-racing: Monza hosts the Italian Grand Prix every September. The Formula I track, built in 1922, is 15km out of town, reached along Viale Monza from Piazzale Loreto.

Skiing and Winter Sports: Lombardy's most famous ski resort is **Bormio**, at the entrance to Italy's largest national park, which has hosted world events in recent years. Splendidly situated in a mountain basin, it has numerous lifts and an indoor pool. The character of the old towered village has not entirely been lost, hence its popularity as a summer resort and spa too (glacier skiing is practised above the Stelvio pass). Other skiing facilities exist near **Bergamo** and in the province of **Como**. **Malcésine** on the east side of Lake Garda is another well-equipped resort. Facilities in Italy have improved greatly and now compare with other European skiing areas, but are usually less expensive. Prices are highest during Christmas and New Year holidays, in February and at Easter. Most resorts offer *Settimane Bianche* (White Weeks) off-season packages at economical rates. Other winter sports, ice-skating and bob-sleighing, are also available at larger resorts.

Watersports: Riva, on Lake Garda, is the main resort for swimming and watersports, with sailing, diving and windsurfing schools. Try Bouwmeester Windsurfing Centre by the Hotel Pier, ✆ 55 42 30, or Nautic Club Riva, Viale Rovereto 132, ✆ 55 44 40. **Torbole** nearby is another popular windsurfing spot. Contact Centro Windsurf, Colonia Pavese, ✆ (0464) 505 385. Lake Como also has well-equipped sailing and windsurfing schools. **Waterskiing** is possible on all the major lakes. For **swimming**, try the smaller, less crowded lakes like Viverone, Varese and Mergozzo.

Sailing: Fraglia della Vela, ✆ 55 24 60, in Riva can provide plenty of information about sailing on Lake Garda. Yacht charters are available from: Horca Myseria, Via Pelitti 1, 20126 Milan, ✆ (02) 255 2585; Noi Blu, Via S Alessandro Sauli 26, 20127 Milan, ✆ (02) 282 64766; Settemari, Via Rubens 28, 20248 Milan, ✆ (02) 407 5843. For further information, contact the **Italian State Tourist Office** or write to either the *Federazione Italiana Vela* (Italian Sailing Federation), Via Brigata Bisagno 2/17, Genoa, ✆ (010) 56 57 23, or the *Federazione Italiana Motonautica* (Italian Motorboat Federation), Via Piranesi 44/B, Milan, ✆ (02) 76 10 50.

Telephones

Public telephones for international calls may be found in the offices of SIP (*Societa Italiana Telefoni*, Italy's telephone company). They are the only places where you can make reverse-charge calles (*a erre*, collect calls) but be prepared for a wait, as all these calls go through the operator in Rome. Rates for **long-distance calls** are among the highest in Europe. Calls within Italy are cheapest after 10pm; international calls after 11pm. Most phone booths now take either coins, *gettoni* (L200 tokens often given to you in place of change) or phone cards (*schede telefoniche*) available in L5000 or L10,000 amounts at tobacconists and news-stands. In smaller villages and islands, you can usually find *telefoni a scatti*, with a meter on it, in at least one bar (a small commission is generally charged). Try to avoid telephoning from hotels, which often add 25% to the bill. Telephone numbers in Italy currently change with alarming regularity as the antiquated system is updated.

Direct calls may be made by dialling the international prefix (for the UK 0044, Ireland 00353, USA and Canada 001, Australia 0061, New Zealand 0064). If you're calling Italy from abroad, dial 39 and then drop the first 0 from the telephone prefix. Many places have public fax machines, but the speed of transmission may make costs very high.

Time

Italy is one hour ahead of Greenwich Mean Time. From the last weekend of March to the end of September, Italian Summer Time (daylight-saving time) is in effect.

Toilets

Frequent travellers have noted a steady improvement over the years in the cleanliness of Italy's public conveniences, although as ever you will only find them in places like train and bus stations and bars. Ask for the *bagno*, *toilette*, or *gabinetto*; in stations and the smarter bars and cafés there are washroom attendants who expect a few hundred *lire* for keeping the place decent. You'll probably have to ask them for paper (*carta*). Don't confuse the Italian plurals; *signori* (gents), *signore* (ladies).

Tourist Offices

Addresses of Italian tourist offices within Lombardy are listed in the text, under the relevant place-name.

UK: 1 Princes Street, London W1R 8AY, ✆ (071) 408 1254

USA: 630 Fifth Avenue, Suite 1565, New York NY 10111, ✆ (212) 245 4822
12400 Wilshire Blvd, Suite 550, Los Angeles, CA 90025, ✆ (310) 820 0098
500 North Michigan Ave, Suite 1046, Chicago IL 60611, ✆ (312) 644 0990

Canada: 1 Place Ville Marie, Suite 1914, Montréal, Quebec H3B 3M9,
✆ (514) 866 7667

Japan: 2-7-14 Minimi, Aoyama, Minato-Ku, Tokyo 107, ✆ (813) 347 82 051
(also responsible for Australia and New Zealand).

Tourist and travel information may also be available from Alitalia (Italy's national airline) or CIT (Italy's state-run travel agency) offices in some countries.

Weights and Measures

1 kilogramme (1000g)=2.2 lb	1lb=0.45 kg
1 *etto* (100g)=0.25 lb (approx)	1 pint=0.568 litres
1 litre=1.76 pints	1 quart=1.136 litres
1 metre=39.37 inches	1 Imperial gallon=4.546 litres
1 kilometre=0.621 miles	1 US gallon=3.785 litres
	1 foot=0.3048 metres
	1 mile=1.161 kilometres

Where to Stay

All accommodation in Italy is classified by the Provincial Tourist Boards. Price control, however, has been deregulated since 1992. Hotels now set their own tariffs, which means that in some places prices have rocketed. After a period of rapid and erratic price fluctuation, tariffs are at last settling down again to more predictable levels under the influence of market forces. The quality of furnishings and facilities has generally improved in all categories in recent years. But you can still find plenty of older-style hotels and *pensioni*, whose eccentricities of character and architecture (in some cases undeniably charming) may frequently be at odds with modern standards of comfort or even safety. Milan has the most expensive and heavily booked hotels in Italy; check the calendar of events with the tourist office—a major trade fair or conference could put all your travel plans in jeopardy.

Category	Double with Bath
luxury (★★★★★)	L450–800,000
very expensive (★★★★)	L250–450,000
expensive (★★★)	L160–250,000
moderate (★★)	L85–160,000
inexpensive (★)	up to L85,000

Hotels and Guesthouses

Italian *alberghi* come in all shapes and sizes. They are rated from one to five stars, depending what facilities they offer (not their character, style or charm). The star ratings are some indication of price levels, but for tax reasons not all hotels choose to advertise themselves at the rating to which they are entitled, so you may find a modestly rated hotel just as comfortable (or more so) than a higher-rated one. Conversely, you may find a hotel offers few stars in hopes of attracting budget-conscious travellers, but charges just as much as a higher-rated neighbour. *Pensioni* are generally more modest establishments, though nowadays the distinction between these and ordinary hotels is becoming blurred. *Locande* are traditionally an even more basic form of hostelry, but these days the term may denote somewhere fairly chic. Other inexpensive accommodation is sometimes known as *alloggi* or *affittacamere*. There are usually plenty of cheap dives around railway stations; for somewhere more salubrious, head for the historic quarters. Whatever the shortcomings of the décor, furnishings and fittings, you can usually rely at least on having clean sheets.

Price lists, by law, must be posted on the door of every room, along with meal prices and any extra charges (such as air-conditioning, or even a shower in cheap places). Many hotels display two or three different rates, depending on the season. Low-season rates may be about a third lower than peak-season tariffs. Some resort hotels close down altogether for several months a year. During high season you should always book ahead to be sure of a room (a fax reservation may be less frustrating to organize than one by post). If you have paid a deposit, your booking is valid under Italian law, but don't expect it to be refunded if you have to cancel. Tourist offices publish annual regional lists of hotels and pensions with current rates, but do not generally make reservations for visitors. In Milan, a list of inexpensive accommodation (boarding houses, student rooms etc.) is available. **Weekend Milano** is a scheme whereby business hotels offer significant discounts at weekends.

Major railway stations generally have accommodation booking desks; inevitably, a fee is charged. Chain hotels or motels are generally the easiest hotels to book, but are often less interesting to stay in. One of the biggest chains in Italy is Jolly Hotels, always reliable if not all up to the same standard; these can generally be found near the centres of larger towns. Motels are operated by the **ACI** (Italian Automobile Club) or by **AGIP** (the oil company) and usually located along major exit routes.

If you arrive without a reservation, begin looking or phoning round for accommodation early in the day. If possible, inspect the room (and bathroom facilities) before you book, and check the tariff carefully. Italian hoteliers may legally alter their rates twice during the year, so printed tariffs or tourist board lists (and prices quoted in this book!) may be out of date. Hoteliers who wilfully overcharge should be reported to the local tourist office. You will be asked for your passport for registration purposes.

Prices listed in this guide are for double rooms; you can expect to pay about two-thirds the rate for single occupancy, though in high season you may be charged the full double rate in a popular beach resort. Extra beds are usually charged at about a third more of the room rate. Rooms without private bathrooms generally charge 20–30% less, and most offer discounts for children sharing parents' rooms, or children's meals. A *camera singola* (single room) may cost anything from about L25,000 upwards. Double rooms (*camera doppia*) go from about L40,000 to L250,000 or more. If you want a double bed, specify a *camera matrimoniale*. Breakfast is usually optional in hotels, though obligatory in *pensioni.* You can usually get better value by eating breakfast in a bar or café if you have any choice. In high season you may be expected to take half-board in resorts if the hotel has a restaurant, and one-night stays may be refused.

Youth Hostels

There aren't many of these in Italy (where they are known as *alberghi* or *ostelli per la gioventù*), but they are generally pleasant and sometimes located in historic buildings. The *Associazione Italiana Alberghi per la Gioventù* (Italian Youth Hostel Association, or **AIG**) is affiliated to the International Youth Hostel Federation. For a full list of hostels, contact AIG at Via Cavour 44, 00184 Roma, ✆ (06) 487 1152; fax, (06) 488 0492. An international membership card will enable you to stay in any of them (cards can be purchased on the spot in many hostels if you don't already have one). Religious institutions also run hostels; some are single sex, others will accept Catholics only: examples in **Milan** include Casa Famiglia, on Corso Garibaldi 123, or Pensione Benefica Giovani, at Via Formentini 8 (both women only); Fondazione Sacro Cuore, Via Rombone 78 (men only). Other youth hostels are in **Bergamo, Menaggio, Mantua**, and **Como**. Rates are usually somewhere between L12,000 and L18,000, including breakfast. Discounts are available for senior citizens, and some family rooms are available. You generally have to check in after 5pm, and pay for your room before 9am. Hostels usually close for most of the daytime, and many operate a curfew. During the spring, noisy school parties cram hostels for field trips. In the summer, it's advisable to book ahead. Contact the hostels directly.

Camping

Most of the official sites in Lombardy are near lake resorts, though you can camp somewhere near most of the principal tourist centres (Milan's campsite is some way out of the city). Iseo is particularly well served, with about ten separate sites. Camping is not the fanatical holiday activity it is in France, for example, nor necessarily any great bargain, but it is popular with holidaymaking families in August, when you can expect to find many sites at bursting point. Unofficial camping is generally frowned on and may attract a stern rebuke from the local police. Camper vans (and facilities for them) are increasingly popular. You can obtain a list of local sites from any regional tourist office. Campsite charges generally range from about L7000 per adult; tents and vehicles additionally cost about L7000 each. Small extra charges may also be levied for hot showers and electricity. A car-borne couple could therefore spend practically as much for a night at a well equipped campsite as in a cheap hotel. To obtain a camping carnet and book ahead, write to the *Centro Internazionale Prenotazioni Campeggio*, Casella Postale 23, 50041, Calenzano, Firenze, ✆ (055) 882 381, fax (055) 882 3918 (ask for their list of campsites as well as the booking form). The *Touring Club Italiano* (**TCI**) publishes a comprehensive annual guide to campsites and tourist villages throughout Italy. Write to: TCI, Corso Italia 10, Milan, ✆ (02) 85261/852 6245.

UK tour operators offering camping or caravaning holidays in the Lakes include:

Caravan & Camping Service, 69 Westbourne Grove, London W2 4UJ, ✆ (071) 792 1944

Caravan Club, East Grinstead House, West Sussex RJ19 1UA, ✆ (0342) 326944

Club Cantabrica Holiday House, 146–148 London Road, St Albans, Herts AL1 1PQ, ✆ (0727) 866177

Select Sites Reservations, Travel House, Monmouth Road, Abergavenny, Gwent NP7 5HL, ✆ (0873) 859876

Sunsites, Canute Court, Toft Road, Knutsford, Cheshire WA16 0NL, ✆ (0565) 625555

For a breath of rural seclusion, the normally gregarious Italians head for a spell on a working **farm**, in accommodation (usually self-catering) that often approximates to the French *gîte*. Often, however, the real pull of the place is a restaurant in which you can sample some home-grown produce (olives, wine, etc.). Outdoor activities may also be on tap (riding, fishing, and so forth). This branch of the Italian tourist industry has burgeoned in recent years, and every region now has several Agriturist offices. Prices of farmhouse accommodation, compared with the over-hyped 'Tuscan villa', are still reasonable (expect to pay around L40,000–60,000 for a cottage or double room). *Agriturismo* is very popular around the Lakes. To make the most of your rural hosts, it's as well to have a little Italian under your belt. Local tourist offices will have information on this type of accommodation in their areas; otherwise you can obtain complete listings compiled by the national organisation **Agriturist**, Corso Vittorio Emanuele 101, 00186 Rome, ✆ (06) 6512342, or Turismo Verde, Via Mariano Fortuny 20, 00196 Rome, ✆ (06) 3669931. Both publications are available in Italian bookshops.

Agriturist Provincial Offices

Bergamo:	Via Borgo Palazzo 133, 24100 ✆ (035) 244 480
Brescia:	Via Creta 50, 25125, ✆ (030) 222 861
Como:	Via Leoni 13, 22100, ✆ (031) 261 090
Cremona:	Piazza Comune 9, 26100, ✆ (0372) 26 201
Mantua:	Piazza Martiri Belfiore 7, 46100, ✆ (0376) 369 121
Milan:	Via Larga 2, 20122, ✆ (02) 869 2047
Pavia:	Corso Mazzini a/B, 27100, ✆ (0382) 21 715
Sondrio:	Via Trento 56, 23100, ✆ (0342) 214 197
Varese:	Via Magenta 52, 21100, ✆ (0332) 283 425

Alpine Refuges

The Italian Alpine Club operates refuges (*rifugi*) on the main mountain trails (some accessible only by *funivie*). These may be predictably spartan, or surprisingly comfortable. Many have restaurants. For an up-to-date list, write to the **Club Alpino Italiano**, Via Fonseca Pimental 7, Milano, ✆ (02) 2614 1378. Charges average L18,000–L25,000 per person per night, including breakfast. Most are open only from July to September, but those used by skiers are about 20% more expensive from December to April. Book ahead in August.

Self-catering Tour Operators

One of the most enjoyable, and best-value, ways of visiting Italy is to opt for self-catering accommodation. Centralized booking agencies exist in many countries as well as Italy, and can organize holidays in genuinely rural settings, sometimes offering discounted air or ferry fares and fly-drive schemes to egg you on. Watch for the small ads, or see the list below. Lakeside cottages are the classic Lombard self-catering experience.

Auto Plan, Energy House, Lombard Street, Lichfield, Staffs WS13 6DP, ✆ (0543) 257777

Citalia, Marco Polo House, 3–5 Lansdowne Road, Croydon CR9 1L,L ✆ (081) 686 5533

Eurovillas, 36 East Street, Coggeshall, Essex CO6 1SH, ✆ (0376) 561156

Inghams, 10–18 Putney Hill, London SW15 6AX, ✆ (081) 785 7777

Interhome, 383 Richmond Road, Twickenham, Middx TW1 2EF, ✆ (081) 891 1294

International Chapters, 102 St John's Wood Terrace, London NW8 6PL, ✆ (071) 722 9560

Italian Interlude, Triumph House, 189 Regent St., London W1R 7WD, ✆ (071) 494 2031

Magic of Italy, 227 Shepherds Bush Road, London W6 7AS, ✆ (081) 748 7575

Sovereign, Astral Towers, Second Floor, Betts Way, Crawley, West Sussex RH10 2GX, ✆ (0293) 599999

Vacanze in Italia, Bignor, Pulborough, West Sussex RH20 1QD, ✆ (0798) 87426

At Home Abroad, 405 East 56th Street, New York, NY 10022. ✆ (212) 421 9165

CUENDET: Posarelli Vacations, Suzanne T. Pidduck, 1742 Calle Corva, Camarillo, CA 93010. ✆ (805) 987 5278

Hideaways International, PO Box 4433, Portsmouth, New Hampshire 03801, ✆ (603) 430 4433

Homeowners International, 1133 Broadway, New York, NY 10010, ✆ (212) 691 2361

RAVE (Rent-a-Vacation-Everywhere), 383 Park Ave, Rochester, NY 14607, ✆ (716) 256 0760

Women Travellers

Italian men, with the heritage of Casanova, Don Giovanni, and Rudolph Valentino as their birthright, are very confident in their role as Great Latin Lovers, but the old horror stories of gangs following the innocent tourist maiden and pinching her bottom are way behind the times. Most Italian men these days are exquisitely polite and flirt on a much more sophisticated level, especially in the more 'Europeanized' north. Milan is a much easier city for single women than Rome or Naples. Still, women travelling alone may frequently receive hisses, wolf-whistles and unsolicited comments (complimentary or lewd, depending on your attitude) or 'assistance' from local swains—usually of the balding, middle-age-crisis variety. A confident, indifferent poise is usually the best policy. Failing that, a polite 'I am waiting for my *marito*.' (avoiding damaged male egos which can turn nasty), followed by a firm '*no!*' or '*Vai via!*' (Scram!) will generally solve the problem. Risks can be greatly reduced if you use common sense and avoid lonely streets and train stations after dark. Choose hotels and restaurants within easy and safe walking distance of public transport. Travelling with a companion of either sex will buffer you considerably from such nuisances (a guardian male, of course, instantly converts you into an inviolable chattel in Italian eyes). Avoid hitchhiking alone in Italy.

History

Quarrelsome Celts,
  Imperialistic Romans   44

The Height and Depths of Empire   44

Fairly Good Goths and
  Really Nasty Lombards   45

Threshold of the Middle Ages   46

The Rise of the *Comune*   48

Guelphs and Ghibellines,
  and the Renaissance   49

Three Grim Centuries of Foreign Rule 50

From Napoleon to Italian Unification   52

Lombardy Takes Off   53

Finally in the Driver's Seat:
  Lombardy and Milan Today   54

Quarrelsome Celts, Imperialistic Romans

The first known inhabitants of Lombardy, from about 3000 BC, left us something to remember them by: the thousands of mysterious symbols they incised on the rocks of the Val Camonica north of Lake Iseo. In a remarkable example of cultural continuity, these inscriptions continued to be made well into Roman times, while various peoples passed across the stage, notably the quiet folks who lived in Bronze Age villages built on piles over the water at Lakes Orta, Varese, and Ledro.

By 400 BC, when most of the peninsula was inhabited by the 'Italics'—a collection of distinct Indo-European tribes with similar languages—northwest Italy stood apart. Most of the area north of the Po was occupied by various Celtic and related Ligurian tribes. A century later, when the Romans arrived, they thought of this region as not Italy at all; their name for it was **Cisalpine Gaul**, 'Gaul this side of the Alps'. The two peoples were bound to come into conflict, and whenever there was war they usually found themselves on opposite sides. The Celts, skilled warriors who made whacking good swords, and gave the Romans their word for 'chariot', often got the best of it, notably in 390 BC, when they occupied Rome itself; only the famous cackling of the geese, warning the Romans of a night attack on their last citadel within the city, saved Rome from complete extinction. From then on, though, the tide turned, and even the chariots couldn't keep out the legions a hundred years later, in a general Italian conflagration called the **Third Samnite War** that pitted the Romans against the Samnites, Northern Etruscans and Celts. The Romans beat everyone once and for all and annexed most of Italy by 283 BC. As in Italy, to solidify their hold the Romans founded colonies throughout Cisalpine Gaul and populated them with army veterans; these included Mediolanum (Milan), Brixia (Brescia), Como, and Cremona.

Being a less developed area, Cisalpine Gaul suffered less from Roman misrule than other parts of Italy. There was little wealth to tax, and little for rapacious Roman governors to steal. The region managed to avoid most of the endless civil wars, famines and oppression that accompanied the death throes of the Roman Republic elsewhere. It did endure a last surprise raid by two Celtic tribes, the Cimbri and Teutones, who crossed over the Riviera and the Alps in a two-pronged attack in 102 BC. **Gaius Marius**, a capable though illiterate Roman general, defeated them decisively, using his popularity to seize power in Rome soon after.

The Height and Depths of Empire

In the Pax Romana of Augustus and his successors, the northern regions evolved from wild border territories to settled, prosperous provinces full of thriving new towns. Of these, the most important was **Mediolanum**. The lakes became a favourite holiday desti-nation for Rome's élite. Trade flourished along new roads like the Via Postumia to Cremona, and Mantua gave birth to Virgil just in time to put Rome's faith in its divine destiny into words. But after over two centuries at the glorious noonday of its history, in the 3rd century the Roman empire began to have troubles from without as well as within:

a severe, long-term economic decline coinciding with a military balance that was shifting to the favour of the barbarians on the frontiers. **Diocletian** (284–305) completely revamped the structure of the state, converting it into a vast bureaucratic machine geared solely to meeting the needs of its army; Diocletian also initiated the division of the empire into western and eastern halves, for reasons of military and administrative necessity. The western emperors after Diocletian usually kept their court at army headquarters in Mediolanum, a convenient place to keep an eye on both the Rhine and Danube frontiers. Through most of the 4th century that city was the western empire's de facto capital, while Rome itself decayed into a marble-veneered backwater.

Times were hard all over the west, and, although northern Italy was relatively less hard-hit than other regions, cities decayed and trade disappeared, while debt and an inability to meet high taxes pushed thousands into serfdom or slavery. The confused politics of the time were dominated by **Constantine** (306–337), who ruled both halves of the empire, and adroitly moved to increase his political support by the Edict of Milan (313), declaring Christianity the religion of the empire. Later in the century Milan became an important centre of the new faith under its great bishop, **St Ambrose**.

The inevitable disasters began in 406, when the Visigoths, Franks, Vandals, Alans and Suevi overran Gaul and Spain. Italy's turn came in 408, when Western Emperor Honorius had his brilliant general Stilicho (who himself happened to be a Vandal) murdered. A Visigothic invasion followed; Alaric sacked Rome in 410; and in Milan St Augustine, probably echoing the thoughts of most Romans, wrote that it seemed the end of the world must be near. Italy should have been so lucky; judgement was postponed long enough for Attila the Hun to pass through in 451.

So completely had things changed, it was scarcely possible to tell the Romans from the barbarians. By the 470s the real ruler in Italy was a Gothic general named **Odoacer**, who led a half-Romanized Germanic army and probably thought of himself as the genuine heir of the Caesars. In 476 he decided to dispense with the lingering charade of the Western Empire. The last emperor, **Romulus Augustulus**, was retired to Naples, and Odoacer had himself crowned king at Italy's new Gothic capital, Pavia.

Fairly Good Goths and Really Nasty Lombards

At the beginning, the new Gothic-Latin state showed some promise; certainly the average man was no worse off than he had been under the last emperors. In 493, Odoacer was replaced (and murdered) by a rival Ostrogoth, **Theodoric**, nominally working on behalf of the Eastern Emperor at Constantinople. Theodoric proved a strong and able, though somewhat paranoid ruler; his court witnessed a minor rebirth of Latin letters, most famously in the great Christian philosopher Boethius, while trade revived and cities were repaired. A disaster as serious as those of the 5th century began in 536 with the invasion of Italy by the Eastern Empire, part of the relentlessly expansionist policy of Emperor **Justinian**. The historical irony was profound; in the birthplace of the Roman Empire, Roman troops now came not as liberators, but foreign, largely Greek-speaking conquerors. Justinian's brilliant generals, Belisarius and Narses, ultimately prevailed over the Goths in a series of terrible wars that lasted until 563, but the damage to an already stricken society was incalculable.

Italy's total exhaustion was exposed only five years later, with the invasion of the **Lombards**, a Germanic people who worked hard to maintain the title of Barbarian; while other, more courageous tribes moved in to take what they could of the empire, the Lombards had ranged on the frontiers like mean stray curs. Most writers, ancient and modern, mistakenly attribute the Lombards' name to their long beards; in fact, these redoubtable nomads scared the daylights out of the Italians not with beards but with their long *bardi*, or poleaxes.

Narses himself first invited the Lombards in, as mercenaries to help him overcome the Goths. Quickly understanding their opportunity, they returned with the entire horde in 568. By 571 they were across the Apennines; Pavia, one of the old Gothic capitals and the key to northern Italy, fell after a long siege in 572. The horde's progress provided history with unedifying spectacles from the very start: King Alboin, who unified the Lombard tribes and made the invasion possible, met his bloody end at the hands of his queen, Rosmunda—whom he drove to murder by forcing her to drink from her father's skull.

They hadn't come to do the Italians any favours. The Lombards considered the entire population their slaves; in practice, they were usually content to sit back and collect exorbitant tributes. Themselves Arian Christians, they enjoyed oppressing both the orthodox and pagan. Throughout the 6th century their conquest continued apace. The popes, occasionally allied with the Lombards against Byzantium, became a force during this period, especially after the papacy of the clever, determined **Gregory the Great** (590–604), who in 603 managed to convert the Lombard queen **Theodolinda** and her people to orthodox Christianity. By then things had stabilized. Northern Italy was the Lombard kingdom proper, centred at Pavia and Monza, while semi-independent Lombard duchies controlled much of the peninsula.

In Pavia, a long succession of Lombard kings made little account of themselves. However, under the doughty warrior king **Liutprand** (712–744), Byzantine weakness made the Lombards exert themselves to try to unify Italy. Liutprand won most of his battles, but gained few territorial additions. A greater threat was his ruthless successor, **Aistulf**, who by 753 conquered almost all of the lands held by the Byzantines, including their capital, Ravenna. If the Lombards' final solution was to be averted, the popes would have to find help from outside. The logical people to ask were the **Franks**.

Threshold of the Middle Ages

At the time, the popes had something to offer in return. For years the powerful **Mayors of the Palace of the Frankish Kingdom** had longed to supplant the Merovingian dynasty and assume the throne for themselves, but needed the appearance of legitimacy that only the mystic pageantry of the papacy could provide. At the beginning of Aistulf's campaigns, Pope Zacharias had foreseen the danger, and gave his blessing to the change of dynasties in 750. To complete the deal, the new king Pepin sent his army over the Alps in 753 and 756 to foil Aistulf's designs.

By 773 the conflict remained the same, though with a different cast of characters. The Lombard king was Desiderius, the Frankish his cordially hostile son-in-law, **Charlemagne**, who also invaded Italy twice, in 775 and 776. Unlike his father, though, Charlemagne meant to settle Italy once and for all. His army captured Pavia, and after deposing his father-in-law he took the Iron Crown of Italy for himself.

The new partnership between pope and king failed to bring the stability both parties had hoped for. With Charlemagne busy elsewhere, local lordlings across the peninsula scrapped continually for slight advantage. Charlemagne returned in 799 to sort them out, and in return got what must be the most momentous Christmas present in history. At Christmas Eve, while praying in St Peter's, Pope Leo III crept up behind him and deftly set an imperial crown on the surprised king's head. The revival of the dream of a united, Christian empire changed the political face of Italy forever, beginning the contorted *pas de deux* of pope and emperor that was to be the mainspring of Italian history throughout the Middle Ages.

Charlemagne's empire quickly disintegrated after his death, divided among squabbling descendants, and Italy reverted to anarchy. Altogether the 9th century was a rotten time, with Italy caught between Arab raiders and the endless wars of petty nobles and battling bishops. To north Italians, the post-Carolingian era is the age of the *reucci*, the 'little kings', a profusion of puny rulers angling to advance their own interests. After 888, when the Carolingian line became extinct, ten little Frankish kings of Italy succeeded to the throne at Pavia, each with less power than the last. Their most frequent antagonists were the Lombard **Dukes of Spoleto**, though occasionally foreign interlopers like Arnolf of Carinthia (893) or Hugh of Provence (932) brought armies over the Alps to try their luck. Worse trouble for everyone came with the arrival of the barbarian **Magyars**, who overran the north and sacked Pavia in 924.

The 10th century proved somewhat better. Even in the worst times, Italy's cities never entirely disappeared. Maritime powers like Venice and Pisa led the way, but even inland cities like Milan were developing a new economic importance. From the 900s many were looking to their own resources, defending their interests against the Church and nobles alike. A big break for the cities came in 961 when **Adelheid**, the beautiful widow of one of the *reucci*, Lothar, refused to wed his successor, Berengar II, Marquis of Ivrea. Berengar had hoped to bring some discipline to Italy, and began by imprisoning the recalcitrant Adelheid in a tower by Lake Como. With the aid of a monk she made a daring escape to Canossa and the protection of the Count of Tuscany, who called in for reinforcements from the king of Germany, **Otto the Great**. Otto came over the Alps, got the girl, deposed Berengar, and was crowned Holy Roman Emperor in Rome the following year. Not that any of the Italians were happy to see him, but the strong government of Otto and his successors beat down the great nobles, divided their lands, and allowed the growing cities to expand their power and influence.

The Rise of the *Comune*

At the eve of the new millennium, business was very good in the towns, and the political prospects even brighter. The first mention of a truly independent *comune* (a free city state; the best translation might be 'commonwealth') was in Milan, where in 1024 the first popular assembly (*parlamento*) met to decide which side the city would take in the imperial wars. And when that was done, Milan's archbishop Heribert invited the German Frankish king Conrad to be crowned in Milan, founding a new line of Italian kings.

Throughout this period the papacy had declined greatly, a political football kicked between the emperors and the Roman nobles. In the 1050s a monk named **Hildebrand** (later Gregory VII) worked hard to reassert Church power, beginning a conflict with the emperors over investiture—whether the church or secular powers would name church officials. Fifty years of intermittent war followed, including the famous 'penance in the snow' of Emperor Henry IV in Canossa (1077). The result was a big revival for the papacy, but more importantly the cities of Lombardy and the rest of the north used the opportunity to increase their influence, and in some cases achieve outright independence, razing the nobles' castles and forcing them to move inside the town.

While all this was happening, of course, the First Crusade (1097–1130) occupied the headlines, partially a result of the new militancy of the papacy begun by Gregory VII. For Italy the affair meant nothing but pure profit. Trade was booming everywhere, and the accumulation of money helped the Italians to create modern Europe's first banking system. It also financed the continued independence of the *comuni*, who began to discover there simply wasn't enough Italy to hold them all. Cremona had its dust-ups with Crema, Bergamo with Brescia, while Milan, the biggest bully of them all, took on Pavia, Cremona, Como, and Lodi with one hand tied behind its back.

By the 12th century, far in advance of most of Europe, Italy had attained a prosperity unknown since Roman times. The classical past had never been forgotten; free *comuni* in the north called their elected leaders 'consuls', and artists and architects turned ancient Roman styles into the Romanesque. Even Italian names were changing, an interesting sign of the beginnings of national consciousness; suddenly the public records show a marked shift from Germanic to classical and Biblical surnames: fewer Ugos, Othos, and Astolfos, more Giuseppes, Giovannis, Giulios, and Flavios.

Emperors and popes were still embroiled in the north. Frederick I—**Barbarossa**—of the Hohenstaufen, or Swabian dynasty, was strong enough back home in Germany, and he made it his special interest to reassert imperial power in Italy. In 1154, he crossed the Alps for the first of five times, settling local disputes against Milan and Tortona in favour of his allies Pavia, Como and Lodi. As soon as he was back over the Alps, Milan set about undoing all his works, punishing the cities that had supported him. Back came Frederick in 1158 to starve Milan into submission and set up imperial governors (*podestàs*) in each *comune*; and, when Milan still proved defiant, he destroyed it utterly in 1161. And back over the Alps he went once more, confident that he had taught Lombardy a lesson.

What he had taught northern Italians was that the liberties of their *comuni* were in grave danger. A united opposition, called the **Lombard League**, included by 1167 every major city between Venice and Asti and Bologna (except Pavia), with spiritual backing in the person of Frederick's enemy Pope Alexander III. Twice the Lombard League beat the furious emperor back over the mountains, and when Frederick crossed the Alps for the fifth time in 1174 he was checked at Alessandria, in Piedmont, and forced by the league to raise his siege; then, in 1176, while his forces were in Legnano preparing to attack Milan, the Milanese militia surprised and decimated his army, forcing Frederick to flee alone to Venice to make terms with Pope Alexander. The truce he signed with the League became the **Peace of Constance**, which might as well have been called the Peace of Pigheads: all that the *comuni* asked was the right to look after their own interests and fight each other whenever they pleased.

Guelphs and Ghibellines, and the Renaissance

Frederick's grandson **Frederick II** was not only emperor but King of Sicily, thus giving him a strong power base in Italy itself. The second Frederick's career dominated Italian politics for 30 years (1220–50). With his brilliant court, his half-Muslim army, his dancing girls, eunuchs and elephants, he provided Europe with a spectacle the like of which it had never seen. The popes excommunicated him at least twice. Now the battle had become serious. All Italy divided into factions: the **Guelphs**, under the leadership of the popes, supported religious orthodoxy, the liberty of the *comuni*, and the interests of their emerging wealthy merchant class. The **Ghibellines** stood for the emperor, statist economic control and (sometimes) religious and intellectual tolerance. Frederick's campaigns and diplomacy in the north met with very limited success, and his death in 1250 left the outcome very much in doubt.

His son Manfred, not emperor but merely King of Sicily, took up the battle with better luck. In 1261, however, Pope Urban IV began an ultimately disastrous precedent by inviting in Charles of Anjou, the ambitious brother of the King of France. As champion of the Guelphs, Charles defeated Manfred (1266), murdered the last of the Hohenstaufens, Conradin (1268), and held unchallenged sway over Italy until 1282. By now, however, the terms 'Guelph' and 'Ghibelline' had ceased to have much meaning; men and cities changed sides as they found expedient, and the old parties began to seem like the black and white squares on a chessboard.

Some real changes did occur out of all this sound and fury. As elsewhere around the peninsula, some cities were falling under the rule of military *signori* whose descendants would be styling themselves dukes, like the Visconti of Milan and the Gonzaga of Mantua. Everywhere the freedom of the *comuni* was in jeopardy; after so much useless strife the temptation to submit to a strong leader often proved overwhelming. And yet at the same time money flowed as never before; cities built new cathedrals and created incredible skylines of tower-fortresses, dotting the country with medieval Manhattans.

This paradoxical Italy continued through the 15th century, with a golden age of culture and an opulent economy side by side with continuous war and turmoil. With no threats over the border, the myriad Italian states menaced each other joyfully without outside interference. War became a sort of game, conducted on behalf of cities by *condottieri*, leading paid mercenaries who were never allowed to enter the cities themselves. The arrangement suited everyone well. The soldiers had lovely horses and armour, and no real desire to do each other serious harm. The cities were making too much money to really want to wreck the system anyway.

By far the biggest event of the 14th century was the **Black Death** of 1347–8, in which Italy lost one-third of its population. The shock brought a rude halt to what had been 400 years of almost continuous growth and prosperity, though its effects did not prove a permanent setback. In fact, the plague's grim joke was that it actually made life better for most of the Italians who survived; working people in the cities, no longer overcrowded, found their rents lower and their labour worth more, while in the country farmers were able to increase their profits by only tilling the best land.

In the north, the great power was the signorial state of Milan. Under the Visconti, Milan had become rich and powerful, basing its success on the manufactures of the city (arms and textiles) and the bountiful, progressively managed agriculture of southern Lombardy. Its greatest glory came under **Gian Galeazzo Visconti** (1385–1402), who bought a ducal title from the emperor and nearly conquered all of north Italy before his untimely death, upon which the Venetians were able to snatch up tasty titbits on the fringe like Brescia and Bergamo.

And what of the Renaissance? No word has ever caused more mischief for the under-standing of history and culture—as if Italy had been Sleeping Beauty, waiting for some Prince Charming to come and awaken it from a 1000-year nap. On the contrary, Italy even in the 1200s was richer, more technologically advanced and far more artistically creative than it had ever been in the days of the Caesars. The new art and scholarship that began in Florence in the 1400s and spread across the nation grew from a solid foundation of medieval accomplishment. The gilded Italy of the 15th century felt complacently secure in its long-established cultural and economic pre-eminence. The long spell of freedom from outside interference lulled the nation into believing that its political disunity could continue safely forever; except perhaps for the sanguinely realistic Florentine Nicolò Macchiavelli, no one realized that Italy in fact was a plum waiting to be picked.

Three Grim Centuries of Foreign Rule

The Italians brought the trouble down on themselves, when Duke Lodovico of Milan invited the French king **Charles VIII** to cross the Alps and assert his claim to the throne of Milan's enemy, Naples. Charles did just that, and the failure of the combined Italian states to stop him (at the inconclusive Battle of Fornovo, 1494) showed just how helpless Italy was at the hands of new nation-states like France or Spain. When the Spaniards saw how easy it was, they too marched in, and restored Naples to its Spanish king the following year. Before long the German emperor and even the Swiss, who briefly controlled Milan, entered this new market for Italian real estate. The popes did as much as anyone to keep the pot boiling. Alexander VI and his son **Cesare Borgia** carried the war across central Italy in an attempt to found a new state for the Borgia family, and Julius II's madcap policy led him to egg on the Swiss, French and Spaniards in turn, before finally crying, 'Out with the barbarians!' when it was already too late.

By 1516, with the French ruling Milan and the Spanish in control of the south, it seemed as if a settlement would be possible. The worst possible luck for Italy, however, came with the accession of the insatiable megalomaniac **Charles V** to the throne of Spain; in 1519 he emptied the Spanish treasury to buy himself the crown of the Holy Roman Empire, making him the most powerful ruler in Europe since Charlemagne. Charles wanted Milan as a base for communications between his Spanish, German and Flemish possessions, and the wars began anew, bloodier than anything Italy had seen for centuries, climaxing with the defeat of the French at Pavia in 1525, and the sack of Rome by an out-of-control imperial army in 1527. The French invaded once more, in 1529, and were defeated this time at Naples by the treachery of their Genoese allies. All Italy, save only Venice, was now at the mercy of Charles and the Spaniards.

The final peace negotiated at Château-Cambrésis left Spanish viceroys in Milan and Naples, and pliant dukes and counts toeing the Spanish line almost everywhere else. The broader context of the time was the bitter struggles of the Reformation and Counter-Reformation. In Italy, the Spaniards found a perfect ally in the papacy; together they put an end to the last surviving liberties of the cities, while snuffing out the intellectual life of the Renaissance with the help of the Inquisition and the Jesuits.

Nearly the only place where anything creative came out of this new order was Lombardy. In Milan, that incorruptible Galahad of the Counter-reformation, Archbishop **Charles Borromeo** (1538–84) came out of the Council of Trent determined to make his diocese a working model of Tridentine reforms. One of the most influential characters in Italian religious history, he relentlessly went about creating an actively pastoral, zealous clergy, giving the most prominent teaching jobs to Jesuits and cleansing Lombardy of heresy and corruption. By re-establishing the cult of Milan's patron, St Ambrose, he developed a sense of Lombard regional feeling; with his nephew and successor, **Federico Borromeo**, he promoted sorely needed cultural and welfare institutions, instilling in the Lombard élite an industrious Catholic paternalism still noted in the region today.

Despite political oppression, the 16th century was a generally prosperous period for most of Italy, embellished with an afterglow of late-Renaissance architecture and art. After 1600, though, nearly everything started to go wrong for the Italians. The textiles and banking of the north, long the engines of prosperity, both withered in the face of foreign competition. The old mercantile economies built in the Middle Ages were failing, and the wealthy began to invest their money in land instead of risking it in business or finance.

Italy in this period hardly has any history at all; as Spain slouched into decadence, most of Lombardy dozed on as part of the Duchy of Milan, ruled by a Spanish viceroy. In 1713, after the War of the Spanish Succession, the Habsburgs of Austria came into control of the

Duchy, and the tiny Duchy of Mantua. The Austrians improved conditions somewhat. Especially during the reigns of **Maria Theresa** (1740–80) and her son **Joseph II** (1780–92), two of the most likeable Enlightenment despots, Lombardy and the other Austrian possessions underwent serious, intelligent economic reforms—the head-start over the rest of Italy that helped Milan to its industrial prominence today.

From Napoleon to Italian Unification

Napoleon, that greatest of Italian generals, arrived in 1796 on behalf of the French revolutionary Directorate, sweeping away the Austrians and setting up republics in Lombardy (the 'Cisalpine Republic') and elsewhere. Italy woke up with a start from its Baroque slumbers, and local patriots gaily joined the French cause. In 1799, however, while Napoleon was off in Egypt, the advance through Italy by an Austro-Russian army, aided by Nelson's fleet, restored the status quo. In 1800 Napoleon returned in a campaign that saw the great victory at Marengo, giving him the opportunity to once more reorganize Italian affairs, and to crown himself King of Italy in Milan cathedral. Napoleonic rule lasted only until 1814, but in that time important public works were begun and laws, education and everything else reformed after the French model; Church properties were expropriated, and medieval relics everywhere put to rest. The French, however, soon wore out their welcome, through high taxes, oppression, and the systematic looting of Italy's artistic heritage. When the Austrians came to chase the French out in 1814, no one was sad to see them go.

Though the postwar **Congress of Vienna** put the Italian clock back to 1796, the Napoleonic experience had given Italians a taste of the opportunities offered by the modern world, as well as a sense of national feeling that had been suppressed for centuries. Almost immediately, revolutionary agitators and secret societies sprang up all over Italy; sentiment for Italian unification and liberal reform was greatest in the north, and in the decades of the national revival, the **Risorgimento**, Lombardy in particular would contribute more than its share.

In March 1848, a revolution in Vienna gave Italians under Austrian rule their chance to act. Milan's famous *Cinque Giornate* revolt began with a boycott of the Austrian tobacco monopoly. Some troops, conspicuously smoking cigars in public, caused fighting to break out in the streets. In five incredible days, the populace of Milan rose up and chased out the Austrian garrison (led by Marshal Radetzky, he of the famous march tune). Events began to move rapidly. On 22 March, revolution spread to Venice, and soon afterwards Piedmont's King Carlo Alberto declared war on Austria, and his army crossed the Ticino into Lombardy. The Piedmontese won early victories, including one important one at Goito, on 30 May, but under the timid leadership of the king they failed to follow them up, and the Austrians were back in control by the end of July. The other Italian revolts, in Rome and Venice, were not put down until 1849.

Despite failure on a grand scale, the Italians knew they would get another chance. Unification, most likely under the House of Savoy that ruled Piedmont, was inevitable. In 1859, with the support of Napoleon III and France, the Piedmontese tried again and would have been successful had the French not double-crossed them and signed an armistice with Austria in the middle of the war; as a result, though, Piedmont gained Lombardy and Tuscany. That left the climactic event of unification to be performed by the revolutionary adventurer **Giuseppe Garibaldi**. When Garibaldi sailed to Sicily with a thousand volunteers in May 1860, nearly half his men were from Lombardy. Their unexpected success in toppling the Kingdom of Naples, launched the Piedmontese on an invasion from the north, and Italian unity was achieved.

Lombardy Takes Off

While life under the corrupt and bumbling governments of the new Italian kingdom wasn't perfect, it was a major improvement over the Austrians. The integration of the northern industrial towns into a unified Italian economy gave trade a big boost, and Milan in particular saw its industry expand dramatically. Along with that came the beginnings of the socialist movement, stronger at first in Lombardy than anywhere else; the first socialist party, the **Partito Operaio Italiano**, was founded in Milan in 1882. Strikes and riots were common in the depression of the 90s; over a hundred people were killed in one clash in 1896. Nevertheless, a rapidly increasing prosperity was drawing the northern cities into the European mainstream. The decades before the First World War, a contented time for many Italians, came to be known by the slightly derogatory term *Italietta*, the 'little Italy' of bourgeois happiness, sweet Puccini operas, the first motor cars, blooming 'Liberty'-style architecture, and Sunday afternoons at the beach.

After the war, Milan saw the birth of another movement, Fascism. **Mussolini** founded his newspaper there, the *Popolo d'Italia*, and organized the first bands of *squadri*, toughs who terrorized unions and leftist parties. The upper classes got on well enough with the Fascists, especially during the boom of the 20s, when big Milanese firms like Montecatini-Edison and Pirelli came into prominence. In the Second World War, the industrial cities suffered heavily from Allied bombings after the capture of Sicily in July 1943. After the government signed an armistice with the Allies in September, the German army moved in massively to take control of the north. They established a puppet government, the Italian Social Republic, at the resort town of Salò on Lake Garda, and re-installed Mussolini, though now little more than a figurehead.

The war dragged on for another year and a half, as the Germans made good use of Italy's difficult terrain to slow the Allied advance. Meanwhile Italy finally gave itself something to be proud of, a determined, resourceful Resistance that established free zones in many areas of Lombardy and other regions, and harassed the Germans with sabotage and strikes. The *partigiani* caught Mussolini in April 1945, while he was trying to escape to Switzerland; after shooting him and his mistress, they hung him by the toes from the roof of a petrol station in Milan where the Germans had shot a number of civilians a week before.

With a heavy dose of Marshall Plan aid and some intelligent government planning, Milan (and Turin) led the way for the 'economic miracle' of the 50s. Meaningful politics almost ceased to exist, as the nation was run in a permanently renegotiated deal between the Christian Democrats and smaller parties, but Lombard industry surged ahead, creating around Milan a remarkably diverse economy of over 60,000 concerns, ranging from multinational giants like Olivetti to the small, creative, often family-run firms that are the model of what has been called 'Italian capitalism'. Milan's most glamorous industry, fashion, began to move to the city from Florence around 1968, owing to the lack of a good airport there. The climax of the boom came in 1987, when it was announced that Italy had surpassed Britain to become the world's fifth largest economy; '*Il Sorpasso*', as Italians called it, was a great source of national pride—even though it was later discovered that government economists had had to fiddle the figures to make the claim.

Finally in the Driver's Seat: Lombardy and Milan Today

With some 8,500,000 people, Lombardy is the most populous region of Italy. And also the richest, by far; it produces a quarter of the gross national product and a third of Italy's exports. The average income is twice that of the south, and higher than any region of Britain or France. Even in the current recession, Lombardy isn't doing badly; on Milan's frantic stock market the number of shares traded in a day occasionally exceeds New York's. Along with prosperity has come a number of serious worries: a big increase in corruption and crime, and severe pollution, in the Lakes, in the air and in Europe's filthiest river, the Po. Some 250,000 immigrants have moved to Milan since the war from southern Italy and Sicily, and the inability of many of them to adapt and get ahead, largely thanks to the bigotry of the Lombards, fuels a host of intractable social problems.

The Milanese believe their city is the real capital of Italy—because it pays the bills. But, following its old traditions, the city has remained largely indifferent to politics, and stolidly unproductive in the arts. Milan can offer fashion and industrial design—both of course highly profitable; it is the nation's publishing centre, and probably its art centre, with more galleries than anywhere else. Endlessly creative in business, it has so far had little else to offer the world.

In politics, at least, the indifference may be gone forever. The lid blew off Italy's cosily rotten political system in 1992 in Milan, with the exposure of the Byzantine web of bribery and kickbacks that has come to be known as *Tangentopoli*—'Bribe City'; a determined group of judges in that city, in the continuing operation called *Mani Pulite*, or 'Clean Hands', is still trying to get to the bottom of it.

In Palermo, the courthouse, or *Palazzo di Giustizia*, is a fortress, surrounded by concrete blocks to deter car bombs and guarded by a brigade of Bersaglieri, Italy's élite troops, dressed in full combat gear and armed to the teeth; helicopters occasionally circle around, surveying the neighbourhood. Forgive the judges and prosecutors if they seem a little nervous. Without all the security the building might not be there. The Mafia did try once to bomb it with rockets, unsuccessfully, but as things are their hoods must lurk outside in the shadows, forced to take their shots at the Honoured Society's tormentors when they're outside the fortress. They have had some success, blowing up the cars of the courageous prosecutors Giovanni Falcone and Paolo Borsellino, despite precautions as great as those made for the US President or any other world leader. The good guys have got their licks in too; with an angry and mobilized public, a wave of highly ranked Mafia *pentiti*, or informers and the recent arrest of *capo di tutti capi* Salvatore Riina, the Mafia is in worse shape than at any time since the 40s.

Up north in Milan, things seem more civilized and relaxed. The security is much less fierce, and the curious queue up every day to witness the latest episode of the biggest show in Italy, unfolding in the courtrooms of Judge Antonio di Pietro and the other five judges on his *Mani Pulite* team. For over a year, the best of the proceedings have been televised, and they have drawn some of the highest ratings on Italian television. Italians can't get enough of it—the spectacle of their entire political class being dragged through the dock, along with some of the best known magnates of industry and finance. With every passing month di Pietro gets closer to the big shots, the top Christian Democrats and their political allies who ran the country as their personal cash cow for decades.

It will make a good film some day—no doubt somebody's already working on the screen-play. Antonio di Pietro was a poor boy from Italy's most obscure region, the Molise. He worked in electronics while studying law at night in Milan, and became a judge in the early 80s. The electronics background gave him a thorough knowledge of computers and what they could do, and he used them skilfully to pile up and collate evidence and connec-tions. He first made a name for himself in 1987, breaking open bribe scandals in the vehicle licence bureau and city bus company. In 1992, a divorced woman wrote him a letter complaining of how her ex-husband, an official in a city old age hospice, was driving around in a new Alfa and wearing silk suits while claiming he couldn't afford her alimony. That man was the now famous Mario Chiesa, a hapless grafter and Socialist party hack who had been skimming off L100,000 from undertakers for every corpse they took out of the place. He was had, and he squealed, revealing a wealth of interesting information about similar shady deals all over Milan.

One thing led to another—to put it mildly. Even di Pietro was amazed at how information on one racket tied in inevitably with others, each one bigger than the last. Two years into the affair, now known around the world as *Tangentopoli*, or 'Bribe City', hundreds of leading politicians and businessmen have been convicted or are awaiting their turn. One of the country's most respected business leaders, Raul Gardini, has committed suicide in his cell. The Christian Democrat and Socialist parties have been utterly annihilated, and the face of Italy's politics changed forever. Di Pietro still has enough work on his books to last him until 1996, even if nothing else new turns up.

Right now, in 1994, media polls declare di Pietro the most popular man in Italy. After the last election, Berlusconi asked him to be his Minister of Justice, a possible co-opting that the judge refused. In Italy there are dark hints that the new government will try to put a stop to *Mani Pulite* before it gets too close to some of its members' own dubious pasts.

Today, unfortunately for the Milanese, everyone knows where Bribe City really is. All along, it seems, the two extremities of the nation have had their separate and distinct ways of doing business—the Sicilians' was just a little more colourful. For every proud, honest citizen of the city of silk suits and Alfas, the events of the last two years must be a profound revelation. Paradoxically, the tremendous drama of indictments, trials and retaliations, north and south, may become the greatest impetus towards a true Italian unity since Giuseppe Garibaldi. Italians have only to look at what is happening to realize that they're all in the same boat, that Palermo and Milan aren't so different after all.

Even before all that started, the Lega Lombarda, led by the noisy yet enigmatic **Umberto Bossi**, the only Italian political figure to dress badly since the time of King Aistulf, made its breakthrough in the 1990 elections, and became the leading party of the region in 1992. On most issues the Lega's position can change by the hour, but its basic tenet of federalism, to cut out the voracious politicians and bureaucrats in Rome, and allow the wealthy north to keep more of its profits for itself, has understandably struck a deep chord in the Lombard soul; other 'leagues' have emerged and prospered in other northern regions, and together they found their way into the government after the 1994 elections as the Lega Nord. At the time of writing, Mr Bossi is about to get his day in the *Mani Pulite* court, accused of the same sort of campaign–funding sins that have brought down so many other politicians, not to mention entire parties.

That leaves Milan's other gift to Italian politics, **Silvio Berlusconi**. He is in fact the essence of Milan distilled into a single individual, the self-made man (self-made with the help of his connections, notably to Socialist kingpin Bettino Craxi) whose empire includes half of Italy's television audience, a third of its magazine readership, books, newspapers, a department-store chain and now the Italian state. Only a few years ago, no journalist or author ever dared to mention some of things about Italy that everyone knew—say, the close alliance between the Christian Democrats and the Mafia and Camorra. Today, you won't find anyone in Italy or anywhere else looking very closely into how Berlusconi came by all these prizes, or more interestingly, into his membership of P2, the shadowy clique of top politicians, industrialists and security chiefs that managed Italy's institutional corruption in the last decades, and created or manipulated most of the terrorist groups of the 60s and 70s.

Berlusconi's new government is planning to reduce bureaucracy, fight corruption and make it easier for business to compete and survive; if he is sincere, much good work can be done. As for the problem delicately called a 'conflict of interest'—a democratic leader willing and able to completely dominate public opinion through the media, Berlusconi says don't worry: 'common sense will sort it out'. Italian democracy, a flickering candle at best, has so far survived the Christian Democrats, the Mafia, P2, and any number of smaller bogeys; we will all have to wait and see whether it can survive Berlusconi.

Prehistoric and Roman 58

Early Middle Ages
  (5th–10th centuries) 58

Romanesque and Late Medieval
  (11th–14th centuries) 58

Renaissance (15th–16th centuries) 59

Baroque (17th–18th centuries) 61

Neoclassicism and Romanticism
  (late 18th–19th century) 62

20th Century 62

Art & Architecture, & Where to Find it

Like the rest of Italy, Lombardy is packed to the gills with notable works of art and architecture, and it's hard to find even the smallest village without a robust Romanesque chapel, or curlicued Baroque *palazzina*, or a mysterious time-darkened painting by a follower of Leonardo or Caravaggio. Because the 'art cities' of this region flourished at different periods, there is no one dominant 'golden age' comparable to the Renaissance in Tuscany or Venice, or the Baroque in Rome. On the other hand, you'll find examples of art of all periods, and of nearly every school. For what the Lombards didn't make, they had the money to buy, so their churches and galleries are endowed with masterpieces.

Prehistoric and Roman

The most remarkable works from the Neolithic period up to the Iron Age are the thousands of graffiti rock incisions in isolated Alpine valleys north of Lake Iseo, especially in the **Val Camonica**, where they are protected in a national park (others are in the Upper Valtellina at **Teglio** and **Grósio**); at an islet in **Lake Varese** and by **Lake Ledro** you can visit the site of Neolithic and Bronze Age lake communities, where houses were built on piles over the water. Apart from the odd menhir and pot the Ligurians and Celts have left few traces, and even the arches and amphitheatres dutifully put up by their Roman conquerors in their colonies and towns have almost disappeared as these grew to become the region's modern capitals. Scanty Roman remains can be seen at the 'Villa of Catullus' at **Sirmione** on Lake Garda, in **Brescia** and in the archaeological museum in **Milan**.

Early Middle Ages (5th–10th centuries)

Although the brilliant mosaics such as those in Ravenna, Venice, and Rome—the delight of this period in Italy—are rare here (the only survivors are in chapels in **Milan**'s Sant'Ambrogio and San Lorenzo Maggiore), the work of the native population under its Lombard rulers was certainly not without talent. There was a marked proclivity in the Italian Dark Ages towards unusual geometric baptistries and churches, some of which may be seen here: **Milan** cathedral, **Lomello**, and the Duomo Vecchio in **Brescia**. A 10th-century church with frescoes may be seen at **Cantù**; during the Second World War remarkable murals from the 8th century were discovered at **Castelséprio**. The Cappella della Pietà in Milan's San Satiro is another rare survivor from the 9th century. Some of the most beautiful works from this period may be seen in the Museum of Christian Art and Abbey of San Salvatore, in **Brescia**); at **Monza**, the treasury of 6th-century Lombard Queen Theodolinda in the cathedral; the Civic Museum in **Pavia**; and from the year 1000, San Pietro al Monte, near **Civate**.

Romanesque and Late Medieval (11th–14th centuries)

In many ways this was the most exciting and vigorous phase in Italian art history, when the power of the artist was almost that of a magician. Some of Europe's best Romanesque churches were built by Lombard architects and masons, especially the school of builders and sculptors hailing from shores of Lake Lugano (the **Campionesi Masters**) and Lake Como (the **Comaschi Masters**). The church of Sant'Ambrogio in **Milan**, last rebuilt in the 1080s, was the great prototype of the Lombard Romanesque, characterized by its decorative rows of blind rounded arches, sometimes called 'Lombard arcading'; by a broad, triangular façade, sometimes decorated with sculpture or carved friezes; by gabled porches supported by crusty old lions (usually having a human for lunch) or hunchbacked telamones; and by passages under exterior porticoes or an atrium and a rib-vaulted interior with aisles separated by arches (in some churches supporting internal galleries). Especially impressive are the cathedrals of **Cremona** and **Monza**, Sant'Abbondio in **Como**, and San Michele and San Pietro in Ciel d'Oro in **Pavia**.

With such a strong local building tradition, it not be surprising that Gothic ideas imported from France never made much of an impression. Gothic caught on only briefly—but long enough to reach a singular climax, and vastness, in the spire-forested cathedral of **Milan**. The transition from pointy, vertical Gothic to the more rounded, classically proportioned Renaissance is wonderfully evident in the Duomo in **Como**, built half in one style, and half in the other; while the abbey of **San Benedetto Po** near Mantua offers a fine mix of Romanesque, Gothic, and Renaissance art and architecture.

Renaissance (15th–16th centuries)

The fresh perspectives, technical advances and discovery of the individual that epitomize the Renaissance were born in quattrocento Florence and spread to the rest of Italy at varying speeds. Lombardy played a major role in the Renaissance, having the capacity to patronize and appreciate talent. Outdoor frescoes—one of the most charming features of the region—were within the realm not only of the nobility but of merchants and bankers. Celebrated patrons of indoor art include Cardinal Branda Castiglioni, who hired the Florentine Masolino (d. 1447) to paint the charming frescoes in **Castiglione Olona**. Lodovico il Moro sponsored the Milanese sojourns of **Leonardo da Vinci.** Leonardo's smoky shading (*sfumato*) so dazzled the local talent that the next generation or two lay heavily under his spell. Most talented of his followers (Boltraffio, Giampietrino, Cesare da Sesto, Andrea Solario, Salaino, and Marco d'Oggiono) was **Bernardino Luini** (d. 1532), whose masterpiece is the fresco cycle in Santa Maria degli Angioli in **Lugano** (also San Maurizio and Brera Gallery in **Milan** and in **Saronno**). Among the sculptors inspired by Leonardo was **Cristoforo Solari** (1439–1525), whose tombs of Lodovico il Moro and Beatrice d'Este are among the treasures at the **Certosa di Pavia**.

The perfect symmetry and geometrical proportions of Renaissance architecture were introduced into **Milan** and the north in the 1450s by Francesco Sforza, who hired **Filarete** to design the city's revolutionary Ospedale Maggiore after Brunelleschi's famous Ospedale degli Innocenti in Florence. Lodovico il Moro brought architect **Donato Bramante** of Urbino (d. 1514) to Milan, where he designed the amazing, illusionistic 97-centimetre-deep apse of Santa Maria presso San Satiro, the great tribune of Santa Maria delle Grazie, and the cloisters of Sant'Ambrogio before going on to Rome. Most Tuscan of all, however, is the Cappella Portinari in Sant'Eustorgio, built for an agent of the Medici bank, perhaps by the Florentine Michelozzo.

Elsewhere in Lombardy, **Mantua** became one of Italy's most influential art cities of the Renaissance, thanks to the sophisticated, free-spending Gonzaga dukes. The Gonzaga's court painter was **Andrea Mantegna** (d. 1506), the leading artist in northern Italy along with his brother-in-law Giovanni Bellini; for the dukes Mantegna produced the famous frescoes of the *Camera degli Sposi* (1474). Mantegna studied the ancients with an intensity only rivalled by the great Florentine theorist and architect **Leon Battista Alberti** (d. 1472), who designed two churches in Mantua, most notably **Sant'Andrea**, in an imaginative re-use of the forms of Vitruvius. Ideal cities, designed from scratch according to Renaissance theories of symmetry and urban planning, were a popular concept, but Vespasiano Gonzaga was one of few to ever actually build one, **Sabbioneta.**

Uncomfortable next to such refined idealism in Mantua is the Mannerist masterpiece of Raphael's star pupil, **Giulio Romano** (d. 1546): Federico Gonzaga II's pleasure palace, the Palazzo del Tè (1527–34). The 1527 Sack of Rome, an event that shook Italians to the core, brought madness to some of the artists who witnessed it (like Rosso Fiorentino). Giulio Romano fled to Mantua, but in the Palazzo del Tè one can sense reverberations of the event: art and architecture become ambiguous, their limits confused; delight and illusion mingle with oppression; violent contrasts between light and dark echo the starkly defined good and evil of the Counter-Reformation.

Elsewhere in Lombardy, the region's traditional art of sculpture reached its florid epitome in the Renaissance in the person of **Giovanni Antonio Amadeo** of Pavia (d. 1522), best known for the extraordinary ornate façade of the **Certosa di Pavia** and for the design and decoration of the Colleoni Chapel in **Bergamo**. Even more prolific than Amadeo was his follower **Bergognone**, sculptor and painter, whose work turns up everywhere.

Bergamo was the home town of Lorenzo Lotto (1480–1556) and Palma Vecchio, more closely associated with Venice, though Lotto left some works behind for the folks at home (Accademia Carrara, and at San Bernardino and San Spirito). **Brescia** became a minor centre of Renaissance painting, beginning with **Vicenzo Foppa** (d. 1515), one of the leaders of the Lombard Renaissance, a school marked by a sombre tonality and atmosphere; Foppa was especially known for his monumental style (works in **Bergamo** (Accademia Carrara) and **Milan** (Sant'Eustorgio). Later, when Brescia came under Venetian rule, its artists also turned east: Alessandro Bonvicino, better known as **Moretto da Brescia** (d. 1554), was more influenced by Titian, and painted the first-known full-length Italian portrait (1526; works in **Brescia**—Duomo Vecchio and the Galleria Tosio-Martinengo). His Bergamasque pupil, **Giovanni Battista Moroni** (d. 1578), painted many run-of-the-mill religious works, but penetrating portraits of the first calibre (in **Bergamo's Accademia Carrara**). A third painter of this period was **Girolamo Romanino** (d. 1561), whose works combine the richness of Titian with the flatter Lombard style (Santa Maria delle Neve in **Pisogne** and **Cremona** cathedral). The rather naïve works of the prolific **Giovanni Pietro da Cemmo**, a quattrocento painter from Brescia's Val Camonica, turn up in many a country parish; in the Valtellina you'll see many works by **Cipriano Valorsa** (c. 1510–1570) of Grósio, nicknamed the 'Raphael of the Valtellina' for the sweet idealism of his work.

Besides the followers of Leonardo da Vinci and the Brescians, Lombardy did produce two extraordinary native geniuses: Arcimboldo and Caravaggio. **Giuseppe Arcimboldo** (d. 1593) of Milan, painted portraits made up entirely of seafood, vegetables, or flowers which anticipate the Surrealists and the collages of *objets trouvés*. Unfortunately Arcimboldi became the court painter to the Habsburgs in Prague, and has left works only in **Milan** (Castello Sforzesco) and **Cremona** (Museo Civico). More immediately influential, not only in Italy but throughout 17th-century Europe, was **Michelangelo Merisi da Caravaggio** (1573–1610), who, despite a headlong trajectory through life (perhaps the first true bohemian—anarchic, rebellious, wild, and homosexual, he murdered a man over a tennis game, was thrown out of Malta by the Knights, and was almost killed in Naples before dying on a Tuscan beach), managed to leave behind paintings of dramatic power. He was revolutionary in his use of light, of foreshortening, and of simple country people as models in major religious subjects. Although most of his paintings are in Rome, where he moved in 1590, there are some works in **Milan** (Ambrosiana and Brera Gallery).

Baroque (17th–18th centuries)

Architecturally, in these centuries the real show in north Italy took place in Piedmont, notably in the revolutionary works of Juvarra and Guarini. In **Milan** these two centuries were far more austere, in part thanks to St Charles Borromeo, who wrote a guide book for Counter-Reformation architects. **Fabio Mangone** (d. 1629) epitomized this new austerity (the façade of the Ambrosiana, Santa Maria Podone); the more interesting **Lorenzo Binago** (d. 1629) designed San Alessandro, with its innovative combination of two domed areas. Most important of all Baroque architects in Milan was **Francesco Maria Ricchino** (d. 1658), whose San Giuseppe follows Binago's San Alessandro with its two Greek crosses; he created a style of crossings and domes that enjoyed tremendous success (other works include the Palazzo di Brera and the Collegio Elvetico, now the Archivo di Stato, the first concave palace façade of the Baroque).

Milan's best painters of the age all worked in the early 1600s—the mystic and somewhat cloying Giovanni Battista Crespi (called **Cerano**, d. 1632) and the fresco master of Lombardy's sanctuaries, Pier Francesco Mazzucchelli, called **Morazzone** (d. 1626; works at **Varese**). These two, along with the less interesting Giulio Cesare Procaccini, teamed up to paint the Brera Gallery's unusual 'three master' painting of *SS. Rufina and Seconda.* A fourth painter, Antonio d'Enrico, **Il Tanzio** (d. 1635), was inspired by Caravaggio, with results that range from the bland to the uncannily meticulous.

After 1630, when Milan and its artists were devastated by plague, **Bergamo** was left holding the paintbrush of Lombard art, in the portraits of **Carlo Ceresa** (d. 1679) and **Evaristo Baschenis** (1617–77), whose precise still-life paintings of musical instruments are among the finest of a rather non-Italian genre. From **Brescia** came **Giacomo Ceruti** (active in the 1730s–50s), nicknamed 'il Pitocchetto', whose sombre pictures of idiots, beggars, and other social outcasts are as carefully obsessive. In sculpture, **Antonio Fantoni** (1659–1734) from Rovetta stands out with his scrolly, elegantly decorative Rococo altarpieces and pulpits (works in the Valle Seriana, especially **Alzano Lombardo.**

Two Late Baroque painters marched to a different drummer: **Alessandro Magnasco** (1667–1749) of Genoa, who worked mainly in Milan, and produced with quick, nervous brushstrokes weird, almost surreal canvases haunted by wraiths of light, and **Giuseppe Bazzani** (1690–1769), of Mantua, who used similar quick brushstrokes to create the unreal and strange.

Neoclassicism and Romanticism (late 18th–19th century)

Baroque proved to be a hard act to follow, and in these centuries Italian art and architecture almost cease to exist. Three centuries of stifling oppression had take their toll on the national imagination, and for the first time Italy not only ceased to be a leader in art, but failed even to a make a significant contribution.

The vast Galleria Vittorio Emanuele in **Milan** is a 19th-century triumph of engineering, while the **Villa Carlotta**, on the banks of Lake Como, is a triumph of Neoclassicism, with statues by the master of the age, **Antonio Canova** and his meticulous follower, **Thorvaldsen.** Works by romantic Lombard artists, the *Scapigliati* ('Wild-haired ones') are in **Milan**'s Civic Gallery of Modern Art.

20th Century

Italian Art Nouveau, or Liberty-style, left its mark in the grand hotels of the Lakes, in the residential area around Corso Venezia in **Milan**, and reached an apotheosis in the spa palaces of **San Pellegrino Terme**. But Liberty's pretty, bourgeoise charm and the whole patrimony of Italian art only infuriated the young **futurists**, who produced a number of manifestos and paintings which attempted to speed into modern times (*see* **Milan**'s Civic Gallery of Modern Art, the Brera Gallery, and the Civico Museo dell'Arte Contemporanea). This same urge to race out of the past ('Never look back' was Mussolini's motto after the day he ran over and killed a child) also created modern Italy's most coherent and consistent sense of design. Fascist architecture may be charmingly naïve in its totalitarianism, or warped and disconcerting (**Brescia**'s Piazza Vittoriale or its domestic variety, D'Annunzio's bizarre villa in **Gardone Riviera** on the shores of Lake Garda). A remarkable exception is the little-known work of the visionary architect Giorgio Terragni (Casa del Fascio, **Como**).

However uneven the Fascist contribution, modern Italian architects have yet to match it, hardly ever rising above saleable and boring modernism (Milan's 1960 **Pirelli Building** by Gio Ponti and Pier Luigi Nervi is the pick of the bunch). The aforementioned museums in Milan also have collections of modern works. But most artistic talent these days is sublimated into film, or the shibboleth of Italian design—clothes, sports cars, furniture, kitchen utensils—and even these consumer beauties tend to be more packaging than content.

The Caffè of Italian Enlightenment   64

Guelphs, Ghibellines and
  Old Red Beard   65

The Best Fiddles in the World   66

Romans of the Lake   67

The Immortal Fool   68

Topics

Java had little to do with it, but *Il Caffè* had the same effect as an espresso on sleepy 18th-century Lombardy—a quick jolt of wakeful energy. This was in fact the name of Italy's first real newspaper. It was published for only two years in the 1760s, by brothers Pietro and Alessandro Verri and a small circle of young Milanese aristocrats led who called themselves the *Accademia dei Pugni*, 'the Fists'.

The opinions it published derived from England and the philosophers and encyclopaedists of France. They wrote of the need for economic, humanitarian and judicial reforms, not once challenging the authority of the absolute monarchy of the Austrian Habsburgs in Lombardy, or even suggesting anything as radical as Italian unity. But at a time when Italy was still languishing in the enforced ignorance of the Church and foreign rulers, this newspaper, such as it was, was revolutionary for merely encouraging people to think.

When *Il Caffè* was published, only a few thousand lay Italians were literate enough to read it. But they were the élite of the system, and it was their opinions that the Verri brothers hoped to influence in their editorials. Also, conditions in Milan, if nowhere else in Italy, were ripe for change. Lombardy's sovereign, Maria Theresa of Austria, was a benevolent, enlightened despot prepared to tolerate a certain amount of local autonomy and opinion; while Milan was starting to wake up, on the verge of its great capitalist destiny, the rest of Italy snored away, festering under papal and Spanish Bourbon rule.

The most important fruit of the Fists' endeavours came from the youngest member of the Academy, a plump stay-at-home mamma's boy named Cesare Beccaria. Pietro Verri saw potential in this muffin that no one else could fathom and assigned him the task of writing a pamphlet on the group's opinions on justice—not a pleasant subject: torture was the most common way of extracting a confession and in Milan alone someone was executed nearly every day. There was even a strict hierarchy of death: nobles got a quick decapitation with a sharp axe and cardinals had the right to be strangled with a gold and purple cord, while the lower classes could expect to have their tongues and ears chopped off, their eyes put out and their flesh burned with hot irons before being allowed to die.

No one suspected Beccaria of any talent whatsoever, and all were astonished when he roused himself to produce the brilliant, succinct *Dei Delitti e delle Pene* (*Of Crimes and Punishments*), published in 1764 in Livorno, out of the reach of local censors. Although the Church hastily consigned the work to its Index of prohibited books, it can be fairly said that no other work on jurisprudence had such an immediate effect on the day-to-day lives of everyday men and women. Beccaria's eloquent logic against torture and the death penalty, his insistence on equality before the law and for justice to be both accountable and public, moved Voltaire to write in his commentary on the work that Beccaria had eliminated 'the last remnants of barbarism'. The absolute monarchs of the day (with the notable exception of Louis XVI) moved at once to follow Beccaria's precepts, at least in part: Maria Theresa in Austria, Charles III in Spain, Catherine the Great in Russia, Frederick the Great of Prussia, Ferdinand I in Naples, and most of all Peter Leopold in

Tuscany, who went the furthest of all by completely abolishing torture and capital punishment. Beccaria wrote of the 'greatest happiness shared by the greatest number', a phrase adopted by Jeremy Bentham and Thomas Jefferson, who used Beccaria's ideas of equal justice for all as a starting point in framing the American constitution.

Guelphs, Ghibellines and Old Red Beard

The origins of the conflict between Guelphs and Ghibellines are lost in the mists of legend. One medieval writer blamed two brothers of Pistoia named Guelph and Gibel, one of whom murdered the other and began the seemingly endless factional troubles that to many seemed a God-sent plague, meant to punish the proud and wealthy Italians for their sins. Medieval Italy may in fact have been guilty of every sort of jealousy, greed and wrath, but most historians trace the beginnings of the party conflict to two great German houses, *Welf* and *Waiblingen* (Edmund Spenser, looking on amusedly from England, fancifully suggested the names were the origins of our 'Elfs' and 'Goblins').

Trouble was brewing even before the conflict was given a name. The atmosphere of contentious city states, each with its own internal struggles between nobles, merchants and commons, crystallized rapidly into parties. In the beginning, at least, they stood for something. The Guelphs, largely a creation of the newly wealthy bourgeois, were all for free trade and the rights of free cities; the Ghibellines from the start were the party of the German emperors, nominal overlords of Italy who had been trying to assert their control ever since the days of Charlemagne. Naturally, the Guelphs found their protector in the emperors' bitter temporal rivals, the popes.

Nothing unifies like a common enemy, though, and in 12th-century Lombardy the battle-lines between Guelphs and Ghibellines broke down in face of the terror sown by the biggest Goblin of them all, Emperor Frederick Barbarossa (1152–90). Barbarossa understood his election as a mission to restore the lost dignity of the Roman Empire. He even got the Bologna University masters of jurisprudence to proclaim that, according to ancient Roman law, only the Emperor had power over the appointment of magistrates, taxes, ports and such.

To maintain the fond fiction that he was the heir of the Caesars required that Barbarossa possess Italy. His sheer ruthlessness in attempting to do so in seven different forays over the Alps was enough to make him one of Hitler's heroes: to subdue Crema, he captured a number of children and bound them to the front of his siege engine as a human shield, where their parents could hear their pathetic cries. But the Cremaschi hated Barbarossa so much that they fought determinedly on, and after a six-month siege Barbarossa razed their city to the ground—his usual technique in dealing with independent-minded city states. The original Lega Lombarda, or Lombard League, united against him and finally crushed the big thug at Legnano. (This victory over northern tyranny that found an echo in the 19th-century struggles of the Risorgimento and in Verdi's rambunctious opera of 1848, *La Battiglia di Legnano*. Verdi's personality, and many of his operas, made him a rallying point for partisans of Italian unity. Crowds at the Scala in the 1850s would shout 'VERDI!,

VERDI!' whenever there were any Austrians around to hear it, and the composer probably didn't mind that the real message, as everyone knew, was 'Vittorio Emanuele, Re D'Italia!')

Ironically, Barbarossa himself was at that same time a symbol for those Germans who wanted their own national unity. The Germans will tell you that Barbarossa wasn't such a bad fellow after all, that the Italians simply invented most of the horror stories, as Italians are wont to do. In later legend—severely embroidered by Romantic poets—the old emperor slept under a mountain called the Kyffhäuser, like King Arthur; sitting around a table with his knights, his red beard growing through the table as he slept, he would wake up once every hundred years, and the raven perched on the back of his throne would tell him whether Germany was yet united—only then could Barbarossa finally rest in peace.

After Legnano Barbarossa was forced to make peace with his arch enemy, Pope Alexander III, kneeling to pay him homage in the atrium of San Marco (the Venetians triumphantly installed a stone to mark the exact spot). The Pope brokered the Peace of Constance of 1183, in which the *comuni* maintained their sovereign rights while recognizing the overall authority of the emperor. Perhaps this was some small consolation to Barbarossa, who shortly afterwards departed for the Crusades, only to fall off his horse crossing a shallow river in Turkey and drown in six inches of water.

The Best Fiddles in the World

The modern violin, developed in Cremona in the 16th century in the workshops of Guarneri, Stradivarius and the two Amatis, was the perfect instrument to usher in the opulent pageant of Baroque. Its rich, sonorous tone, its capacity for thrilling emotions and drama, equalled rarely even by the human voice, was enough to make the typical Baroque dome's population of saints and angels pause on their soaring flight to heaven to let a tear fall for the earth they were leaving behind.

The sensuous shape of the violin and the very complexity of its manufacture are as Baroque as its sound. Stradivarius and company used the finest wood from the Dolomites and from the dense groves that covered the Lombard plain. The main body of the violin was made from maple and spruce, the neck and other bits from poplar, pear and willow. The fluted edges and scrolls and the beautiful curves come straight from the vocabulary of Cremona's Baroque architecture. Shaped and preserved with an alchemist's varnish, the violins made by the 16th- and 17th-century masters have mellowed and aged over the years like bottles of the finest Sauternes, to develop a quality of sound so powerful, rich and luscious that the violins themselves seem to have a soul. The priceless examples displayed in Cremona's Palazzo del Comune are taken out at least once a week and given a bit of exercise, a caress over the old strings, because there is something alive in them.

The year after Andrea Amati fathered the first violin prototype (1566) Cremona gave birth to Claudio Monteverdi. Growing up amid the rich music flowing from the violinmakers' shop must have had a seminal influence on his career. As a pioneer composer of opera and *maestro di cappella* of St Mark's in Venice, his sumptuous polyphonic music for four to six choirs got him in trouble with the Church, which complained that no one could make out a word of the sacred texts. But that's Baroque for you—the beauty and feeling is the meaning. And perhaps it's not surprising in our strange modern Baroque world, that an organization called the *Associazione Cremonese Luitai Artigiani Professionisti* is attempting to revive the intricate, painstaking craftsmanship that made Cremona's violins the happiest of all instruments of passion.

Romans of the Lakes

Pliny the Elder (Gaius Plinius Secundus), born in Como in the year AD 23, was a man with an endless capacity for collecting facts, gossip and hearsay. The result can be read in his greatest work, the 37 books of the *Historia Naturalis*, the world's first encyclopaedia, which he himself proudly claimed contained '20,000 matters worthy of consideration'. Though above all a scholar and a natural scientist, Pliny died with his boots on—he was the admiral of the fleet in Campania when Vesuvius erupted in AD 70, and as he went closer to inspect the phenomenon he was suffocated in the fumes.

There's hardly a subject Pliny failed to expound on in his master work—geography, botany, agriculture, minerology, zoology and medicine are all there, much of it taken from lost Greek works. What can be traced back to an original source shows that Pliny often ill-digested what he read, and failed to apply much critical judgement; the truth is, much of the *Historia Naturalis* is pure poppycock—like the accounts of blue men in India who hopped around on a single foot, or others who fed only on the scent of flowers—although that hardly stopped it from being one of the most plagiarized works of all time.

Less known, perhaps, is the influence wielded in the Renaissance by Pliny's entries on art and artefacts (again from Greek sources—the Romans themselves were far too practical to theorize about such things). In the 15th and 16th centuries, most artists were of humble origin, and got about as much respect as the local baker. In Pliny (translated into Italian in 1473) they found justifications for their obsession with mathematics, for painting nude figures, and for their search for ever more accurate illusions of reality. Best of all to their minds were Pliny's anecdotes on the honour and respect given by the ancient Greeks to artists. One of their favourites was the story of how Alexander the Great gave his mistress Campaspe to Apelles, when he noticed that the artist had fallen for her while painting her in the nude.

If the Greeks that the Elder Pliny studied so intensely were great classicists in their shunning of all excess and search for beauty in simple, everyday things, the Romans always preferred realism (their finest achievements in sculpture were portrait busts showing all the warts and wrinkles, exactly the opposite of the idealizing Greeks). Long doses of ugly realism, however, are hard to bear, and lead almost inevitably to an escape into the imagination, into romance. Although today we tend to lump all Greek and Roman literature together as 'classics', the greatest Roman writers in the golden age of Augustus were, as the very name suggests, the first Romantics, from Virgil (born in Mantua in AD 70) down to Petronius.

Perhaps the immeasurable, excessive beauty of Lake Como and Lake Garda had something to do with the fact that two other important Roman romantics grew up on their shore. Pliny's own nephew, Pliny the Younger (born in AD 61 in Como), was a famous lawyer and consul whose *Letters* are an invaluable source for his times. But he also wrote of his quiet villas on the lake, to evoke the magic of the scenery—not something the Romans had ever paid much attention to, except when working out where to build the next aqueduct.

To Garda, however, goes the honour of hosting the most highly strung Romantic of them all, the poet Catullus, born in AD 87 in Verona, although he spent most of his time at the family villa at Sirmione—the delicious descriptions by the Younger Pliny of fishing out of his bedroom window resulted in a veritable craze among the first century's smart set to build their own holiday homes there. Catullus' burning, tortured poems for his mistress Lesbia deserve a chapter of their own in the literature of love; she is a grand married woman of the world living on the Palatine Hill, who is gradually won by the young poet's passionate verses. But she soon tires of him and takes new lovers by the score; in despair Catullus flees to Sirmione, only to be summoned back to Rome a decade later by the ageing Lesbia for one last bitter fling. He finds her holding reckless orgies, and about to go on trial for having murdered her husband; in his final poem, shortly before his early and perfectly romantic death from consumption and unrequited love, he leaves a picture of his old flame worthy of a final scene in a Puccini opera:

> *Caelius, Lesbia—she, our Lesbia—Oh, that*
> *only Lesbia, whom Catullus only*
> *loved as never himself and all his dearest,*
> *now on highways and byways seeks her lovers,*
> *strips all Rome's noble great-souled sons of their money.*

trans. by Edith Hamilton

The Immortal Fool

The first recorded mention of Arlecchino, or Harlequin, came when the part was played by a celebrated actor named Tristano Martinelli in 1601—the year that also saw the début of *Hamlet*. Theatre as we know it was blooming all over Europe in those times: Shakespeare and Marlowe, Caldéron and Lope de Vega in Spain, the predecessors of Molière in France. All of these learned their craft from late-Renaissance Italy, where the *commedia dell'arte* had created a fashion that spread across the continent. The great companies, such as the Gelosi, the Confidenti and the Accesi, toured the capitals, while others shared out the provinces. Groups of ten or twelve actors, run as co-operatives, they could do comedies, tragedies or pastorals, to their own texts, and provide music, dance, magic and juggling between acts. The audiences liked the comedies best of all, with a set of masked stock characters, playing off scenes between the *magnificos*, the great lords, and the *zanni*, or servants, who provide the slapstick, half-improvised comic relief. To spring the plot there would be a pair of lovers, or *innamorati*—unmasked, to remind us that only those who are in love are really alive.

It had nothing to do with 'art'. *Arte* means a guild, to emphasize that these companies were made up of professional players. The term was invented in 1745 by Goldoni (who wrote one of the last plays of the genre, *Arlecchino, servitore di due padroni*); in the 1500s the companies were often referred to as the *commedia mercenaria*—they would hit town, set up a stage on trestles, and start their show within the hour. Cultured Italians of the day often deplored the way the 'mercenary' shows were driving out serious drama, traditionally written by scholarly amateurs in the princely courts. In the repressive climate of the day, caught between the Inquisition and the Spanish bosses, a culture of ideas survived only in free Venice. Theatre retreated into humorous popular entertainment, but even then the Italians found a way to say what was on their minds. A new stock character appeared, the menacing but slow-witted 'Capitano', who always spoke with a Spanish accent, and Italians learned from the French how to use Arlecchino to satirize the hated Emperor Charles V himself—playing on the French pronunciation of the names *harlequin* and *Charles Quint*.

Arlecchino may have been born in Oneta, a village north of Bergamo (*see* p.187), but he carries a proud lineage that goes back to the ancient Greeks and Romans. From his character and appearance, historians of the theatre trace him back to the antique *planipedes*, comic mimes with shaved heads (everyone knew Arlecchino wore his silly nightcap to cover his baldness). Other scholars note his relationship to the 'tricksters' of German and Scandinavian mythology, and it has even been claimed that his costume of patches is that of a Sufi dervish. No doubt he had a brilliant career all through the Middle Ages, though it was probably only in the 1500s that he took the form of the Arlecchino we know. At that time, young rustics from the Bergamasque valleys would go to Venice, Milan and other cities to get work as *facchini*, porters. They all seemed to be named Johnny—*Zanni* in dialect, which became the common term for any of the clownish roles in the plays; it's the origin of our word 'zany'.

The name 'Arlecchino' seems actually to have been a French contribution. At the court of Henri III, a certain Italian actor who played the role became a protégé of a Monsieur de Harlay, and people started calling him 'little Harlay', or Harlequin. The character developed into a stock role, the most beloved of all the *commedia dell'arte* clown masks: simple-minded and easily frightened, yet an incorrigible prankster, a fellow as unstable as his motley dress. His foil was usually another servant, the Neapolitan Puricinella, or Puncinella—Punch—more serious and sometimes boastful, but still just as much of a buffoon. Try to imagine them together on stage, and you'll get something that looks very much like Stan Laurel and Oliver Hardy. No doubt these two have always gone through the world together, and we can hope they always will.

History	74
Getting to and from Milan	78
Getting Around	80
Tourist Information	81
Piazza del Duomo	81
Brera and its Accademia	88
West of the Duomo	91
South of the Duomo: Porta Romana	95
The Ticinese Quarter	96
The Navigli District	96
Sports and Activities	97
Where to Stay	97
Eating Out	100
Entertainment and Nightlife	102
Short Excursions from Milan	105

Milan

La Scala

71

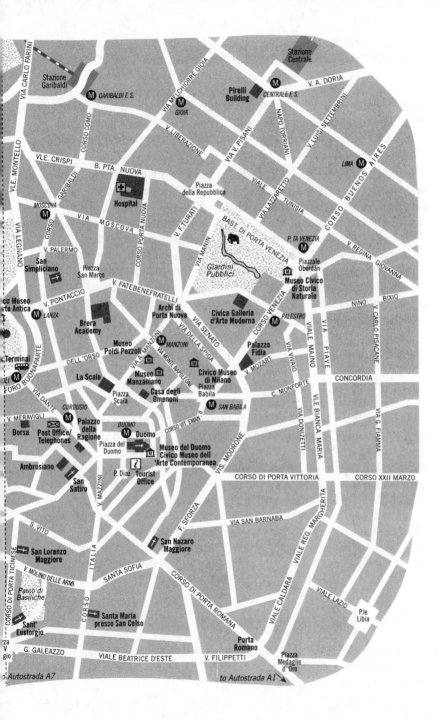

73

Most tourists don't come to Italy looking for slick and feverishly busy Milan, and most of those who somehow find themselves here take in only the obligatory sights—Leonardo's *Last Supper*, La Scala, the Duomo, and the Brera Gallery—before rushing off in search of designer fashions. Most Italians (apart from the almost 4,000,000 Milanese, that is) have little good to say about their second city, either: all the Milanese do is work, all they care about is money, and they defiantly refuse to indulge the myth of *la dolce vita*.

The Italians who deride Milan (most of whom work just as many hours themselves) are mostly envious, and the tourists who whip through it in a day are mostly ignorant of what this great city has to offer. Milan is indeed atypical, devoid of the usual Italian daydreams and living-museum mustiness. Like Naples it lives for the present, but not in Naples' endearing total anarchy; as one of Europe's major financial centres and a capital of fashion, Milan dresses in a well-tailored, thoroughly cosmopolitan three-piece suit. The skills of its workers, above all in the luxury clothing trades, have been known for centuries—as evoked in the English word *millinery*.

And yet, as the Milanese are the first to admit, Milan has made its way in the world not so much by native talent as through the ability to attract and make use of those from other places, from St Ambrose and Leonardo Da Vinci to its most celebrated designer of the moment. It has produced no great music of its own, but La Scala opera house is one of the world's most prestigious places to sing; it has produced but one great artist of its own (the extraordinary Arcimboldo) but managed to amass enough treasures to fill four first-class galleries. Milan is Italy's New York, its greatest melting pot, the Italians' picture window on the modern world, where the young and ambitious gravitate to see their talents properly appreciated and rewarded. Here history seems to weigh less; here willowy Japanese models slink down the pavement with natty young gents whose parents immigrated from Calabria. Luigi Barzini complained that foreigners are interested only in dead Italians, but Milan is one city where the live ones are equally captivating and overflowing with ideas.

History

Milan was born cosmopolitan. Located far from any sea or river, in the middle of the fertile but vulnerable Lombard plain, it nevertheless lies at the natural junction of trade routes through the Alpine passes, from the Tyrrhenian and Adriatic ports, and from the river Po. A great advantage commercially, this strategic position has also put Milan right in the path of every conqueror tramping through Italy.

Mediolanum, as it was originally called, first became prominent in the twilight of the Roman Empire, when, as the headquarters of the Mobile Army and the seat of the court and government of the West, it became the de facto capital for long periods of time; Diocletian preferred it to Rome, and his successors spent much of their time here. The Christianization of the Empire was given official support here in 313, when Constantine the Great established religious toleration with his Edict of Milan.

St Ambrose (Sant'Ambrogio)

No sooner had Christianity received the stamp of approval than it was split between two camps: the orthodox, early-Catholic tradition and the followers of Arianism. Arians, followers of the Egyptian bishop Arius, denied that Christ was of the same substance as God, and the sect was particularly widespread among the peoples on the fringes of the Roman Empire. An early bishop of Milan was an Arian and persecutor of the orthodox, and a schism seemed inevitable when he died. When the young consular governor Ambrose spoke to calm the crowd during the election of the new bishop, a child's voice suddenly piped up: 'Ambrose Bishop!' The cry was taken up, and Ambrose, who hadn't even been baptized, suddenly found himself thrust into a new job.

According to legend, when Ambrose was an infant in Rome, bees had flown into his mouth, attracted by the honey of his tongue. Ambrose's famous eloquence as bishop (374–97) is given much of the credit for preserving the unity of the Church; when the widow of Emperor Valentine desired to raise her son as an Arian, demanding a Milanese basilica for Arian worship, Ambrose and his supporters held the church through a nine-day siege, converting the Empress's soldiers in the process. His most famous convert was St Augustine, and he also set what was to become the standard in relations between Church and Empire when he refused to allow Emperor Theodosius to enter church until he had done penance for ordering a civilian massacre in Thessalonika. St Ambrose left such an imprint on Milan that even today genuine Milanese are called Ambrosiani; their church, practically independent from Rome until the 11th century, still celebrates Mass according to the Ambrosian rite. The Milanese even celebrate their own civic carnival of Sant'Ambrogio in March.

The Rise of the *Comune*

During the barbarian invasions of the next few centuries 'Mediolanum' was shortened to Mailand, the prized Land of May, for so it seemed to the frostbitten Goths and Lombards who came to take it for their own. In the early 11th century Milan evolved into one of Italy's first *comuni* under another great bishop, Heribert, who organized a *parlamento* of citizens and a citizen militia. The new *comune* at once began subjugating the surrounding country and especially its Ghibelline rivals Pavia, Lodi, and Como. To inspire the militia Heribert also invented that unique Italian war totem, the *carroccio*, a huge ox-drawn cart that bore the city's banner, altar and bells into battle, to remind the soldiers of the city and church they fought for.

It was Lodi's complaint about Milan's bullying to Holy Roman Emperor Frederick Barbarossa that first brought old Red Beard to Italy in 1154. It was to prove a momentous battle of wills and arms between the Emperor and Milan, one that would define the relationship of Italy's independent-minded *comuni* towards their nominal overlord. Barbarossa besieged and sacked Milan in 1158; the Ambrosiani promised to behave but attacked his German garrison as soon as the Emperor was back safely over the Alps. Undaunted, Barbarossa returned again, and for two years laid waste to the countryside around Milan, then grimly besieged the defiant city. When it surrendered he was merciless, demanding the surrender of the *carroccio*, forcing the citizens to kiss his feet with ropes around their necks, and inviting Milan's bitterest enemies, Lodi and Como, to raze the city to the ground, sparing only the churches of Sant'Ambrogio and San Lorenzo.

But this total humiliation of Milan, meant as an Imperial example to Italy's other *comuni*, had the opposite effect to that intended; it galvanized them to form the Lombard League against the foreign oppressor (only Pavia hated Milan too much to join). Barbarossa, on his next trip over the Alps, found the *comuni* united against him, and in 1176 was soundly defeated by the Lombard League at Legnano. Now the tables had turned and the empire itself was in danger of total revolt. To preserve it, Barbarossa had to do a little foot-kissing himself in Venice, the privileged toe in this case belonging to Pope Alexander III, whom Barbarossa had exiled from Rome in his attempt to set up a pope more malleable to his schemes. To placate the Lombard *comuni*, the Treaty of Constance was signed after a six-year truce in 1183, in which the signatories of the Lombard League received all that they desired: their municipal autonomy and the privilege of making war—on each other! The more magnanimous idea of a united Italy was still centuries away.

The Big Bosses

If Milan was precocious in developing government by the *comune*, it was also one of the first cities to give it up. Unlike their counterparts in Florence, Milan's manufacturers were varied in their trades (though mainly involved in textiles and armour) and limited themselves to small workshops, failing to form the companies of politically powerful merchants and trade associations that were the power base of a medieval Italian republic. The first family to fill Milan's vacuum at the top were the Torriani (della Torre), feudal lords who became the city's *signori* in 1247, only to lose their position to the Visconti in 1277.

The Visconti, created dukes in 1395, made Milan the strongest state in all Italy, and marriages into the French and English royal houses made the family prominent in European affairs as well (they fêted a certain Geoffrey Chaucer, in town to find a princess for a Plantagenet). Most ambitious of all the Visconti was Gian Galeazzo (1351–1402), married first to the daughter of the king of France, and then to the daughter of his powerful and malevolent uncle Bernabò, whom Gian Galeazzo neatly packed off to prison, before conquering most of northern Italy, the Veneto, Romagna, and Umbria. His army was ready to march on Florence, the gateway to the rest of the peninsula, when he suddenly died of plague. In his cruelty, ruthlessness, and superstitious dependence on astrology, and in his love of art and letters (he founded the Certosa of Pavia, began the Duomo, held a court second to none in its lavishness, and supported the University of Pavia) Gian Galeazzo was one of the first 'archetypal' Renaissance princes. The Florentines and the Venetians took advantage of his demise to carry off pieces of his empire, and while his sons, the obscene Gian Maria (who delighted in feeding his enemies to the dogs) and the gruesome, paranoid Filippo Maria, did what they could to regain their father's conquests, Milan's influence was eventually reduced to Lombardy, which its leaders ran as a centralized state.

Filippo Maria left no male heirs, but a wise and lovely daughter named Bianca, whom he betrothed to his best condottiere, Francesco Sforza (1401–66). After Filippo Maria's death, the Milanese declared the Golden Ambrosian Republic, which crumbled without much support after three years, when Francesco Sforza returned peacefully to accept the dukedom. One of Milan's best rulers, he continued the scientific development of Lombard agriculture and navigable canals and hydraulic schemes, and kept the peace through a friendly alliance with the Medici. His son, Galeazzo Maria, was assassinated, but not before fathering Caterina Sforza, the great Renaissance virago, and an infant son, Gian Galeazzo II.

Lodovico il Moro

It was, however, Francesco Sforza's second son, Lodovico il Moro (1451–1508) who took power and became Milan's most cultured and intriguing leader. He was helped by his wife, the delightful Beatrice d'Este, who ran one of Italy's most sparkling courts until her early death in childbirth. Lodovico was a great patron of the arts, commissioning the *Last Supper* and many of Leonardo da Vinci's engineering schemes, as well as his theatrical pageants. Nevertheless Lodovico bears the blame for one of the first great Italian political blunders, when his quarrel with Naples grew so touchy that he invited King Charles VIII of France to march through the peninsula to claim the Kingdom of Naples. Charles took him up on it and marched unhindered through the country. Lodovico soon realized it was a terrible mistake, and joined the last-minute league of Italian states that united to trap and destroy the French at Fornovo. They succeeded, partially, but the damage was done: the French invasion had shown the Italian states, beautiful, rich and full of treasures, to be disunited and vulnerable. Charles VIII's son, Louis XII, took advantage of a claim on Milan through his Visconti grandmother and captured the city, and Lodovico with it. He died a prisoner in a Loire château, an unhappy Prospero, covering the walls of his dungeon with bizarre symbols and graffiti that perplexes tourists to this day. After more fights between French and Spanish, Milan ended up a strategic province of Charles V's empire, ruled by a Spanish Viceroy.

In 1712 the city came under the Habsburgs of Austria, and with the rest of Lombardy profited from the enlightened reforms of Maria Theresa, who did much to improve agriculture (especially the production of rice and silk), rationalize taxes, and increase education; under her rule La Scala opera house was built, the city's greatest art gallery, the Brera Academy, was founded, and most of central, neoclassical Milan was built. After centuries of hibernation the Ambrosiani were stirring again, and by the time Napoleon arrived the city welcomed him fervently. With a huge festival Milan became the capital of Napoleon's 'Cisalpine Republic' and was linked with Paris via the new Simplon Highway.

The Powerhouse of United Italy

Austrian rule was restored once more after Napoleon's collapse in 1814, but Milan was to be an important centre of Italian nationalist sentiment during the Risorgimento, and rebelled against the repressive Habsburg regime in 1848. The city's greatest contribution during this period, however, was the novelist Manzoni, born in Lecco on Lake Como, whose masterpiece, *I Promessi Sposi*, caused a sensation through his use of language—a new, popular, national Italian that everyone could understand, no small achievement in a country of a hundred dialects, where the literary language had remained practically unchanged since Dante. It was also a work that observed history from the point of view of the common man, and was a landmark in sparking feelings of Italian unity.

After joining the kingdom of Italy, Milan rapidly took its place as Italy's economic and industrial leader, attracting thousands of workers from the poorer sections of the country. Many of these workers joined the new Italian Socialist Party, which was strongest in Lombardy and Emilia-Romagna. In Milan, too, Mussolini founded the Fascist Party and launched its first campaign in 1919. The city was bombed heavily in air raids during World War II. In May 1945 its well-organized partisans liberated it from the Germans before the Allies arrived, and when Mussolini's corpse was hung up on a meat hook in the Piazzale Loreto the Milanese turned out to make sure that the duke of delusion was truly dead before beginning to rebuild their battered city on more solid ground.

Milan was, again, perhaps *the* centre of Italy's postwar economic miracle when it began to take off in the late fifties, drawing in still more thousands of migrants from the south. Despite economic ups and downs and a few hiccups, the city's wealth has continued to grow by near-mathematical progression ever since, while its political affairs were dominated from the seventies onwards by the Socialist Party and their ineffable boss Bettino Craxi. Since the beginning of the nineties, however, as anyone exposed to any of the Italian media has not been allowed to forget for even one minute, the whole structure has of course come crashing down, for it was in Milan, too, that the first allegations of the large-scale taking of *tangenti* (bribes) came to light, initially involving the Socialists, though the mud later spread to touch all the established parties. Craxi and his cronies have virtually disappeared from the political map, and power in Milan's affairs is now disputed between a left/green alliance and the regionalist Northern League. The effects of this new broom are awaited with a mixture of hope, curiosity and apprehension.

Getting to and from Milan

The transport hub of northern Italy, Milan is naturally well served by a full range of international services—with two international **airports**, several **train stations** and many long-distance **coach** services. It is also the centre of the Italian **motorway** (*autostrada*) network, and the main point of arrival for many roads from the north through or across the Alps, though anyone driving to the city would be well advised to leave their car wherever they are staying as soon as possible, and do any sightseeing by public transport. Milan's expanding Metro network is, as well as one of the best means of getting from A to B, a very useful aid to orienting oneself within the city, and stops (indicated **Ⓜ**) are listed in the text below.

by air

Both of Milan's airports, **Linate** (8km from the centre) and the larger **Malpensa** (50km to the west) receive national and international flights (*see* **Travel** pp.2–3). As a rule, intercontinental flights use Malpensa, while Linate handles most of the European and domestic traffic—but be sure to check. For all flight enquiries for both airports call ✆ 74852200. Buses run every 20 minutes between Linate and Porta Garibaldi station or Piazza Luigi di Savoia, next to the Stazione Centrale, in Milan. City bus 73 also runs to Linate from Piazza San Babila (**Ⓜ** *line 1*) in the city centre. Ticket prices are the same as for other city buses (L1200). For Linate bus information call ✆ 66984509.

Buses to and from Malpensa also run from Porta Garibaldi and Piazza Luigi di Savoia, 2½ hours before each flight. Check the full schedule in the nearby **Agenzia Dorea**, or call for information on ✆ 40099260/80. Tickets cost L12,000 each way.

by rail

Milan's splendiferous main **Stazione Centrale** (**Ⓜ** *lines 2, 3*), designed in the thirties with the travelling Fascist satrap in mind, dominates the Piazza Duca d'Aosta northeast of the centre. Centrale (information ✆ 675001) handles nearly all international trains, as well as most of the domestic routes. From Centrale you can take tram 1 to Piazza Scala and Nord Station, and 33 to Stazione Garibaldi and the Cimitero Monumentale; bus 60 goes to Piazza del Duomo and Castello Sforzesco and bus 65 runs down Corso Buenos Aires, Corso Venezia and through the centre to Corso Italia.

Stazione Garibaldi (**Ⓜ** *2*) is the terminus for car-train services, as well as trains for Pavia, Monza, Varese, Como, and Bergamo. **Stazione Lambrate** (**Ⓜ** *2*), on the east side of the city, has connections to Genoa, Bergamo, and towards the Simplon Pass. **Milano-Nord** (**Ⓜ** *Cadorna*) is the main station of Lombardy's regional railway network, with connections to Lake Como, Varese, Novara, Lake Maggiore and several other local destinations. *See* **Travel**, pp.3–4 and 9–11, for further details about tickets and trains in Italy.

by long-distance bus

Most intercity buses (*see* **Travel**, p.4) arrive in the Piazza Castello (**Ⓜ** *Cairoli*), where several bus companies have their offices. **Autostradale** (✆ 801161) is the largest, and it's worth giving them a call if you're aiming for one of the less frequented lake shores or Alpine valleys with no train link.

The various *autostrade*, from France and Turin in the west and across to Venice in the east (A4), to Genoa (A7) and to Bologna, Florence and the south (A1), all link up around Milan with the *tangenziale* ring road, which like the *autostrade* is a toll road. From there several streets connect with the three inner ring roads and the centre; one of the most direct is the Viale Certosa, from the north west. To the north the A8 runs from the *tangenziale* towards Domodossola and the Simplon Pass, and the A9 towards Lake Como and into Switzerland via Lugano. *See* **Travel** pp.11–13 for more details on driving in Italy.

Getting Around

Milan is not a difficult place to find your way around—unless you've brought a car.

by bus and tram

The buses and rather dashing Art Deco trams run by the Milan transport authority (ATM) are convenient and their routes well marked. As usual in Italy you must purchase **tickets** (L1200) in advance at tobacco shops, news-stands, or in the coin-gobbling machines at the main stops, and stamp them in the machines on board; one ticket is valid for 75 minutes' travel anywhere on the network, regardless of how many transfers you need to make. You will find that most bus routes run from about 6am to midnight, after which time special night bus routes operate with reasonable frequency.

If you plan to be riding around a fair bit, buy a one-day pass (L4100), which is valid for buses, trams and the Metro, and is available from the tourist office, tobacconists, or the ATM information office in the Piazza del Duomo, ✆ 89010797. The ATM also publishes a very useful, but cheap, large map showing all the bus routes and metro stops, the *Guida Rete dei trasporti pubblici*, available from the same outlets.

by metro

The **Metropolitana Milanese** (Ⓜ), begun in the sixties, is sleek and well run, and a boon for the bewildered tourist. There are three lines, the Red (Ⓜ*1*), Green (Ⓜ*2*), and Yellow (Ⓜ*3*), the last of which was only completed in 1990. The Red and Green Lines intersect at Cadorna and Loreto; the Yellow and Green lines cross only at Stazione Centrale, while the Yellow and Red meet at Duomo. The Metro is open from 6am to midnight daily, and tickets are the same as those used for the buses or trams.

Milanese taxis are yellow, and their drivers generally honest and reliable. If it's not possible to flag a free cab down in the street they can be found waiting at ranks in the Piazza del Duomo, by the Stazione Centrale, and in several other central piazzas. Alternatively, call for a taxi on ✆ 8585.

by car

Driving in Milan requires chutzpah, luck, and good navigation skills. One-way streets are the rule, signs are confusing, parking impossible (outside of a handful of usually full underground garages, *see* **Travel**, p.11), and bringing a vehicle into the city centre between 7 and 10am or trying to park during rush hours is not only foolhardy but illegal. Also, remember that even though Milan looks like a bloated amoeba on the map, since it has grown outwards in concentric circles, most of its sights are in the highly walkable innermost ring, the *Cerchia dei Navigli.*. Within this area, getting anywhere by car is usually the least convenient means of doing so. Traffic moves only slightly more freely within the second ring, the *Viali.*

Milan ✆ (02–)   **Tourist Information**

The main tourist office is in the Piazza del Duomo on Via Marconi 1, ✆ 809662, fax 72022999. Other branch offices are at the Stazione Centrale, ✆ 6990432, and Linate Airport, ✆ 744065. All three will make free hotel reservations on the spot, and provide good city maps and other practical information; they also organize daily coach tours of the city, departing from the Piazza del Duomo, and boat trips on the canals in summer. The information office in the Galleria Vittorio Emanuele, ✆ 870545, is especially good for information on exhibitions, concerts, and other special events. Other good places to find out what's on are Milan's excellent daily *Corriere della Sera*, and the weekly tabloid *Viva Milano*.

Piazza del Duomo

In the exact centre of Milan towers its famous **Duomo**, a monument of such imposing proportions (third largest in the world after St Peter's and Seville Cathedral) that on clear days it is as visible from the distant Alps as the Alps are visible from its dome. Bristling with 135 spires, defended by 2244 marble saints and one sinner (Napoleon, who crowned himself King of Italy here in 1805), guarded by some 95 leering gargoyles, energized by sunlight pouring through the largest stained-glass windows in Christendom, Milan Cathedral is a remarkable bulwark of the faith. And yet for all its monstrous size, for all the hubbub of its Times-Squarish piazza of throbbing neon signs, traversed daily by tens of thousands of Milanese and tourists, the Duomo is utterly ethereal, a rose-white vision of pinnacles and tracery woven by angels.

Gian Galeazzo Visconti founded it in 1386 as a votive offering to the Mother of God, hoping that she would favour him with a male heir. His prayers for a son were answered in the form of Giovanni Maria, a loathsome degenerate assassinated soon after he attained power; as the Ambrosiani have wryly noted, the Mother of God got the better of the deal.

The Making of a Cathedral

Gian Galeazzo Visconti was the Man who Would be King—King of Italy, or whatever fraction of it he could snatch. An overwhelming, well-nigh psychotic ambition drove the frantic career of this paradigm of Renaissance princes, and such an ambition required a fitting symbol. Milan was to have a new cathedral, the biggest in Italy, dedicated to the greater glory of God, Milan and the Visconti. The demolition of a huge part of the city centre made a space ready for it by 1386, when building began.

All Gian Galeazzo's schemes and aggressions came to nothing, as the little empire he built disintegrated after his death, but Milan did get its cathedral as a kind of consolation prize. From the beginning, the Duke called in all the most skilled builders of the day who were available. Their names are recorded: men such as Bonino da Campione and Matteo da Campione, two of the 'Campionese masters', heirs to medieval Lombardy's great architectural traditions, and also a number of foreigners—Gamodia of Gmünd, Walter Monich and Peter Monich from Germany, and a Parisian known as Mignot. In the court of the Duke, they argued over the sacred geometry appropriate to the task, over the relative merits of beginning the work *ad triangulum* or *ad quadratum*, that is, whether the plans and the measures should be based on the proportions of the equilateral triangle or the square. The latter, the more common form, was decided on, and in the lodge constructed for them the builders would have set up a large open space on the floor, for tracing out the detailed plan and elevation with compass and straight-edge. After that, over the months and years to come, they would work out all the details, every vault, column, buttress and pinnacle, from the same set of proportions.

The building would be the a major drain on Gian Galeazzo's budget—almost as expensive as his endless wars. A normal, modest cathedral would have been hard enough. To get the Candoglia marble they meant to use for the job, for example, the master builders had to design and build roads and even canals, to bring the stone down from the quarries around Lake Maggiore; traces of these can be made out today. The Duke's passion for decoration made it even more difficult. The cathedral was to be embellished with angelic legions of statuary—over 2000 on the exterior and 700 more inside. As many as 300 sculptors found employment at one time in the cathedral workshops. These too came from all over Europe; names like Pietro di Francia and Fritz di Norimberga on the pay lists are a reminder of the Christian, pan-European universality of the age. Men might speak different tongues, but for all the language of faith and art were the same.

How did Milan and the Duke pay for all this? The available records mention a big campaign by local Church authorities to sell religious indulgences, while the state contributed sums from a steep increase in fines in the courts. It wouldn't have been enough. The financing would have been a formidably complex matter, no doubt partially arranged by loans from the Lombard and Tuscan bankers, but no one can say exactly how deeply the Duke dug into his own pockets, how much he coaxed or squeezed out of the other great families, how much the pope, Milan's ally, threw in and how much was wrung out of the poor. New technology helped to lower the costs, especially the machines invented by a master named Giovanni da Zellino for hoisting stone more easily—it's often forgotten how the late Middle Ages was a time of dizzying technological progress, creating new advances in everything from navigation to farming to the first mechanical clocks. For all the complexity of the task, the Duke and his builders knew what they were about; though the façade had to wait for Napoleon, the cathedral was substantially complete by 1399.

However, by the time they got to the façade, the Gothic style—which the Italians never liked much to begin with—had become unfashionable. This bewildered front went through several overhauls of Renaissance and Baroque, then back to Gothic, with the end result, completed in 1809 under Napoleon's orders, resembling a shotgun wedding of Isabelline Gothic with Christopher Wren. In the 1880s there were plans to tear it down and start again, but no one had the heart, and the Milanese have become used to it. Walk around, though, to the glorious Gothic apse, to see what its original builders were about. The subjects of the bas-reliefs on the bronze doors, all cast in this century, are a Milanese history lesson: the Edict of Constantine, the Life of St Ambrose, the city's quarrels with Barbarossa, and the history of the Cathedral itself.

The remarkable dimensions of the interior challenge the eyes to take in what at first seems like infinity captured under a canopy. Its tremendous volume is defined into five aisles by 52 pillars of titanic dimensions, crowned by rings of niches and statues, and is dazzlingly lit by acres of stained glass; the windows of the apse, embellished with flamboyant Gothic tracery, are among the most beautiful anywhere. In them you can see the mysterious alchemical symbol adopted as the Visconti crest, and now the symbol of the city: a twisting serpent in the act of swallowing a man. All other decorations seem rather small afterthoughts, but you may want to seek out in the right transept Leoni's fine Mannerist tomb of Gian Giacomo de' Medici, better known as *Il Medeghino*, the pirate of Lake Como—erected by his brother Pope Pius IV. Near Il Medeghino's tomb is the most disconcerting of the cathedral's thousands of statues: that of San Bartolomeo being flayed alive, with an inscription assuring us that it was made by Marco Agrate and not by Praxiteles, just in case anyone couldn't tell the difference. Other treasures include the 12th-century Trivulzio Candelabrum, by Nicola da Verdun, as well as medieval ivory, gold, and silver-work in the Treasury, located below the main altar by the crypt, where St Charles Borromeo (nephew of Il Medeghino; *see* below, 'Arona' on Lake Maggiore) lies in state. Near the entrance of the cathedral is a door leading down to the **Baptistry of St Ambrose** (*open 10–12, 3–5, daily; adm*), excavated in the 1960s, containing the octagonal baptismal font where the good bishop baptized St Augustine.

For a splendid view of Milan, take a walk through the enchanted forest of spires and statues on the **Cathedral roof** (*open 9–5.30 daily; steps, or lift from outside the cathedral; adm*). The 15th-century dome by Amadeo, topped by the main spire with the gilt statue of *La Madonnina* (who, at 4m tall, really isn't as diminutive as she seems 100m from the ground) offers the best view of all—on a clear morning all the way to the Matterhorn.

Museo del Duomo and Palazzo Reale

On the south side of the cathedral, the **Museo del Duomo** (*open 9.30–12.30, 3–6, Tues–Sun; adm; disabled access*) is housed in a wing of the Palazzo Reale, for centuries home of Milan's rulers, from the Visconti to the Austrian governors. The latter were responsible for its current neoclassical make-up. The museum contains artefacts related to the Duomo, including some of the original stained glass and fine 14th-century French and German statues and gargoyles, tapestries, and a Tintoretto among many other artworks. Other rooms document the history of the cathedral's construction, including a magnificent wooden model built in 1519, designs from the 1886 competition for the new façade, and castings from the bronze doors.

In the main core of the Palazzo Reale is the recently installed **Civíco Museo dell'Arte Contemporanea (CIMAC)** (*open 9.30–5.30 Tues–Sun; disabled access*), with temporary exhibits on the second and the main collection on the third floor. It's devoted to   mainly Italian art of this century, and has early works by the futurists (especially Boccioni), as well as others by Modigliani, De Chirico, Morandi, De Pises, Melotti, the mystical Carrà, and current artists like Tancredi and Novelli.

Behind the palace, on Via Palazzo Reale, be sure to note the beautiful 14th-century **campanile di San Gottardo**, formerly belonging to the palace chapel. The main flanks of the Piazza del Duomo are occupied by porticoes sheltering some of the city's oldest bars; in the centre stands a florid equestrian statue of Vittorio Emanuele II.

The Galleria and La Scala

Opening up from the north side of the Piazza del Duomo is Milan's majestic drawing room, the elegant **Galleria Vittorio Emanuele**, a great glass-roofed arcade designed by

Giuseppe Mengoni, who tragically fell from the roof the day before its inauguration in 1878. Here are more elegant bars (especially the venerable **Il Salotto**, serving perhaps Milan's best cup of coffee) and some of the city's finest shops. In the centre, under a marvellous 48m glass dome, is a ring of mosaic figures of the zodiac; the Milanese believe it's good luck to step on Taurus's testicles.

At the other end of the Galleria lies the **Piazza della Scala**, address of one of the world's great opera houses, the modest-looking neoclassical **La Scala Theatre**, its name derived from the church of Santa Maria alla Scala which formerly stood on the site. Inaugurated in 1778 with Salieri's *Europa Riconosciuta*, La Scala saw the premieres of most of the 19th-century classics of Italian opera, and when bombs smashed it in 1943, it was rebuilt as it was in three years, reopening under the baton of its great conductor Arturo Toscanini. The **Museo Teatrale alla Scala** (*open June–Oct 9–12, 2–6, daily; Nov–May Mon–Sat only; adm*), entered through a door on the left, has recently been rearranged to house better its excellent collection of opera memorabilia, scores, letters, portraits and photos of legendary stars, and set designs; there's even an archaeological section with artefacts related to ancient Greek and Roman theatre. From the museum you can look into the beautiful 2800-seat theatre, with its great chandelier; try to imagine the scene in 1859, when the crowded house at a performance of Bellini's *Norma* took advantage of the presence of the Austrian governor to join in the rousing war chorus.

An unloved 19th-century statue of Leonardo stands in the middle of the Piazza della Scala, while opposite the theatre the imposing **Palazzo Marino** is a fine 16th-century building hiding behind a 19th-century façade; now the Palazzo Municipale, it has one of the city's loveliest courtyards. A few steps away, on Via Catena, the unusual 1565 **Casa degli Omenoni** is held up by eight uncomfortable giants; around the corner on the lovely cobblestoned Piazza Belgioioso, the **Museo Manzoniano** (*open 9.30–12, 2–4, Tues–Fri*) is located in the fine old house where Manzoni lived, and contains items relating to the novelist's life and work, including illustrations from *I Promessi Sposi* and an autographed portrait of his friend Goethe. For more on the man (incidentally the grandson of Cesare Beccaria) *see* 'Lecco', p.169.

Museo Poldi-Pezzoli

In front of La Scala runs one of Milan's busiest and most fashionable boulevards, the **Via Manzoni**. Verdi lived for years and died in a room in the Grand Hotel (No.29); at No.10 is the lovely 17th-century palace of Gian Giacomo Poldi-Pezzoli, who decorated his home to fit his fabulous art collection, then willed it to the public in 1879. Repaired after bomb damage in the War, the **Museo Poldi-Pezzoli** (*open 9.30–12.30, 2.30–6, Tues–Fri; 2.30–7.30pm Sat; closed Sun pm April–Sept, and Sat in Aug; adm*) houses one of Italy's best-known portraits, the 15th-century *Portrait of a Young Woman* by the Tuscan Antonio Pollaiuolo, depicting an ideal Renaissance beauty. She shares the most elegant room of the palace, the Salone Dorato, with the other jewels of the museum: Mantegna's Byzantine *Madonna*, Giovanni Bellini's *Pietà*, Piero della Francesca's *San Nicolò* and from a couple of centuries later, Guardi's *Grey Lagoon*. Other outstanding paintings include Vitale da

Bologna's *Madonna*, a polyptych by Moretti, and works by Luini, Foppa, Turà, Crivelli, Lotto, Cranach (portraits of Luther and wife) and a crucifix by Raphael. The museum also has a fine Islamic collection of metalwork and rugs, including a magnificent 1532 Persian carpet depicting a hunting scene (in the Salone Dorato), medieval and Renaissance armour, Renaissance bronzes, Flemish tapestries, Murano glass, and much more.

Via Montenapoleone

A couple of blocks up Via Manzoni from the museum is Milan's high fashion vortex, the palace-lined **Via Montenapoleone** and a bit beyond, the elegant, pedestrian-only **Via della Spiga**. Even if you're not in the market for astronomically priced clothes by Italy's top designers, these exclusive lanes make for good window-shopping and perhaps even better people-watching. It's hard to remember that up until the 1970s Florence was the centre of the Italian garment industry. When Milan took over this status, thanks mainly to its superior transportation network, it added the essential ingredient of public relations to the Italians' innate sense of style to create a high-fashion empire rivalling Paris, London and New York.

There are two recently established museums in the sumptuous 18th-century Palazzo Morando Bolognini, on Via S. Andrea 6, between 'Montenapo' and Via della Spiga: the **Civico Museo di Milano** and the **Civico Museo di Storia Contemporanea** (*both open 9.30–5.30 Tues–Sun; disabled access*), the first documenting the story of the city, the second devoted to Italian history between the years 1914 and 1945.

Near the intersection of Via della Spiga and Via Manzoni, the **Archi di Porta Nuova**, the huge stone arches of a gate, are one of the few survivals of the 12th-century walls. The original moat that surrounded the walls was enlarged into a canal to bring in the marble for the construction of the cathedral; it was covered in the 1880s when its stench became

greater than its economic benefits. (A useful bus, no.96/97, from the Piazza Cavour makes the circuit of the former canal, and is convenient for reaching the Castello Sforzesco, Santa Maria delle Grazie, or Sant'Ambrogio.)

Giardini Pubblici

From Piazza Cavour, Via Palestro curves between the two sections of Milan's Public Gardens. The Romantic **Giardini di Villa Reale** (Ⓜ *Palestro*) were laid out in 1790 for the Belgiojoso family by Leopoldo Pollak, who also built the Villa Reale, Napoleon's residence while in town. This is now the **Civica Galleria d'Arte Moderna** (*open 9.30–5.30 Tues–Sun; disabled access*); it specializes in Lombard art of the 19th century, in which local artists reflected international movements and invented one of their own, the self-consciously Romantic *Scapigliati* (the 'Wild-haired Ones'). Besides the Italians, there are works by Millet, Corot, Cézanne, Gauguin, Manet, and Van Gogh. A third section contains early 20th-century works by the futurists and others, while a recent donation has added paintings by Picasso, Renoir, and Matisse.

The **Giardini Pubblici** proper, with its fine old trees, lies between Via Palestro and the Corso Veneziaand was laid out in 1782; artificial rocks were added to this shady corner of arcadia to compensate for Milan's flat terrain. A good place to take the children, with its zoo, swans, peddle cars, and playgrounds, it is also the site of Italy's premier **Natural History Museum** (*open 9.30–12.30, 2.30–5.30, Tues–Fri; 9.30am–7.30pm Sat, Sun*), near the Corso Venezia; another victim of the War, it has been rebuilt in its original neomedieval style. Look out for the Canadian cryptosaurus, the stuffed white rhino, the Colossal European lobster, the Madagascar aye-aye and the 40-kilo topaz.

Corso Venezia itself is one of Milan's most interesting thoroughfares, with its neo-classical and Liberty style palaces—most remarkably, the 1903 **Palazzo Castiglione** at No.47 and the neoclassical **Palazzo Serbelloni**, Milan's press club, on the corner of Via Senato. The quarter just west of the Corso Venezia was the most fashionable in the city in the 1920s. It has a smattering of unusual buildings: on Via Malpighi 3, off the Piazza Oberdan, the **Casa Galimberti** with a colourful ceramic façade; the good Art Deco foyer at Via Cappuccini 8; the eccentric houses on Via Mozart (especially No.11); and the romantic 1920s **Palazzo Fidia** at Via Melegari 2.

Lo stile Liberty

'Liberty style' is the name given in Italy to Art Nouveau, the short-lived artistic and architectural movement that flourished in many European countries around the turn of the century. It refers, curiously, to Liberty's, the London shop, whose William Morris-influenced, flower-patterned fabrics and ceramics were some of the first articles in the style imported into Italy, and became enormously popular at the time (the style is also, less commonly, known as the *stile floreale*). The ethos behind the movement was an avoidance of architectural precedents, an embracing of 'naturalistic' ornament and smooth, flowing lines, and a desire to 'integrate' all the arts—hence the importance given not just to painting and fine art, but also to architecture and interior and practical design. Decoration, an integral part of every design, was the key.

Liberty style was never as important in Italy as were its equivalents in France, Austria or Catalonia—nor was it usually as extravagant as they often were—but it did for a time become the vogue among the newly wealthy middle classes of Italy's industrializing north. As the prosperity of this class grew in the 1900s, so too did demand for Liberty-style buildings and products—seen most notably in the villas around the lakes, or along the Riviera. Perhaps the most important figure working in the style in Italy was Giuseppe Sommaruga (1867–1917), whose achievements include the Palazzo Castiglione in Milan and the Hotel Tre Coli, near Varese. Both are characterized by their richly ornamental lines and an uninhibited use of space. In a similar style, but more refined, is the architecture of Raimondo D'Aronco (1857–1932), who worked mainly on public buildings, particularly for conferences and exhibitions. His most famous work is the Palazzo Comunale in Udine.

There are few examples of Liberty style in the less affluent, less industrialized South. Most are in Sicily, thanks to the exceptional talent of architect-designer Ernesto Basile (1857–1932) whose chief works, the Villa Igiea and Villino Florio (both in Palermo), are marked by an almost vertiginous degree of sinuous decoration.

Northwest of the Giardini Pubblici, the **Piazza della Repubblica** has many of the city's hotels; the Mesopotamian-scale Stazione Centrale, blocking the end of Via Vittor Pisani, is the largest train station in Italy. The nearby skyscraper, the **Pirelli Building**, is one that the Milanese are especially proud of, built in 1960 by Gio Ponti. Pier Luigi Nervi designed its concrete structure. It's now the seat of Lombardy's regional government, and you can see most of the city from its terrace (call ahead, © 67651).

Brera and its Accademia

Another street alongside La Scala, Via G. Verdi, leads into the **Brera**, one of the few old quarters to survive in central Milan. Although some of the old cobblestone streets of Brera have maintained their original flavour (especially the Corso Garibaldi), local trendies are busily turning the remainder into Milan's version of Greenwich Village, full of antique and curiosity shops, late night spots, and art galleries.

At the corner of Via Brera and the pungently named Via Fiori Oscuri ('Street of the Dark Flowers') is the elegant courtyard of the **Brera Academy** (*open 9–5.30 Tues–Sat; 9–12.30 Sun; adm; free on 1st, 3rd Sun, and 2nd, 4th Sat of each month*), one of Italy's most important hoards of art. Credit for the collection goes mainly to Napoleon, whose bronze statue, draped in a toga, greets visitors as they enter; a firm believer in centralized art as well as central government, he stripped northern Italy's churches and monasteries of their treasures to form a Louvre-like collection for Milan, the capital of his Cisalpine Republic. The museum first opened in 1809.

Perhaps the best known of the Brera's scores of masterpieces is Raphael's *Marriage of the Virgin*, a Renaissance landmark for its evocation of an ideal, rarefied world, where even the disappointed suitor snapping his rod on his knee performs the bitter ritual in a graceful dance step, all acted out before a perfect but eerily vacant temple in the background. In the same room hangs Piero della Francesca's last painting, the *Pala di Urbino*, featuring among its holy personages Federico da Monfeltro, Duke of Urbino, with his famous nose. The Venetian masters are well represented: Carpaccio, Veronese, Tintoretto, Jacopo Bellini and the Vivarini, but especially Giovanni Bellini, with several of his loveliest madonnas and the great *Pietà*, as well as a joint effort with his brother Gentile, of *St Mark Preaching in Alexandria*; there are luminous works by Carlo Civelli and Cima da Conegliano; and several paintings by Mantegna, including his remarkable study in foreshortening, the *Cristo Morto*. Other Italian works include a unique panel by Bramante, Caravaggio's striking *Supper at Emmaus*, the *Pala Sforzesca* by an unknown 15th-century Lombard artist, depicting Lodovico il Moro and his family; a polyptych by Gentile da Fabriano; and fine works by the Ferrarese masters, da Cossa and Ercole de' Roberti.

Outstanding among the foreign artists' works are Rembrandt's *Portrait of his Sister*, El Greco's *St Francis*, and Van Dyck's *Portrait of the Princess of Orange*. When the Great Masters become indigestible, take a breather in the new 20th-century wing of the gallery, populated mainly by futurists like Severini, Balla, and Boccioni, who believed that to achieve speed was to achieve success, and the metaphysical followers of De Chirico, who seem to believe just the opposite.

Brera's other principal monument is **San Simpliciano**, just off the Corso Garibaldi to the north. Founded perhaps by St Ambrose, it retains its essential palaeo-Christian form in a 12th-century wrapping, with an excellent fresco in the apse by Bergagnone, one of the leading 15th-century Lombard painters.

Castello Sforzesco

Open 9.30–5.30 Tues–Sun; disabled access.

Marking the western limits of the Brera quarter, the **Castello Sforzesco** is one of Milan's best-known monuments. Originally a fortress in the walls, the Visconti made it their castle, and as a symbol of their power it was razed to the ground by the Ambrosian Republic in 1447. Three years later, with the advent of Francesco Sforza, it was rebuilt, though since then its appearance has suffered many vicissitudes. Air raids damaged it and its treasures, and when it was rebuilt, its stout towers were made to double as cisterns. Today it houses the city's main art collection, the **Civico Museo d'Arte Antica del Castello**. The entrance is located across the vast Piazza d'Armi, in the lovely Renaissance Corte Ducale. Housed in what was the principal residence of the Sforza, the museum contains intriguing odds and ends from Milan's history—the equestrian tomb of Bernabò Visconti and a beautiful 14th-century monument of the Rusca family; reliefs of Milan's triumph over Barbarossa, and the city's gonfalon. Leonardo designed the ilex decorations of the **Sala delle Asse**. The next room, the **Sala dei Ducali**, contains a relief by Duccio from Rimini's Tempio Malatestiano; the Sala degli Scarlioni contains the two finest sculptures in the museum, the *Effigy of Gaston de Foix* (1525) and Michelangelo's unfinished *Rondanini Pietà*, a haunting work that the artist laboured on for nine years, off and on, until his death.

Upstairs, most notable among the fine collection of Renaissance furnishings and decorative arts, are the 15th-century Castello Roccabianca frescoes illustrating the popular medieval tale of Patient Griselda. The **Pinacoteca** contains a tender *Madonna with Child* by Giovanni Bellini, his brother-in-law Mantegna's more austere, classical madonna in the *Pala Trivulzio*, and the lovely *Madonna dell'Umiltà* by Filippo Lippi. From Lombardy there are several fine works by Bernardino Bergagnone (especially the serene *Virgin with SS. Sebastian and Gerolamo*) and Il Bramantino, one of the strangest of mannerists, with an eerie *Noli me tangere*. There's a roomful of Leonardo's followers, then a painting by Milan's Giuseppe Arcimboldi (1527–1593), who was no one's follower at all, but the first surrealist. Before going on to become court painter for the Habsburgs in Prague, he left this *Primavera*, a portrait of a woman made up entirely of flowers. From 18th-century Venice, Francesco Guardi's *Storm* could be the precursor of another school—Impressionism.

The castle's third court, the beautiful **Cortile della Rocchetta**, was designed by the Florentines Bramante and Filarete, both of whom worked for several years for Francesco Sforza. Filarete also built Milan's great Ospedale Maggiore (1450s, the centrepiece of the Università degli Studi) with ornate brickwork and terracotta and the first cross-shaped wards, and wrote an architectural treatise on the ideal city he called *Sforzinda* in honour of his patron. The basement of the cortile is filled with the *comune*'s extensive **Egyptian collection** of funerary artefacts and the **Prehistoric collection** of items found in Lombardy's Iron Age settlements. The first floor houses the **Museum of Musical Instruments** with a beautiful collection of string and wind instruments, and a spinet that was played by Mozart. The **Sala della Balla**, where the Sforza played ball, now contains the *Tapestries of the Months* designed by Bartolomeo Suardi, better known by his nickname 'Bramantino' for having been Bramante's pupil.

Parco Sempione and Cimitero Monumentale

Behind the Castello lies the **Parco Sempione**, Milan's largest city park, the site of De Chirico's **Metaphysical Fountain**; the 1930s **Palazzo dell'Arte**, used for exhibitions; the **Arena**, designed in 1806 after Roman models, where 19th-century dilettantes staged mock naval battles; and the imposing triumphal arch, **Arco della Pace**, marking the terminus of Napoleon's great highway (Corso Sempione) that extended from Milan to the Simplon Pass. The arch, originally intended to glorify Napoleon, was instead dedicated to peace by the Austrians. The **Casa Rustici** at Corso Sempione 36, designed in 1931 by Terragni, has proportions that follow Euclid's Golden Rule; many consider it Milan's finest modern building.

Further out (tram 4 from Piazza Scala) lies the **Cimitero Monumentale** (*open 8.30am–5pm daily*), the last rendezvous of Milan's well-to-do burghers. Their lavish monuments—Liberty-style temples and pseudo-ancient columns and obelisks—are just slightly less flamboyant than those of the Genoese. The cemetery keeper has guides to the tombs—Manzoni, Toscanini, and Albert Einstein's father are among the best-known names; the memorial to the 800 Milanese who perished in German concentration camps is the most moving.

West of the Duomo

Milan's greatest painting, Leonardo da Vinci's *Last Supper* (or the *Cenacolo*), is in the refectory of the convent of **Santa Maria delle Grazie** (Ⓜ *Cadorna, then Via Boccaccio and left on Via Caradosso; open 8.15–1.45 daily; adm; disabled access*). But before entering, get into the proper Renaissance mood by first walking around the 15th-century church and cloister. Built by Guiniforte Solari, with later revisions by Bramante under Lodovico il Moro, it is perhaps the most beautiful Renaissance church in Lombardy, its exterior adorned with fine brickwork and terracotta. Bramante's greatest contribution is the majestic Brunelleschi-inspired tribune, added in 1492; he also designed the choir, the unusual crossing under the dome, the sacristy, and the elegant little cloister, the **Chiostrino** (*open 7–12, 3–7, daily*).

The Last Supper

 Leonardo painted three of his masterpieces in Milan, the two versions of the mystery-laden *Virgin of the Rocks* and *The Last Supper*. The former two are in London and the Louvre; the latter would have been in Paris too, had the French been able to figure out a way to remove the wall. Unfortunately, the ever-experimental artist was not content to use proper, established fresco technique (where the paint is applied quickly to wet plaster) but painted with tempera as if on a wood panel (*fresco secco*), enabling him to return over and over to achieve the subtlety of tone and depth he desired. The result was exceedingly beautiful, but almost immediately the moisture in the walls began its deadly work of flaking off particles of paint. As the painting deteriorated, various restorers through the centuries have come to try their hand at this most challenging task, with mixed success. In the Second World War the refectory was decimated by a bomb, and the *Last Supper* only preserved thanks to precautionary measures. Since 1977 restorers have been at work once again, this time cleansing the work of its previous restorations, and stabilizing the wall to prevent further damage; scaffolding will hide portions of the work for several years.

Deterioration or no, the *Last Supper* still thrills, especially in the mellow afternoon light. Painted at the moment when Christ announces that one of his disciples will betray him, it is a masterful psychological study, an instant caught in time, the apostles' gestures of disbelief and dismay captured almost photographically by one of the greatest students of human nature. According to Vasari, the artist left the portrait of Christ purposely unfinished, believing himself unworthy to paint divinity; Judas was another problem, but Leonardo eventually found the proper expression of the betrayer caught guiltily unawares but still nefariously determined and unrepentant.

Monastero Maggiore

From Santa Maria delle Grazie the Corso Magenta leads back towards the centre; at the corner of Via Luini stands the Monastero Maggiore. The monastery's pretty 16th-century church of **San Maurizio** (*open 9.30–12, 3.30–6.30, Wed, Sat, Sun only; closed*

June–Sept) contains exceptional frescoes by Bernardino Luini, one of Leonardo's most accomplished followers. The former Benedictine convent (entrance at Corso Magenta 15) houses the city's Etruscan, Greek, and Roman collections in the **Civico Museo Archeologico** (*open 9.30–5.30 Tues–Sun*), with good Greek vases, Roman glass, a 1st-century AD head of Jove discovered under the Castello Sforzesco, finds from Caesarea in the Holy Land, and Etruscan funerary objects. As important as Milan was in the late Empire, next to nothing has survived the city's frequent razing and rebuilding.

Sant'Ambrogio

The last resting place of Milan's patron saint, the ancient church of Sant'Ambrogio, lies just off San Vittore and Via Carducci (**Ⓜ** *Sant'Ambrogio*) behind the restored medieval gate, the **Pusterla di Sant'Ambrogio**. Founded by St Ambrose in 379, it was enlarged and rebuilt several times, the last time in the 1080s; the result became the prototype of Lombardy's Romanesque basilicas.

The church (*open 7–12, 2–7, Mon–Sat; 7–1, 3–8, Sun*) is entered through a porticoed **Atrium**, lined with fragments of tomb which sets off the simple, triangular façade with its rounded arches and ancient towers; the one to the right, the Monks' Campanile, was built in the 9th century, while the more artistic Canons' Campanile on the left was finished in 1144. The bronze doors, in their decorated portals, date from the 10th century. In its day the finely proportioned interior was revolutionary for its new-fangled rib vaulting; rows of arches divide the aisles, supporting the women's gallery, or

S. Ambrogio – Milano

Matroneum. On the left, look for the 10th-century bronze serpent (said to symbolize Moses' staff) and the **pulpit**, one of the masterpieces of Italian Romanesque. The apse is adorned with 10th–11th century mosaics of the Redeemer and saints, while the sanctuary contains two ancient treasures: the 9th-century *Ciborium* (a casket on columns containing the Host) and a magnificent gold, silver, enamel and gem-studded **altar** (835), portraying scenes from the lives of Christ and St Ambrose. In the crypt below moulder the bones of Saints Ambrose, Gervasio, and Protasio. At the end of the south aisle the 4th-century **Sacello di San Vittore in Ciel d'Oro** ('in the sky of gold') contains brilliant 5th-century mosaics in its cupola and a presumed authentic portrait of St Ambrose.

After working on Santa Maria delle Grazie, Bramante spent two years on Sant'Ambrogio, contributing the unusual **Portico della Canonica** (entered from the door on the left aisle) and the two cloisters, now incorporated into the adjacent Università Cattolica; these display Bramante's new interest in the ancient orders of architecture, an interest he was to develop fully when he moved on to Rome. The upper section of the Portico houses the **Museo della Basilica di Sant'Ambrogio** (*open 10–12, 3–5, Mon, Wed–Fri; 3–5 Sat, Sun; adm*), which contains illuminated manuscripts, medieval capitals and other architectural fragments, as well as ancient fabrics and vestments, some dating back to the 4th century, known as the 'Dalmatiche di Sant'Ambrogio' tapestries, and paintings by Luini and Bergognone. The 1928 **War Memorial** in the Piazza Sant'Ambrogio was designed by Giovanni Muzio and inspired by Athens' Tower of the Winds.

Museum of Science and Technology

From Sant'Ambrogio Via San Vittore leads to the former Olivetan convent of San Vittore, repaired after the War to house the **Leonardo da Vinci Museum of Science and Technology** (*open 9.30–4.30 Tues–Sun; adm; disabled access*). Most of this vast and diverse collection, still arranged in its original 1950s format, is rather mysterious for the uninitiated, and if you're not keen about smelting and the evolution of batteries you may want to head straight 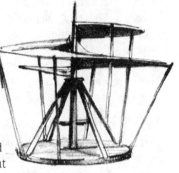 for the **Leonardo da Vinci Gallery**, lined with wooden models and explanations of his machines and inventions.

Leonardo in Milan

 In 1481, Leonardo wrote to Duke Ludovico Sforza, applying to work in his court. He had been recommended to the duke as musician and player of the lyre, of all things, and in his letter of introduction Leonardo boasts of his ability to design war machines, and mentions only at the end of the letter that he could paint, too, if required. In fact, exactly what he did and for whom seemed to matter little. 'I work for anyone who pays me,' he said, and directly after his Milan period he got a job with the nefarious Cesare Borgia. For Leonardo the results of his genius weren't half as important as the quest. In Milan he filled notebook after notebook with studies of nature, weather and anatomy and ideas for inventions in the applied sciences—you can see them displayed in the Ambrosiana. His most practical work in canal-building Milan, however, was in hydraulic engineering. He painted occasionally; besides the *Virgin of the Rocks* and the *Last Supper*, he did a range of portraits including one of Sforza's mistress, Cecilia Gallerani, called the *Lady with an Ermine* (in Cracow). Although the effortless master of the most beautiful painting technique of his time, Leonardo was chiefly interested in solving problems in composition, and once solved, he left most of his painting unfinished out of boredom. Yet more than any other painter he was responsible for the intellectualizing of what had hitherto been regarded as a mere craft–culminating the Renaissance evolution that began with the rediscovery of the works of the Elder Pliny (*see* **Topics**, pp.67–8).

Other rooms include musical instruments and displays on optics, radios, computers, clocks and astronomy; downstairs you can push buttons and make waterwheels turn. Another building is devoted to trains, and another to ships and naval history.

Milan's Financial District

Between Sant'Ambrogio and the Duomo lies what has been the centre of Milan's merchant guilds, bankers, and financiers for centuries, the bank-filled **Piazza Cardusio** (Ⓜ *Cardusio*), and the area around the Via degli Affari and the Via Mercanti, which gives into the Piazza del Duomo. Milan's imposing **Borsa** (stock exchange) was founded by Napoleon and is now the most important in the nation. On Via Mercanti, the 13th-century **Palazzo della Ragione**, the old Hall of Justice, was given an extra floor with oval windows by Maria Theresa. It has recently been restored and is adorned on the Via Mercanti side with a curious statue of a sow partly clad in wool that recalls the city's Roman name, Mediolanum, which could be translated as 'half-woolly'; on the Piazza Mercanti side the building is adorned with a beautiful early 13th-century equestrian relief.

The Ambrosiana

In the Piazza Pio XI (off Via Spadari and Via Cantù) is the most enduring legacy of the noble Borromeo family, the **Ambrosiana**, founded by Cardinal Federico Borromeo (cousin of Charles), who amassed one of Italy's greatest libraries here in 1609, containing 30,000 rare manuscripts, including ancient Middle Eastern texts collected to further the Cardinal's efforts to produce a translation of the Bible, a 5th-century illustrated *Iliad*, Leonardo da Vinci's famous *Codice Atlantico*, with thousands of his drawings, early editions of *The Divine Comedy*, and many more unique items. Unfortunately, the library is currently indefinitely closed for restoration.

The restoration hasn't affected the Cardinal's art collection, the **Pinacoteca** (*open 9.30–5 Mon–Fri, Sun; adm*), housed in the same building. Although a number of paintings have been added over the centuries, the gallery is a monument to one man's taste—which showed a marked preference for the Dutch, and for the peculiar; the art here ranges from the truly sublime to some of the funniest paintings ever to grace a gallery: here are Botticelli's lovely *Tondo,* and his *Madonna del Baldacchino* nonchalantly watering lilies with her milk; a respectable *Madonna* by Pinturicchio and the strange, dramatic *Transito della Vergine* by Baldassarre Estense. Further along an *Adoration of the Magi* by the Master of Santo Sangue is perhaps the only one where Baby Jesus seems thrilled at receiving the wise men's gifts. A small room is illuminated by a huge pre-Raphaelitish stained-glass window of Dante by Giuseppe Bertini (1865), and contains the glove Napoleon wore at Waterloo, a 17th-century bronze of Diana the Huntress, so ornate that even the stag wears earrings, and a number of entertaining paintings by Cardinal Borromeo's friend Jan Brueghel the Younger, who delighted in a thousand and one details and wasn't above putting a little pussycat in Daniel's den of lions.

These are followed by more masterpieces: Giorgione's *Page*, Luini's *Holy Family with St Anne* (from a cartoon by Leonardo), Leonardo's *Portrait of a Musician*, a lovely portrait of Beatrice d'Este attributed to Ambrogio De Predis , and then Bramantino's *Madonna in*

Trono fra Santi, a scene balanced by a dead man on the left and an enormous dead frog on the right. Challenging this for absurdity is the nearby *Female Allegory* by 17th-century Giovanni Serodini, in which the lady, apparently disgruntled with her lute, astrolabe and books, is squirting herself in the nose.

The magnificent cartoon for Raphael's *School of Athens* in the Vatican is as interesting as the fresco itself; the copy of Leonardo's *Last Supper* was done by order of the Cardinal, who sought to preserve what he considered a lost work (the copy itself has recently been restored). A 16th-century *Washing of Feet* from Ferrara has one Apostle blithely clipping his toenails. Another room contains pages of drawings from Leonardo's *Codice Atlantico*. The first Italian still-life, Caravaggio's *Fruit Basket*, is also the most dramatic; it shares the space with more fond items like Magnasco's *The Crow's Singing Lesson*. Further on is Titian's *Adoration of the Magi*, painted for Henri II of France, and still in its original frame.

San Satiro

On the corner of Via Spadari and busy Via Torino is the remarkable Renaissance church of **San Satiro** (officially Santa Maria presso San Satiro), rebuilt by Bramante in 1476, his first Milanese project, but with a mostly 19th-century façade. Faced with a lack of space in the abbreviated, T-shaped interior, Bramante came up with the ingenious solution of creating the illusion of an apse with *trompe l'œil* stucco decorations. Bramante also designed the beautiful octagonal **Baptistry** off the right aisle, decorated with terracottas by Agosto De Fondutis; to the left the **Cappella della Pietà** dating from the 9th century is one of the finest examples of Carolingian architecture in North Italy, even though it was touched up in the Renaissance, with decorations and a Pietà by De Fondutis. San Satiro's 11th-century **Campanile** is visible on Via Falcone.

South of the Duomo: Porta Romana

This corner of Milan is the main traffic outlet of Milan towards the *autostrada* to the south. Tram 13 will take you past its two monuments—firstly, **San Nazaro Maggiore** on Corso Porta Romana, a church that has undergone several rebuildings since its 4th-century dedication by St Ambrose, and last restored in the Romanesque style. The most original feature of San Nazaro is the hexagonal **Cappella Trivulzio** by Bramantino, with the tomb of the condottiere Giangiacomo Trivulzio, who had inscribed on his tomb, in Latin: 'He who never knew rest now rests: Silence.' Trivulzio did have a busy career; a native Milanese who disliked Lodovico Sforza enough to lead Louis XII's attack on Milan in 1499, he became the city's French governor, then went on to lead the League of Cambrai armies in thumping the Venetians at Agnadello (1509), when they threatened to create a land empire as great as the one they already possessed at sea. Further down Corso Porta Romana, in the Piazza Medaglie d'Oro, is one of the original Renaissance gates of the city, the **Porta Romana** (1598).

Corso Italia, another main artery to the south, leads to **Santa Maria presso San Celso**, finished in 1563; its façade is a fine example of the Lombard love of ornament, which reaches almost orgiastic proportions in the Certosa di Pavia (*see* p.110). Within, beyond an attractive atrium, the interior is paved with an exceptional marble floor and decorated with High Renaissance paintings by Paris Bordone, Bergognone, and Moretto. The adjacent 10th-century church of **San Celso** has a charming interior restored in the 19th century, and a good original portal.

The Ticinese Quarter

Southwest of the city centre, Via Torino leads into the artsy quarter named for the Ticino river, and traversed by the main thoroughfare, Corso di Porta Ticinese (tram 15 from Via Torino). In the Ticinese you can find pieces of Roman Mediolanum, which had its centre in modern **Piazza Carrobbio**: there's a bit of the Roman circus on Via Circo, off Via Lanzone, and the **Colonne di San Lorenzo**, on the Corso: these 16 Corinthian columns, now a rendezvous of Milanese teenagers but originally part of a temple or bath, were transported here in the 4th century to construct a portico in front of the **Basilica di San Lorenzo Maggiore**. This is considered the oldest church in Milan, perhaps dating back to the palaeo-Christian era. It acquired its octagonal form, encircled by an ambulatory, in the 4th century. Along with Sant'Ambrogio it was preserved when Barbarossa sacked the city in 1164, but since then it has suffered severe fires, and in the 16th century came near total collapse. The dome and interior were then rebuilt, conserving as much of the old structure as possible. The most interesting section of the church is the **chapel of Sant'Aquilino** (*adm*) with beautiful 5th-century mosaics of Christ and his disciples and an early Christian sarcophagus.

Near the neoclassical **Porta Ticinese** built in the Spanish walls, stands another 4th-century church, **Sant'Eustorgio**, rebuilt in 1278 and modelled along the lines of Sant'Ambrogio, with its low vaults and aisles. The pillars have good capitals, and the chapels are finely decorated with early Renaissance art. One chapel is dedicated to the Magi, and held their relics until Frederick Barbarossa took them to Cologne. The highlight of the church, however, is the pure Tuscan Renaissance **Cappella Portinari**, built for Pigello Portinari, an agent of the Medici bank in Milan. Attributed to Michelozzo and often compared with Brunelleschi's Pazzi Chapel in Florence in its elegant simplicity and proportions, the chapel is crowned by a lovely dome, adorned with stucco reliefs of angels. This jewel is dedicated to one of the more dreadful saints, the Inquisitor St Peter Martyr (who was axed in the head in 1252), whose life was frescoed on the walls by Vincente Foppa and whose remains are buried in the magnificent *Arca di San Pietro Martire* (1339) by the Pisan Giovanni di Balduccio.

The Navigli District

Beyond Porta Ticinese is Milan's Navigli district (Ⓜ *Porta Genova*, or tram 8 or 19) named for the navigable canals, the **Naviglio Grande** and **Naviglio Pavese**, that break up the endless monotony of streets, and meet to form the *Darsena* near the Porta Ticinese. Up until the 1950s Milan, through these canals, handled more tonnage than seaports like Brindisi, and, like any good port, the Navigli was then a funky working class district of warehouses, workshops, sailors' bars, and public housing blocks. Although some of this lingers, Navigli is Milan's up and coming trendy area, where many of the city's artists work, and much of the city's new night spots are opening up.

Shopping

Milan is *the* place to shop in the region. (*See* **Practical A–Z** pp.30–33).

Sports and Activities

A dip in one of Milan's public **swimming pools** can make a hot day of summer sightseeing far more tolerable: two of the nicest and most convenient are situated in the **Parco Solari**, Via Solari and Via Montevideo (Ⓜ *Sant'Agostino*), and the outdoor **Lido di Milano**, Piazzale Lotto 15 (Ⓜ *Lotto*). East of town, the **Parco dell'Idroscalo**, built around an artificial lake designed as a 'runway' for seaplanes in the 20s, has a lovely complex of three pools known as Milan's Riviera (Viale dell'Idroscalo 1), reached by a special bus departing from Piazza Cinque Giornate.

The best **golf** course in the Milan area is the **Golf Club Milano**, in the delightful Parco di Monza in Monza, a short distance north of the city (*see* p.105). A popular **bicycle excursion** from Milan is to pedal along the Naviglio Grande canal from the Darsena to the Ticino river (around 40km), passing by way of **Cassinetta di Lugagnano**, which has one of Italy's finest restaurants (*see* p.101). Like the Venetians with their villas along the Brenta canal, the 18th-century Milanese built sumptuous summer houses along the Naviglio. Only one, the 15th-century frescoed **Villa Gaia** in Robecco, is open to visitors, and only if you call ahead (Ⓒ 9470512). Bicycles can be **rented** for any period of time from Vittorio Comizzoli's shop in Via Washington 60, Ⓒ 4984694 (Ⓜ *Wagner*).

Milan's two prestigious first division football clubs, AC Milan and Inter, play on alternate Sundays during the September-May season at **San Siro** stadium, Via Piccolomini 5 (Ⓜ *Lotto*, then walk). Arrive early to be sure to get a ticket; alternately, tickets for AC games can be bought in branches of the Cariplo bank, and for Inter games in branches of the Banca Popolare Milano. American football (the 'Rhinos') and rugby are semi-professional and can often be seen at the Giurati sports centre. Milan has a good basketball team, which plays in the Super Palatenda sports facility, on Via Sant'Elia. There are two race tracks, the Ippodromo and the Trottatoio for trotters, both near San Siro. For a real escape, travel agencies throughout Milan can book you a week's package holiday in the mountains, for skiing or hiking.

Milan Ⓒ *(02–)*   ## Where to Stay

Milan has basically two types of accommodation: smart hotels for expense-accounted business people, and seedy dives for new arrivals from the provinces, still seeking their first job in the city. This bodes ill for the pleasure traveller, who has the choice of paying a lot of money for an up-to-date modern room with little in the way of atmosphere, or paying less for a place where you may not feel very comfortable (or, worse, very safe). Reserve in advance if possible, because the exceptions to the rule are snapped up fast. Tourist offices (*see* p.81) provide a free hotel reservation service. Bear in mind also that in August in Milan only a handful of shops, restaurants and so on remain open, so that at this time it can be surprisingly easy to find a hotel. On the other hand, during the city's great trade fairs (especially the big fashion show in March and autumn, and the April Fair) you may find no room at the inn.

luxury

Milan's deluxe hotels are clustered between the centre and the Stazione Centrale; four are owned by the reliable and imaginative CIGA chain.

★★★★★ **Excelsior Gallia**, Piazza Duca d'Aosta 9, © 6785, fax 66713239, is a deluxe hotel near the Stazione Centrale that has hosted most of Milan's visiting potentates since it first opened in 1932. Lately spruced up with briarwood furnishings and oriental rugs, its spacious, elegant, and air-conditioned rooms are equipped with satellite television that receives English channels; the Health Centre offers Turkish baths, massages, solarium and beauty treatments, and the Baboon Bar (ask how it got the name during the War) is a mellow place to while away the evening.

★★★★★ **Hotel Palace**, Piazza della Repubblica 20, © 6336, fax 654485, is a CIGA hotel that caters primarily for executives who demand heated towel racks in addition to very tasteful bedrooms and public rooms; many have balconies, and there's a nice roof garden as well.

★★★★★ **Hotel Principe di Savoia**, Piazza della Repubblica 17, © 6230, fax 6595838, is the most elegant and prestigious of the CIGA hotels, originally built in 1927 and since lavishly redecorated. Rooms and service are designed to pamper and please even the most demanding clients—when Margaret Thatcher and Jerry Lewis are in Milan, they stay here. The hotel has its own buses to the airports, a good bar, and private garage.

very expensive

★★★★ **Cavour**, Via Fatebenefratelli 21, © 6570251, fax 6592263. An elegantly furnished hotel in the Brera, a few blocks from the Giardini Pubblici and Via Montenapoleone, and a good choice in the 4-star category.

★★★★ **De La Ville**, Via Hoepli 6, © 867651, fax 866609, is a modern hotel that's very centrally located, between the Duomo and La Scala, and has antique furnishings and courteous service.

★★★★ **Diana Majestic**, Viale Piave 42, © 29513404, fax 201072, (Ⓜ *Porta Venezia*) is a stylish CIGA hotel built at the turn of the century, with charming rooms and views over a garden.

Manin, Via Manin 7, ✆ 6596511, fax 6552160, is a comfortable hotel facing the shady Giardini Pubblici, in one of central Milan's quieter corners; reception is friendly and the rooms modern.

expensive

Ariosto, Via Ariosto 22, ✆ 4817844, has more character than most Milanese hotels of its class, and is conveniently close to Ⓜ *Conciliazione*. An early 20th-century mansion converted to a hotel in 1969, it has a lovely little courtyard, overlooked by the nicer rooms.

Hotel Manzoni, Via Spirito Santo 20, ✆ 76005700, fax 784212. This pleasant and tranquil hotel enjoys one of the most privileged locations in Milan—on a quiet street in easy walking distance of Montenapoleone and La Scala, with the plus of a private garage. Its cheap prices for its location, however, make it extremely popular, so book well in advance.

Soperga, Via Soperga 24, ✆ 6690541, fax 66980352, two blocks east of the Stazione Centrale, is rather expensive, but has good, safe rooms, all with baths.

moderate

Antica Locanda Solferino, Via Castelfidardo 2, ✆ 6570129, fax 26571361. Among the less expensive offerings, the most enjoyable is this 19th-century inn in Brera that has been brought back to life, complete with its former furnishings. All 11 rooms are different in shape and decoration, though the baths are modern. This is another place that requires advance reservations.

London, Via Rovello 3, ✆ 72020166, fax 8057037. Between the castle and the cathedral, this hotel lacks the charm of the Solferino, but offers good rooms with baths, and breakfast included.

Giulio Cesare, Via Rovello 10, ✆/fax 72003915, near the London and among the more pleasant and wholesome of Milan's cheaper accommodation; it even has air-conditioning.

inexpensive

Pensione Valley, Via Soperga 19, ✆ 6692777. Good budget hotels in Milan are thin on the ground, but this one, a short distance from the Stazione Centrale, has comfortable rooms at accessible prices, some with baths.

Sabrello, Via Sammartini 15, ✆ 6697786. Also very conveniently situated near the station, very clean, and exceptional value for the city.

cheap

Ostello Piero Rotta, Via Salmoiraghi 2, ✆ 367095, Milan's modern youth hostel, near San Siro stadium and Ⓜ *QT8* on line 1. An IYHF card is required, and it is open all year, 7–9am, 5–11pm, and costs L20,000 per person per night, including breakfast.

In moneyed Milan you'll find some of Italy's finest restaurants, and some of its most expensive; an average meal will cost you considerably more than it would almost anywhere else in Italy. Butter is preferred in local cooking to oil, and polenta appears more often on the menu than pasta. Perhaps the best-known Milanese speciality, found even in the most obscure corners of Calabria, is the breaded cutlet (*cotoletta alla milanese*), with *risotto alla milanese* (prepared with broth and saffron) a close second. The Lombards also favour hearty dishes like *ossobuco alla milanese* (veal knuckle braised with white wine and tomatoes, properly served with risotto) and *cassoeula* (a stew of pork, cabbage, carrots and celery). Milan also lays claim to minestrone and *busecca*, tripe soup with eggs and cheese. The Milanese cake *panettone,* filled with raisins and fruit, has become a Christmas tradition all over the country.

Good Lombard wines include the reds from the Valtellina (Grumello, Sassella, or the diabolical sounding Inferno); the various wines from Oltrepó Pavese, or Franciacorta's crisp dry whites and mellow reds. Visconti's Lugana is a very pleasant and dry white; Barbacarlo, a dry, fruity red; Buttafuoco, a dry, rathermore hearty red.

In August (and on Sundays, for that matter) so few restaurants remain open that their names are printed in the paper; in the past few years the *comune*, taking pity on the famished hordes, has operated an open-air mess hall in August in the Parco Sempione providing inexpensive meals. At other times, the best places to find a sizeable selection of cheaper restaurants are in the Brera, Ticinese and Navigli districts.

very expensive

Savini, © 8058343, (*closed Sun*), in the Galleria Vittorio Emanuele (since 1867), is considered the most traditional Milanese restaurant of all, a cultural institution where you can try Lombard classics at the pinnacle of perfection—here the often-abused *cotoletta* and risotto retain their primordial freshness, as do the more earthy *cassoeula* and *ossobuco*. Oenophiles will appreciate the vast cellar of Italian and French wines. Another culinary bastion is **La Scaletta**, Piazzale Stazione Porta Genova 3, © 8350290, (*closed Sun, Mon; reservations strongly advised*). Don't let the location, in one of the city's more banal corners, fool you; this little restaurant is the workshop of Italy's *nuova cucina* sorceress, Pina Bellini, who does exquisite things to pasta and risotto, fish and rabbit, all beautifully presented. Excellent desserts and wines finish off a truly memorable meal. If you prefer the ultimate in traditional Italian cuisine, **Aimo e Nadia**, Via Montecuccoli 6, © 416886, (*closed Sat midday, Sun*), in another dull, out-of-the-way corner north of the Stazione San Cristoforo, will serve you such mouth-watering delights as hot ricotta with radicchio (that slightly bitter red chicory from the Veneto), an exquisite liver paté, risotto with zucchini (courgettes) and white truffles, sole tarragon, and pigeon with artichokes. Fantastic light desserts top off the meal. Alternatively, if you're looking for delectable gourmet treats, **Peck**, Via Victor Hugo 4, © 876774, is a name that has meant the best in Milan for over a hundred years, either in its epicurean delicatessen and shop at Via Spadari 9, or here, at its restaurant, which offers different tantalizing fixed-price menus every week. If you need a break from Italian cuisine, **Suntory**, Via G. Verdi 6, © 8693022, (*closed Sun*), serves some of the best Japanese food in all Italy, and is much patronized by Milan's large Japanese business community.

Although it's 20km from Milan, along the Naviglio Grande in Cassinetta di Lugagnano, the **Antica Osteria del Ponte**, © 9420034 (*closed Sun, Mon*), is known as a holy temple of Italian cuisine that shouldn't be missed by any serious gourmet, featuring heavenly dishes like ravioli filled with lobster and zucchini, fresh foie gras, marvellously prepared fish, cassata with pistachio sauce and perfect little pastries—nearly every dish based in Italian traditions. The décor is beautiful, intimate and elegant. There is a fixed-price menu in the evening.

expensive

For a glimpse of Milanese intellectuals like Umberto Eco and fashion's trend-setters, dine at their favourite restaurant, **Decio Carugati**, in the Navigli at Vias Vigevano and Corsico, © 860036, where *la cucina nuova* is as interesting as its elegant patrons. **La Zelata**, Via Anfossi 10 (off Corso Porta Vittoria) © 5484115 (*closed Sun*), is a quiet and refined place run by the former head chef of the Palace hotel. Specialities here include the unusual *raviolone* (one big raviolo, with a delightful sauce) and turbot in a delicate sauce of zucchini flowers; there are also great desserts, and a fine French and Italian wine list. **Trattoria del Ruzante**, Corso Sempione 17, © 316102, has gained a reputation for its exquisite and utterly simple approach to Lombard dishes, especially their famous *tagliatelle alle verdure*. **Aurora**, Via Savona 23 (in the Navigli), © 89404978 (*closed Mon*), has lovely belle epoque dining rooms and an equally lovely cuisine, with an emphasis on mushrooms and truffles; another speciality is the cart of boiled meats, from which you can chose a vast array of sauces, or the salad cart, which offers a quick lesson in Italian olive oil and vinegar dilettantism—the former especially is treated as circumspectfully as vintage wine. Yet another cart will overwhelm you with its bewildering array of cheeses. Exceptional value for this quality of cuisine, the Aurora has been greatly praised by readers.

Another good, but again out-of-the-way place, **Osteria del Binari**, Via Tortona 1 (by the Porta Genova station), © 89409428, has delightful Lombard and Piedmontese specialities, served outdoors in a shady garden in the summer, complemented by homemade bread and pasta, and fine wines.

moderate

Championship pizzas, with a vast selection to choose from, are the speciality at **Vecchia Napoli Da Rino**, Via Chavez 4 (between Stazione Centrale and Parco Lambro), © 2919056 (*closed Mon*); besides pizzas, they also do good *antipasti*, gnocchi, and fish dishes. The **Osteria del Pallone**, Via Gorizia, is a popular, noisy traditional *osteria* with an old-style Milanese atmosphere on the banks of the Naviglio Grande canal, serving hearty Lombard cuisine at good-value prices. It's also a popular bar, and they have exquisite ice cream.

Inexpensive by Milanese standards, anyway. Besides the places listed below, Milan is well endowed with American and Italian fast-food joints, for those without the money or time for a genuine Italian sit-down feast.

Pizzeria Carmignani Angelo e Gianfranco, Corso S. Gottardo 38 (Navigli district), ℂ 8391959, (*closed Tues, Wed*), offers excellent value and tasty pizza from a wood oven as well as good fish, pasta, and other dishes. In Brera, spaghetti-lovers will want to try one of the over 100 varieties offered at **Emilio**, Viale Piave 38, ℂ 29401982 (*closed Mon, Tues midday*). Late-night eaters, except on Sundays, can find delicious victuals at **Topkapi**, Via Ponte Vetero in Brera, ℂ 808282, (*closed Wed*)—good pizza, risotto, *involtini* and more, topped off with homemade pies. One of the best bargains in town is the **Grand'Italia**, Via Palermo 5, Brera, ℂ 877759, which serves up good pizza and *focacce* (Ligurian pizza), as well as a daily if limited choice of first and second courses. Exceptionally cheap but nevertheless full-sized meals are also available at one of Brera's best-known bars, the **Bar Giamaica** (*see* below).

Entertainment and Nightlife

opera, classical music and the theatre

For many people, an evening at **La Scala** is one of the major reasons for visiting Milan. The opera season traditionally opens on 7 December, St Ambrose's Day, and continues until July, while a symphony concert season runs from September through November. The programme is posted outside the theatre, and the box office is located on the left side of the façade. For information, ℂ 807041; reservations ℂ 809126, but be warned that finding a good seat at a moment's notice is all but impossible. You can try through your hotel's concierge, or show up at the box office an hour before the performance to see what's available. Chances are it'll be a vertiginous gallery seat, just squeezed in under the ceiling, but what you can't see you can at least hear. More **classical music** is performed in the Giuseppe Verdi Conservatorio, Via del Conservatorio 12, ℂ 701755, and at the Angelicum, Piazza Sant'Angelo 2, ℂ 6592748. The city of Milan sponsors a series of **Renaissance and Baroque music concerts** in the lovely church of San Maurizio on Corso Magenta, while the province puts on, between October and June, a series of contemporary concerts called *Musica nel nostro tempo*. Keep an eye out for posters and banners, and tourist offices will have full details.

Milan is also the home of Italy's best **theatre** company, the **Piccolo Teatro**, Via Rovello 2, near Via Dante, © 872352. Founded after the Second World War and run for years by brilliant director Giorgio Strehler, the Piccolo is ideologically sound, with a repertory ranging from Commedia dell'Arte to the avant-garde. Tickets are priced low so anyone can go—but reserve in advance as far as possible. Sometimes the Piccolo performs at the much larger **Teatro Lirico**, near the Duomo at Via Larga 14, © 876889. Even if your Italian is only so-so you may enjoy a performance at the puppet theatre, the **Teatro delle Marionette**, Via Olivetani 3/b, © 4694440, near Piazza Sant'Ambrogio. **Films** in English are shown regularly at the Angelicum, Piazza Sant'Angelo 2. The *Corriere della Sera* has complete listings of theatre and films, but if the films aren't listed under *Versione Originale* you can be sure they're dubbed.

jazz

The *Corriere* also lists under 'Ritrovi' the cabarets and nightclubs with live music; for **jazz** Milan's best club is **Scimmie**, Via Ascanio Sforza 45, in Brera, with diverse but high-quality offerings from Dixieland to fusion. The more informal **Capolinea**, Via Lodovico il Moro, at the end of the no.19 tramline (in the Navigli), has attractive low prices and often excellent sessions. Two spots in Brera offer jazz on a more intimate scale: **Il Ponte**, Via Brera 32, and **Club Due**, Via Formentini 2, with live music in the basement.

cafés and bars

Milan has some good, lively **bars**, concentrated in the Brera, Navigli and Ticinese quarters. The old rendezvous of artists and intellectuals in the twenties and thirties, the **Bar Giamaica**, is still open for business at Via Brera 26, as is another old bar, **Moscatelli**, Corso Garibaldi 93, a beloved Milanese oasis for the fashion-weary. **El Tumbun de San Marc**, Via San Marco 20, serves some of Milan's best beer, but for a hearty atmosphere, and a balm to the heart of a homesick Brit, try the **Matricola** pub, tram no.23 to corner of Vias Giovanni Pascoli and Romagna (*open 11pm–1am Mon–Sat; L8000/pint*), a Guinness-owned place with the black stuff on tap plus full pub lunches and 'English' breakfasts served.

As in the rest of Italy, a favourite evening activity is a promenade topped off with an ice cream stop at the *gelateria*. Traditional favourites include **Pozzi**, Piazza Gen. Cantore 4, in the Navigli, and **Passerini**, Via Hugo 4, near the Duomo. **Viel** in Piazza Castello (Via Beltrami) has the most surprising flavours, while totally natural ingredients go into the treats at the **Ecologica**, Corso di Porta Ticinese 40.

After a hard day's shopping Milanese also like nothing more than to pop in for a drink at **Taveggia**, near the Duomo, a traditional bar that has a tapas-style selection of free food. The **Pois**, by the Colonne di San Lorenzo in the Ticinese, is a place for the young and stylish. If you have James Bondish tastes and the wallet to match, the exclusive **Champagneria**, Via Clerici 1 (near La Scala), will soothe your palate with 850 labels of champagne, to wash down the equally vast selection of caviars.

For a sophisticated drink try too **Bar Magenta**, Via Carducci 13, near Ⓜ *Cadorna*, renowned for the models to be found among its young and trendy crowd. A place popular for both lunchtime and evening drinking is **Bar Cavour**, Via Meravigli (Ⓜ *Cordusio*), a large, well-lit bar, open till 2am, which attracts a fairly smart crowd and gets very busy at weekends. For a less formal night out try **Tropical Latino**, Via Ozanam (Ⓜ *Lima*), a Mexican bar with food, lots of imported Mexican beer, salsa music, and a loud atmosphere. Arrive early to avoid queueing.

clubs and discos

The **club scene** in Milan, as in the rest of Italy, is concerned more with appearance than dancing. However, it is possible to discover some places where the emphasis is reversed—though you have to look hard. Generally, places open every day until 3am (though this is often extended at weekends), and the admission fee entitles you to one free drink.

One of the biggest clubs in town, the warehouse-style **City Square**, Via Castelbarco 11–13 (*adm*), near the university, plays techno and house to a young crowd. There's an incredible light show, and live bands during the week, when admission is substantially cheaper. Milan's very fashion-conscious rock'n'rollers get down at the **Rolling Stone**, Corso XXII Marzo 32, (bus 90/91), perhaps the most famous club in town. The atmosphere is relaxed, the music—anything from rock to rap to reggae—and clientele are varied, and despite a capacity of 1000, it's still advisable to arrive early (before midnight).

The recently trendy **Zimba**, Via Gratosoglio 108 (*open Tues–Sun*), plays a mixture of African/Tribal/Reggae sounds and occasionally presents a top-name band in that genre, while the wonderful, bizarre and very chic **Plastico**, Viale Umbria 120 (*open Mon–Sat; adm*) is Milan's version of Studio 54—small and shiny with a very eclectic clientele and fussy doormen. It also has a sizeable gay following. Milan's foremost gay club, though, the biggest in the country, is **Nuova Idea**, Via Castiesa 30.

The super-exclusive, membership-only **Soul 2 Soul** (*adm*) plays a mixture of jazz, hip-hop and R&B in an ultra-modern setting. The other big disco **Time**, Corso Lodi, has three dance-floors playing three different types of music and a capacity of 1500. The emphasis is on techno, and sometimes it gets so hot that the whole place steams up.

By way of contrast, **Stella Alpina**, Via Bocconi (*adm/*, is small and trendy and plays an interesting mixture of jazz/disco and salsa (tram 29/30). Brazilian music and drinks are on tap at Brera's **Leoncino**, Corso Garibaldi 50.

Monza

Only 15 minutes by train from the Porta Garibaldi Station, or 20 minutes by bus from Piazza IV Novembre, Monza is synonymous with the Italian Grand Prix, which is held in early September on the famous Monza racecourse. The course, built in 1922, lies in the heart of one of greater Milan's 'lungs', the beautiful Parco di Monza, formerly part of the Villa Reale of the kings of Italy. It includes the 27-hole **Golf Club Milano** as well as other recreational facilities in its acres and acres of greenery; the single sombre note is struck behind the 18th-century residence—an expiatory chapel built by Vittorio Emanuele III that marks the spot where his father Umberto was assassinated by an anarchist in 1900.

Monza itself is a pleasant if industrial town, once highly favoured by the Lombard Queen Theodolinda, who founded its first cathedral in the late 6th century after being converted from Arianism by Pope Gregory the Great. The present **Duomo** on Via Napoleone dates from the 13th century, and bears a lovely if crumbling multicoloured marble façade by the great Campionese master, Matteo (1390s), who also did some of the fine carvings inside. Theodolinda's life is depicted in a series of 15th-century frescoes near her tomb, honouring the good queen who left Monza its most famous relic, preserved in the high altar: the **Iron Crown of Italy**, a crown believed to have belonged to the Emperor Constantine, named after the iron strip in the centre said to be one of the nails from the True Cross. In the old days, new Holy Roman Emperors would stop in Monza or Pavia to be crowned King of Italy, before heading on to Rome to receive the Crown of Empire from the Pope. The cathedral's precious treasury is displayed in the **Museo Serpero** (*open 9–11.30, 3–5, Tues–Sun*) and includes many objects that once belonged to Theodolinda: a processional cross given her by Gregory the Great, her crown and her famous silver hen and seven chicks symbolizing Lombardy and its provinces.

Lodi

The southeast corner of the province of Milan, watered by the river Adda, is called La Bassa. La Bassa's main city, **Lodi**, was a fierce rival of Milan until the year 1111, when the Milanese ended the feud by decimating Lodi, leaving only the ancient church of San Bassiano intact; they then forbade the citizens of Lodi from returning. Even in the cruel and bitter period of inter-city rivalries Milan's treatment was unduly harsh, and in 1153 Lodi brought a formal complaint to the newly elected Emperor Frederick Barbarossa, hoping he would act as a referee. The emperor warned Milan to leave Lodi alone, and when the proud Ambrosiani mocked his threats he levied a terrible penalty, the brutal sacking of Milan. He also founded a new city of Lodi, but it showed its gratitude by joining Milan in the Lombard league as soon as the Emperor was safely back across the Alps—the first Italian city to learn that calling in foreign intervention was a Pandora's box best left closed. History, though, was to repeat itself over and over again before 1796, when another emperor, Napoleon, won an important battle over the Austrians here.

Besides the ancient church of **San Bassiano** in Lodi Vecchio (Old Lodi, 5km to the east), Lodi's greatest monument is its elegant Renaissance church of the 1490s, **La Incoronata**, an octagon in the style of Bramante, lavishly decorated within with blue and gold and paintings by Bergognone. It is located near the city's large central arcaded Piazza della Vittoria, site of its Broletto and 12th-century **Duomo**, with a fine porch and Romanesque statuary within; another church, **San Francesco**, has a lovely rose window and 14th–15th-century frescoes.

Saronno

Northwest of Milan, on the road and rail line to Varese, lies industrial Saronno, synonymous with *amaretti* biscuits, but also an Italian art scholarship with its **Santuario della Madonna dei Miracoli**, built by Giovanni Antonio Amadeo, begun in the 1430s and finished in 1498, and decorated with major frescoes by Gaudenzio Ferrari and Bernadino Luini, including the former's innovative and startling *Assumption* (1535).

Pavia

The Lombard Plain

Pavia	108
Around Pavia: Lomello and Vigévano	113
Cremona	113
Around Cremona: Soncino and Crema	118
Mantua	119
Around Mantua	128

The three small capitals of the Lombard plain are among Italy's most rewarding art cities, each maintaining its individual character: Pavia, the capital of the ancient Lombards and the region's oldest centre of learning, embellished with fine Romanesque churches and its famous Renaissance Certosa; Cremona, the graceful city where the raw medieval fiddle was reincarnated as the lyrical violin; and Mantua, the dream shadow capital of the wealthy Gonzaga dukes and Isabella d'Este.

Pavia

Pavia is one of those rare cities that had its golden age in the three-digit years before the millennium, that misty half-legendary time that historians have shrugged off as the Dark Ages. But these were bright days for Pavia, when it served as capital of the Goths, and saw Odoacer proclaimed King of Italy after defeating Romulus Augustulus, the last Roman Emperor in the West. In the 6th century the heretical Lombards led by King Alboin captured Pavia from the Goths and formed a state the equal of Byzantine Ravenna and Rome, making Pavia the capital of their *Regnum Italicum*, a position the city maintained into the 11th century; Charlemagne came here to be crowned (774), as did the first King of Italy, Berenguer (888), and Emperor Frederick Barbarossa (1155). At the turn of the millennium, the precursor of Pavia's modern university, the *Studio*, was founded, and among its first students of law was the first Norman Archbishop of Canterbury, Lanfranc, born in Pavia in 1005.

Pavia was a Ghibelline *comune*, the 'city of a hundred towers' and a rival of Milan, to whom it lost its independence in 1359. It was favoured by the Visconti, especially by Gian Galeazzo, who built the castle housing his art collection and founded the **Certosa di Pavia**, one of the most striking landmarks in Italy. It, with many other churches in the city, bears the mark of Pavia's great, half-demented sculptor-architect of the High Renaissance, Giovanni Antonio Amadeo.

Getting to and from Pavia

There are **buses** roughly every 45 minutes between Milan and Pavia, and this is also the best way to travel if you wish to stop off and visit the Certosa, some 8km north of Pavia. Buses arrive in and depart from Via Trieste, in the brand-new station-cum-shopping centre. Frequent **trains** link Pavia to Milan (30mins) and Genoa (1½ hours), and there are less frequent services to Cremona and Mantua, Alessandria and Vercelli, and Piacenza. The train station is an easy walk from the centre, at the end of Corso Cavour and Via Vittorio Emanuele II. *See* **Travel** pp.3–4 and 9–11 for further details about tickets and trains in Italy.

If you're travelling by **car**, Pavia can be reached very quickly from Milan by the A7 *autostrada*, or in a more leisurely fashion by the SS35, which has the advantage of passing by the Certosa.

Via Fabio Filzi 2, ℂ (0382) 22156, fax 32221, very near the new shopping centre.

The Duomo and San Michele

Pavia retains its street plan from the days when it was the Roman city of *Ticinum*, the cardus (Corso Cavour) and the decumanus (Strada Nuova) intersecting by the town hall, or **Broletto**, begun in the 12th century, and the **Duomo**. Begun in 1488, the cathedral owes its imposing design to Amadeo, Leonardo da Vinci, Bramante and a dozen other architects, and its strange, unfinished appearance—from a distance it looks as if it's covered with corrugated cardboard—to an unusual lack of interest and funds. The last two apses in the transept were added only in 1930, while the vast cupola that dominates the city skyline was added in the 1880s. Next to the cathedral is the rubble of what was once the singularly unattractive 12th-century **Torre Civica**, the collapse of which in 1989 prompted serious attention to its rather more famous Pisan relation.

From the Duomo, the Strada Nuova continues south down to the river and the pretty **Covered Bridge**, which has replaced the original Renaissance model damaged during the last War. From Strada Nuova Via Maffi leads to the small brick 12th-century **San Teodoro**, notable for its early 16th-century fresco of Pavia when it still had a forest of a hundred towers and the original covered bridge.

East of the Strada, Via Capsoni leads in a couple of blocks to Pavia's most important church, the Romanesque **Basilica di San Michele**, founded in 661 but rebuilt in the 12th century after its destruction by lightning. Unlike the other churches of Pavia, San Michele is made of sandstone, mellowed into a fine golden hue, though the weather has been less kind to the intricate friezes that cross its front like comic strips, depicting a complete 'apocalyptic vision' with its medieval bestiary, mermaids, monsters, and human figures involved in the never-ending fight between Good and Evil. The solemn interior, where Frederick Barbarossa was crowned Emperor, contains more fine carvings on the capitals of the columns; the most curious, which is the fourth on the left, portrays the 'Death of the Righteous'. Along the top runs a Byzantine-style women's gallery, while the chapel to the right of the main altar contains the church's most valuable treasure, a 7th-century silver crucifix.

The University and Castello Visconteo

The great yellow neoclassical quadrangles of the **University of Pavia**, famous for law and medicine, occupy much of the northeast quadrant of the ancient street plan. The ancient Studio was officially made a university in 1361. St Charles Borromeo, a former student, founded a college here (still supported by the Borromei in Milan), while Pope Pius V founded another, the Collegio Ghislieri, in 1569. In the 18th century Maria Theresa worked hard to bring the university back to life after scholarship had hit the skids, and financed the construction of the main buildings. Three of Pavia's medieval skyscrapers, or **Torri**, survive in the middle of the university, in the Piazza Leonardo; the roof in the

Piazza shelters what is believed to be the crypt of the demolished, 12th-century **Sant'Eusebio church**; nearby you can meet some of the university's 17,000 students (many of whom commute from Milan), at the Bar Bordoni, on Via Mentana. In the Piazza Cairoli, northeast of the main university, the 1228 **San Francesco d'Assisi** was one of the first churches in Italy dedicated to the saint; it has an unusual façade, adorned with lozenge patterns and a triple-mullioned window.

At the top of Strada Nuova looms the mighty **Castello Visconteo**, built in 1360 by the Campionese masters for Gian Galeazzo II, but partially destroyed in the Battle of Pavia, on 24 February 1525, when Emperor Charles V captured Francis I of France, who succinctly described the outcome in a letter to his mother: 'Madame, all is lost save honour'. Three sides of the castle and its beautifully arcaded courtyard with terracotta decorations managed to survive as well, and now house Pavia's **Museo Civico** (*open 10–12, 2.30–4, Tues–Sun; Dec, Jan, July, Aug 9am–1pm only, Tues–Sun*). The archaeological and medieval sections contain finds from Roman and Gaulish Pavia, as well as robust Lombard and medieval carvings salvaged from now-vanished churches, and colourful 12th-century mosaics. One room contains an impressive wooden model of the cathedral, built by the architect Fugazza in the early 16th century. The picture gallery on the first floor contains works by Giovanni Bellini, Correggio, Foppa, Van der Goes and others.

San Pietro in Ciel d'Oro

Behind the castle, Via Griziotti (off Viale Matteotti) leads to Pavia's second great Romanesque temple, **San Pietro in Ciel d'Oro** ('St Peter in the Golden Sky'), built in 1132 and named for its once-glorious gilded ceiling, mentioned by Dante in Canto X of the *Paradiso*. The single door in the façade is strangely off-centre; within, the main altar is one of the greatest works of the Campionese masters, the **Arca di Sant'Agostino**, a magnificent 14th-century monument built to shelter the bones of St Augustine, which, according to legend, were retrieved in the 8th century from Carthage by the Lombard king Luitprand, staunch ally of Pope Gregory II against the Iconoclasts of Byzantium. Luitprand himself is buried in a humble tomb to the right, and in the crypt lies another Dark Age celebrity, the philosopher Boethius, slain by Emperor Theodoric of Ravenna in 524.

There are two other notable churches in Pavia. In the centre of town (walk down the Piazza Petrarca from Corso Matteotti), **Santa Maria del Carmine** (1390s) is an excellent example of Lombard Gothic, with a fine façade and rose window and, inside, a beautifully sculptured lavabo by Amadeo. Outside the centre, to the west (Corso Cavour to Corso Mazzoni and Via Riviera) it's a 15-minute walk to the rather plain, vertical, 13th-century **San Lanfranco**, especially notable for its lovely memorial, the *Arca di San Lanfranco*, sculpted by Amadeo in 1498, his last work (though Archbishop Lanfranc was actually buried in Canterbury); the same artist helped design the church's pretty cloister.

The Certosa di Pavia

The pinnacle of Renaissance architecture in Lombardy, and according to Jacob Burckhardt 'the greatest decorative masterpiece in all of Italy', the Certosa, or Charterhouse, of Pavia, was built over a period of 200 years. Gian Galeazzo Visconti laid the cornerstone in 1396, with visions of the crown of Italy dancing in his head, and the desire to build a splendid pantheon for his hoped-for royal self and his heirs. Although many architects and artists worked on the project (beginning with the Campionese masters of Milan cathedral), it bears the greatest imprint of Giovanni Antonio Amadeo, who with his successor Bergognone worked on its sculptural programme for 30 years and contributed the design of the lavish façade.

Napoleon disbanded the monastery, but in 1968 a small group of Cistercians reoccupied the Certosa. The monks of today live the same style of contemplative life as the old Carthusians, maintaining vows of silence. A couple, however, are released to take visitors around the complex (*open 9–11.30, 2.30–6pm, Tues–Sun in summer; it closes at 5pm in the spring and autumn, and 4pm in winter; weekends are often very crowded*). If you arrive by the Milan-Pavia bus, the Certosa's a 1½km walk from the nearest stop, a beckoning vision at the end of the straight, shaded land, surrounded by well-tended fields and rows of poplars once part of the vast game park of the Castello Visconteo in Pavia.

Once through the main gate and **vestibule** adorned with frescoes by Luini, a large grassy court opens up, lined with buildings that served as lodgings for visitors and stores for the monks. At the far side rises the sumptuous, detailed façade of the **church**, a marvel of polychromatic marbles, medallions, bas reliefs, statues, and windows covered with marble embroidery from the chisel of Amadeo, who died before the upper, less elaborate level was begun. The interior plan is Gothic but the decoration is Renaissance, with later Baroque additions. Outstanding works of art include Bergognone's five statues of saints in the chapel of Sant'Ambrogio (sixth on the left); the tombs of Lodovico il Moro and his young bride Beatrice d'Este, a masterpiece by Cristoforo Solari; the beautiful inlaid stalls of the choir, and the tomb of Gian Galeazzo Visconti, all works of the 1490s and surrounded by fine frescoes. The old sacristy contains a magnificent early cinquecento ivory altarpiece by the Florentine Baldassarre degli Embriachi, with 94 figures and 66 bas reliefs.

From the church, the tour continues into the **Little Cloister**, with delicate terracotta decorations and a dream-like view of the church and its cupola, a rising crescendo of arcades. A lovely doorway by Amadeo leads back into the church. The **Great Cloister** with its long arcades is surrounded by the 24 house-like cells of the monks—each contains a chapel and study/dining room, a bedroom upstairs and a walled garden in the rear. The frescoed **Refectory** contains a pulpit for the monks who read aloud during otherwise silent suppers.

Pavia ✆ (0382–)

Where to Stay

Most people visit Pavia as a day trip from Milan, but light sleepers or budget-minded souls could always take in Milan as a day trip from Pavia.

expensive and moderate

★★★★ **Moderno**, Viale Vittorio Emanuele II 45, ✆ 303401, the most comfortable, if expensive hotel in town, next to the railway station.

★★★★ **Ariston**, Via A. Scopoli 10/d, ✆ 34334, fax 25667. Conveniently centrally located, this hotel has a slightly more old-fashioned touch, with air-conditioning, private bath and television in each room, for much less than you'd pay in Milan.

★★★ **Excelsior**, Piazza Stazione 25, ✆ 28596, fax 23060, also conveniently located, and slightly cheaper.

inexpensive

★★ **Aurora**, Via Vittorio Emanuele II 25, ✆ 23664. There are not many options in this category, but this is another hotel near the station, which has showers in all the rooms.

★ **Splendid**, Via XX Settembre 11, ✆ 24703. Elderly but friendly, the Splendid has plenty of rooms, though none of them has baths.

Pavia ✆ (0382–)   **Eating Out**

Pavia is well endowed with good restaurants. Specialities include frogs, salami from Varzi and *zuppa pavese* (a raw egg on toast drowned in hot broth); good local wines to try are from the Oltrepó Pavese region, one of Lombardy's best. Cortese is a delicious dry white, Bonarda a meaty, dry red, Pinot a fruity white.

expensive

For excellent, innovative cuisine, eat at the small but chic **Locanda Vecchia Pavia**, right under the cathedral on Via Cardinal Ribodi 2, ✆ 304132 (*closed Wed, Aug*); its young chefs base the day's menu on what looks good in the market, with some surprising but delicious results like salmon and caviar tartare, truffle-filled ravioli, and equally fine desserts. Pavia's other temple of fine cuisine is **Al Cassinino**, Via Cassinino 1, ✆ 422097 (*closed Wed, Christmas*), just outside the city on the Giovi highway. Sitting on the Naviglio, the restaurant is done out in the style of a medieval inn, complete with rare antiques. Dishes are whatever the market provides—from truffles to frogs' legs, oysters to caviar.

moderate and inexpensive

Osteria della Madonna, Via de Liguri, ✆ 302833, (*closed Sun, Mon, Aug*), is a jumping place featuring good, solid lunches for around L20,000 and more elaborate dinners, often with live entertainment, for L50,000. In the old 16th-century mill of the Certosa, the **Vecchio Mulino**, Via al Monumento 5, ✆ 925894, (*closed evenings Sun, Mon*), serves up delicious food with ingredients garnered from the fertile countryside—foie gras, risotto with crayfish or asparagus, frog's legs, *coniglio al Riesling* (rabbit in wine), crêpes filled with artichokes, and much more. The wine list has nearly every label produced in Lombardy. Cheapest of all, **Il Senatore**, on the street of the same name, serves good, solid local fare at a very reasonable price in a cosy atmosphere.

Around Pavia: Lomello and Vigévano

West of Pavia and the Certosa lies the little-known Lomellina, a major rice-growing and frog-farming district, irrigated by canals dug by order of the Visconti in the 14th century. The feudal seat, **Lomello**, retains some fine early medieval buildings, most notably a lovely little 5th-century polygonal **Baptistry** near the main church, the 11th-century **Basilica di Santa Maria**.

Also in the Lomellina is the old silk town of **Vigévano** (better known these days for its high-fashion footwear manufacturers), the site of another vast **castle** of the Visconti and Sforza clans; it was the birthplace of Lodovico il Moro, and for the past few years has been undergoing a lengthy restoration process. Below it lies the majestic rectangular **Piazza Ducale**, designed in 1492 by Bramante (with help from Leonardo) as Lombardy's answer to Venice's Piazza San Marco. Originally a grand stairway connected the piazza to one of the castle towers, though now the three sides are adorned with slender arcades, while on the fourth stands the magnificent concave Baroque façade of the **Cathedral**, designed by a Spanish bishop, Juan Caramuel de Labkowitz. Inside there's a good collection of 16th-century paintings and a 15th-century Lombard polyptych on the life of St Thomas of Canterbury, and an especially rich treasury (*open 3–5pm public holidays only, or upon request*), containing illuminated codices, Flemish tapestries, and golden reliquaries.

Cremona

Charming Cremona is famous for two things: the stupendous complex of its Romanesque cathedaral and its equally stupendous violins. It has been the capital of the latter industry since 1566, when Andrea Amati developed the modern violin in his Cremona workshop. The next two centuries were a musical golden age for the city, the era when Andrea's son Nicolò Amati, and his famous pupils Antonio Stradivarius and Giuseppe Guarneri, built the workshops (*Botteghe Liutarie*) that today still house some 50 violin masters, many of whom have learnt their trade in Cremona's International School of Violin-making. To celebrate the tradition the city hosts a festival of stringed instruments every third October (the next in 1994). Violins even seem to be reflected in the curving spiral cornices and pediments that adorn Cremona's elegant brick and ornate terracotta palaces, while the sweetness of their tone is recalled in the city's culinary specialities—*torrone*, a nougat made of almonds and honey and sold in bars throughout the city, and *mostarda di Cremona*—candied cherries, apricots, melons, and so on in a sweet mustard sauce, served with boiled meats.

violin making

In the 14th century the *comune* of Cremona was captured by Milan, and the city's history is closely linked with the Lombard capital. In 1441 it was given to Bianca Maria Visconti as her dowry when she married Francesco Sforza, marking the change of the great Milanese dynasties. The city enjoyed a happy, fruitful Renaissance as the apple of Bianca's eye, and the fertile countryside is littered with lovely villas and castles.

Getting to and from Cremona

Even Cremona's railway station is delightful: there are frequent **train** services there from Milan (about 2 hours journey), Pavia, Mantua, Brescia, and Piacenza, as well as three times a day from Bergamo. If you are coming from Parma or Bologna, change in Fidenza. The station lies north of the centre, at the end of Via Palestro. **Buses** arrive in and depart from Piazza Marconi, southeast of the Piazza del Comune, for Genoa, Trieste, Mantua, Bergamo, Padua, Milan, Iseo and all destinations in Cremona province; for information, call © (0372) 29212.

Travelling **by car**, the most convenient road to take from Milan is the SS415 via Crema, leaving Milan by the Corso Lodi. If you are approaching from the west or the east, Cremona is also near the A21 Brescia-Turin *autostrada*.

Tourist Information

Piazza del Comune 5, © (0372) 23233. If you're in the market for a violin or just want to visit a workshop, ask for their free list of *Botteghe Liutarie*. The tourist office also operates a useful **museum entry scheme**—a single L5000 ticket, valid for a three-day period, gives admission to all the town's main museums.

Via Palestro to the Piazza del Comune

Cremona can be easily visited by foot in a day, starting from the station and the Via Palestro. Here, behind a remodelled Baroque façade at No.36, the 15th–16th-century **Palazzo Stanga**'s courtyard is an excellent introduction to the Cremonese fondness for elaborate terracotta ornament. The **Museo Stradivariano** nearby at No.17 (*open 9am–6pm Tues–Sat, 9–12.30, 3–6, Sun; closed Aug; adm*) is an equally good introduction to the cream of Cremona's best known industry, featuring casts, models, and drawings explaining how Stradivarius did it. Just around the corner, on Via Dati, the Palazzo Affaitati (begun in 1561) houses a grand theatrical staircase added in 1769 and the **Museo Civico** (*open 9am–6pm Tues–Sat; 9–12.30, 3–6, Sun; closed Aug; adm*), which has sections devoted to art, with paintings by the Cremonese school (Boccaccino and the Campi family), and one of the 16th-century surrealist Arcimboldo's most striking portraits, *Scherzo con Ortaggi*, a vegetable face with onion cheeks and walnut eyes spilling out of a bowl. The interesting archaeology section includes a fine labyrinth mosaic from the Roman colonia at Cremona; another section houses the Cathedral Treasury, with some fine Renaissance illuminations.

Via Palestro becomes Via C. Campi, and at an angle runs into the boxy, Mussolini-era Galleria Venticinque Aprile, leading to the **Piazza Roma**, a little park; along Corso

Mazzini is Stradivarius' tombstone, transferred from a demolished church. Corso Mazzini forks after a block; near the split, at Corso Matteotti 17, is Cremona's prettiest palace, the 1499 **Palazzo Fodri** (now owned by the Banca d'Italia; ask the guard to unlock the gate), with a courtyard adorned with frescoed battle scenes and terracottas.

The Duomo and its Torrazzo

By now you've probably caught at least a glimpse of the curious pointed crown of the tallest bell tower in Italy, the 112m **Torrazzo**, looming high over Cremona's equally remarkable Duomo in Piazza del Comune, itself a square seductive enough to compete in any urban beauty contest. The Torrazzo, only slightly shorter than Milan Cathedral, was built in the 13th century, and has battlements as well as bells, though any warlike purpose it may have had is belied by a fine astronomical clock, added in 1583 by Giovanni Battista Divizioli, and the twin 'wreaths' and spire on top. The stout-hearted can ascend to the top for an eye-popping view of Cremona. An added attraction on the lower levels is a violin workshop, a reproduction of one of Stradivarius' time, where a violin-maker often works and explains his art (*open Mar–Oct 10–12, 3–6.30, Tues–Sat; 10–12.30, 3–7, Sun; Nov–Feb 3–6pm Sat only; adm*).

The **Duomo**, linked to the Torrazzo in the early 15th century by a double loggia, the *Bertazzola*, is the highest and most exuberant expression of Lombard Romanesque, with a trademark Cremonese flourish in the façade's graceful curls and immense rose window. Built by the Comacini masters after an earthquake in 1117 destroyed its predecessor, the cathedral is just as captivating, especially the main door **Porta Regia**, flanked by two nearly toothless lion telamones and four flat prophets, and crowned by a small portico, known as the Rostrum, where 13th- and 14th-century statues of the Virgin and two saints silently but eloquently hold forth above a frieze of the months by the school of Antelami.

The cathedral was begun as a basilica, but as Gothic came into fashion it was decided to add arms to make a Latin cross; the new transepts, especially the north one, are almost as splendid in their exteriors as the marble-coated main façade. Inside, the nave and apse have opulent frescoes (early 15th century) by Romanino, Boccaccino, Pordenone and others, and fine Flemish tapestries. The twin pulpits have reliefs attributed to Amadeo or Pietro da Rho. Among the individual paintings, look for the Pietà in the left transept by Antonio Campi—not a great painter, but a strange one. The choir has stalls inlaid in 1490 by G. M. Platina.

Before leaving the cathedral, look at the medieval capital in the presbytery supported by tired telamones, while behind them an impassive mermaid holds up her forked tail—a Romanesque conceit nearly as popular as the two lions by the main door. Such mermaids, displaying the entrance to the womb, with birds or dragons whispering in their ears, come straight from medieval mysticism, perhaps as a symbol of the cosmic process: the sirens, representing desire, become the intermediaries by which nature's energy and inspiration (here represented by the birds) are conducted into the conscious world.

Completing the divine ensemble in Piazza del Comune is the octagonal **Baptistry di San Giovanni** (1167), with another pair of lions supporting the portico, and two sides of marble facing to match the cathedral. Across from the Duomo, the Gothic **Loggia dei Militi** was used as a rendezvous by the captains of the *comune*'s citizen militia; the outdoor pulpit between two of the arches is a relic of the charismatic, itinerant preachers like San Bernadino of Siena, whose sermons were so popular they had to be held outside. Behind it lies the 13th-century **Palazzo del Comune** (*open 9am–6pm Tues–Sat, 9–12.30, 3–6, Sun; closed Aug; adm*), a lavish town hall that retains some of its original frescoes, doorways, and windows; one room has been converted into a **Saletta dei Violini**, which contains the municipal collection, where you can see some of the greatest products of some of Cremona's greatest craftsmen, such as Stradivarius' golden 'Cremonese 1715', which retains its original varnish—as mysterious as the embalming fluids of ancient Egypt. Another of Stradivarius' secrets was in the woods he used for his instruments; like Michelangelo seeking just the right piece of marble in the mountains of Carrara, Stradivarius would visit the forests of the Dolomites looking for perfect trees that would one day sing. Other violins on display are 'Charles IX of France' by Andrea Amati, one of 24 violins commissioned in the 1560s by the French sovereign from the father of modern fiddles; the 'Hammerle', by Nicolò Amati (1658); Giuseppe Guarneri's 'Del Gesù' (formerly owned by Pinchas Zukerman) and the 1689 'Quarestini', also by Guarneri.

Back Towards the Station

Behind the Palazzo del Comune lies Piazza Cavour and Corso Vittorio Emanuele, leading to the River Po. En route it passes one of Italy's earliest and most renowned small-town theatres, the **Teatro Ponchielli**, built in 1734, and rebuilt after a fire in 1808; its name recalls composer Amilcare Ponchielli (*see* p.118) who premiered several of his operas on its little stage. A street to the left of the theatre leads back to San Pietro al Po, coated with 16th-century stuccoes and paintings, none individually as effective as the sum.

North of the Corso Vittorio Emanuele, on Via Plasio, stands the 14th-century church of **Sant'Agostino**. Its Gothic façade is adorned with fine terracotta decorations, and within are good Renaissance frescoes by Bembo; the fifth chapel on the left contains a lovely *Madonna with Saints* (1494) by Perugino. Further up Via Plasio joins the Corso Garibaldi, site of the 11th-century church of **Sant'Agata**, hiding behind a neoclassical façade; inside are more frescoes and a medieval masterpiece, the 13th-century wooden panel painted with the life of St Agatha. Across the street stands (just barely) the dilapidated 1256 **Cittanova**, former headquarters of the Guelph party in Cremona, now attached to the flamboyant but phoney Gothic façade of the **Palazzo Trecchi**. Further up Corso Garibaldi, the pink and white **Palazzo Raimondi** (1496) is the home of the **International School of Violin-making**; while across the street stands the city's most peculiar palace, crowned with strange iron dragons. Further up, near the station, **San Luca** has a beautiful terracotta façade and a little detached octagonal baptistry.

One other church, **San Sigismondo**, is 1km east of the centre, beyond the Piazzale Libertà, on Via A. Ghisleri. Built in 1463 by Bianca Maria Visconti to commemmorate her marriage in an earlier church on the same site, it is adorned with colourful Renaissance frescoes by the Cremona school, in a harmonious marriage of art and architecture.

Boating on the River Po is possible at **SNI**, Via Robolotti 7, © (0372) 25546. Or, for dinosaur-obsessed children (and adults!), there is a **Prehistoric Zoo Park** in nearby **Rivolta d'Adda**, © (0373) 78184, with over 20 life-size reproductions of various prehistoric animals in their natural habitat.

Cremona © (0372–) **Where to Stay**

moderate

★★★★ **Continental**, Piazza della Libertà 27, © 434141. Cremona has a small selection of fairly good hotels, and this is near the top of the moderate price range. It's modern, comfortable and near the centre, and has a display of its own collection of Cremona-made fiddles. All rooms have bath and television, and there's parking in the garage.

★★★★ **Impero**, Piazza Pace 21, © 460337. Another very nice option, just behind the main square. Rooms are stylish and modern, and good value.

★★★ **Duomo**, Via Gonfalonieri 13, © 35242, on a street leading from the main square, with a very nice restaurant as well as comfortable rooms.

★★★ **Astoria**, Via Bordigallo 9, © 461616, fax 461810, a cheaper option, a very pleasant hotel in a quiet street near the Duomo and the Piazza Roma.

inexpensive

It's worth remembering that hotels at the lower end of the price scale are virtually all closed from late July to early September. Those that aren't, however, include:

★ **Albergo Touring**, Via Palestro 3, © 36976, a good, simple choice midway between the centre and the station.

★ **Bologna**, Piazzale Risorgimento 7, © 24258, right by the station and perhaps the most reasonably priced.

★ **Ideale,** just down from the station on the corner of Via Trieste, with clean, if rather noisy, doubles.

Farming Holidays are also available in the area—information can be obtained either from the tourist office, or c/o Piere d'Olmi, Azienda Borlenga, © 63670.

Eating Out

Cremona is not one of Italy's gastronomic capitals, but you can dine very well at the elegant **Ceresole**, at Via Ceresole 4, © (0372) 23322 (expensive; reservation advisable), near the Piazza del Comune. Recently remodelled, it serves a balance of traditional and innovative dishes—eel with leeks, *gnocchetti* with ricotta and herbs, and duck are among the specialities. An older, rather more traditional restaurant, the

Trattoria Bissone, Via F. Pecorari 3 (moderate), features boiled meats with *mostarda di Cremona* and other hearty fare. On Via Bordigallo, a Chinese restaurant, **Fou-Lu**, offers full meals adapted for Italian tastes, in the same price category. In the inexpensive range, **Marechiaro**, Corso Campi 49, serves fairly basic, but very tasty, fare at very reasonable prices. **Bar Voglia Pizza**, Corso Garibaldi 38, is the place to go for *pizza al taglio* (by the slice).

On the northwest outskirts of **Crema**, in Via Crocicchio, is the **Trattoria Guada il Canal**, © (0373) 200133 (expensive), considered the finest restaurant in the whole province, with a warm, country atmosphere. The cuisine is based entirely on seasonal availability, and though the menu is usually brief, everything is sublime, from the pâtés to the various pasta dishes (try the *tagliolini* with scallops and broccoli), the well-prepared seafood, succulent rack of lamb with thyme, and many more specialities.

Around Cremona: Soncino and Crema

Lying between the rivers Po and Oglio, the mainly agricultural province of Cremona is fortified with a number of castles and towers that recall the days when the Italians had nothing better to do than beat each other up. The best surviving one, the **Castello Sforza**, (*open for visits, but check at Cremona's tourist office before setting out*) is in **Soncino** on the river Oglio; originally built in the 12th century, it was expanded in 1473 by Galeazzo Maria Sforza as an advance base against the Venetians, who possessed the Brescian-built fortified town of Orzinuovi directly across the river. The castle's now-dry moat and dungeons survive, as well as its imposing quadrangle of towers .

Between Cremona and Crema (the two Italian towns that most sound like dairy products) lies **Paderno**, birthplace of 'the Italian Tchaikovsky', Amilcare Ponchielli (1834–86). Italy has produced scores of 'one opera' composers, but Ponchielli can claim two that are performed with some frequency: *La Gioconda* and *Marion Delorme*; and as the teacher of Puccini and Mascagni can claim to be grandfather of many others. His humble birthplace is now the **Museo Ponchiellano**, devoted to his life and works (*open Mon–ri, 3–7 pm*).

In 1449, Francseco Sforza offered the attractive little town of **Crema** to Venice in exchange for the Serenissima's support of his dukedom. To this day it bears a white marble lion of St Mark on its town hall, recalling a pleasant occupation that endured for three centuries and left a touch of elegance rare in Lombard towns. In the same piazza as the marble lion stands Crema's delightful pink brick **Duomo**, a little Gothic present from the 14th century, with a high, ornate façade and finely worked windows decorated with curling vines. Next to it stands the charming and whimscal campanile, made of baked clay, that so ravished historian John Addington Symonds. In the former convent of Sant' Agostino in Via Dante, the **Museo Civico di Crema** (*open 2.30–6.30pm Tues–Fri; 9am–12 midday Sat; 10am–1pm Sun and holidays*) has an interesting collection of medieval Lombard armour discovered in local tombs. The refectory contains a ruined but lovely fresco of the Last Supper (1498) by Giovan Pietro da Cemmo, from Brescia. An

S. Maria della Croce

architect from Cremona, Faustino Rodi, designed the fine **Porta Serio**, Crema's chief neoclassical monument. And there are fine palazzi to see, specially the ambitious uncompleted Baroque **Palazzo Terni de Gregori**. A kilometre or so north of Crema, the rotund **Santa Maria della Croce** is a lovely Renaissance church inspired by Bramante, with three orders of loggias encircling the façade, and four polygonal chapels with spherical cupolas. Crema also has a number of fine palaces and villas dating from its Venetian period, of which the 18th-century **Villa Ghisetti-Giavarina** in nearby Ricengo is the most interesting and stately, with fine arches and statues.

Mantua

By its setting Mantua (Mantova) hardly answers to many people's expectations of Italy, sitting as it does in a fertile, table-flat plain, on a wide thumb of land protruding into three swampy, swollen lakes formed by the River Mincio. Its climate is moody, soggy with heat and humidity in the summer and frosty under blankets of fog in the winter. The local dialect is harsh, and the Mantuans, when they feel chipper, dine on braised donkey with macaroni. Verdi made it the sombre setting of his opera *Rigoletto*. And yet this former capital of the art-loving, fast-living Gonzaga dukes is one of the most atmospheric old cities in the country, masculine and stern, dark and handsome, with none of neighbouring Cremona's gay architectural arpeggios—melancholy with memories of past glories, poker-faced but holding in its hand a royal flush of dazzling Renaissance art.

History

Mantua gained its fame in Roman times as the beloved home town of the poet Virgil, who recounts the legend of the city's founding by the Theban soothsayer Manto, daughter of Tiresias, and her son, the hero Ocnus. Virgil was born around 70 BC, and not much else was heard from Mantua until the 11th century, when the city formed part of the vast domains of Countess Matilda of Canossa. Matilda was a great champion of the pope against the Emperor; her adviser, Anselmo, Bishop of Lucca, became Mantua's patron saint. Even so, as soon as Mantua saw its chance it allied itself with the opposition, beginning an unusually important and lengthy career as an independent Ghibelline *comune*, dominated first by the Bonacolsi family, and then the Gonzaga.

Naturally defended on three sides by the Mincio, enriched by river tolls, and enjoying the protection and favour of the emperor, Mantua became prominent as a neutral buffer state between the expansionist powers of Milan and Venice. The three centuries of Gonzaga rule, beginning in 1328, brought the city unusual peace and stability, while the refined tastes of the marquesses brought out artists of the highest calibre: Pisanello, Alberti, and especially Andrea Mantegna, who was court painter from 1460 until his death in 1506. Gianfrancesco I Gonzaga invited the great Renaissance teacher, Vittorino da Feltre, to open a school in the city in 1423, where his sons and courtiers, side by side with the children of Mantua's poorer families, were taught according to Vittorino's humanist educational theories, which gave equal emphasis to the intellectual, the physical, and the moral. His star pupil was Ludovico (1412–78), who was considered one of the most just princes of his day, and did much to embellish Mantua according to Florentine principles. Ludovico's grandson, Gianfrancesco II, was a military commander, who lead the Italians against the French at Fornovo, but is perhaps best known in history as the husband of the brilliant and cultivated Isabella d'Este, the foremost culture vulture of her day as well as an astute diplomat, handling most of Mantua's affairs of state for her not very clever husband.

The family fortunes reached their apogee under Isabella's two sons. The eldest, Federico II (1500–40), godson of Cesare Borgia, married Margherita Palaeologo, the heiress of Monferrato, acquiring that duchy for the family, as well as a ducal title for the Gonzaga; he brought Raphael's pupil, the great Giulio Romano (called 'that rare Italian master' by Shakespeare in *The Winter's Tale*), from Rome to design and adorn his pleasure dome, the Palazzo del Te. When he died his worthy brother, Cardinal Ercole, served as regent for his son Guglielmo, and both of these men, too, proved to be busy builders and civic improvers. The last great Gonzaga, Vicenzo I, was a patron of Rubens and Monteverdi, who composed the first modern opera, *L'Orfeo*, for the Mantuan court in 1607.

The Gonzaga and Mantua suffered a mortal blow in 1630 when their claims for Monferrato came into conflict with the Habsburgs, who sent Imperial troops to take and sack the city. The Gonzaga's great art treasures were stolen or sold, including Mantegna's great series, the *Triumphs of Caesar*, now at Hampton Court. The duchy, under a cadet branch of the family, limped along until the Austrians snatched Mantua in 1707, eventually making it the southwest corner of their Quadrilateral.

Getting to and from Mantua

Mantua is linked directly by **train** with Verona, Milan, Modena, and Cremona, and indirectly with Brescia and Parma (change at Piadena). There are also **buses** to Lake Garda and frequent services to towns in the province, such as Sabbioneta (*see* below). Both the bus and train stations are near Piazza Porta Belfiore, at the end of Corso Vittorio Emanuele, about 10 minutes walk from the centre.

By car the quickest way to get to Mantua from Milan is to take the A4 *autostrada* towards Venice, and then take the exit onto the SS236 just beyond Brescia. A more interesting route is to take the SS415 to Cremona, and then continue on the SS10 to Mantua. Mantua is also close to the A22 *autostrada*, between Modena and the Brenner Pass.

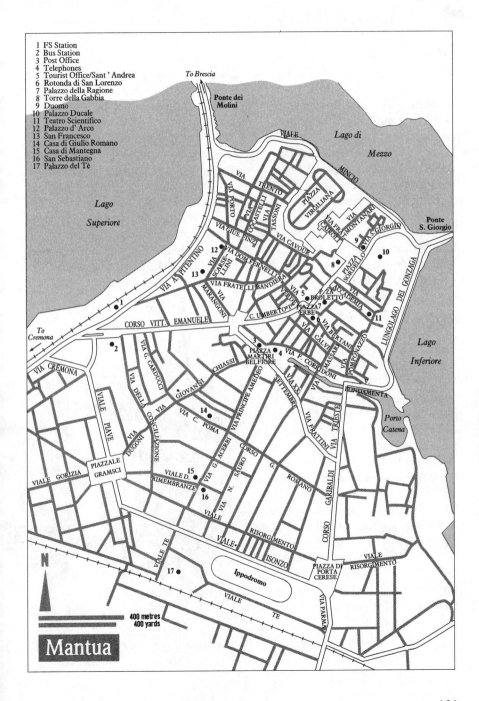

1 FS Station
2 Bus Station
3 Post Office
4 Telephones
5 Tourist Office/Sant'Andrea
6 Rotonda di San Lorenzo
7 Palazzo della Ragione
8 Torre della Gabbia
9 Duomo
10 Palazzo Ducale
11 Teatro Scientifico
12 Palazzo d'Arco
13 San Francesco
14 Casa di Giulio Romano
15 Casa di Mantegna
16 San Sebastiano
17 Palazzo del Tè

To Brescia

Ponte dei Molini

Lago di Mezzo

Ponte S. Giorgio

Lago Superiore

To Cremona

Lago Inferiore

Porto Catena

PIAZZALE GRAMSCI

Ippodromo

N

400 metres
400 yards

Mantua

Piazza Mantegna

From the station, Corso Vittorio Emanuele and Corso Umberto I lead straight into the Renaissance heart of Mantua, where the narrow cobbled streets are lined with heavy porticoes. Rising up above the rest of the city, in Piazza Mantegna, is the lofty dome of Mantua's great basilica, **Sant'Andrea**, built by Leon Battista Alberti in 1472 to house the Gonzaga's most precious holy relic, a chalice of Christ's blood, said to have been given to St Andrew by St Longinus, the Roman centurion who pierced Christ's side with his lance. Ludovico Gonzaga had asked Alberti to create a truly monumental edifice to hold the relic and form a fitting centrepiece for the city, and Alberti complied. In Florence Alberti had found himself constrained as an architect by his patrons' tastes, but in Mantua he was able to experiment and play with the ancient forms he loved. Sant'Andrea is based on Vitruvius's idea of an Etruscan temple, with a single barrel-vaulted nave supported by side chapels, fronted with a unique façade that combines a triumphal arch and a temple. Inside, Andrea Mantegna is buried in the first chapel on the left, next to a rather stern self-portrait in bronze. He designed much of the decoration in the spacious interior, later executed by his pupils.

On the east side, the unfinished flank of the basilica is lined with the porticos and market stalls of the **Piazza dell'Erbe**. Across the square is the attractive 1082 **Rotonda di San Lorenzo**, built by the Countess Matilda over an earlier Lombard structure, and restored in 1908 after many centuries of neglect; fragments of medieval frescoes in the beautiful apse were discovered by the restorers. Also on the Piazza dell'Erbe, the lovely **Casa di Boniforte** has delicate stucco decoration, almost unchanged since it was built in 1455, while the 13th-century **Palazzo della Ragione** has a stout clock tower topped by an odd little temple and astronomical clock, added during Ludovico's restoration of the palace. The adjacent **Broletto**, built in 1227, faces the Piazza del Broletto, with a medieval figure of Virgil seated near the door.

Piazza delle Erbe

An archway leads into the grand, cobbled **Piazza Sordello**, traditional seat of Mantua's ruling lords. On one side rise the sombre palaces of the Bonacolsi, the Gonzaga's predecessors, with their **Torre della Gabbia**, named for the iron torture cage (*gabbione*) they kept to suspend prisoners over the city (though the Mantuans claim it was only used once). At the head of the piazza stands Mantua's **Duomo**, with a silly 1756 façade topped with wedding-cake figures that hides a lovely Renaissance interior by Giulio Romano. The 15th-century house at No.23 has been restored as the official **Casa di Rigoletto**, and contains a little exhibition on the opera.

Palazzo Ducale

Open 9–1, 2.30–6, Mon–Sat; 9–1 Sun; guided tours every half-hour; adm.

Opposite the Bonacolsi palaces stands that of the Gonzaga, its unimpressive façade hiding one of Italy's most remarkable Renaissance residences, both in its artwork and in sheer size. The never-satisfied Gonzaga kept on adding on until they had some 500 rooms in three main structures—the original **Corte Vecchia**, first built by the Bonacolsi in 1290, the 14th-century **Castello**, with its large towers overlooking the lake, and the **Corte Nuova**, designed by Giulio Romano. Throw in the Gonzaga's **Basilica di Santa Barbara** and you have a complex that occupies the entire northeast corner of Mantua. If you go in the winter, dress warmly—it's as cold as a dead duke.

Although stripped of its furnishings and many of its artworks, the palace is still imposing, majestic, and seemingly endless. One of the first rooms on the tour, the former **chapel**, has a dramatic if half-ruined 14th-century fresco of the Crucifixion, attributed by some to Tommaso da Modena, while another contains a painting of a battle between the Gonzaga and the Bonacolsi in the Piazza Sordello, in which the Gonzaga crushed their rivals once and for all, in 1328—although the artist, Domenico Monore, painted the piazza as it appeared later in 1494. More fascinating than this real battle is the vivid **fresco of Arthurian knights** by Pisanello, Italy's Gothic master. For centuries the work was believed lost, until layers and layers of plaster were stripped away in 1969, revealing a remarkable, if unfinished, work that was commissioned by Gianfrancesco Gonzaga in the mid 15th century to commemorate his receiving from Henry VI the concession to use the heraldic SS collar of the House of Lancaster, an insignia that forms the border of Pisanello's mural, mingled with the marigold motif of the Gonzaga.

Beyond this are the remodelled **neoclassical rooms**, holding a set of Flemish tapestries based on Raphael's Acts of the Apostles cartoons (now in the Victoria and Albert Museum). Woven in the early 1500s, these copies of the Vatican originals are in a much better state of preservation; note the curiously pagan borders. Beyond these lies the **Sala dello Zodiaco**, with vivacious 1580 frescoes by Lorenzo Costa il Giovane, and the **Sala del Fiume**, named for its fine views over the river, and the **Galleria degli Specchi**, with its mirrors and mythological frescoes, and, by the door, a note from Monteverdi on the days and hours of the musical evenings he directed there in the 1600s.

The Gonzaga were mad about horses and dogs, and had one room, the **Salone degli Arcieri**, painted with *trompe l'œil* frescoes of their favourite steeds standing on upper ledges; they were used in a family guessing game, when curtains would be drawn over the figures. Sharing the room are works by Tintoretto and a painting by Rubens of the Gonzaga family, so large that Napoleon's troop had to cut it into pieces to carry it off. Further on lie the duke's apartments, with the family's fine collection of classical statuary, including busts of the emperors, a Hellenistic torso of Aphrodite, and the 'Apollo of Mantova', a Roman copy of a Greek original. The **Sala di Troia** has vivid 1536 frescoes by Giulio Romano and his pupil, Rinaldo Mantovano, while another ducal chamber has a beautiful seicento labyrinth on the ceiling, each path inscribed in gold with 'Maybe yes, maybe no'. From some of the rooms you can look out over the grassy **Cortile della Cavallerizza**, with rustic façades by Giulio Romano.

The **castle** is reached by a low spiral ramp, built especially for the horses the Gonzaga apparently could never bear to be long without. Here, in the famous **Camera degli Sposi**, are the remarkable frescoes by Mantegna, who like a genie captured the essence of the Gonzaga in this small bottle of a room. Recently restored to their brilliant, original colours, the frescoes depict the life of Ludovico Gonzaga, with his wife Barbara of Brandenburg, his children, dwarves, servants, dogs, and horses, and important events— greeting his son Francesco, recently made a cardinal, and playing host to Emperor Frederick III and King Christian I of Denmark. The portraits are unflattering and solid, those of real people not for public display, almost like a family photo album. The effect is like stumbling on the court of the Sleeping Beauty; only the younger brother, holding the new cardinal's hand, seems to suspect that he has been enchanted. Wife Barbara and her stern dwarf stare out, determined to draw the spectator into the eerie scene. And in truth there is a lingering sorcery here, for these frescoes are fruit of Mantegna's fascination with the mysterious new science of perspective that gave artists the power to recreate three-dimensional space. The beautiful backgrounds of imaginary cities and ruins reflect Mantegna's other love, classical architecture, and add another element of unreality, as do his *trompe l'œil* ceiling decorations.

From here the tour continues to the **Casetta dei Nani**, residence of the dwarfs, tiny rooms with low ceilings and shallow stairs, although there are party-poopers who say the rooms had a pious purpose, and were meant to bring the sinning dukes to their proud knees. The last stop is the **suite of Isabella d'Este**, designed by her as a retreat after the death of her husband. In these little rooms Isabella held court as the Renaissance's most imperious and demanding patroness of art, practically commanding Leonardo and Titian to paint her portrait; at one point she commissioned an allegorical canvas from Perugino so exacting that she drew a sketch of what she wanted and set spies to make sure the painter was following orders. Given an excellent classical education in her native Ferrara, she surrounded herself with humanists, astrologers, poets and scholars. Her fabulous art collection has long gone to the Louvre, but the inexplicable symbols she devised with her astrologers remain like faint ghosts from a lost world on the walls and ceiling.

Other Sights

There are several sights within easy walking distance of the Palazzo Ducale. On Via Accademia, just east of the Broletto, Piazza Dante, has a monument to the poet and the **Teatro Scientifico** (*open 9.30–12.30, 3–6, Mon–Sat; adm*). Also known as the Teatro

Bibiena, it was built by Antonio Galli Bibiena, a member of the famous Bolognese family of theatre builders. Mozart, aged 13, performed at the inaugural concert in 1770; father Leopold thought it was the most beautiful theatre he had ever seen.

West of the Piazza Sordello, Via Cairoli leads to the city's main park, the **Piazza Virgiliana**, with a Mussolini-era statue of Virgil. The **Museo Gonzaga**, Via Cairoli 55 (*open April–June, Sept, Oct 9.30–12, 2.30–5, Tues–Sun; July–Aug Thurs, Sat, Sun only; Nov–Mar Sun only; adm*), contains a variety of artefacts and treasures that once belonged to the family.

Further west, in the Piazza d'Arco, the 18th-century **Palazzo d'Arco** has been opened to the public (*open Mar–Oct 9–12, 3–5, Thu, Sat, Sun, 9–12 only Tues, Wed, Fri; Nov–Feb 9–12, 2.30–4, Sun and holidays only; adm*); former residence of the Contes d'Arco, it contains furnishings, instruments, and a section of the original 15th-century palace, with beautiful zodiac frescoes. The nearby 1304 church of **San Francesco** was rediscovered in 1944, when a bomb hit the arsenal that had disguised it for a century and a half. Restored to its original state in 1954, it contains frescoes attributed to Tommaso da Modena.

South of the medieval nucleus lies Mantua's second great sight, the Palazzo del Te; on the way there, just off the main Via Principe Amedeo, you can take a look at **Giulio Romano's House**, designed by the artist, as was the quaint palace decorated with monsters opposite. Mantegna also designed his dream house, the **Casa di Mantegna**, in the same neighbourhood, at Via Acerbi 47 (*open 9–12.30, 3–6, daily*). Designed as a cube built around a circular courtyard, he intended it partially as his personal museum. Embellished with classical 'Mantegnesque' decorations, the house is used for frequent art exhibitions. Nearby stands the rather neglected **San Sebastiano**, the second church in Mantua designed by Alberti, this one in the form of a Greek cross.

Palazzo del Te

At the end of Via Acerbi is Giulio Romano's masterpiece, the marvellous **Palazzo del Te** (*open 10am–6pm Tues–Sun; adm exp*), its name derived not from tea, but from *tejeto*, a local word for a drainage canal. The palace grounds were formerly swampland, drained for a horsey Gonzaga pleasure ground. In 1527 Federico II had Giulio expand the stables to create a little palace for his mistress, of whom his mother, Isabella d'Este, disapproved. The project expanded over the decades to become a guest house suitable for the emperor Charles V.

In the Palazzo del Te Giulio Romano created one of the great Renaissance syntheses of architecture and art, combining *trompe l'œil* with a bold play between the structure of the room and the frescoes; in the **Sala dei Giganti** the Titans, wrestling with pillars, seem to be bringing the ceiling down upon the spectator's head. Another room has more life-size Gonzaga horses up on ledges, and another, the **Camera di Psiche**, is painted with lusty scenes from *The Golden Ass* of Apuleius, all in contrast with the serene Pompeii-style decorations in between. In the garden Giulio Romano added the little **Casino della Grotta**, adorned with pretty stuccoes.

Several **boat** companies operate on the lakes and the river Mincio around Mantua, among them **Andes**, Piazza Sordello 8, ✆ (0376) 322875, fax 322869. A pleasant 1½hr trip costs L10,000 (less for children).

Mantua ✆ (0376–)

Where to Stay

expensive

★★★★ San Lorenzo, Piazza Concordia 14, ✆ 220500. Housed in a restored late Renaissance building, with all modern comforts, in the centre's pedestrian zone, this hotel has many rooms with views over the Piazza dell'Erbe.

moderate

★★★★ Rechigi, Via Calvi 30, ✆ 320781. Mantua has a small selection of typical hotels, and this is the best, conveniently located in the historic centre. All rooms have private bath, air conditioning, and comfortable furnishings, and the hotel has ample parking.

★★★ Due Guerrieri, ✆ 325596. Another pleasant hotel housed in an older building overlooking the Piazza Sordello and the Palazzo Ducale. There are baths in every room, and parking nearby.

★★ Albergo Bianchi, Piazza Don Leoni, ✆ 321504. Near the station, and handy for train travellers.

inexpensive

★ ABC Moderno, ✆ 322329. Next door to the Bianchi, this good-value hotel has small cell-like rooms arranged around an inner courtyard with space for parking.

★ Rinascita, Via Concezione 4, ✆ 320607, a spotlessly clean budget hotel off Piazza Virgiliana, has a delightful inside garden and marble floors throughout.

Villa Schiarino-Lena, ✆ 398104. Under a programme initiated in the last few years, five old country **villa-farmhouses** have been developed as inexpensive accommodation, averaging around L20,000 per person per night. This one is only a few km from Mantua, on the other side of Lago Superiore; the rooms around a 16th-century agricultural courtyard have been converted into apartments.

Feniletto, ✆ 650262. Also under the scheme mentioned above, this is a fully functioning farm, 13km from Mantua at Rodigo, in the midst of the Regional Park of the Mincio; boating excursions are possible on the river. Reserve well in advance, as there are only five beds.

Due Madonne, ✆/fax (0386) 40056. This villa-farmhouse, a few kilometres south-east of Mantua in Serravalle a Po, offers horse riding, walking and cycling as well as hearty local cooking.

For more information on stays in traditional buildings in the Mantuan countryside, contact the tourist office.

cheap

Ostello Sparafucile, Lunetta di San Giorgio, © 372465, is Mantua's exceptional **youth hostel**, located just outside the city. The hostel is in a cinquecento castle, popularly believed to be the headquarters of the baddie in Rigoletto. The interior has been remodelled, but without losing any of its character. The charge is L14,000 a person a night, with breakfast; cheap meals are also available.(*Closed 15 Oct–1 April; to get there, take bus nos.2 or 9 from Piazza Cavallotti.*)

Mantua © (0376–)   **Eating Out**

During the long reign of the Gonzaga the Mantuans developed their own cuisine, which other Italians regard as a little peculiar. The notorious *stracotto di asino* (donkey stew) heads the list, but the Mantuans also have a predilection for adding Lambrusco to broth and soup. The classic Mantuan *primi* include *agnoli* stuffed with sausage and cheese in broth, risotto *alla pilota*, with sausage sauce and local grana cheese, or *tortelli di zucca* (little pasta caps stuffed with pumpkin, served with melted butter). The local lake and river fish—deep-fried frog's legs, catfish, eel, crayfish, pike and bass—are traditional second courses.

Mantua is also a good place to taste true, natural Lambrusco, which must be drunk young (a year or so old) to be perfectly lively and sparkling; the test is to see if the foam vanishes instantly when poured into a glass. There are three main kinds: the grand *Lambrusco di Sorbana*, the mighty *Lambrusco di Santa Croce*, and the amiable *Lambrusco di Castelvetro*.

expensive

Long considered Mantua's finest restaurant, **Il Cigno**, Piazza d'Arco, © 327101, does many local specialities in a very elegant setting. The menu changes according to season—when it's cold, the *agnoli* in broth with Lambrusco will take off the chill; the eel in balsamic vinegar is a delicious second course (*closed Mon, first part of Aug*).

The lovely **Aquila Nigra**, Vicolo Bonaclosi 4, © 350651, offers both local dishes and some from other regions, including seafood and risotto with scampi. There's a large selection of Italian and French wines, and delicious desserts like chestnut torte (*closed Sun, Mon, most of Aug*). **Al Garibaldini**, Via S. Longino 7, © 328263, is right in the historic centre of Mantua, in a fine old structure with a shady garden for al fresco dining in the summer. The menu features many Mantuan dishes, with especially good risotto and *tortelli di zucca*, fish, and meat dishes (*closed Wed, most of Jan*).

For no atmosphere but delicious Mantuan cooking at a very accessible price try the **Trattoria al Lago**, Piazza Arche 5, © 323300. The **Due Cavallini**, Via Salnitro 5 (near Lago Inferiore, off Corso Garibaldi), © 322084, is the place if you want to bite into some donkey meat—though it has other, more typical dishes as well (*closed first part of July*).

Around Mantua

Although the Po plain isn't generally known for its natural beauty, Mantua's western lake, **Lago Superiore**, is noted for its delicate lotus blossoms, planted in the 1930s as an experiment. They have since thrived, and bloom in July and August around the city's park, the **Valletta Belfiore**. Another of Mantua's parks, the **Bosco della Fontana**, lies 5km to the north off the road to Brescia. The Bosco's ancient, broad-leafed trees are believed to be a relic of the ancient forest that once covered the Po plain, and its shady paths and streamlets are a tempting retreat from the afternoon heat. Within its confines stand the ruins of a 12th-century Gonzaga castle. If you're in Mantua in the middle of August, be sure to visit the **Sanctuary of the Madonna delle Grazie**, on the banks of Lago Superiore at Curtatone, where there's an unusual art competition, for the *madonnari*—artists who draw sidewalk chalk portraits of the Madonna—among other diversions. Inside, the church is chock-full of votive offerings, some curious and some inexplicable, left in thanks by people who invoked the name of the Madonna in an hour of need. There is also a stuffed crocodile hanging from the roof, apparently the last in the area when the remaining land around the church was drained.

San Benedetto Po

Some 22km southeast of Mantua (connected in the summer by small tourist boats, sailing down the Mincio to the Po), San Benedetto Po grew up around the Benedictine abbey of **Polirone** (*open 8am–7pm daily*), the 'Monte Cassino of the North', established in the year 1007 and especially favoured by the feisty Countess Matilda of Canossa (d.1115), whose alabaster sarcophagus survives in the apse of the **Basilica**, rebuilt in the 1540s by Giulio Romano. The basilica is connected to the 12th-century Church of Santa Maria, which has a fine contemporary mosaic. There are several cloisters from various periods, and a refectory with recently discovered frescoes attributed to Correggio. Another part of the monastery contains the **Museo della Cultura Popolare Padana**, © 615977, (*open June–Oct 9–12, 3–6.30, Tues–Sun; Mar–May 9–12.30, 2–5.30 daily; Nov–Mar, call in advance; adm*), devoted to the traditions and culture of the surrounding countryside.

Sabbioneta

An hour's bus ride southwest of Mantua on the Parma road lies Sabbioneta, designed in the late 16th century as an ideal city by the Prince of Bozzolo, Vespasiano Gonzaga, member of a cadet branch of the Gonzaga family. Vespasiano was a firm believer that the city should be a rational expression of humanistic ideals, that it should have a content and a function. In his 'Little Athens' he and Vincenzo Scamozzi, Palladio's greatest pupil, designed not only palaces but schools, a mint, hospital, library, theatre, printing office and an enormous Gallery of Antiques.

A New Renaissance City

The idea of building a whole new city in the lifetime of a single man had already been made possible by technological advances on the construction site. Many of these techniques first came into being during the construction of Brunelleschi's dome over Florence Cathedral; one thing Brunelleschi did was abolish the old medieval 'mechanical' system, composed of skilled workers working under master masons, in favour of a 'liberal' system in which there was only one planner and his manual labourers.

Equally fundamental was the evolution of the city from the Middle Ages, when it was an organic body, founded on a community of interest between the merchants and craftsmen whose lived in it, to the view in the 15th and 16th centuries, when the cities lost their liberties and became nothing more than the seat of a higher power, a *signore* or a king—a reflection of his greater glory. Public buildings became increasingly grand, and open spaces arranged as a stage for the ceremonies of church and state. Architects and artists were inspired by Leon Battista Alberti's monumental *De re aedificatoria* (1452), which drew on Vitruvius in its aim to orchestrate the humanist recreation of the ancient city and its monuments. For the first time since antiquity, changes in a city's structure and plan were brought about from above, by a prince and his architects. Architectural treatises of the time are filled with geometrical designs of ideal cities, usually set in massive defensive works around polygonal walls, often star-shaped, the better to deflect bullets and cannonballs. According to Alberti, single buildings must always be conceived in their urban context, the whole plan of which must follow the rule of perspective, proportion and symmetry—leading to the fanciful urban backgrounds of many Renaissance paintings. Vespasiano Gonzaga was one of the few readers of Alberti to ever actually to build his city and apply his ideals. One of these was a great tolerance and respect for ancient learning, something that attracted many Jewish settlers; the press they established was famous for the excellence of its Hebrew editions.

Unfortunately for Sabbioneta, humanism was out of fashion even before the city was built. When its creator died, it reverted to a small rural breakwater, a silent little museum city with a declining population that has the haunting, empty air of De Chirico painting. To see the interiors of the historic centre you should contact the Pro Loco on Via V. Gonzaga 31, © (0375) 52039 (*open April–Sept 9–12, 2.30–6, Tues–Sun; Oct–Mar 9–12, 2.30–5, Tues–Sun; adm*).

Prince Vespasiano laid out Sabbioneta in polygonal star-shaped walls with two gates linked by the central axis of the main street. The street plan is rectangular and has for a centre Piazza Castello, where Vespasiano constructed a lengthy frescoed corridor, the **Galleria**

degli Antichi, to display his collection of classical statues (now in Mantua's Palazzo Ducale). At one end lies the **Palazzo del Giardino**, the prince's pleasure palace, richly adorned with frescoes and stuccoes by the school of Giulio Romano.

The next piazza contains the symmetrical **Palazzo Ducale** with its five arches, housing wooden equestrian statues of Vespasiano and his kin; other rooms, with fine frescoes and ceilings, include the **Sala d'Oro** with its golden ceiling, the **Sala degli Elefanti** with elephants, or the **Sala delle Città Marinare** with paintings of port towns and a small **Museum of Sacred Art**. Behind the palace, the 1586 church of the **Incoronata** houses Vespasiano's mausoleum, with a bronze statue of the prince in classical Roman garb. The last stop on the tour is the small 1588 **Teatro Olimpico**, designed by the Vicenzan Scamozzi after Palladio's theatre in Vicenza. Twelve plaster statues of the ancient Olympians grace the balcony, and some of the original Venetian frescoes have recently been rediscovered. Also in the centre of town is the 16th-century **Synagogue**, derelict for the past 50 years.

Eating Out

In Sabbioneta, the **Ca' d'Amici**, Via d'Aragona 2, © (0375) 52318, (*expensive*), is the best restaurant, featuring local and national specialities. For a real treat, however, just getting into the very expensive price range, drive 20km north to Canneto sull'Oglio (just beyond Piadena), where you can feast at one of Lombardy's finest and most tranquil restaurants, **Dal Pescatore**, Via Runate 13, © (0376) 70304, (*closed Mon, Tues, mid-Aug, two weeks Jan*), located in an old and elegant country house. The menu and its preparation are authentic and delightful; offerings include *tortelli* with pumpkin, grilled eel, delectable fish dishes and magnificent desserts and wines.

Sirmione

Lake Orta and Domodossola   133
Lake Maggiore   141
Stresa   143
Between Lakes Maggiore and Lugano   150
Lake Lugano   153
Lake Como   157
The City of Como   159

The Italian Lakes

Lecco and its Lake   169
La Brianza   177
Beyond Como: the Valleys of Sondrio 173
Bergamo   180
Lake Iseo and the Val Camonica   188
Brescia   195
Lake Garda   203
Sirmione   207

Just to mention the Italian Lakes is to evoke a soft, dreamy image of romance and beauty, a Latin Brigadoon of consumptive gentlemen and gentle ladies strolling through gardens, sketching landscapes, and perhaps indulging in a round of whist on the villa veranda in the evening. The backgrounds to their fond pleasures are scenes woven of poetry, of snow-capped peaks tumbling steeply into ribbons of blue, trimmed with the silver tinsel of olives and the daggers of dark cypress; of mellowed villas gracing vine-clad hillsides and gold-flecked citrus groves; of spring's excess, when the lakes become drunken with colour, as a thousand varieties of azaleas, rhododendrons, and camellias spill over the banks. For even though the Swiss border is just around the corner, the three largest lakes—**Maggiore, Como** and **Garda**—cover enough area to create their own climatic oases of Mediterranean flora, blooming even at the foot of the starlit Alps.

Lake holidays faded from fashion in the post-War era, when a suntan became a symbol of leisure instead of manual labour and summer's mass trek to the seashore became as fixed a ritual as the drowning of lemmings. But the lakes are simply too lovely to stay out of fashion for long, and today a new generation is busily rediscovering what their grandparents took for granted, polishing up the old Belle Epoque fixtures of the villas and grand hotels. For better or worse, the Italians have ringed the lakes with finely engineered roads, making them perhaps too accessible, whereas before visitors had to make do with small boats, or leisurely steamers. Prices have risen with demand, and between July and September rest and relaxation, or even peace and quiet, may seem a Victorian relic, unless you book into one of the grander villa hotels. Quiet havens, however, still exist on the smaller, less developed lakes of Iseo and Orta, the east shores of lakes Maggiore and Como, and in the mountain valleys to the north of the lakes, around Domodossola and in the beautiful Valtellina.

Lake resorts are generally open between April and October. The best times to visit are in spring and autumn, not only because there are fewer crowds, but because the lakes themselves are less subjected to winter mists and summer haze. In the restaurants, look for lake fish and trout, served either fresh or sun-dried. The finest wines from the lake district come from Bardolino on the east shore of Lake Garda; try too the reds from the Valtellina, or the vintages from Franciacorta near Lake Iseo or La Brianza near Lake Como.

Below, the lakes are described geographically from west to east, from Piedmont's Lake Orta and the valleys around Domodossola, through Lombardy's lakes and the Valtellina, the art cities, Bergamo and Brescia, and then to Lake Garda on the border of the Veneto.

Lake Orta and Domodossola

Westernmost of the Italian Lakes, Orta (the Roman *Lacus Cusius*) is neither a contender for the largest, stratching a mere 13km at its longest point, nor the most majestic—its mountains aren't as high, nor are its villas as opulent as some of its neighbours'. But what Orta does have is an exceptional dose of charm; a lake 'made to the measurements of man', that can be encompassed by a glance, surrounded by hills made soft with greenery, a haven from the worst excesses of international tourism that sometimes scar the major lakes. Nietzsche, who never fell in love, did so on its soft green shores. He didn't get the girl, but the world got *Thus Spake Zarathustra*.

The green waters of Lake Orta run still and quiet, and in the centre they hold a magical isle, illuminated on summer nights, to hang like a golden fairy castle in the dark. On a more mundane level, the villages around the lake produce most of Italy's kitchen and bathroom taps, and some of its finest chefs; so many come from Armeno that in November it holds an annual reunion of cooks and waiters.

Getting Around

The main resorts on Lake Orta, Orta San Giulio and Omegna are easily reached from Turin or Milan on **trains** heading north to Domodossola and the Simplon Pass. There are also frequent **buses** from Orta to Arona, on Lake Maggiore, and from Omegna to Verbania. A small railway makes the trip between Domodossola and Locarno, in Switzerland, while the other mountain valleys are served by bus from the town of Domodossola.

By **road** Orta is easily accessible from Milan by the *autostrada* A8, which also connects with the A26 from Turin, Alessandria and Genoa, and from Switzerland via the Simplon Pass road, which meets the A8.

On the lake itself, *Navigazione Lago d'Orta* provides service between the ports of Oria, Omegna, Punta di Crabbia, Pettanasco, L'Approdo, Orta, Isola San Giulio, Pella, San Filiberto and Lagna, at least twice a day. The company also offers a midnight cruise from Orta, Pella and Pettanasco on Sat and Sun in July and Aug.

Tourist Information

There are three tourist offices in the area: in **Orta San Giulio**, at Via Orlina, ✆ (0322) 90355; in **Macugnaga**, Piazza Municipio, ✆ (0324) 65858; and in **Santa Maria Maggiore**, at Piazza Risorgimento 5, ✆ (0324) 95091.

Lake Orta

The east bank of Lake Orta is dominated by the district's highest peak, the 1491m **Mottarone**; under its shadow, on its own little garden peninsula, is the lake's charming main village, **Orta San Giulio**. Life in Orta is centred in its sombrely handsome main

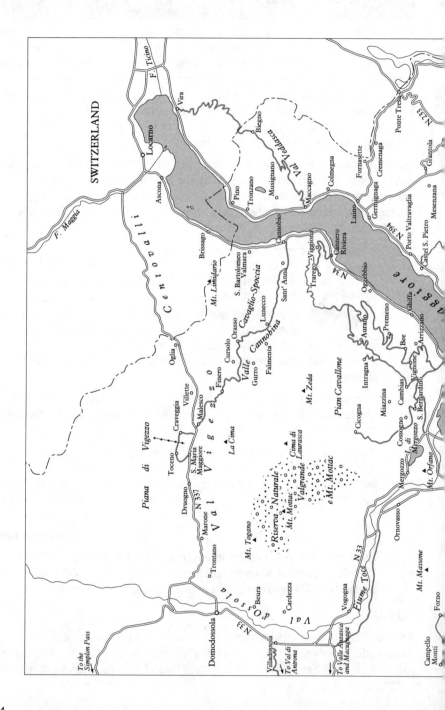

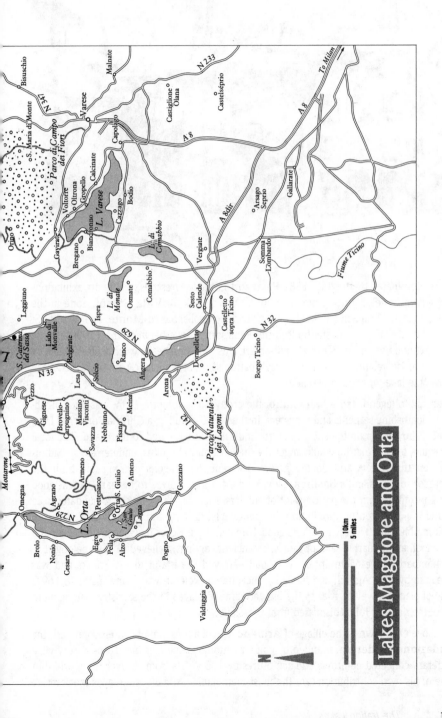

Lakes Maggiore and Orta

square, dominated by the little 1582 **Palazzotto** of faded frescoes, where art exhibitions are frequently held. Among the villas in the town, look for **Villa Crespi**, done in the Alhambra style. Orta San Giulio also has its own acropolis, **Sacro Monte**, dedicated to St Francis; its 21 chapels, mostly built in the Renaissance style between the 1590s and the 1660s, contain yet more 3D Piedmontese art, this time frescoes and terracotta statues by different artists relating to the life of Italy's patron saint, St Francis. A path from the village follows the lake for about a kilometre.

According to legend, **Isola San Giulio**, the pretty islet facing the Orta, was once inhabited by loathsome serpents and monsters. In the year 390 Julius, a Christian preacher from Greece, showed up on the shores of Orta and asked to be rowed to the island. The local fishermen, fearing that he would anger the dragons, refused; Julius, undeterred, spread his cloak on the waters and floated across. He sent the dragons packing and built the precursor to the island's **Basilica**, by yoking a team of wolves to his cart—a feat good enough to make him the patron saint of builders. Most of what you see today dates from around the 12th century, including the giant eagle, griffons and serpents carved on the black marble pulpit. There are some good 15th-century frescoes by Gaudenzio Ferrari and his school, and a marble sarcophagus with ancient carvings, believed to have belonged to the Lombard Duke Meinulphus, who had betrayed the island to the Franks and was beheaded by King Agilulf; and indeed a decapitated skeleton was found inside in 1697. Pride of place, however, goes to the big vertebrae displayed in the sacristy, belonging to one of the dragons Julius dismissed from the island.

Just above Orta town is the village of **Armeno**, site of a museum of contemporary art, the **Fondazione Calderara**, founded by painter Antonio Calderaras in a 16th-century villa. Calderara collected paintings and sculptures by 133 artists from all over the world, but some of his own contributions are the most memorable—still-life landscapes that capture the spirit of the lake better than any photograph. The south point of Orta, by **Gozzano**, is overlooked by the **Torre di Buccione**, first built in the 4th century and rebuilt by the Lombards in the Dark Ages; in times of trouble its bells were loud enough to warn all the communities on the lake. **Villa Junker**, near Gozzano, has the finest garden on the lake, despite its name.

Round on the west shore, a majestic rocky outcrop supports the **Santuario della Madonna del Sasso**, which isn't as impressive as the rocks, but affords a grand view over the lake and the villages of Pella and Alzo near the shore. On the northern tip of the lake, the main town and port is **Omegna** (Roman *Vomenia*), where you can stand in the Piazza del Municipio and look for the famous contrary river, the Nigoglia, the only one in Italy to flow towards the Alps. From Omegna a road curls up in ringlets through chestnut forests to **Quarna**, divided into Sotto and Sopra (lower and upper). Quarna Sotto has been manufacturing musical instruments for over 150 years, and has a small museum devoted to them; Quarna Sopra has spectacular views over Lake Orta. A second valley radiating from Omegna, the **Valstrona**, is less intensely spectacular, but **Forno** is a fine sleepy little place where dogs can sleep in the middle of the street; the last hamlet in the valley, **Campello Monti**, is another kind of Sunday afternoon destination, where you can walk off too many *tortellini.*

From Lake Orta to Domodossola: the Ossola Valleys

Unspoiled, and mostly unnoticed by visitors plunging down the motorway to more Mediterranean delights, the Ossola valleys cut deep into the Alps, following the course of the river Toce and its tributaries on their way to Lake Orta. Napoleon drove the first road through here, from Milan to the Simplon Pass, but even the improved communications couldn't help the Fascists and Nazis when the inhabitants booted them out and formed an independent republic that lasted 40 days. Nowadays the valleys are visited for their forests, rustic hospitality, and Alpine lakelets so blue they hurt.

North of Omegna the main road heads north towards **Gravellona Toce**, an important crossroads in the shadow of the mighty granite dome of Mount Orfano, which the locals are slowly whittling away to make flowerpots. Mount Orfano in its turn guards an orphan lake, **Lago Mergozzo**, which formed an arm of Lake Maggiore until the 9th century, when sediment from the Toce plugged it, a loss perhaps in prestige compensated by the fact that Mergozzo is now much cleaner than its larger neighbour.

The main town on the lake, also called **Mergozzo**, lost most of its importance as a transit centre with the constructiuon of the Simplon road. Its main attraction is the 12th-century church of **San Giovanni**, made of Orfano granite; the small **Antiquarium of Mont'Orfano** contains local pre-Roman and Roman artefacts. The next town up the valley, **Candoglia**, is the site of the quarry which for the past six centuries has been worked for the marble to build the Duomo in Milan.

The first valley splitting off to the west, the enchanting **Valle Anzasca**, leads straight towards the steep east face of Monte Rosa (buses there can be caught from Domodossola or from the station at Piedimulera at the foot of the valley). A number of attractive little villages lie scattered among the woods and vineyards—tiny **Colombetti**, its slate roofs huddled under a lofty cliff; **Bannio-Anzino**, the 'capital' of the valley, across and above the river Anza, with modest ski facilities and a 7ft-tall, 16th-century bronze Christ in its parish church, brought here from Flanders. **Ceppo Morelli** has a famous, vertiginous bridge over the Anza, which traditionally divides the valley's Latin population from the Walser. Beyond Ceppo the road plunges through a gorge to the old mining town of **Pestarena**, mining in this case meaning gold; the upper Valle Anzasca has Italy's largest gold deposits, extracted in galleries stretching 40km.

The various hamlets that comprise **Macugnaga**, the Valle Anzasca's popular resort, lie under the majestic frowning face of **Monte Rosa** (4638m). As in the Valle d'Aosta's Val Gressoney on the southern side of Monte Rosa, Macugnaga was settled by German-speaking Swiss from the Valais (the Walser) in the 13th century. A small museum in **Staffa**, the chief village of Macugnaga, is devoted to Walser folklore, while other old Swiss traces remain in the parish church, built in the 13th century. Macugnaga has a number of ski lifts, and a chair lift that operates in the summer as well, to the magnificent **Belvedere** with views over the Macugnaga glacier; a cableway from Staffa to the **Passo Monte Moro** (2868m) is used by skiers in both the winter and summer seasons. From Macugnaga, fearless alpinists can attempt the steep east flank of Monte Rosa, one of the most dangerous ascents in the Alps; walkers can make a three day trek over the mountains to Gressoney-St-Jean and other points in the Valle d'Aosta (trail map essential).

North of the Valle Anzasca, the much less visited **Val d'Antrona** is a pretty wooded valley famed for its trout fishing. The valley begins at **Villadossola**, from where you can catch a bus to the chief village **Antronapiana**, a pleasant place lost in the trees, near the lovely lakelet of Antrona, created by an avalanche in 1642. The north branch of the valley winds up and to **Cheggio**, a wee resort with refuges, restaurants and another lake.

Domodossola

The largest town in the Valley of the River Toce, or Valle d'Ossola, Domodossola was a Roman settlement, perhaps best known in Italy as the largest town in the republic beginning with the letter D, and for its location at the foot of the **Simplon Pass** (*Passo del Sempione*), through which, after the Battle of Marengo, Napoleon constructed his highway from Geneva to Lombardy, completed in 1805. Exactly 100 years later the even more remarkable Simplon Tunnel was completed—the longest in the world at 19.8km.

Domodossola is a pleasant old town with an arcaded main square and an interesting **Museo Civico**, which incorporates a medieval church and has something for every taste: natural history, paintings, Roman finds from the 3rd century AD necropolis at Gurro, in the Val Cannobina; exhibits relating to the construction of the Simplon tunnel and the flight of the Peruvian Georges Chavez, the first man to fly over the Alps (29 September 1910), only to die in a crash near Domodossola. You can also find a monument to him in Piazza Liberazione.

The road and railway line between Domodossola and Locarno (the largest Swiss town on Lake Maggiore) pass through the extraordinary **Val Vigezzo**, a romantic beauty of woodlands and velvet pastures that has attracted and produced so many artists through the years that it's earned the name 'the Valley of Painters'; it also claims to have given birth to the 18th-century formulators of the first *acqua di colonia*, or cologne. If the valley's sylvan charms tempt you to linger, stay in the main town, **Santa Maria Maggiore**; see its **Scuola di belle arti**, where you can see some of the paintings that gave the valley its sobriquet, or perhaps take in the odd little **Museo dello Spazzocamino** (a chimney-sweep museum; we couldn't find it, but maybe you can). From nearby Malesco a road descends the Val Cannobina to Cannobio on Lake Maggiore (*see* below, p.147).

Buses from Domodossola also plunge north towards the San Giacomo Pass, through the spectacular scenery of the **Valli Antigorio e Formazza**, colonized in the 13th century by German families from the Valais. Their charming scattered villages are planted with vines and figs, and offer bases for excursions to some genuinely obscure little Alpine lakes. The valley's spa, **Crodo**, is famous in Italy for bottling a ludicrously chipper soft drink called Crodino, as well as iron-laced mineral water; further north, **Baceno**'s parish church, **San Gaudenzio** (11th–16th century) is the finest church of the Ossola valleys and a national monument to boot; it has a fine front portal with sirens and a cartwheel window, and 16th-century Swiss stained-glass and carved wooden altarpiece. In Premia, along the Toce, you can visit the steep gorges sliced by the river over the millenia. The bus from Domodossola terminates at **Ponte** (with a chair lift), but one of the most breath-taking waterfalls in all the Alps is 6km up the road from Ponte: the **Cascata della Frua** (or del Toce), though like all of Italy's best waterfalls it is almost always dry, its water diverted for hydroelectric power. However, if you come between 10 and 20 August, or on a Sunday or a holiday between 9am and 5pm from June until September, you can be over-whelmed by a thundering 300m veil of mist, released by the power company, plummeting down a series of terraces.

Where to Stay

Orta San Giulio

★★★★ **San Rocco**, Via Gippini 11, ✆ (0322) 905632, fax 905635 (very expensive) is the lake's most luxurious hotel, located in a former 17th-century monastery with a pretty garden right on the water. All rooms have private baths and balconies, and air-conditioning.

★★★ **Orta**, ✆ (0322) 90253, fax 905646 (moderate). On the main square, opposite the island, the Orta is modern and stylish with big rooms and bathrooms.

★★★ **Leon d'Oro**, ✆ (0322) 905666, fax 90303 (moderate). Also on the main square, this hotel has rather smaller rooms and is not quite as stylish as its neighbour, but is slightly cheaper.

★★★ **La Bussola**, Via Panoramica 24, ✆/fax (0322) 90198 (moderate). Set back on a quiet hill, this 16-room hotel (all rooms with bath) enjoys a magnificent panorama of the lake; there's a pretty garden with a swimming pool and a good restaurant.

★   **Antico Agnello**, Via Olina 18, ✆ (0322) 90259 (inexpensive). In the centre of the village is this simple, inexpensive little inn with warm, cosy rooms and an excellent restaurant (*see* 'Eating Out').

Pettenasco

★★★   **Hotel Giardinetto**, Via Provinciale 1, ✆ (0323) 89118, fax 89219 (moderate). A friendly, family-run hotel, also right on Lake Orta, with beautiful views of the Isoletta di San Giulio, which offers reduced rates for children; there's a swimming pool, private beach, and water sports facilities, and an excellent restaurant. All rooms have private bath or shower. (*Open April–Oct only.*)

Omegna

★★   **Vittoria**, Via Zanoia 37, ✆ (0323) 62237 (inexpensive) This is the pick of the inexpensive-range *locande.*

Valle Anzasca

Most of the Valle Anzasca's accommodation is clustered in Macugnaga.

★★★   **Nuova Pecetto**, in the hamlet of Pecetto, ✆ (0324) 65025 (moderate). A charming tiny, traditional hotel with a garden and fine views of Monte Rosa. All rooms have baths.(*Closed mid-Sept–Nov.*)

★★★   **Zumstein**, Via Monte Rosa 63, ✆ (0324) 65118 (moderate). The largest and most luxurious choice in Staffa has attractive rooms in a pretty location. (*Open mid-Dec–April, mid-June–mid-Sept.*)

★★   **Chez Felice**, ✆ (0324) 65229 (inexpensive). Also in Staffa, this is a little mountain villa which has both simple but charming rooms with bath and the best restaurant in the valley (*see* below).

Domodossola

★★★   **Europa**, ✆ (0324) 481032, fax 481011 (moderate). Above the town in the suburb of Calice, 4km away; it has fine views and a garden, and the rooms all have private bath and toilet.

Santa Maria Maggiore

★★   **La Jazza**, Via Domodossola, ✆ (0324) 94471 (inexpensive). A pleasant hotel with a garden. (*Open all year.*)

Eating Out

The nicest restaurant in Orta is the **Antico Agnello** inn (*see* above). The menu changes with the season and varies between traditional dishes like fish from the lake, and more unusual fare such as pumpkin soup and *torta di* *verdura* (vegetable pie). Add to this a charming atmosphere an extensive wine list and excellent service and you have a perfect recipe. It's still in the moderate price category, but reservations are necessary. Also in Orta San Giulio, **Sacro Monte**, Via Sacro Monte 5, © (0322) 90220 (*closed Tues*), has delicious food and wine with the Piedmontese touch, in the same price range.

In Staffa **Chez Felice** (*see* above, moderate) is a lively haven of mountain *nuova cucina*, where you can find salmon mousse with herbs, warm artichokes with a sauce of anchovies and capers, delicious soups, risotto with almonds, cheese and herb soufflé and many other delights; for afters, there's a magnificent array of local cheeses and exquisite desserts. (*Closed Thurs, and reservations advisable if you're not staying at the hotel.*)

Lake Maggiore

> *Have you not read in books how men when they*
> *see even divine visions are terrified?*
> *So as I looked at Lake Major in its halo*
> *I also was afraid ...*

Hilaire Belloc, *The Path to Rome*

Italy's second-largest lake after Garda, Lago Maggiore winds majestically between Piedmont and Lombardy, its northern corner lost in the towering, snow-capped Swiss Alps. In Roman times Maggiore was called *Lacus Verbanus*, for the verbena that still grows luxuriantly on its shores. What really sets the lake apart, though, are its three jewel-like islands, which for many people make it the best lake to visit if there's only time for one. These, the fabled Borromean isles, still belong to the Borromeo family of Milan, who also possess the fishing rights over the entire lake—as they have since the 1500s.

The western shore of the lake, especially in the triad of resorts Stresa, Baveno, and Verbania, are the most scenic places to aim for, with the best and most varied accommodation. Unless you reserve well in advance, however, avoid July and August.

Getting Around

Trains from Milan's Stazione Centrale to Domodossola stop at Arona and Stresa; from Porta Garibaldi station in Milan trains go to Luino on the east shore. A third option is the regional railway from Milano-Nord, which goes by way of Varese to Laveno. Trains from Turin and Novara go to Arona and Stresa. By **road** Lake Maggiore is directly connected with Milan by both the A8 *autostrada* and the SS33, and with Turin, Alessandria and Genoa by the A26.

From Lake Orta, there are **buses** from Omegna to Verbania, every 20 minutes. Buses that connect the two lakes also run from Stresa and Arona stations.

Navigazione Lago Maggiore runs **steamers** to all corners of the lake, with the most frequent services in the central lake area, between Stresa, Baveno, Verbania, Pallanza, and Laveno; **hydrofoils** buzz between Arona and Locarno (in Switzerland). Frequent services by steamer or hydrofoil from Stresa sail to the Borromean Isles—a ticket for the furthest, Isola Madre, entitles you to visit all. **Car ferries** run between Intra and Laveno. Pick up a boat schedule at one of the tourist offices, or from the company's headquarters at Viale F. Baracca 1, in Arona.

Tourist Information

There are several tourist offices around the lake: at **Luino**, Viale Dante Alighieri 6, ✆ (0332) 530019; in **Stresa**, Principe Tommaso 70, ✆ (0323) 30150, fax 32 561; in **Verbania**, Corso Zanitello 6, ✆ (0323) 503249; in **Baveno**, Corso Garibaldi 4, ✆/fax (0323) 924632; and in **Arona**, at Piazza Duca d'Aosta, ✆/fax (0322) 243601.

Arona

Arona is the southernmost steamer landing, and the most interesting town in the southern reaches of Lake Maggiore. Even if you're just passing through it is hard to avoid **San Carlone**, a copper colossus towering 35m high above the old town. San Carlone (St Big Chuck) is perhaps better known as Charles Borromeo (1538–84), born in the now-ruined **Castle of Arona**, and the statue was erected by a family member in 1697.

The World's Biggest Saint

Charles Borromeo, son of Count Gilbert Borromeo and a Medici mum, was the most influential churchman of his day, appointed 'Cardinal Nephew and Archbishop of Milan' at the age of 22 by his maternal uncle, Pope Pius IV. In Rome he was a powerful voice calling for disciplinary reforms within the Church, and was an instigator of the Council of Trent, that decade-long Counter-Reformation strategy session in which he played a major role. There was one legendary point in the Council when the cardinals wanted to ban all church music, which by the 16th century had degenerated to the point of singing lewd love ballads to accompany the Te Deum. Charles and his committee, however, decided to let the musicians have one more go, and gave Palestrina the chance to compose three suitable masses that reflected the dignity of the words of the service (and Charles reputedly told the composer that the cardinals expected him to fail). To their surprise, and to the everlasting benefit of Western culture, Palestrina succeeded, and sacred music was saved.

After the death of his uncle-pope, Charles went to live in his diocese of Milan, the first archbishop to do so in 80 years. Following the mandate of the Council of Trent to the letter, he at once began reforming the cosy clergy to set the example for other bishops. In Milan he was so hated that he narrowly escaped an assassination attempt (the bullet bounced off his heavy brocade vestments). He was a bitter enemy of original thought and not someone you would want to have over for dinner, but for a queer sensation walk up the steps in his statue's hollow heart for the view.

The Borromeo family's chapel in **Santa Maria**, also in the upper part of town, contains a lovely 1511 altarpiece by Ferrari.

More Borromeana (including the saint's knickers) are displaced at **Angera**, across the lake in Lombardy and the first steamer call. Angera has an interesting, well-preserved castle, the **Rocca di Angera** (*open April–June, Sept–Oct 9.30–12, 2–5 daily; July–Aug 9.30–12.30, 3–7, daily; adm*). The original owners, the Visconti, had it frescoed in the 14th century with battle scenes from their victory over the Della Torre family, still to be seen in all their medieval splendour in the Sala degli Affreschi. The Borromei picked it up in 1439, and have lately added frescoes from their palace in Milan, along with personal items relating to the family saint, including every pair of knickers he ever wore.

From Arona to Stresa

From Arona the state road for the Simplon Pass hugs the lakeshore, through **Meina**, the medieval Màdina. Màdina was owned by the Benedictines of Pavia, and later came under the rule of Milan's Visconti and Borromeo families; from the 18th century, when it first became fashionable, it still has a sprinkling of neoclassical villas. Meina is the base for visiting **Ghevio** and **Silvera**, little villages immersed in the green of the hills of Colle and Vergante. Further up the west shore lies **Belgirate**, with its Gothic church of Santa Marta and Villa Carlotta, a favourite retreat of Italy's 19th-century intellectuals, now a hotel.

Stresa

Beautifully positioned between the lake and monte Mottarone lies the 'Pearl of Verbano', **Stresa**. A holiday resort since the last century, famous for its lush gardens and mild climate, it soared in popularity after the construction of the Simplon Tunnel in 1906; Hemingway used its **Grand Hotel des Iles Borromées** as Frederick Henry's refuge from war in *A Farewell to Arms*. The town is also a favourite of international congresses, and in late summer sponsors a music festival, *see* p.145. Among the villas and gardens, the star attraction is the Villa Pallavicino and its colourful gardens, where saucy parrots rule the roost, along with a small collection of other animals.

While Stresa itself is lovely, bursting with flowers and sprinkled with fine old villas, it serves primarily as a base for visiting the isles and **Monte Mottarone** (1491m), via the cableway beginning at Stresa Lido. The views are famous, taking in a vision of glacier-crested Alpine peaks, stretching all the way from Monte Viso (far west) and Monte Rosa over to the eastern ranges of Ortles and Adamello by Lake Garda, as well as the Lombard plain and the miniature islands below. Stresa's golf course is on the slopes of Monte Mottarone, at **Vezzo** (9 holes); both it and **Gignese**, site of a curious little **Umbrella Museum** (*open April–Sept, mornings only*), can be reached from Stresa by bus.

Stresa

★★★★★ **Des Iles Borromées**, Corso Umberto I 67, © 30431, fax 32405, (luxury). Opened in 1863, this hotel is opulent in both its aristocratic Belle Epoque furnishings and its modern conveniences. Overlooking the lake, the islands, and a lovely flower-decked, palm-shaded garden, the hotel has a pool, beach, tennis courts, and the *Centro Benessere* ('well-being') where doctors are on hand to give you a check-up, exercises and improve your diet. There's even a heli-pad, should you need one. The magnificent rooms all have sumptuous private bathrooms and minibars. (*Open all year.*)

★★★★ **Regina Palace**, Corso Umberto I, © 933777, fax 933776, (very expensive). Some 40 years younger than the above, this is a lovely, bow-shaped palace with Liberty-style touches, tranquil in its large park. It has a heated swimming pool, tennis courts, beach, and splendid views.(*Open April–Oct.*)

★★★★ **Milan au Lac**, Piazza Marconi, © 31190, fax 32729, (expensive) Another lake-front hotel, with good-size rooms, many with balconies and, of course, wonderful views.

★★★★ **Villaminta**, at Stresa Lido, on the Sempione road, © 933818, fax 933955 (expensive). A hotel that enjoys the most ravishing view of the islands. In addition to its comfortable rooms, there's a beach, pool, and tennis courts, and its good restaurant serves excellent lake fish and dishes from nearly every region in Italy. (*Open mid-Mar–Oct.*)

★★★ **Primavera**, Via Cavour 39, © 31286, fax 33458, (moderate) A friendly hotel with a touch of style, and pretty balconies, but no restaurant.

★★★ **Moderno**, at Via Cavour 3, © 933773, fax 93375, (moderate). A charming place, with rooms set round an inner patio. All have TV and minibar, and there are also two very good restaurants.

★★★ **Italia e Suisse**, Piazza Marconi, © 30540, fax 32621, (moderate) Near the lake and the steamer landing. (*Open all year.*)

★★ **Elena**, Piazza Cadorna 15, © 31043, fax 33339, (inexpensive). This is a good budget option in Stresa, with big, modern rooms, many with balcony and TV. It also has a garage.

Stresa

Stresa's gourmet haven, **Emiliano**, is on the lakefront at Corso Italia 52, © 31396, (very expensive), and offers *nuova cucina* with a Bolognese touch, with specialities such as their delicious seafood dishes, a beef and lobster 'mosaic' and calves' liver in balsamic vinegar. They also have excellent desserts, and a superb wine list. The grand *menu degustazione* is L90,000, but others are less.

La Chandelle, Via Sempione 23, ✆ 30097, (expensive), offers a mixed Italian-French menu in an elegant atmosphere; fondues, escargot, French onion soup, and curried shrimp are some of the choices on the menu.

Entertainment and Nightlife

From the last week of August through September the town of Stresa sponsors a highly acclaimed series of music weeks, the *Settimane Musicali di Stresa*, featuring orchestras from around the world. As to nightlife, Maggiore has a more sedate feel than the other lakes, and the place is awash with softly tinkling piano bars. In Stresa, for a quiet drink in atmospheric surroundings, the **Casa del Caffè**, Via A. M. Bolognaro 26, is ideal.

The Borromean Islands

Rare and probably myopic is the visitor to Lake Maggiore who can resist a trip to at least one of these lush beauties, dotting the mouth of the wide bay of Pallanza. Actually, the three Borromean Islands include the **Isola dei Pescatori** in the middle, with its almost too quaint and picturesque fishing village, and another private islet called **San Giovanni**, just off the shore at Pallanza, with a villa once owned by Toscanini. Stresa has the most boats to the islands (you can even rent a rowing boat in town to avoid the crowds), but there are also frequent excursions from Baveno and Pallanza.

The closest island to Stresa, **Isola Bella**, is also the most celebrated. It was a barren rock until the 17th century, when Count Carlo III Borromeo decided to make it a garden for his wife, Isabella (hence the name of the islet), hiring the architect Angelo Crivelli to plan its impressive series of 10 terraces and formal arrangements. Later 17th-century Borromei added the palace and 'artificial grottoes' and finished the gardens, endowing them with statuary, fountains, and perhaps the first of its famous white peacocks. The only problem is that the 17th century was not an auspicious time for doing much of anything, especially art, and on Isola Bella sighs of raptures over the splendour of the views and gardens intermingle with groans of disbelief at the 'art'. The conducted palace tour goes down best after a few drinks (*open Mar–Oct 9–12, 1.30–5.30, daily; adm exp*).

The delightful, larger **Isola Madre** stands in interesting contrast to Isola Bella, planted with a colourful and luxuriant botanical garden, dominated by a giant Kashmir cypress. On its best days few places are more conducive to a state of perfect languor, at least until one of the isle's bold pheasants tries to stare you out. Like Isola Bella, Mother Island has its palace, though smaller and more refined, with an interesting collection of Borromeo family portraits, and the family's 18th-century marionette theatre, antique dolls, and puppets (*opening times and adm as Isola Bella*).

Isola dei Pescatori

★★★   **Verbano,** © 30408, fax 33129, (moderate). A lovely, quiet little hotel on the lake, which offers the chance to see the picturesque island after the hordes return to the mainland. It also has a good restaurant.

★   **Belvedere,** ©/fax (30047, (inexpensive). A less expensive choice, with doubles at very reasonable prices.

Beyond Stresa

Baveno, Verbania and the Villa Taranto Gardens

Baveno is Stresa's quieter sister, connected by a beautiful, villa-lined road. Known for its quarries of pink stone, it has been fashionable among the international set ever since 1879, when Queen Victoria spent a summer at the Villa Clara, now Castello Branca. In the centre of Baveno, the church of **Santi Gervasio e Protasio**, founded in the 11th century, has retained its original plain square façade, though the frescoes inside are workaday Renaissance. Next to the church stands a charming little octagonal baptistry founded in the 5th century. A pretty road leads up **Monte Camoscio,** behind Baveno, while another leads back to the little Lake Mergozzo, a corner of Lake Maggiore that has been cut off in the last 100 years by silt from the river Toce. The main shore road carries on to **Pallanza**, which has a famously mild winter climate. Pallanza was united with Suna and Intra in 1939 to form **Verbania** (from the old Roman name of the lake), although each of the towns retains its own identity. Pallanza has several manmade attractions: the pretty Renaissance **Madonna di Campagna** church, inspired by Bramante, with a curious gazebo-like arcaded drum and a Romanesque campanile, and the 16th-century Palazzo Dugnani, site of the **Museo del Paesaggio**, with Renaissance frescoes and local archaeological finds.

The glory of greater Verbania is the **Villa Taranto**, built on the Castagnola promontory between Intra and Pallanza by a certain Count Orsetti in 1875. In 1931, the derelict villa was purchased by a Scots captain, Neil McEacharn, who had one of the world's greenest thumbs and pockets deep enough to afford to import exotic plants from the tropics to the tune of some 20,000 varieties, planted over 20 hectares. The aquatic plants, including giant Amazonian water lilies and lotus blossoms, the spring tulips and autumn colour are exceptional, as are some of the rarer species—the handkerchief tree, bottle bush, and copper-coloured Japanese maple. The house is used by the Italian prime minister for special conferences (*otherwise open April–Oct 8.30am–sunset; adm*).

Intra, Verbania's industrial and business quarter, has a large market each Saturday and is the departure point for a ferryboat across to Laveno. From here also, buses wind up to the Imtrasca valley, past quiet, woodsy holiday towns like **Arizzano, Bèe**, and most importantly **Premeno**, mountain resort overlooking Maggiore, with skiing in the winter and a beautiful 9-hole golf course. In 1950, some 4th-century AD Roman tombs were discovered in Premeno's **Oratorio di San Salvatore**. The road continues up to the mountain refuge of Pian Cavallo, then across to **Aurano**, a lovely base for walks in the woods and pastures, and two fine belvederes: **Intragna**, from where you can see almost all of Lake Maggiore, and **Miazzina**, an old stone village known as the Balcony of Lake Maggiore.

Back on the lake, north of Intra, **Ghiffa** is a pretty, rural place, with a waterside promenade and, in its suburb of Ronco, the Trinità Sanctuary, another 17th-century Piedmontese series of chapels. **Cannero Riviera**, further up the shore, is a quiet resort set amid glossy green citrus groves and facing two islets, formerly haunted by the five brothers Mazzarditi, medieval banditti defeated in 1414 by the Visconti. On the largest islet, a ruined castle surges straight out of the water; though once the Mazzarditi stronghold, in the twilight it could easily pass for a lost isle of Avalon.

Cannobio, the last stop before Switzerland, is an ancient market town, one that, though in Piedmont, is famous for adhering to the Milanese Ambrosian Rite (*see* p.75), itself revived by Cardinal Charles Borromeo in an effort to promote local pride. It has a fine Bramante-inspired Santuario della Pietà, with an altarpiece by Ferrari.

Cannobio lies at the foot of the sparsely populated and seldom visited **Val Cannobina**, which rises up to meet the Val Vigezzo and Domodossola. Just a few kilometres in from Cannobio, you can hire a boat to visit the dramatic **Orrido di Sant'Anna**, a deep, narrow gorge carved by the Cannobio river and waterfall. Further up the valley lies a cluster of wee hamlets of stone houses, known collectively as **Cavaglio Spoccia**, where you can follow the valley's first road, the Via Borromeo, and its old mossy bridges. **Falmenta**, a tiny vilage on the other side of the valley, has among its quaint black houses a 1565 parish church with a rare wooden altarpiece, crowded with small figures, from the 1300s. The next village, **Gurro**, has retained its medieval centre and keeps alive its folk traditions, with a little museum of local customs and products. **Orasso** has a 13th-century Visitazione church, and another finely carved wooden altarpiece in the 15th-century parish church, San Materno. Buses continue to Malesco, in the Val Vigezzo.

Swiss Lake Maggiore

Beyond Cannobio and the Swiss frontier, the first town of any importance is bustling **Brissago**; from its Porto Ronco boats sail to the two little **Brissago islands**, one with the ruins of a stronghold, the other with a beautiful botanical garden. Striking lake and mountain views continue along the shore to **Ascona**, its older neighbourhoods a retreat of artists and writers from the 16th century to the present. Near the northernmost tip of Maggiore is **Locarno**, one of the chief towns of the Swiss canton Ticino, and a well-equipped resort, its lakeside promenade lined with beautiful trees. From Locarno a rope railway ascends 365m to the Santuario della Madonna del Sasso, founded in 1497, where the star work of art is a *Flight into Egypt* by Bramantino. From here, you can rise into the clouds, by way of the cableway and chair-lift to **Cimetta Cardada** (1671m) for a fabulous view of the lake and snow-capped Alps.

The Eastern Shore and Santa Caterina del Sasso

Maccagno, the first sizeable town on the east shore back in Italy, is a quiet haven, with only a crenellated tower recalling its medieval heyday, when it even had the right to mint its own coins. Maccagno is the base for visiting the wild, woody **Val Veddasca**, with venerable alpine villages like **Curaglia**, accessible only on foot. Another road from Maccagno leads up to little Lake Delio, a pretty retreat.

To the south, where the river Tresa flows into Lake Maggiore—from Lake Lugano—is the most important town on the Lombard shore, **Luino** (with a big market on Wednesdays). Luino is the presumed birthplace of Leonardo da Vinci's chief follower, Bernadino Luini, who left a fresco on the campanile of the **Oratorio di Santi Pietro e Paolo**. In the hills above Luino, a narrow road leads up to **Dumenza** and **Agra**, the latter enjoying a mighty view over Maggiore; offshore towers a photogenic rocky pinnacle called **Sas Galet**, which, depending on your point of view, could be a praying nun or the Smog Monster.

To the south is the ceramics town of **Laveno**, where boats wait to ferry your car over to Verbania-Intra; if you're taking the train from Milan or Varese, the Milano-Nord line will leave you right next to the lake and quay. The best thing to do in Laveno is to take the cable car up to the **Sasso del Ferro** (1062m), from where you can walk up for a marvellous view over the lake. In the Palazzo Perabò, in nearby Cerro, you can take in the municipal ceramics collection. Or come at Christmas-time when Laveno claims Italy's only underwater *presepio* (Christmas crib), floodlit and visible from terra firma—and no, the figures don't wear snorkels!

Hanging—literally—further down the Lombard shore between Reno and Cerro is the deserted Carmelite convent of **Santa Caterina del Sasso**. Suspended on the sheer cliffs of the Sasso Ballaro over the water, with grand views over the Borromean islands and mountains, the convent is visible only from the lake (if you're driving, follow the signs from the shore road after Leggiuno and take the path down; boats call here between April and September).

According to legend, in the 12th century a wealthy merchant and usurer named Alberto Besozzi was sailing on the lake when his boat sank. In deadly peril he prayed to St Catherine of Alexandria, who saved him from the waves and cast him upon this rock-bound shore. Alberto henceforth repented of his usury and lived as a hermit in a cave, becoming famous for his piety. When his prayers brought an end to a local plague, he asked that as an *ex voto* the people construct a church to St Catherine. Over the centuries, other buildings were added as the cave of 'Beato Alberto' became a popular pilgrimage destination, especially after a huge boulder fell on the roof, only to be miraculously wedged just above the altar, sparing the priest who was saying mass. The boulder finally crashed through in 1910, without harming anyone, because nobody was there; the monastery had been suppressed in 1770 by Joseph II of Austria. In 1986 a 15-year long restoration of Santa Caterina was completed, revealing medieval fresco fragments (especially notable is one in the Sala Capitolare, of 13th-century armed men). And don't miss the 16th-century fresco of the *Danse Macabre* in the loggia of the Gothic convent.

Sports and Activities

There are any number of beaches around the lake, though many are privately-owned, often by hotels. There are 9-hole **golf courses** near Stresa, at Vezzo, and in the mountain resort of Premeno, reached by bus from Verbania. Premeno also offers good **skiing** in winter.

Where to Stay

Easter and July to mid-September are the high season on Lake Maggiore, when you should definitely reserve.

Verbania-Pallanza

★★★★ **Majestic**, Via Vittorio Veneto 32, © (0323) 504305, fax 556379, (expensive). A very comfortable grand old hotel, right on the lake, endowed with a good restaurant and plenty of amenities—an indoor pool, tennis, park and private beach.(*Open April–Oct.*)

★★★ **Belvedere**, Viale Magnolia 6, © (0323) 503202, fax 504466, (moderate). A good hotel for thie price-range, located on the lake near the steamer landing.

★★★ **Pace**, Via Cietti 1, © (0323) 557207, fax 557341, (moderate) Excellent value, with modern rooms and bathrooms and old-style writing desks and other furniture.(*Open Mar–Oct.*)

★ **Villa Serena**, Via Crocetta 26, © (0323) 556015, (inexpensive). A hotel which enjoys a lovely position in a park near the lake.

Cannero Riviera

★★★ **Hotel Cannero**, Lungolago 2, © (0323) 788046, fax 788048, (moderate). A fine hotel with terraces overlooking the lake. There's a swimming pool, better than average food in the restaurant, and a garage. Guests must stay for a minimum of three days. (*Open end Mar–Oct.*)

Luino

★★★★ **Camin**, © (0332) 530118, fax 537226, (expensive). A hotel in the old style, with big rooms, plush fittings and heavy wooden furniture, combined with the modern: TV (and in some rooms, video), hydro-massage baths and twin basins in marble.

★★ Internazionale, ℰ (0332) 530193, fax 537882, (inexpensive). Opposite the station, this has a smart modern interior, with fully equipped and good-size rooms, and parking facilities.

★ Elvezia, Via XXV Aprile 107, ℰ (0332) 531219, (inexpensive). Just down from the station, the Elvezia is neat, clean, convenient; it's towards the top of this price range, but still good value.

★★★ Ancora, on the main square, ℰ/fax (0332) 530451, (inexpensive). A bit basic for this price range, but enjoys fine views.

Eating Out

Pallanza

The best place to eat in Pallanza, the **Milano**, Corso Zanitello, ℰ (0323) 556816 (expensive), is located in a fine old villa on the lake, with dining out on the terrace for a very romantic evening. The food is some of the finest on Maggiore: wonderful *antipasti* and lake fish prepared in a number of delicious styles. (*Closed Tues.*)

Ranco

North of Angera, on the Lombard side of the lake, is **Del Sole**, Piazza Venezia 5, ℰ (0331) 976620, (very expensive), the finest restaurant on the lake, in a lovely old inn with a charming terrace for outdoor dining in summer. The exquisitely and imaginatively prepared lake fish and crayfish are worth the journey; they're complemented by magnificent wine lists and delicate desserts.(*Closed Mon evenings, Tues, and all Jan.*)

Entertainment and Nightlife

Lake Maggiore is one of the quieter lakes; however, if you do feel the need to dance, **Kursaal**, in Pallanza, at Via Veneto 16 (*adm*), is a big, plush place in its own grounds, and with occasional live acts too.

Between Lakes Maggiore and Lugano

The triangle formed by Lakes Maggiore, Lugano and the Swiss border is called the **Prealpi Varesine**, not exactly a destination you'll see in Thomas Cook's posters. Obscure, yes, but dull, no: besides three small and hygienic lakes and the Campo dei Fiori natural park, it has villages with frescoes, ranging in date from the 8th century to last year, including some exquisite works by that Tuscan charmer, Masolino, in the early Renaissance town of Castiglione Olona.

Varese, the main town between the lakes, is served by the FS and Milano-Nord **trains** from Milan—the stations in Varese are next to each other. There's also a station at Castiglione Olona. **Buses** from Varese go to Castiglione, Arsago, Casteséprio, Lake Varese, and Campo dei Fiori.

The tourist office in Varese is at Via Carrobbio 2, ✆ (0332) 283604.

Lake Varese

Lake Varese, an 8½km-long sheet of water set in its low hills, is the big, sleepy head of the 'minor lakes'. Its main settlement, **Gavirate**, is famous for its hand-carved pipes. For carvings of a different nature, go to Voltorre, just south of Gavirate, where you can visit the 11th-century Cluniac monastery of **San Michele** (now a cultural centre); the cloister has great sculpted capitals, attributed to the Comacino master Lanfranco. The monastery's campanile has one of the oldest bells in Italy, and sounds like it, too.

The best thing to do at Lake Varese is catch the little boat from Biandronno on the west shore for Isolino Virginia, a wee wooded islet inhabited three millennia ago by a people who built their homes on pile dwellings just off the shore. The islet's **Museo Preistorico di Villa Ponti** chronicles the settlement, which endured into Roman times. Isolino Virginia is a good spot for a picnic, or you can lunch in the little island restaurant.

The finest beaches on the lake, such as they are, are at Schiranna and Bodio, while to the southwest the lake dissolves into marshlands, not as much fun for humans as for waterfowl; the same holds true for the reed beds in Lake Varese's twin baby sisters to the west, **Lago di Monate** and **Lago di Comabbio**.

Arsago Séprio to Castiglione Olona

South of the lakelets, to the east of Somma Lombardo, **Arsago Séprio** has remains of another ancient civilization, the 9th-century BC Iron-Age Golasecca culture, the first known inhabitants of Lake Maggiore, named after their cemetery in Golasecca with their little mementoes tidied off into the Civic Museum. Later residents in the 9th century (AD this time) gave the village a Romanesque gem of a church, the **Basilica di San Vittore**, with a lovely façade, aisles lined with Roman columns, three apses, and a 9th-century campanile that has bells looped on top. In the 11th century, an unusual hexagonal **baptistry** was added, crowned with a round drum dressed in blind arches; it has a serenely harmonious interior. There are traces of ancient frescoes, but real fresco-lovers should carry on 19km to the east, to **Castelséprio**, an ancient Lombard *castrum* designed on the Roman model. Ruins of the walls and castles survive, but the main reason to stop is to visit the little church of **Santa Maria Foris Portas**, once the parish church of a town destroyed in the 13th century. Its unique, 8th-century frescoes were discovered during the

Second World War by a partisan hiding here; no one knows who painted them, but the style shows an exotic, Eastern influence.

More lovely, though, is the little Renaissance town of **Castiglione Olona**, southeast of the lake (there's a local station about 3km away, on the Milano-Nord line to Varese). Castiglione Olona owes its quattrocento Florentine charm to Cardinal Branda Castiglioni (1350–1443), a native who went on to serve as a bishop in Hungary and briefly in Florence, where he was so enchanted by the blossoming Renaissance that he brought Masolino and other Florentine artists home with him to do up the town. Among their works are the frescoes in the cardinal's birthplace, the **Casa dei Castiglioni**, with Masolino's fresco of Veszprem, Hungary, as decribed to him by the cardinal; and the Brunelleschi-style **Chiesa di Villa** on Piazza Garibaldi, a cube surmounted by a hemispherical dome. Walk up Via Cardinal Branda to the Gothic-Lombard **Collegiata**, built over the Castiglioni castle. It contains beautiful frescoes, with Masolino contributing several on the life of the Virgin; his greatest work is in the separate **Baptistry**, the old tower of the castle. On the first Sunday of each month, Castiglione holds the *Fiera del Cardinale*, an antiques fair and flea market.

Varese and Campo dei Fiori

Varese, a pleasant little garden city of shoe-manufacturers, has had a very minor role in history: Maria Theresa gave it briefly to the Duke of Modena, Francesco III d'Este (1765–1780), whose main contribution was to build himself a suitable residence, **Palazzo Estense**, now the Municipio; usually you can visit the gaudiest room, the Salone Estense, on request. Behind the palace, the duke's formal park, modelled on the Schönbrunn gardens in Vienna, is now the **Giardino Pubblico**. Next to this garden is the pretty English garden of the eclectic Villa Marabello, this now the seat of Varese's **Museo Civico** (*open 9–12, 3–5, Tues–Sun*), with a hodgepodge of local archaeology and art, including artefacts from the prehistoric Golasecca culture, which flourished near modern Sesto Calende. Another public park, at Biumo Superiore, is built around a quaint neoclassical villa, **Villa Fabio Ponti**, now used as a congress centre.

Varese's landmark, the quirky garlic-domed 17th-century **Campanile del Bernascone**, rings the chimes for Varese's most imprtant church, the **Basilica di San Vittore**, an ancient foundation rebuilt on a design by Pellegrino Tibaldi, with a neoclassical façade pasted on; inside the most important paintings are by Morazzone. The neighbouring **Baptistry** is an austere relic of the 12th century, containing some of its original frescoes. In the far northwestern corner of Varese, on the Gavirate road, stands the small **Castello di Masagno**, containing a rare cycle of secular frescoes by the 15th-century Lombard school, including a lady with a mirror, preening her elaborate muffin of hair. In the opposite direction, the neighbouring town of **Malnate** has a **Museum of Transport** (horse-drawn trams, steam locomotives, old bicycles etc.) in its Villa Rachele-Ogliari.

Varese serves as a departure point for visiting Lakes Maggiore or Lugano, Castiglione Olona or **Sacro Monte**, reached by northbound bus from the station. Supposedly founded by St Ambrose, in gratitude for Lombardy's safe deliverance from the Arian heresy,

Sacro Monte's church of **Santa Maria del Monte** has since been lavishly rebuilt in the Rococo style; pilgrims ascend from the Prima Cappella along the Sacred Way, marked by fourteen 11th-century chapels dedicated to the Mysteries of the Rosary. There are fine views from Sacro Monte, and even finer ones if you continue up to the karst massif of the **Parco Naturale di Campo dei Fiori**, pocked with deep, meandering grottoes for expert pot-holers (spelunkers) only, especially the 480m-deep Grotta Marelli, next to a grand but abandoned Liberty-style hotel, the Albergo Campo dei Fiori, built in 1912.

If you're not up (or down!) to journeying to the centre of the earth, the Campo dei Fiori offers other points of interest within easy walking distance: a botanical garden at **Zambeletti**, and the path to the panoramic western peak, **Vetta Paradiso** (1227m), with its astronomical observatory and views as far as Monte Rosa. At Brinzio the road through Campo dei Fiori forks; the left branch with some zigzags will eventually take you towards **Casalzuigno**, where Villa Bozzolo has another fine Itlian garden. Just beyond Casalzuigno, a winding road cuts up the wooded flank of Monte Nudo for **Arcumeggia**, an ancient hamlet, where the stone houses are piled one atop the other, and where, after the First World War, the locals decided to turn their home into a work of art by inviting Italy's best-known artists to fresco the old stone walls. None of their efforts is particularly riveting, but they add a cheerful 1950s note. An easy path from Arcumeggia leads to **Sant'Antonio**, with splendid views over Lake Maggiore.

From Varese to Lugano

From Varese there are two valley routes to Lake Lugano, the prettiest, N233, cutting through the Valganna to Ponte Tresa, a route that takes in the Liberty-style brewery at Grotte, the **Birreria Liberty Poretti**, the 11th-century **Badia di San Gemolo** at Ganna, and little **Lake Ghirla** beside a village of the same name. The second, easterly route from Varese to Porto Ceresio passes by **Bisuschio**, site of the Villa Cicogna Mozzoni (*see* below, p.156). **Viggiù**, just to the east, is a little resort and belvedere, and was the birthplace of early Baroque architect Martino Longhi, who worled mainly in Rome.

Lake Lugano

Zigzagged Lake Lugano with its steep, wooded fjord-like shores is more than half Swiss; the Italians, when they want to make a point about it, call it Lake Ceresio. Its most important town, Lugano, is the capital of the Canton of Ticino. The Swiss snatched it from Milan way back in 1512, and when the canton had a chance to return to Italy a couple of centuries later it stalwartly refused. Nevertheless, Italy maintains a wee island of territory in the middle of the lake, Campione d'Italia, which is just big enough to support a prosperous casino that more than welcomes Swiss francs. If you can't beat them, soak them.

Getting Around

The main approach to the lake is from Varese, which has a **train** to Porto Ceresio and a bus to Ponte Tresa. Both of these are **steamer** calls on

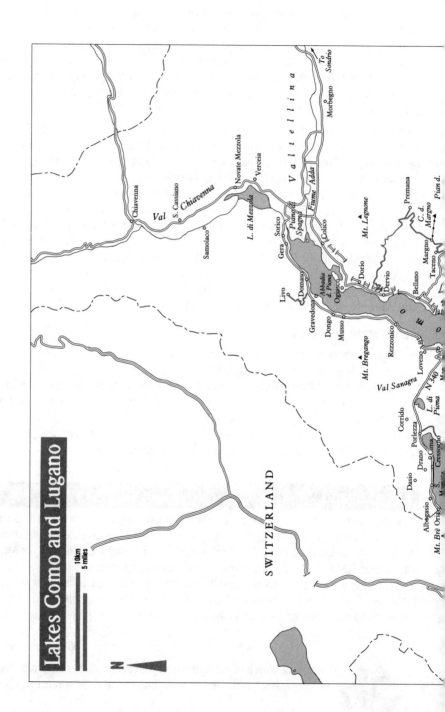

Lakes Como and Lugano

10km
5 miles

N

SWITZERLAND

Val Chiavenna

Chiavenna
S. Cassiano
Samolaco
Novate Mezzola
Verceia
L. di Mezzola
Sorico
Gera
Piano di Spagna
Colico
Fiume Adda
Valtellina
To Sondrio
Morbegno

Mt. Legnone
Premana
C. d. Margno
Pian d.
Margno
Taceno
Dorio
Dervio
Bellano
Livo
Domaso
Abbadia d. Piona
Ogiesco
Gravedona
Dongo
Musso
Mt. Bregango
Rezzonico
Loveno
Val Sanagra
N 340
L. di Piona
Corrido
Porlezza
Drano
Dasio
Cima
Cressogno
S. Mamete
Albogasio
Mt. Brè Origo

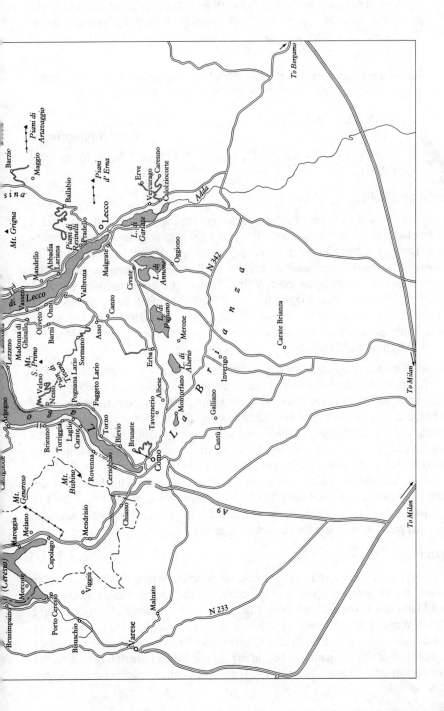

the *Società Navigazione Lago di Lugano* line, with several links daily to Lugano, from where you can continue east back to Italian territory (Porlezza or Osteno). You can also approach from Lake Como; **buses** from Como or Menaggio will take you to Porlezza.

By road you can approach the lake from Milan via Varese, to reach the Italian side, on the A8, or via Como on the A8 and then the A9, directly to Lugano.

Tourist Information

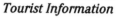

There is a tourist office in Campione d'Italia, at Via Volta 16, © (091) 685051.

Campione d'Italia

Lugano slowly drains its rather polluted waters into Lake Maggiore through the Tresa, a river that forms the border between the Italian and Swiss halves of the village of **Ponte Tresa**. There's not much to see in either half beyond the steamer landing, but if from Varese you head instead to Lugano's other Italian landing at **Porto Ceresio**, you can take in along the way the pretty 16th-century **Villa Cicogna Mozzoni** (*open May–Oct 9–12, 2–6, daily*) at Bisuschio, near **Viggiù**; the villa is especially interesting for its frescoes by the Campi brothers and their school, and also has a fine garden. From Porto Ceresio the steamer enters Swiss territory (bring your passport), passing the pretty village of **Morcote** en route to **Campione d'Italia**.

In the Middle Ages, before state-sanctioned gambling was invented, the once-independent fief of Campione was celebrated for its master builders, who like other medieval artists worked anonymously, and are known to history only as the Campionesi Masters. They had a hand in most of Italy's great Romanesque cathedrals—in Cremona, Monza, Verona, Modena, and Sant'Ambrogio in Milan—and such was their reputation that when the Hagia Sophia in Constantinople began to sag, the Byzantine Emperor hired the Campionesi Masters to prop it up. In their hometown they left only a small sample of their handiwork, **San Pietro** (1326). A later, Baroque-coated church of the **Madonna dei Ghirli** (Our Lady of the Swallows), has a fine exterior fresco from 1400 of the Last Judgement, and several others from the same period in the interior. Campione uses Swiss money and postal services and has no border formalities.

Lugano

The scenery improves as you near Lugano, set between Monte Brè and Monte San Salvatore. A popular resort, it has two main sights, the 16th-century Franciscan church of **Santa Maria degli Angioli**, containing striking frescoes by Bernardino Luini, considered his greatest masterpiece; Ruskin, who wrote that Luini was 'ten times greater than Leonardo', saw these frescoes and gushed, 'Every touch he lays is ethereal; every thought he conceives is beauty and purity...' The second sight, the **Villa Favorita**, has a collection of paintings amassed by Baron Heinrich von Thyssen-Bornemisza: most of the Old Masters are at present showing in Madrid and Barcelona, but the villa retains a permanent exhibition of European and American modern art. A popular excursion is to continue down the south arm of the lake to **Capolago** and take the rack railway up to the summit of Monte Generoso for the fabulous view.

East of Lugano, the lake returns to Italy, in the province of Como. **Santa Margherita** on the south shore has a cableway up to the panoramic Belvedere; 2km above the Belvedere, from the resort of **Lanzo d'Intelvi**, there are even more wide ranging views. **San Mamete**, a steamer landing on the north shore, is the prettiest village in the area, with its castle and the quiet Valsolda behind. **Osteno** has fine views of the lake, and boat excursions up the watery ravine of the River Orrido. From **Porlezza** you can catch a bus for Menaggio on Lake Como, passing on the way the tiny, enchanting Lago di Piano.

Where to Stay and Eat

In San Mamete, the ★★★**Stella d'Italia**, ✆ (0344) 68139, fax 68729 (*open April–Oct*), is a lovely, moderate-range lakeside hotel, with a lido, garden, and waterside terraces. Each room has a balcony looking over a tranquil vision of mountain and lake, and you can borrow the hotel's boat for outings. All rooms have private bath. In Porlezza there are more choices; try the inexpensive ★★**Rosen-Garden**, ✆ (0344) 62228, which has ten comfortable rooms, all with bath near the lake, and is open all year, or, in the moderate price category, ★★**Regina**, ✆/fax (0344) 61228, with quiet and simple rooms on the lake, all with bath. The Regina also has a fine restaurant, featuring good homemade pasta and specialities such as breast of duck served with grapes (moderate).

An attractive villa of 1821, in Induno Olona (a few km from Varese) has been converted into an elegant, beautifully restored 34-room hotel, the ★★★★**Villa Castiglioni**, Via Castiglioni 1, ✆ (0332) 200 201 (very expensive); Garibaldi and Mazzini were guests here, and as you stroll the shady park, or go for a swim or a game of tennis, and doze in one of the canopy beds, you can easily forget that this is a hotel (until you come to pay the bill!).

Lake Como

Sapphire Lake Como has been Italy's prestige romantic lake ever since the earliest days of the Roman empire, when the Plinys wrote of the luxuriant beauty surrounding their several villas on its shores. It was just the sort of beauty that enraptured the children of the Romantic era, inspiring some of the best works of Verdi, Rossini, Bellini, and Liszt, as well as enough good and bad English verse to fill an anthology. And it is still there, the Lake Como of the Shelleys and Wordsworths, the grand villas and lush gardens, the mountains and beloved irregular shore of wooded promontories. The English still haunt their traditional English shore, but most of the visitors to Como these days are Italian, and there are times when the lake seems schizophrenic, its nostalgic romance and mellowed dignity battered by modern demands that it be the Milanese Riviera. Even so, Como is large and varied enough to offer retreats where, to paraphrase Longfellow's ode to the lake, no sound of Vespa or high heel breaks the silence of the summer day.

Third-largest of the lakes, 50km long but only 4.4km at its widest point, Como (or Lario) is one of the deepest lakes in Europe, plunging down 410m near Argegno. It forks in the middle like a pair of legs, the east branch known as the Lago di Lecco for its biggest town, while the prettiest region is the centre, where Como appears to be three separate lakes, and where towns like Tremezzo and Bellagio have been English enclaves for 200 years. The seven excellent golf courses in the province are a legacy of the English, while the waters around Domaso are excellent for windsurfing. As a rule, the further you go from the city of Como, the cleaner the lake, and the mnore likely you are to find '*lucias*', the traditional fishing boats topped with hoops, and wooden racks of fat twaite shad, drying in the sun. The winds change according to the time of day; the *breva* blows northwards from noon to sunset, while the *tivà* blows south during the night.

Getting Around

There are frequent FS **trains** from Milan's Centrale or Porta Garibaldi stations, taking you in some 40 minutes to Como's main San Giovanni Station (information ✆ (031) 261494. Slower trains run on the regional Milano-Nord line to the lakeside station of Como-Lago. From Como, trains to Lugano and Lecco all depart from San Giovanni. Lecco is connected by rail with Milan, Como, and Bergamo; from Lecco the line up to the Valtellina follows the eastern shore as far north as Cólico (Lecco rail information ✆ (0341) 364130. **Buses** from Como run to nearly every town on the lake.

To get to the west shore of the lake **by road** from Milan the most direct route is to take the A8 *autostrada* out of the city, and then the A9, which leads directly past Como town. For Lecco and the eastern lake the main roads are the SP42 from Milan and the SS342 from Bergamo.

A **steamer**, **motor boats** and **hydrofoils** are operated by *Navigazione Lago di Como*, based on the lake in Como at Piazza Cavour, ✆ (031) 304060, and in Lecco at Lungolario C Battisti, ✆ (0341) 364036, where you can pick up schedules and tourist passes. There are frequent connections between Como, Tremezzo, Menaggio, Bellagio, Varenna, and Cólico, with additional services in the central lake, and at least one boat a day to Lecco. **Car ferries** run between Bellagio, Menaggio, Varenna, and Cadenabbia. Some services stop altogether in the winter.

Tourist Information

In **Como** there are tourist offices at Piazza Cavour 17, ✆ (031) 262091, fax 261152, and in the San Giovanni railway station, ✆ (031) 267214. They distribute a free monthly booklet, *Turismo Proposte*, with a complete list of events and concerts around the lake. There are also offices in **Bellagio**, Lungolago A. Manzoni 1, © (031) 950204; **Cernobbio**, at Via Regina 33b, © (031) 510198; **Lecco**, Via Nazario Sauro 6, © (0341) 362360, fax 286231; **Menaggio**: Via Lusardi 8, © (0344) 32924; and **Tremezzo**, at Piazza Fabio Filzi 2, © (0344) 40493.

The City of Como

Magnificently located at the southern tip of the lake, Como was captured from the Gauls by the Romans in the 2nd century BC. In AD 23 it was the birthplace of Pliny the Elder, compiler of antiquity's greatest work of hearsay, the *Natural History*, and later of his nephew and heir, Pliny the Younger, whose letters are one of our main sources for the cultured Roman life of the period. In the 11th century Como enjoyed a brief period as an independent *comune*, but it was too close to Milan and the Visconti to remain so for long, and from 1335 on it has been ruled by Milan. For centuries it has been the leading Italian silk city, and while silk worms are no longer raised on the lake, Chinese thread is woven and dyed here to the specifications of the Milanese fashion industry (as displayed in Como's biggest silk shop, Centro della Seta, at Via Volta 64 and Via Bellinzona 3). Even if you're passing through to the more serene resorts, Como merits a visit; part of its charm is that the historic centre, still bearing the imprint of its Roman plan, is closed to traffic.

Life in Como revolves around the busy lakeside **Piazza Cavour**, with its cafés, hotels, steamer landing and pretty views. West of Piazza Cavour, the *Giardini Pubblici* have two landmarks: the circular neoclassical **Tempio Voltiano**, dedicated to Como's electrifying native son, physicist Alessandro Volta, which contains a display of his instruments (*open April–Sept 10–12, 3–6, Tues–Sun; Oct–Mar 10–12, 2–4, Tues–Sun; adm*); and the War Memorial by futurist architect Antonio Sant'Elia.

From Piazza Cavour Via Plinio leads back to the elegant Piazza Duomo, adorned with the colourful striped town hall, or **Broletto**, the **Torre del Comune** (both early 13th century), and the magnificent **Duomo**, considered Italy's best example of the transition from Gothic to Renaissance. The Gothic is revealed in the lovely rose window and in the pinnacles on the main façade; over the side doors note the fine carving by the Rodari brothers, while on either side of the central portal under delicate stone canopies are Renaissance statues of Pliny the Elder on the left and Pliny the Younger on the right.

What, you might ask, are ancient Romans doing on a cathedral? Although Pliny the Younger did once write a famous letter to Emperor Trajan on the subject of Christians, praising their hard work and suggesting that they be left alone, in fact the Renaissance tended to look at all noble figures of antiquity as honorary saints. Inside, the three Gothic aisles combine happily with a Renaissance choir and transept. The aisles of the nave are hung with 16th-century tapestries, which lend the cathedral a palatial elegance; a pair of Romanesque lions near the entrance are survivors from the cathedral's 11th-century predecessor. But most of the art is from the Renaissance: in the right aisle six reliefs with scenes from the Passion by Tommaso Rodari, and fine canvases by two of Leonardo's followers, Gaudenzio Ferrari (*Flight into Egypt*) and Luini (*Adoration of the Magi* and the famous *Madonna with Child and four saints*). The left aisle has more by the same trio: Rodari's *Deposition* on the fourth altar; Ferrari's *Marriage of the Virgin*, and Luini's *Nativity*, as well as a 13th-century sarcophagus.

Down the main street, Via Vittorio Emanuele, the 12th-century **San Fedele** has a unique pentagonal apse and a doorway carved with portly medieval figures. Further up the street, in the Piazza Medaglie d'Oro Comasche, the **Museo Civico** (*open 9.30–12.30, 2–5, Tues–Sat; 9.30–12.30 Sun*) is the city's attic of artefacts, dating from the Neolithic era up until the Second World War. Como also has a small **Pinacoteca**, Via Diaz 84 (*open 9.30–12.30, 2–5, Tues–Sat; 9.30–12.30 Sun; adm*), which contains carved capitals and wonderful medieval paintings from the old monastery of Santa Margherita del Broletto. Particularly striking are a placid *St Sebastian* shot through with arrows, and the poignant *Youth and Death*, both anonymous.

From the Piazza Medaglie d'Oro Comasche, continue down Via Giovio to the **Porta Vittoria**, a striking gate from 1192 topped with five tiers of arches. Como's Romanesque gem, the 11th-century **Sant'Abbondio**, is a short walk away in an industrial suburb; from the Porta Vittoria, follow Viale Cattaneo to Viale Roosevelt, cross and turn left to Via Sant'Abbondio. Well restored in the 19th century, the church has five aisles, and 14th-century frescoes of knights in medieval armour coming to arrest Christ in Gethsemane. In this same part of town look up the **Guardia di Finanza**, housed in Giorgio Terragni's Casa del Fascio, built in 1936 but a good 50 years ahead of its time. Unlike the heavy travertine buildings constructed under Mussolini in the south, the Casa del Fascio is practically transparent, an essay in light and harmony, the masterpiece of the only coherent architectural style Italy has produced in the 20th century.

For great views over the lake take the funicular up **Brunate**, the hill overlooking Como. The station is on the Lungolario Trieste, near the main beach at Villa Genio.

From Como, the lace-making town of **Cantù** is only a short hop away on the train towards Lecco. Cantù's landmark is the tall, minaret-like Romanesque campanile of its parish church, but its main point of interest, the 10th-century **Basilica di San Vicenzo**, is a 20-minute walk to the east of the station, in the neighbouring hamlet of Galliano (follow the signs) and is decorated with a remarkable fresco cycle painted just after the millennium (*check opening hours in the Como tourist office before setting out*).

Sports and Activities

There are good public beaches in Como, and the city also has a full 18-hole golf course 4km away in Monteforno. From Como, as from other towns around the lake, there are superb walks; *see* 'Sports and Activities', p.167, for details of activities outside the city.

Como

★★★★ **Palace Hotel**, Lungolago Trieste 16, © 303303, fax 303170, (very expensive), one of the newest and most luxurious hotels in town. Partly built in the former palace of the Archbishop, its rooms are big and modern, and some have fax machines. There are extensive conference facilities, and a huge banqueting hall.

★★★★ **Barchetta Excelsior**, © 3221, fax 302622, (expensive) On Como's main Piazza Cavour, overlooking the lake, a grand old hotel, with many rooms boasting balconies over the piazza and lake. (*Open all year.*)

★★★★ **Villa Flori**, Via Cernobbio 12, © 573105, fax 570379, (expensive). In a garden, just outside Como on the west shore. All rooms with bath. (*Open all year.*)

★★★★ **Le Due Corti**, Piazza Vittoria 15, © 328111, fax 328800, (expensive). For character, charm and a large amount of history, this is *the* place to stay in Como. Originally an ancient monastery, and then a post house, it reopened in 1992 as a hotel. Rooms are arranged around the original monastic courtyard and all are individual, preserving much of their original architecture. Design is meticulous, with only local fabrics used, antique furniture and old prints on the walls. Concessions to modernity include air-conditioning, satellite TV, minibar and jacuzzis in some bathrooms. The suites are particularly lovely.

★★★ **Park Hotel**, Viale Rosselli 20, © 572615, fax 574302, (moderate). A medium–sized establishment near the lake, without a restaurant.

★★★ **Marco's**, Via Coloniola 43, © 303628, fax 302342, (moderate). This is also a good choice, with 11 small rooms, all with TV, phone, bathroom and balcony.

★ **Sole**, Via Borgovico 89/91, ©/fax 573382, (inexpensive). A clean, cosy and friendly little hotel, with a small restaurant.

Como

Como is one of those towns where the restaurants tend to process clients with slipshod food and service, especially in summer. **Perlasca**, Piazza de'Gasperi 8, ©/fax (031) 303936 (expensive) run by four brothers, two in the kitchen and two out front, is one place that does not. The menu changes almost every day and according to season, and features typical dishes like *filetto di laverello*, a fish only found in this part of the lake, and *fettuccine e funghi*, a peerless pasta with local mushrooms. The restaurant also enjoys wonderful views over the lake. **Sant'Ana**, Via Filippo Turati 3, © (031) 505266, (expensive) is also a good, old, family establishment, more frequented by toilers in the silk trade than tourists, featuring well-prepared if unadventurous Lombard specialities: good risotto with radicchio, and trout with almonds. (*Closed Mon.*)

There are not many good cheap restaurants in the area, but in Como the **Sole** hotel (inexpensive) has a pleasant little restaurant with reasonable prices.

Around Lake Como to Tremezzo

Zigzagging back and forth from shore to shore, the steamer (*see* 'Getting Around', p.158) is the ideal way to travel around the lake, allowing you to drink in the marvellous scenery. The first steamer landing, **Cernobbio**, is an old resort, the 1816–17 retreat of Queen Caroline of England, who held her wild parties in what is now the fabulous Hotel Villa d'Este. The best views in the neighbourhood are to be had from atop **Monte Bisbino**, a dizzy 17km drive up from Cernobbio.

Across the lake, near the steamer landing of ancient **Torno**, is **Faggeto Lario** and the 16th-century **Villa Pliniana**, which so

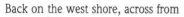

charmed Shelley that he tried to buy it; its name is derived from its peculiar intermittent spring described in a letter of Pliny the Younger (*check at the Como tourist office to see if it's been reopened for visits.*) Stendhal lived here for a period, as did Rossini who composed *Tancredi* during his stay.

Back on the west shore, across from Torno, **Villa Passalacqua** at **Moltrasio** has a lovely Italianate garden decorated with ceramics, open for visits in the spring, while nearby **Villa Salterio** is where Vincenzo Bellini composed *Norma* in 1831. **Argegno** enjoys one of the most privileged positions on the lake, with views of the snow-clad mountains to the north and access to the west into the pretty Val d'Intelvi, which culminates at the summer/winter resort of **Lanzo d'Intelvi**, overlooking Lake Lugano.

Beyond Argegno (still on the west shore), lies the pretty islet of **Comacina**, sprinkled with the ruins of ancient churches, many destroyed by raiders from Como in the 1190s; by some twist of fate it was owned by the King of Belgium, who donated it as a retirement home for Milanese artists. The islet comes blazingly alive on the Saturday or Sunday nearest St John's Day for the festival of the *lumaghitti*, when hundreds of tiny lamps in snail shells decorate the lanes. This is followed by an immense show of fireworks and a

Sunday parade of boats decked with flowers and islanders in 18th-century garb. On the east shore, you can take a boat to visit **Lézzano**'s version of Capri's Blue Grotto, the **Grotta dei Búlberi**.

Tremezzina

In the west-shore district of **Tremezzina**, the description of the lake as the 'mirror of Venus' hardly seems extravagant. Totally sheltered, the Tremezzina enjoys the most benign climate on Lake Como, lined in the spring with carpets of azaleas, agaves, camellias, rhododendrons and magnolias under the towering cypresses and palms. **Lenno**, the southernmost village, is believed to have been the site of Pliny the Younger's villa 'Comedia'; in one of his letters he describes how he could fish from his bedroom window. No remains of the villa have ever been found, but you can visit the fine 11th-century octagonal **baptistry** of the parish church. It was in this lovely setting, in front of a villa in nearby **Mezzegra**, that Mussolini and his mistress Claretta Petacci were executed by local partisans. They had been captured along the north lakeshore, attempting to flee in a German truck to Switzerland. Claretta was killed trying to shield *Il Duce* from the bullets.

Villa Carlotta

The main towns of the Tremezzina are the popular English resorts of **Tremezzo** and **Cadenabbia**, served by an old Anglican church. Between the two lies the most popular attraction on Lake Como, the **Villa Carlotta** (*open Mar, Oct 9–12, 2–4.30, daily; April–Sept 9am–6pm daily; adm exp*). Originally built in 1747 as the Villa Clerici, the villa took its name from its subsequent owner, Princess Carlotta of the Netherlands, who received it as a wedding gift from her mother upon her marriage to the Duke of Saxony-Meiningen in the 1850s. Carlotta laid out the magnificent formal gardens and park, and in April and May the thousands of azaleas and rhododendrons put on a dazzling display of colour. But no matter when you come you can also take in the neoclassical interior with its cool, virtuoso, irritatingly insufferable neoclassical statuary, among which Canova's passionate *Cupid and Psyche* holds pride of place. Ponder, if you can, the Icelander Bertel Thorvaldsen's frieze of Alexander entering Babylon, commissioned by Napoleon but completed after Waterloo for another client who picked up the considerable tab. In another villa in Cadenabbia, Verdi composed *La Traviata*.

Where to Stay

Cernobbio

★★★★★**Villa d'Este**, © (031) 511471, fax 512027, (luxury). This famous hotel, the most palatial on Lake Como, was originally built in 1557 by Cardinal Tolomeo Gallio, the son of a local fisherman who went on to become one of the most powerful men in the Vatican—besides this villa, he had seven along the road to Rome so he never had to spend a night not under his own roof. Queen Caroline was not the only crowned head to make use of the Cardinal's old digs, and since 1873 it has been a hotel. Each room is individual, furnished with antiques or fine reproductions, the public rooms are regal, the food is superb, and the glorious gardens in themselves a reason to stay. There is a swimming pool literally on the lake, another indoor pool, a fine golf course, squash, tennis, sailing, nightclub, dancing and more. Be warned that the rooms cost a king's ransom too, at L600,000 or more for a double. (*Open April–Oct.*)

★★ **Terzo Crotto**, Via Volta 21, ✆ (031) 512304, (moderate). Nine rooms, all with bath, and also an excellent good-value restaurant.

Tremezzo

★★★★ **Grand Hotel**, Tremezzo, ✆ (0344) 40446, fax 40201, (expensive). A large, comfortable 19th-century hotel next door to Villa Carlotta. Besides its garden and pool, it has large rooms with good views on all sides. (*Open mid-Feb–mid-Dec.*)

★★ **Villa Marie**, ✆ (0344) 40427 (inexpensive). An intimately Victorian hotel with 15 pleasant rooms overlooking the lake and a shady garden. (*Open April–Oct.*)

Cadenabbia

★★★★ **Bellevue**, ✆ (0344) 40418, fax 41466, (moderate). On the western shore in Cadenabbia, right on the lake and charmingly old-fashioned, a large but very pleasant place to stay, with plenty of sun terraces, garden, and pool. (*Open 20 Mar–10 Oct.*)

★★★ **Britannia Excelsior**, ✆ (0344) 40413, (inexpensive). A cosy old hotel in Cadenabbia set in a piazza overlooking the lake; lots of rooms with balconies, some without bathrooms. (*Open April–Oct.*)

Eating Out

Cernobbio

The restaurant in the **Terzo Crotto** in Cernobbio (moderate, *see above*) provides delicious dinners for around L35,000.

Comacina

The islet of Comacina, dotted with the interesting ruins of its numerous churches, is deserted except for a restaurant, the 50-year-old **Locanda dell'Isola Comacina**, ✆ (0344) 55083 . For one fixed price (L50,000) you are picked up in a boat at Cala Comacina or Ossuccio (near Lenno), and given a fine meal including an antipasto followed by grilled trout, fried chicken, wine, and dessert, and a return trip to the mainland. (*Open April–Nov.*)

Tremezzo

The best place to dine in the area of Tremezzo is, by common consent, **Velu**, ✆ (0344) 40510, 1½km up in the hills at Rogara di Tremezzo. From the terrace you can see the lake shimmering below, once the home of the fish on the menu. Good basic Italian meat courses are served as well, and excellent fresh vegetables. (*Open April–Oct; closed Tues.*) Another of the best restaurants in the area is in the **Il Griso** hotel in Malgrate, near Lecco (*see* below). Reservations are essential.

Bellagio, Menaggio and Northern Lake Como

High on the headland where the lake forks, enjoying one of the most scenic positions in all Italy, **Bellagio** (from the Latin *bi-lacus*) is a fine old town that has managed to maintain an air of quiet dignity through the centuries, perhaps because even now, with its silk industry, it doesn't depend totally on tourism. A bus from the pier will take you to the **Villa Serbelloni**, now the Study and Conference Centre of the Rockefeller Foundation. Most scholars believe this stands on the site of Pliny's villa 'Tragedia', higher over the lake than his villa 'Comedia', and so named not only because tragedy was considered a 'loftier' art, but because in his day tragic actors wore high heels. The villa itself is closed to visitors, but you can walk through the park on a two-hour guided tour between April and October (*open 10.30am–4pm Tues–Sun; adm*). Another villa in Bellagio open for visits, the white **Villa Melzi** (*open April–Oct 9am–6.30pm daily; adm*), topped with a score of pointy little chimneys, also has immaculate lawns, a fine terraced garden, a lake of water lilies and a greenhouse, while the villa itself contains a collection of Egyptian sculpture. In the centre of Bellagio, the 12th-century church of **San Giacomo** has interesting carvings.

South of Bellagio is an interesting area called the **Triangolo Lariano**, a wedge of karst that keeps Como doing the eternal spilts, though millenia of dripping water have bored ling caverns in its very intestines—one cave called Tacchi-Zelbio meanders for 9km, and has yet to be explored to its end. A number of paths, best in the spring and autumn, criss-cross the Triangle, especially the **Piani del Tivano**.

Back on the west shore, **Menaggio** is another pleasant resort, with a lovely golf course and beach. It lies at the head of two valleys: the Val Menaggio, which is an easy route to Lake Lugano, and the **Valle Sanagra**, from where you can make one of the finest ascents on the lake, the day-long walk up to panoramic **Monte Bregagno**, departing from the Villa Calabi.

Varenna, and its River of Milk

Varenna, the main village on the east shore of the lake, is near Lake Como's most curious natural wonder, the **Fiumelatte** ('river of milk'), Italy's second shortest river, running only 250m before hurtling down in creamy foam into Lake Como. For the Fiumelatte, as its name implies, is as white as milk. Not even Leonardo da Vinci, who delved deep into the cavern from which it flows, could discover its source, or why it abruptly begins to flow in the last days of March and abruptly ceases at the end of October. The best route up is to follow the signposted path from Varenna, passing a tiny cemetery on the way. The walk takes only 15min, and the views along the way are wonderful. Varenna also has a couple of villas and gardens open for tours, including the **Villa Monastero** (*open April–Sept 10–12.30, 2.30–6.30, daily; adm*), built on the site of a 13th-century convent, suppressed by Charles Borromeo in 1567 for the scandalous and luxurious behaviour of its nuns; the garden, adorned with statues and bas-reliefs, is especially known for its citrus trees. The nearby **Villa Cipressi** (*same times as Villa Monastero, above*) has a very fine garden.

Varenna's most interesting church is the Romanesque **San Giorgio**, adorned with a giant exterior fresco of St Christopher (giant-sized, the better to bring luck to passing travellers), while the nearby **Oratorio di San Giovanni Battista**, built around the millennium, is one of the oldest surviving churches on the lake. The ruined **Castello Vezio** high above Varenna, was, according to legend, founded by Queen Theodolinda; you can drive up for the fantastic view, or it's a 15-minute walk from the village.

Another east-shore village, **Bellano**, lies at the bottom of the steep gorge of the River Pioverna. It has a fine Lombard church, **Santi Nazaro e Celso** (1348), by the Campionese masters (*open Easter–Sept 9.30am–5.30pm, closed Wed*) with a rose window in majolica. A series of steps and gangways threads through the gorge and its bulging walls, offering remarkable views of the river just below. **Dervio**, the next town, has some of Como's widest beaches; steps lead up to the old Castello district, marked by a massive stump of a tower. From Dervio you have the option of turning up the rustic Val Varrone or continuing north along the lake shore to **Corenno Plinio**, a town built around the impressive embattled towers of the **Castello Andreani**. Next to the castle, the early 14th-century church of **St Thomas à Becket** has frescoes and a pretty Tuscan ancona of the Annunciation from the 1500s.

Facing Dervio on the west shore, visitors to Venice will recognize the name of the hamlet of **Rezzonico**, cradle of the family that built one of the grandest palaces on the Grand Canal and produced Pope Clement XIII. Further up, looming over Musso, the lofty, almost inaccessible **Rocca di Musso** was the castle stronghold of Lake Como's notorious pirate, Gian Giacomo de' Medici, nicknamed 'Il Medeghino', born during the Medici exile from Florence in 1498. He gained the castle from Francesco II, Duke of Milan, for helping to remove the French from Milan and assassinating the duke's best friend; he made it the base for his fleet of armed ships that patrolled the lake and extorted levies from towns and traders. He ended his career as the Marquis of Marignano, helping Charles V oppress the burghers of Ghent. His brother became the intriguing Pope Pius IV, while his nephew was St Charles Borromeo, the holy scourge of Milan.

Next on the lake, **Dongo, Gravedona** and **Sorico** once formed the independent republic of the Three Parishes that endured until the arrival of the Spaniards. In the Middle Ages the little republic was plagued by the attentions of the inquisitor Peter of Verona, who sent scores of citizens to the stake for daring to doubt that the pope was Christ's representative on earth. Peter got a hatchet in his head for his trouble—and a quick canonization from the pope as St Peter Martyr.

Gravedona was and still is the most important town of the three; it has a fine 12th-century church, the small **Santa Maria del Tiglio**, believed to have been originally a baptistry, with frescoes of St John the Baptist; it has some fine carvings (the centaur pursuing a deer is Early Christian symbolism, representing the persecution of the Church), and an unusual tower. Nearby is another ancient church, **San Vicenzo**, with a 5th-century crypt.

Back on the east shore, **Cólico**, near the mouth of the Adda, is the gateway to the Valtellina (*see* below). At nearby Fuentes Montecchio you can still trace the perimeters of the massive fort built by the Spanish governor of Milan in 1603 to guard the strategic entrance to the Valtellina. It gave its name to the alluvial and vaguely eerie **Pian di Spagna**. South of Cólico the road passes the peculiar green waters of the Lago di Piona, a basin formed of fossils and garnet notched into the side of Como. On the lick of land enclosing the basin stands the Romanesque **Abbazia di Piona**, with the ruined apse of a 7th-century church, a 'new' church consecrated in 1138, and a very pretty cloister of 1257. The Casamari Cistercians of the abbey distil and sell a potent herb liqueur called *gocce imperiali*, for fire-safety reasons best taken in small doses.

Sports and Activities

There are superb **walks** and hikes of varying degrees of difficulty from virtually every one of the towns around the lake; local tourist offices can suggest possible itineraries. **Boats** too can be hired in most of the lakeside towns, and there are good **beaches** in Como, at Villa Geno, and at the Lido in Menaggio, where there is also a large swimming pool. There are also plenty of **golf courses** around the lake apart from in Como; there is a particularly beautiful course at Menaggio.

Where to Stay

Bellagio

★★★★★ **Grand Hotel Villa Serbelloni**, Via Roma 1, ✆ (031) 950216, fax 951529, (very expensive). Bellagio is one of the most romantic places to stay on the lake, and it has several fine hotels. This is a magnificent ornate villa, set in a flower-filled garden, and enjoying some of Como's finest views. The frescoed public rooms are glittering and palatial, and there's a heated pool and private beach, tennis, boating and water-skiing, and dancing in the evening to the hotel orchestra. The rooms range from palatial suites to some that are a bit faded.(*Open April–Oct.*)

★★★ **Hotel Du Lac**, Piazza Mazzini, ✆ (031) 950320, fax 951 624, (moderate). A genial 16th-century hotel near the centre of Bellagio, located on a terrace next to the lake. The rooftop garden has a fine view over the lake, and the comfortable rooms all have bath.

★★★ **Firenze**, ✆ (031) 950342, fax 951722, (moderate). Located in a 19th-century villa, the Firenze is right next to Bellagio's harbour. The terraces and many of the rooms have lake views, and there's a cosy lobby with heavy beams and a Florentine fireplace. The rooms (some without baths) are good and unpretentious. (*Open mid-April–mid-Oct.*)

★★★ **Excelsior Splendide**, ✆ (031) 950225, fax 951224. Also on the lake-front, this has a touching, fading charm, big, old rooms (most with a view, though be sure to ask), a pool and its own garden.

★★★ **Metropole**, ✆ (031) 950409, fax 951534, (moderate). Lake views, but slightly smaller rooms, and less character.

★ **La Spiaggia**, ✆ (031) 950313, (inexpensive). Simple accommodation available all year round, near the lake; most of its rooms are without baths.

Menaggio

★★★★ **Grand Hotel Victoria**, ✆ (0344) 32003, fax 32992, (expensive). A hotel that was built in 1806 next to the lake, and during recent renovation its original décor was carefully preserved while it was complemented with creature comforts like designer bathrooms, TVs, and minibars. The public rooms are quite elegant, and there's a pool in the garden. (*Open all year.*)

★★★★ **Grand Hotel Menaggio**, ✆ (0344) 32640, fax 32350, (expensive). A more modern establishment which also stands in its own grounds on the lake. Rooms are modern and fully equipped, most of them with a stunning view, and there's a pool and conference facilities.

★★★ **Bellavista**, ✆ (0344) 32136, fax 31793, (moderate). A hotel right on the lake, which also has nice rooms. (*Open Mar–Dec.*)

Ostello La Primula, Via IV Novembre 38, ✆ (0344) 32356, (inexpensive). Menaggio's very fine **youth hostel**, the with beds at L12,000 per night and a restaurant serving some of the best cheap meals in the area. (*Open Mar–Oct.*)

Varenna

★★★★ **Hotel Royal Victoria**, Piazza S. Giorgio 5, ✆ (0341) 830102, fax 830722, (expensive). A fine old hotel on the eastern shore of the lake which was completely renovated in 1981. Right on the lakeside, in the midst of a 19th-century Italian garden, it has 45 very comfortable rooms, all with en suite bath and minibar. (*Open all year.*)

★★★★ **Hotel du Lac**, ✆ (0341) 830238, fax 831081, (expensive). As its name suggests, right on the lake, with rooms and bathrooms that are very small though fully equipped, and its views are marvellous. There's also a good lakeside restaurant at lake level.

★★★ **Albergo Milano**, Via XX Settembre 29, ✆ (031) 830298, (moderate). One of the best places to stay in Varenna, a lovely, family-run place in an exquisite setting, with eight rooms all of which have bathrooms, balconies and wonderful views. The ones to request, though (months in advance), are numbers 1 or 2, with their large terraces, ideal for couples and incurable romantics.

Menaggio

Some of the best cheap meals in the region, at around L12,000, are available in the youth hostel, the Ostello La Primula, in Menaggio (see above).

Lecco and its Lake

The Lago di Lecco, the less touristy leg of Lake Como, resembles a brooding fjord, its granite mountains plunging down steeply into the water, entwined in rushing streams and waterfalls and carved with shadowy abysses—a landscape that so enchanted Leonardo da Vinci as he planned canals and water schemes for Lodovico Sforza that he used it in two of his most celebrated works, the *Virgin of the Rocks* and *The Virgin and St Anne*. The mountains of the east shore—Resegone and the Grigna Range—are wild and pointed sharp dolomitic peaks of limestone shot through with fossils from a primordial sea.

Lecco

An industrial and sombre city, magnificently positioned at the foot of jagged Mount Resegone, Lecco grew up where the River Adda leaves Lake Como to continue its journey south (a typical hearsay entry in Pliny's *Natural History* records how the Adda passes through the entire lake without mingling its waters). In 1336, the river was spanned by the 11-arch **Ponte Azzone Visconti**, built as part of Azzone's defensive line from Lecco to Milan, though now shorn of its towers and most of its character. Another Visconti souvenir, the **Torre Visconti**, stands in the pretty Piazza XX Settembre, where a market has been held every Wednesday and Saturday since 1149. **San Nicolò**, by the lake under the city's tallest campanile, has a chapel frescoed by a follower of Giotto.

Manzoniana

Most Italians, however, come in search of Manzoniana. For Lecco was the childhood home and inspiration of Alessandro Manzoni (born in Milan 1785, died 1873) and the setting of his *I Promessi Sposi* (*The Betrothed*), Italy's 19th-century fictional classic—one that looked at history through the eyes of the common man, and sparked pro-unification sentiments in the breast of every Italian who read it. In its day the *Sposi* was also a sensation for its language—a new, popular national Italian that everyone could understand—no small achievement in a country of a hundred dialects, where the literary language had remained unchanged practically since Dante. Even now the *Sposi* remains required reading for every Italian schoolchild, a sacred cow breathlessly milked by every denizen of Italian culture, but something of a hard slog for the uninitiated.

The principal literary pilgrimage goal is the museum in Manzoni's boyhood home, the **Villa Manzoni**, now lost amid the urban sprawl on Via Guanella (*open Mar–May*

9.30–6, Tues–Sun; June–April 9.30–2, Tues–Sun; adm); on display are Manzoni's cradle, tobacco boxes and nightcap, though it is the house itself, little changed since the 18th century, that forms the main attraction. A gallery of 18th-century Lombard art is being arranged upstairs. In Piazza Manzoni, there's a large **Monument to Manzoni**, the author sitting pensively over a base adorned with scenes in bas-relief from the novel. If it whets your appetitie, ask the tourist office for its special Manzoni brochure that points out the various scenes and buildings from the novel, most of which (Lucia's house, Don Rodrigo's castle, the marriage church) are in **Olate**, a village above Lecco, to the east. At **Pescarenico**, an old fishing village just south of the Ponte Visconti, another scene from the novel took place at Padre Cristoforo's convent, now ruined; the village's quirky, triangular campanile, erected in the 1700s, survives in better condition and has been listed as a national monument. Pescarenico is one of the last true fishing villages on the lake, where the fishermen still use their traditional narrow, thin-bowed boats and nets.

Just east of Lecco towers **Monte Resegone**, a jaggedy, bumpetty Dolomite that got away; on weekends it becomes a major Milanese escape route, especially for rock-climbers. Those not up to grappling on crusty cliffs can take the funicular from Lecco to the **Piani d'Erna**, but mind that it's a clear day, when the view is extraordinary.

Villages up the east shore of the Lago di Lecco include the old silk town of **Abbadia Lariana**, where you can visit and watch live demonstrations at the **Silk Industry Museum** in the 1917 Monti throwing-mill, with an impressive round throwing machine of 432 spools from the 1850s. Just to the north, on a small spur, you can make believe you're walking into an illuminated book in the fresco-covered 15th-century church of **San Giorgio**. Next along the shore, **Mandello del Lario** rolls on a different kind of wheels—those of Guzzi motorcycles, manufactured here since 1921; the plant, at Tonzànico, has a **Motorcycle Museum**, open upon request.

The Grigna Range and its Val Varrone and Valsassina

All the towns on the east shore are overshadowed by the magnificent 'white towers' of the **Grigna Mountains: Grigna Meridionale** (2177m), the southern group, may be approached by footpath from Mandello di Lario, or from **Ballabio Inferiore**, with its long and winding road up to the green saddle of **Piani Resinelli** and its Rifugio Porta, from where you can begin a remarkable trail called the **Direttissima** up to Rifugio Rosalba and awesome, fantastical pinnacles rising over the Val Tesa.

The more massive and taller northern group, **Grigna Settentrionale** (2409m), is bounded on the west by Lake Como and on the east by the **Valsassina**, which begins to the north of Ballabio Inferiore. The road cuts through a gloomy gorge to **Colle di Balisio**, another green saddle, with the crossroads for the popular ski resorts of **Barzio**, **Cremeno**, and little **Maggio**, while the main Valsassina road continues up to **Pasturo**, famous for its soft cheeses and the major market town of the Valsassina. Further up the road, around **Introbio** and its stalwart medieval **Arrigoni Tower**, is a land of abandoned silver, lead, and iron mines. To the east the town is dominated by the **Pizzo dei Tre Signori**

(2554m), so named because it once stood at the border of the dukedom of Milan, the Republic of Venice, and Switzerland, while up the road towards Vimogno is the lovely waterfall, the **Cascata del Troggia**.

Primaluna, the next town, was the cradle of the Della Torre family, who ruled Milan from 1240 to the advent of the Visconti. Their coat-of-arms still emblazons some of the small palace-fortresses in town; the parish church, **San Pietro**, has paintings in the manner of Titian and the beautiful golden 15th-century **Torriani Cross**; neighbouring **Cortabbio**, scholars believe, was the first feudal court of the archbishop of Milan, where the earliest Christian tombstone in Lombardy was discovered (425 AD). At **Cortenova** the road forks again, and a hard choice it is because both routes take in spectacular mountain scenery. To explore Grigna Settentrionale, take the road towards Varenna by way of the little resort of **Esino Lario** and the road to **Cainallo** and Vó di Moncòdeno. The trail from here, while not stupendously difficult (in parts you'll have to hold tight to chains), has enough sheer abysses and infernal pits to make it sufficiently exciting for most. The not-so-daring can take the road from Esino to the plateau of **Ortanella**, a natural balcony over the lake and site of the 1000-year-old church of San Pietro, or take in Esino's **Grigna Mountain Museum**, housing local Gallic and Roman finds, minerals and fossils.

The right fork from Cortenova winds its way to Premana, the Val Varrone, and down to the lake at Dervio. Among the sights here is a waterfall in a 30-metre abyss called the **Tomba di Taìno**, located by Cosmasìra, near Vendrogno; the old hamlet of **Torre**, near Premana, an ancient Milanese stronghold where the older women still wear their traditional costumes; **Premana** itself, an iron town that specializes in scissors and, long ago, in the iron beaks of gondolas, some of which may be seen in the local ethnographic museum. From Premana the road to Dervio follows the **Val Varrone**, dotted with old settlements like **Treménico**, and an interesting church of 1583, **San Martino** at Introzzo, with a pulpit carved by Rococo master Antonio Fantoni and campanile with an excellently preserved clock of 1707.

Lecco ⓒ (0341–)   **Where to Stay**

Lecco

★★★★ **Il Griso** Via Statale 29, ⓒ 202040, fax 202248, (expensive) Just over a kilometre outside Lecco, at Malgrate, is this moderate-sized but elegant hotel with fine views of the lake from its wide terrace. There's a pool in the garden, and one of the region's best gourmet restaurants (*see* below).

★★★ **Moderno**, Piazza Diaz 5, ⓒ 288519, fax 362177, (moderate). Not very characterful, but it has adequate rooms with all modern facilities.

Alberi, Lungolago Isonzo 4, ⓒ 363440, (inexpensive). A tiny hotel which has the advantage of being right on the lake, and has very cheaply priced rooms without bathrooms. (*Open all year.*)

South of Triangolo Lariano, between Como and Lecco, is La Brianza, a region of five little lakes that span the legs of Lake Como like footprints or fragments of sky that *did* fall on Chicken Little. Milanese nobles erected summer villas on their shores in the 18th and 19th centuries, though the two lakes just south of Lecco, especially **Garlate**, are most closely associated with the silk industry; since 1950 the Abegg silk mill on the lake shore has been a **Silk Museum**, where you can find out more about one of the nicest things ever made by worms; exhibits include some 500 tools and machines, most impressive of which are the 19th-century throwing-machines, capable of 10,000 revolutions a minute (open the afternoon of the first Sunday of each month, or by request at Garlate's municipio). La Brianza is also known for its furniture and wine, and for a fine 10th-century church in **Carate Brianza**, on the road back to Milan.

Stendhal came to the banks of **Lake Annone** (the next little lake to the west, and the most interesting to visit) whenever Milan, as much as he loved it, got on his nerves; his farm, the 'Fattorie Stendhal', is now a hotel and restaurant. **Oggiono**, on the south shore of the lake, was the home of one of Leonardo's pupils, Marco d'Oggiono, who left a fine polyptych in **Santa Eufemia church**, which still retains its Romanesque bell tower and an octagonal, 11th-century bapistry. South of Lake Annone, on jagged Monte Brianza, are the romantic ruins of the **Campanone della Brianza**, built by Queen Theodolinda of the Lombards; south of Campanone, the regional **Park of the Curone** (near Missaglia and Montevecchia) offers pretty walks through chestnut and birch woods and some fine rural countryside.

Another Dark Age relic, on the north shore of Annone at **Civate**, is the famous abbey of **San Calocero**, founded in 705 by two reform-minded French Benedictines. In the 1080s it led the post-Patariane reformation in Lombardy, and in the 1590s, after one of its monks became Pope Gregory XIV, it became an Olivetan monastery until its suppression in 1803. In the monastery's basilica, currently undergoing restoration, some unusual 11th-century frescoes were discovered behind the 17th-century vaulting, and in the Romanesque crypt; also to be seen are nothing less than the keys of St Peter, given him by Christ, as well as marble and silver caskets of the 6th and 7th centuries.

Best of all, make the pretty hour's walk up from Civate to **Cornizzolo** for the round 10th-century church of **San Pietro al Monte**, reached by way of a long flight of steps and a door that was borrowed from a giant's oven (before setting out, ask at San Calocero to see if it's open). Inside its twin apses are remarkable 11th-century frescoes and stuccoes inspired by the Apocalypse, especially of the four rivers of the New Jerusalem, St Michael slaying the dragon, and the Christ of the Second Coming liberating the Lady Church; there's a rare *baldacchino* from the 1050s, decorated with reliefs, and the ancient crypt, unusually enough, also has frescoes and stuccoes. The adjacent, centrally planned **Oratorio di San Benedetto** has an unusual 12th-century painted altar.

Erba

★★★★★ **Castello di Pomerio**, Via Como 5, ✆ (031) 627516, fax 628245, (very expensive). Away from the lake itself and halfway between Como and Lecco, a 12th-century castle has been converted into a lovely hotel. The interior has been meticulously restored, right down to the frescoes. Many rooms have fireplaces, and massive wooden beds (but modern bathrooms); the public rooms are furnished with antiques, and it has indoor and outdoor pools and tennis courts.

Viganò Brianza

If you're touring in the Brianza south of Lake Como, the little village of Viganò Brianza, half-way between Como and Milan, is worth a special trip for its restaurant **Piero**, Via XXIV Maggio 26, ✆ (039) 956020, (expensive). Delicious regional specialities complement the chef's own innovations, and there's an excellent wine list. (*Closed Sun evenings, Mon, Aug.*)

Beyond Como: the Valleys of Sondrio

North and east of Lake Como lies the mountainous and little-known province of Sondrio, sandwiched between the Orobie Alps and Switzerland. Its glacier-fed rivers flow not only into Como and the Mediterranean, but through the Danube to the Black Sea and through the Rhine into the North Sea. Only four roads link Sondrio's two main valleys, the Valchiavenna and the Valtellina, with the rest of Italy. The province is among the least-exploited Alpine regions, offering plenty of opportunities to see more of the mountains and fewer of your fellow creatures, especially in the western reaches.

When the Spanish Habsburgs took Milan, the Valtellina, with its many Protestants, joined the Swiss Confederation. Yet even though they didn't possess it, it was of prime importance to the Spaniards during the Counter-Reformation, assuring their trouble-making troops the link between Milan, Austria, and the Netherlands. In 1620, the Spanish in Milan instigated the 'Holy Butchery' of 400 Protestants in the valley by their Catholic neighbours. The valley rejoined Italy only in the Napoleonic partition of 1797.

The Valtellina may seem an unlikely spot for wine, but that doesn't keep the locals from stubbornly tending their knotty vines, hung high above the valley on narrow terraces laboriously cut into the sunny, but steep and stony slopes of the mountains. To create these tiny vineyards, many generations of Valtellinians have carried up baskets of soil on their backs; of necessity everything is done by hand. The Valtellina's four DOC red wines, which are all aged for two years in oak casks, are Sassella, Grumello, Valgello and the diabolical-sounding Inferno, which gets its name from the extra heat and sun the vines receive just east of Sondrio.

Getting Around

At Cólico the **railway** from Milan and Lecco forks, one line heading north as far as Chiavenna, the other heading east as far as Tirano before veering north towards St Moritz. Sondrio is served by an efficient network of **buses**. Several lines run into Switzerland from Sondrio, Tirano, and Chiavenna; and there are direct coach connections to Sondrio from Milan. If you're driving, the road up to the Valchiavenna is the SS36, which runs from Milan via Lecco, and from Bergamo via the SS342. Just north of Cólico the SS38 branches off the SS36 eastwards into the Valtellina.

Tourist Information

The main tourist office in the region is in **Sondrio**, at Via C. Battisti 12, © (0342) 512500, fax 212590. It can provide a full range of maps and information on walks and tracks in the surrounding mountains (*see* below, 'Sports and Activities'). There are also offices in **Aprica**, © (0342) 746113, fax 747732; **Bormio**, Via Stelvio 10, © (0342) 903300, fax 904696; **Chiesa in Valmalenco**, Piazza SS. Giacomo e Filippo 1, © (0342) 451150, fax 452505; **Madesimo**, © (0343) 53015, fax 53782; and **Livigno**, Via Gesa 55, © (0342) 996379, fax 996881.

Valchiavenna

In Roman times Lake Como extended as far north as **Samolaco**; between here and Cólico lies the marshy Pian di Spagna and the shallow Lake Mezzola, an important breeding ground for swans. On the west shore of the lake stands the 10th-century Romanesque chapel of **San Fedelino**; on the east **Novate Mezzola** is the base for walks in the enchanting and unspoiled **Val Codera**, inaccesible to cars. The track up begins at Mezzolpiano (where you can park), and passes a granite quarry lost in the woods, as well as two tiny granite hamlets, **San Giorgio di Cola** and, beyond the chasm of the Gola della Val Ladrongo, **Codera**.

Chiavenna, the chief town in the district, is delightfully situated among the boulders of an ancient landslide in a lush valley. Amidst the rocks are natural cellars, the **Crotti**, which maintain a steady, year-round temperature and have long been used for ripening local cheeses and hams; some have been converted into popular wine cellars, celebrated in mid-September at the annual *Sagra dei Crotti*. The most important church in town, **San Lorenzo**, was begun in the 11th century and contains a treasure with a 12th-century golden 'Pax' cover for the Gospels; also note the carved octagonal font (1156) in the Romanesque Baptistry. Above the Palazzo Baliani you can walk up to **Paradiso** (*open 2–6pm Tues–Sat; 10.30–12.30, 2–6, Sun; adm*), the town's botanical park, with a small archaeological museum; another park, the **Marmitte dei Giganti**, 'the giants' kettles', actually contains remarkable round glacial potholes. The path up to the park passes *crotti* under the horse chestnuts and charming meadows; beyond the potholes a sign directs the way to the *incisioni rupestri*—etchings in the boulders left by prehistoric inhabitants.

East of Chiavenna, in the Val Bregaglia, the road towards Switzerland passes the **Acqua Fraggia**, a waterfall near Borgonuovo; a seemingly endless stair leads to the ancient hamlet of Savogno atop the cascade. In 1618, a huge landslide buried the town of **Piuro**, further up the valley; the excavations of this humble, 17th-century Pompeii, which you can visit, have revealed a number of finds now in the museum of the church of Sant'Abbondio in Borgonuovo. In another nearby village, **Aurogo**, the 12th-century church of **San Martino** contains contemporary frescoes.

North of Chiavenna, the **San Giacomo valley** becomes increasingly rugged and steep, with dramatic landslides, glaciers and waterfalls. There are two summer/winter resorts on the road—**Campodolcino** and the more developed **Madesimo**—before you reach the **Splügen Pass** (2118m), generally closed six months of the year.

The Valtellina

East of Cólico the S38 enters the Valtellina, the valley of the River Adda. The old, vine-wrapped villages and numerous churches along the lower valley are part of the **Costiera dei Cèch**, referring to its inhabitants, the Cèch, whose origin is as mysterious as the name. Their main town is **Morbegno**; from here buses make excursions towards the south, into the two scenic valleys, the **Valli del Bitto**, with iron ore deposits that made them a prize of the Venetians for two centuries, and the rural **Val Tartano**, a 'lost paradise', dotted with alpine cottages, woods, and pastures, its declining population still farming as their ancestors did. The road through the valley was finished only in 1971, though many hamlets in the valley even today are accessible only by foot or mule. A third valley running to the north, the wild granite **Val Másino**, is traversed by the magnificent 'Sentiero Roma', and also serves as the base for the ascent of Monte Disgrazia (3680m) one of the highest peaks in the region. According to legend, it is haunted by the huge and hairy 'Gigiat', a kind of monster goat—the yeti of the Valtellina, seen only by a few intrepid alpinists. The six-day Sentiero Roma, laid out in the 1920s, begins at the little spa of Bagni di Masino, though there are other striking mountain paths from Bagni that can be walked in a single day, especially up to the meadows and torrents of the Piano Porcellizzo. **Val di Mello**, a little branch valley to the east, above San Martino, is equally tempting for its granite bulwarks and crystal streams and waterfalls. Near the village of Cataéggio, the landmark is an awesome granite boulder, the **Sasso Remenno**.

Sondrio

The provincial capital **Sondrio** is a modern town, dotted with a few old palaces and dominated by its oft-remodelled **Castello Masegra**, dating from 1041. The town's Palazzo Quadrio houses the ethnographic **Museo Valtellinese**, with archaeological and art collections. It is temporarily closed for restoration work, but in the same palazzo you can also taste the upper Valtellina's famous red wines (*see* p.25). Rock hunters should not miss the valley north of Sondrio, the **Val Malenco**, mineralogically the richest valley in the Alps with 150 different kinds of minerals, including the commercially mined serpentine, or green marble, locally known as *pietra ollare*, for it was traditionally carved into local cooking pots, called '*laveggi*'. **Chiesa in Valmalenco** and **Caspoggio** are the main towns and ski resorts in the valley; in the summer Caspoggio has stables for riding tours of the region. The former has a small **Museo Storico Etnografico** (*open April–Oct 5–7pm daily; Nov–Mar 4.30–6.30pm Sun, holidays only; adm*), containing various stone objects found in the valley, from Roman times to the present day, such as ancient gourds and jars.

The High Road (*alta via*) of the **Val Malenco** offers a 7-day trekking excursion around the rim of the valley, beginning at Torre di Santa Maria, south of Chiesa; alternatively, the less ambitious can practically drive (or take a 2-hour walk) from San Giuseppe (on the road north of Chiesa, towards Chiareggio) up to the Rifugio Scarscen-Entova, for one of the most spectacular mountain views in the area. Another fine (and easy) excursion is up to the rugged lakes of **Campo Moro**, on the east branch of the valley; a white road will take you as far as the Rifugio Zóia, and from here it's an easy 3-hour hike up to the glacier-blasted peaks around the Rifugio Marinelli.

South of Teglio, the main route 38 heads north to Tirano, while S39 tries its best to continue east through the Val di Corteno towards Edolo (at the head of the Val Camonica). **Aprica** is the principal resort, but you can escape the crowds by continuing east to **Corteno Golgi**, near the head of two remote valleys, the **Val Brandet** and **Val Camovecchio**, both part of a little-known park of firs, rhododendrons, tiny lakes, wooden bridges, and old stone alpine huts. At Corteno you can hire a horse, or drive as far south as Sant'Antonio, where the two valleys fork.

The Upper Valtellina

The highway rises relentlessly through the valley; but if you're driving, take the scenic 'Castel road' running north of the highway and river from Sondrio, via Tresivio and the melancholy ruins of Grumello castle, then on to the old patrician town of **Ponte in Valtellina**. Ponte was the birthplace of astronomer Giuseppe Piazzi (1746–1826), discoverer of the first asteroid, but is mostly visited for its parish church of **San Maurizio**, and its unusual bronze *cimborio* (1578), or lantern, and frescoes by Bernardino Luini.

Further east along the castle road or highway, charming **Teglio** was the most important town of the Valtellina in the Middle Ages. It takes special pride in a dish called *pizzoccheri*, described as 'narcotic grey noodles with butter and vegetables', served up to bewildered visitors at the annual autumn *Sagra dei Pizzoccheri*. Teglio has the finest palace in the whole region, the **Palazzo Besta** (*open 9–12.30, 2.30–5.30, Tues–Sat; 9–12.30 Sun; adm*) from 1539, embellished with fine *chiaroscuro* frescoes in its Renaissance courtyard, and the **Antiquarium Tellinum** (*open April–Sept 9–1, 2.30–5.30 Tues–Sun; Oct–Mar 9–2 Tues–Sun; adm*), housing a fine example of local prehistoric rock carving, the 'Stele di Caven', among other examples of the valley's prehistoric art. **San Pietro** has a fine 12th-century campanile, while above Teglio the mighty stump of its old tower offers fine views of the valley. Among the old lanes, look for the house with the blackened arcades, once the residence of a particularly adept and sought-after executioner.

Tirano, the rail terminus, has a number of 16th- and 17th-century palaces and the Valtellina's Renaissance masterpiece, the **Sanctuary of the Madonna**, built in 1505 a kilometre from the centre; inside is an ornate, inlaid wood organ. Between Tirano and Teglio a road pushes southeast to the winter and summer resort of **Aprica**, with its school of competitive skiing, and beyond to Edolo in the Val Camonica (*see* p.191). Another road from Tirano follows the railway north into Switzerland to St Moritz.

The Stelvio road continues up to **Grosotto**; the organ in its church of the Virgin is a masterpiece of the woodcarver's art. The large old village of **Grosio** has been important since prehistoric times, as witnessed by the engravings in its **Parco delle Incisioni Rupestri**, similar to those in the National Park in the Val Camonica. It's the last village in Lombardy where you can still see women wearing their traditional costumes; in the 16th century it was the birthplace of Cipriano Valorsa, nicknamed the 'Raphael of the Valtellina', who was responsible for most of the frescoes in the region's churches, including those in Grosotto's **San Giorgio** and the **Casa di Cipriano Valorsa**. The imposing if ruined castle and the finest palazzo in town belonged to the local lords, the Visconti-Venosta. **Sóndalo**, the next town, has a modern sanatorium and some courtly 16th-century frescoes in the church of Santa Marta.

Bormio and Stelvio National Park

The seat of an ancient county, not unjustifiably called the 'Magnifica Terra', Bormio is a fine old town with many frescoed palaces, recalling the days of prosperity when Venice's Swiss trade passed through its streets. Splendidly situated in a mountain basin, it is a major ski centre (the 1985 World Alpine Ski Championships were held here), with numerous ski lifts and an indoor pool. The **Chiesa del Crocifisso** has fine 15th-century frescoes, and there's a spa in nearby **Bagni di Bormio**.

Bormio is the main entrance into the **Parco Nazionale Delle Stelvio**, Italy's largest national park, founded in 1935 and encompassing the grand alpine massif of Ortles-Cevedale. A tenth of the park's area is covered with glaciers, including one of Europe's largest, the *Ghiacciaio dei Forni*. The peaks offer many exciting climbs, on **Grand Zebrù** (3850m), **Ortles** (3905m) and **Cevedale** (3778m) among other peaks. It also include's Europe's second-highest pass, the **Passo di Stelvio**, through which you can continue into the Alto Adige and Bolzano between the months of June and October; the pass is also an important winter and summer ski centre.

Some 14km east of Bormio, in the confines of the park, is 'the skier's last white paradise', perhaps better known as **Santa Caterina Valfurva**, a typical alpine village and cradle of ski champions, surrounded by snowy slopes from early autumn to late spring.

From Bormio a white road winds up along the Valle di Fraele, towards the source of the river Adda, into a landscape known as Italy's little Tibet, as much for its quantity of snow as for its rugged mountains. Two towers, the **Torri di Fraele**, once guarded the rocky route into Switzerland, much frequented by smugglers; one route, diverging to the west, is known as the *sentiero dei Contrabbandieri*. The steep gorge of the Adda survives, if not the river (diverted by a power-thirsty hydroelectric industry).

From Bormio the N301 follows the **Valdidentro** west into another part of 'Little Tibet'— the **Valle di Livigno**, though before reaching Livigno town you must first pass through Customs—for this old paradise for smugglers is now Europe's highest duty-free zone, a favourite weekend destination for Bavarians who barrel down through the Drossa tunnel to replenish their stereo or hooch supplies. 'Long live the sun and snow' is Livigno's motto; besides alcohol it has excellent skiing, with snow most of the year; it also preserves many of its old wooden houses.

Sports and Activities

Those interested in a **trekking** holiday through the region's most spectacular scenery should request the Sondrio tourist office's booklet *L'Avventura in Lombardia* which, though in Italian, details a fine 20-day trail from Novate Mezzola through Stelvio National Park down to Capo di Ponte; another booklet from the tourist office has a complete listing of the area's alpine refuges. Tourist offices also have information on **skiing** facilities in winter, but note that at popular resorts such as Bormio it's nearly always necessary to reserve in advance. Travel agents in Milan and other cities will have full information on individual resorts.

The **Stelvio National Park** is administered by the provinces of Sondrio, Trentino and Bolzano, all of which have **park visitors' centres**. Bormio's is at Via Monte Braulio 56, © (0342) 901 582; they can tell you where to find the 1500km of marked trails, and a score of alpine refuges, or the best place to watch for the park's chamois, the not very shy marmots, the eagles, and other wildlife, including the ibex, reintroduced from Paradiso National Park in 1968. Unfortunately, the insatiable Italian hunter shot the last bear in these mountains in 1908. Hunting is now illegal in the Lombard section of the park, but continues in the eastern sections, causing no end of controversy each autumn between the anti-hunting and hunters' factions. At the visitors' centre, the **Giardino Botanico Rezia** contains many of the 1800 species of flora that grow in the park. Among the easiest walks are through the Valle dello Zebrù and through the Valle di Cedec to the Rifugio Pizzini Frattola, from the Albergo dei Forni.

Where to Stay

Prices in Sondrio's resorts are a relief compared to those in the more fashionable mountain regions of the Val d'Aosta and the Dolomites.

Valchiavenna

**** Cascata e Cristallo, © (0343) 53108, fax 54470, (expensive). This large hotel, with a pool and health centre, is at the top of the list of the many hotels in Madesimo. (*Open all year.*)

Valtellina

*** Margna, Via Margna 24, ©/fax (0342) 610377, (inexpensive). A real charmer in Morbegn, in the Valtellina, is this fine old hotel which also has an excellent restaurant featuring local cuisine. All its rooms have baths. (*Open all year.*)

*** Sassella, © (0342) 847272, fax 845880, (inexpensive). This is another fine old hotel and restaurant, in Grosio in the Upper Valtellina (*see* below); the rooms are all fitted with private bath and TV.

*** Chalet Rezia, ©/fax (0342) 451271, (inexpensive). On the north side of the Valtellina, in Chiesa in Valmalenco, is a lovely little chalet in a peaceful setting, with a covered pool, that has been well recommended by readers. All the rooms have baths. (*Open all year.*)

Sondrio

**** Bella Posta, Piazza Garibaldi 19, © (0342) 510404, fax 510210, (moderate). Formerly the old stage post, this grand old hotel is the best place to stay in Sondrio. Its rooms are big with lots of charm, as well as amenities like TV, phone and minibar. Public rooms include a cosy reading room, and a very good restaurant.

Valtartano

** La Gran Baita, © (0342) 645043, (inexpensive). In Tartano, the main village of the serene Valtartano, is this comfortable hotel offering rooms with bath for around L50,000. (*Open all year.*)

Bormio

**** Palace, © (0342) 903131, fax 903366 (very expensive). A modern upmarket establishment with tennis, swimming pool, and very comfortable rooms all with bath and TV. (*Open 20 Dec–25 April, 28 June–6 Sept.*)

*** Baita dei Pini, © (0342) 904346, fax 904700 (expensive). A pleasant place, with very good rooms, all with bath. (*Open Dec–April, 15 June–Sept.*)

** Everest, © (0342) 901291 (inexpensive). This hotel has a garden and pleasant rooms, all with baths. (*Closed Oct, Nov.*)

Eating Out

Sondrio's cuisine is less influenced by international tastes than that in other alpine resort areas. Buckwheat is the stuff of life, in the Valtellina's grey *polenta taragna* and the narcotic noodles, *pizzoccheri*; there are delicious cheeses like *bitto* and the low-fat *matûsh*, chestnut-fed pork and salami, and fresh whipped cream on raspberries for dessert.

Valchiavenna

Madesimo's **Osteria Vegia**, Via Cascata 7, ℂ (0343) 53335, (moderate) has been the place to go for *pizzoccheri* and other local treats for 280 years .

Valtellina

A restaurant that readers have particularly recommended in Chiesa in Valmalenco in the Valtellina is the **Taverna Valtellinese**, Via Rusca, ℂ (0342) 451200, (moderate) which features excellent local cuisine including delicious *pizzoccheri*, and an extensive wine list. Ponte in Valtellina, though, has the restaurant considered to be the region's best, **Cerere**, ℂ (0342) 482284 (expensive), housed in a 17th-century palace. Cerere has long set the standard of classic Valtellina cuisine and its wine list includes the valley's finest. (*Closed Wed, Jul.*)

The **Sassella** hotel in Grosio (moderate, *see* above) serves a refined version of local specialities like *bresaola condita* (local cured beef served with olive oil, lemon and herbs), crêpes with mushrooms and local cheese, smoked trout, and Valtellina wines. Another good place to go wine tasting is Grosio's **Enoteca Valtellinese**, 'Al bun vin', near the centre of the village.

Bormio

Kuerc, in the heart of old Bormio on Piazza Cavour 8, ℂ (0342) 904738, (moderate) is named after the ancient town council of Bormio, and is a good place to try local dishes in an attractive setting.

Bergamo

At the end of *A Midsummer's Night Dream*, Bottom and his pals who played in 'Pyramus and Thisbe' dance a 'Bergamask' to celebrate the happy ending. Bergamo itself is happy and charming in the same spirit as its great peasant dance, a city that has given the world not only a dance but also the maestro of *bel canto* in the composer Gaetano Donizetti, the Venetian painters Palma Vecchio and Lorenzo Lotto, and the great master of the portrait, Gian Battista Moroni.

Built on a hill on the edge of the Alps, the city started out on a different foot, founded by Celts who named it 'Berheim' or hill town, and to this day the Bergamasques speak a dialect that puzzles even the Italians. Bergamo owes much of its grace to the long rule of Venice (1428–1797), but this wasn't a one-way deal. Not only did Bergamo contribute two of Venice's most important late Renaissance artists, but the city's most brilliant and honourable condottiere, Bartolomeo Colleoni (1400–75). Colleoni, whose coat of arms displays a pair of testicles, *coglioni*, as a play on his name, was so trusted by the Great Council that he was given complete control of Venice's armed forces; he also received the unique honour of an equestrian statue in Venice, a city that as a rule never erected personal monuments to anybody—though it helped that Colleoni left the Republic a fortune in his will in exchange for the statue. Somehow there was enough cash left over to build Colleoni a dashing tomb in his home town as well, one of the jewels of the old Città Alta. Bergamo also contributed so many men to Garibaldi in its enthusiasm for the Risorgimento that it received the proud title 'City of the Thousand'.

Getting to and from Bergamo

Bergamo is an hour's **train** ride from Milan, and also has frequent connections to Brescia, but only a few trains a day to Cremona and Lecco; for information, call © (035) 247624. It is also very easily accessible **by road**, as it is just beside the A4 Milan-Venice *autostrada*.

There are regular **bus** services to Lake Iseo, as well as to Como, Lake Garda, the Bergamasque valleys, and Edolo and the Val Camonica. Both train and bus stations are located near each other at the end of Viale Papa Giovanni XXIII. Local bus 1 from the station will take you to the base of the funicular (L1100 one-way) up to the historic upper city, or otherwise will take you there itself. Bergamo also has an **airport**, with flights to Rome and Ancona.

Tourist Information

Bergamo has two tourist offices, one in the Lower Town, very near the train and bus stations. They are at Viale Papa Giovanni XXIII 106, © (035) 242226, fax 242994; and one in the Upper Town, at Vicolo Aquila Nera 3, © (035) 232730.

Up to the Piazza Vecchia

There are two Bergamos: the **Città Alta**, the medieval and Renaissance centre up on the hill, and the **Città Bassa**, pleasant, newer and spacious on the plain below, most of its streets laid out at the beginning of this century. The centre of the Lower Town is the large, oblong **Piazza Matteotti** (from the station, walk up Viale Giovanni XXIII) with the grand 18th-century **Teatro Donizetti** and, on the right, the church of **San Bartolomeo**, containing a fine 1516 altarpiece of the *Madonna col Bambino* by Lotto. Further up Viale Vittorio Emanuele II is the funicular up to the Città Alta; once you're at the top, Via Gombito leads from the upper station in a short distance to the beautiful **Piazza Vecchia**.

Architects as diverse as Frank Lloyd Wright and Le Corbusier have praised this square as one of Italy's finest, for its magnificent ensemble of medieval and Renaissance buildings, all overlooking a low, dignified fountain with marble lions donated by the Contarini of Venice in 1780. At the lower end stands the **Biblioteca Civica** (begun in 1594), designed by Palladio's student, Vincenzo Scamozzi, and modelled after Sansovino's famous library in Venice; one of the treasures inside is Donizetti's autographed score of *Lucia di Lammermoor*. Directly opposite, an ancient covered stair leads up to the 12th-century

Bergamo

Torre Civica, with a 15th-century clock and curfew bell that still orders the Bergamasques to bed at 10pm; there is a lift to take visitors up for the fine views over Bergamo (*temporarily closed at time of writing*). Next to the stair, set up on its large rounded arches, is the 12th-century **Palazzo della Ragione**, with a Lion of St Mark added recently to commemorate the city's golden days under Venice, which seemed blessedly benign compared to some of the alternatives.

One of the best features of the Piazza Vecchia is that through the dark, tunnel-like arches of the Palazzo della Ragione are glimpses of a second square hinting more of a jewel box than an edifice. This is the Piazza del Duomo, and the jewel box reveals itself as the sumptuous, colourful façade of the 1476 **Colleoni Chapel**, designed for the old condottiere by Giovanni Antonio Amadeo while working on the Charterhouse at Pavia. The Colleoni Chapel is even more ornate and out of temper with the times, an almost medieval tapestry that disregards the fine proportions and serenity of the Tuscans for the Venetian love of flourish. Amadeo also sculpted the fine tombs within, of Colleoni and his daughter Medea (Colleoni's, however, is empty—his remains were misplaced after a couple of temporary burials in the chapel before the tomb was finished). For some unknown reason, his empty tomb is double decked, one beautifully carved sarcophagus under another, all under a fine equestrian statue by Sixtus of Nuremberg that makes the condottiere look like a wimp compared to Verrocchio's haughty version in Venice—neither, however, were carved from life. Young Medea's tomb is much calmer, and was brought here in the 19th century from another church. The ornate ceiling is by Tiepolo, and there's a painting of the Holy Family by Goethe's constant companion in Rome, the Swiss artist Angelica Kauffmann.

Flanking and complementing the chapel are two works by Giovanni, a 14th-century master of Campione: the octagonal **Baptistry** and the colourful porch of the **Basilica of Santa Maria Maggiore**, crowned by an equestrian statue of St Alexander. The church itself was begun around 1137 and is austerely Romanesque, behind Giovanni da Campione's window-dressing. He also designed the attractive door with a scene of the Nativity of Mary. The Baroque interior, however, hits you like a gust of lilac perfume. Sumptuous late 16th-century tapestries are hung around the walls; woven in Florence and Flanders, nine show scenes from the *Life of the Virgin* by Alessandro Allori while the others are more secular—one shows a deer hunt. Poor Donizetti deserved better than his tomb tucked in the back of the church; the best and strangest art is up along the balustrade of the altar, where in 1525 the Venetian painter Lorenzo Lotto designed four scenes, executed in intarsia by Capodiferro ('Ironhead') di Lovere, who used an amazing selection of colours and shades of natural wood to work into the vivid scenes. Their subjects are unfathomable allegories and abstractions, a veritable fad at the time, as in Isabella d'Este's mysterious suite in Mantua. The third building on the square is the comparatively insipid **Duomo**, originally designed by Florentine humanist Filarete, and given a late Baroque-ish façade in 1886.

Although lacking in famous monuments, the rest of the Città Alta deserves a stroll; walk along the main artery, the Via Colleoni (the condottiere lived at Nos.9–11) to the old fortress of the **Cittadella**, which houses the city's **Natural History Museum** (*open 8.30–12.30, 2.30–5.30, Tue–Sun*) and the **Archaeological Museum** (*open 9–12.30, 2.30–6, Tues–Sun*). Near the Cittadella is the bottom station of another funicular, up to **San Virgilio**—also a very pleasant, if steep, walk—where there is another fortress, the **Castello**, with superb panoramic views. Another good place to aim for is the ruined 14th-century **Rocca**, the castle of the Visconti, whose unpleasant rule preceded that of the Venetians. Back at the Cittadella, the quiet, medieval Via Arena leads around to the back of the cathedral, passing by way of the elegant 17th-century Palazzo Scotti, now the **Museo Donizettiano** (*open 8–12, 2–5, Mon–Fri*).

A Bitter End

Gaetano Donizetti (1787–1848) was the son of the doorkeeper of Bergamo's municipal pawnshop. In his lifetime he composed 65 of the most lyrical operas of all time—grand old chestnuts of the bel canto repertoire such as *Lucia di Lammermoor*, *L'Elisir d'Amore* and *La Favorita* as well as a score of one-act pieces, down to the much-scoffed-at (by English singers anyway) *Emilia di Liverpool*. By 1843 he was the toast of Europe, when suddenly the deadly syphilis he had contracted in his youth manifested itself during the Paris rehearsals of his *Dom Sébastien*, when the composer, usually as affable and charming as his own music, burst forth in fits of uncontrollable anger. His creeping madness alternated with bouts of helpless despair. When the Paris sanatorium could do no more for him, he was packed off to Bergamo to die, where his friends tried to cheer his last days in the Palazzo Scotti with arias from his most famous operas. Donizetti, reduced to a vegetable state, could no longer respond. The palazzo is now the town conservatory and in the little museum his furniture, little piano portraits and daguerrotypes recall happier days.

The Carrara Academy

Bergamo's great art museum lies half-way between the upper and lower cities. To get there fromthe Città Alta's funicular station, walk along the mighty Venetian walls (the Via Della Mura) and exit through the Porta Sant'Agostino. The first left is the pedestrian-only

Via della Noca, which descends to the **Pinacoteca Carrara**, Piazza dell'Accademia (*open 9.30–12.30, 2.30–5.30, Wed–Mon; adm Mon, Wed–Sat, free Sun*), founded in 1780 and housing one of Italy's great provincial collections. It boasts especially fine portraits— Botticelli's haughty *Giuliano de' Medici*, Pisanello's *Lionello d'Este*, Gentile Bellini's *Portrait of a Man*, Lotto's *Portrait of Lucina Brembati* with a vicious weasel under her arm and a sickly moon overhead, and another strange painting of uncertain origin, believed to be of Cesare Borgia, with an uncannily desolate background. There are fine portraits by Bergamo's master of the genre, Moroni, to whom Titian sent the *Rectors of Venice*, with the advice that only Moroni could 'make them natural'. There are some excellent *Madonne con Bambini* by the Venetian masters, Giovanni Bellini, Mantegna (who couldn't do children), and Crivelli (with his cucumber signature), as well as by the Sienese Landi. The plague saint San Sebastiano is portrayed by three contemporaries from remarkably different aspects—typically naked and pierced with arrows before a silent city, by Giovanni Bellini; well-dressed and rather sweetly contemplating an arrow, by Raphael; and sitting at a table, clad in a fur-trimmed coat, by Dürer. An eerie, black and silver *Calvary* is an unusual work by the same artist, and there is much, much more, by both Italian and foreign artists.

From the Carrara, Via San Tommaso, Via Pignolo and Via Torquato Tasso lead back down to the central Piazza Matteotti. There are fine altarpieces by Lorenzo Lotto along the way, in **San Bernardino** and **Santo Spirito**.

Bergamo ☎ (035–)   **Where to Stay**

very expensive

★★★★ **Excelsior San Marco**, Piazzale Repubblica 6, ☎ 366111, fax 223201. The city's finest hotel, well located between the upper and lower towns, which offers air-conditioned, modern rooms, all with TV and bath, as well as one of Bergamo's best restaurants (*see* below).

expensive

★★★★ **Capello d'Oro e del Moro**, Viale Giovanni XXIII 12, ☎ 232503, fax 242946. Also now one of the top choices in town, with well-equipped modern rooms with satellite TV, lovely bathrooms, and a very good restaurant.

moderate

★★ **Agnello d'Oro**, Via Gombito 22, ☎ 249883, fax 235612. Most of Bergamo's hotels are in the Città Bassa, but this, one of the most atmospheric, is up in the medieval centre. It's a fine old 17th-century inn with cosy rooms, all with bath; the restaurant is also quite good.

★★ **Sole**, Via Rivola 2, ☎ 218238, fax 240011. Another hotel in the Upper Town, on the corner of the Piazza Vecchia. A shade noisier, but homely, with baths in all the rooms.

★   **Caironi**, Via Toretta 6, ✆ 243083. A good cheaper option in the Lower Town, which involves a 20min walk or bus nos.5, 7 or 8.

★   **Sant'Antonio**, Via Paleocapa 1, ✆ 210284, fax 212316. Also in the Lower Town; most rooms are without baths.

Bergamo ✆ (035–)   ***Eating Out***

expensive

Bergamo prides itself on its cooking, and the city is well endowed with excellent restaurants. Many, surprisingly, feature seafood—Bergamo is a major inland fish market. The classic for fish, **Da Vittorio**, Viale papa Giovanni XXIII 21, ✆ 218060, specializes in seafood prepared in a number of exquisite ways, as well as a wide variety of meat dishes, polenta, risotto, and pasta, and a superb *bouillabaisse* (*closed Wed, three weeks Aug*). The other great fish restaurant is **Dell'Angelo**, Via S. Caterina 55, ✆ 237103, a 17th-century inn with tables outdoors in a courtyard in summer, and delicacies like smoked *balik* salmon fillets and aubergine with ricotta. The great speciality of the house is baked sea bass with seashell crust. Also in the Lower Town, the Excelsior San Marco hotel (*see* above) houses another of the town's best eating places, the very modern and imaginative **Colona**, featuring both local and international specialities.

Taverna dei Colleoni, on the Piazza Vecchia, ✆ 232596, features more classical Italian cuisine, and specialities including swordfish with mushrooms and *concerto di porcini.*

moderate

An excellent choice in the Città Alta, just below the Piazza Vecchia, is the **Trattoria Tre Torri**, Piazza Mercato del Fieno 7, ✆ 244366, a tiny, atmospheric place, featuring hearty cuisine and lots of delicious local specialities cooked in individual ways. As an antipasto, try the *guanciale* (pig cheek), followed by *casoncelli* (a kind of ravioli), and, as a main course, *polenta di Bergamo* with rabbit. There's an extensive wine list, including many labels from the restaurant's own vineyards, excellent service and friendly prices.

inexpensive

For good pizza by the slice and bread shaped like Commedia dell'Arte figures, try **Il Fornaio**, Via V. Colleoni near Piazza Vecchia.

Around Bergamo

The year after Bartolomeo Colleoni was appointed Captain General of Venice he purchased a ruined castle at **Malpaga** (on the Cremona road), which he had restored; his heirs in the cinquecento added a fine series of frescoes commemorating a visit to the castle by King Christian I of Denmark in 1474, portraying Colleoni hosting the *de rigueur* splendid banquets, jousts, hunts and pageants of Renaissance hospitality. It's open for visits if you call ahead, ✆ (035) 840003.

East of Bergamo in Trescore Balneario, on the road to Lovere, the oratory of the **Villa Suardi** at Novale has a charming fresco cycle by Lorenzo Lotto, painted in 1524 during his 15-year stint in Bergamo. A native Venetian, he had been driven from his home by the merciless 'Triumvirate' of Titian, Sansovino and poison-pen master Aretino. The subject of the frescoes is the story of St Barbara, patroness of artillerymen, architects and gravediggers. Her life reads like a fairy-tale—basically her pagan father locked her in a tower, and after various adventures had her martyred for being a Christian, although he paid for his wickedness by being struck down by a bolt of lightning—and Lotto gave it just the treatment it deserved.

Southwest of Bergamo, **Caravaggio** was the birthplace of Michelangelo Merisi da Caravaggio and is the site of a popular pilgrimage sanctuary designed in a cool Renaissance style by Pellegrino Tibaldi. **Treviglio**, a large, rather dull town nearby, has an exquisite 15th-century polyptych in the Gothic church of San Martino; to the south **Rivolta d'Adda** boasts the **Zoo di Preistoria** (*open Wed–Mon; adm*), with lifesize replicas of the denizens of the region in the Mesozoic era. An even more mind-boggling roadside attraction beckons in **Capriate San Gervasio**, off the *autostrada* towards Milan, where the **Parco Minitalia** (*open daily*) cuts Italy down to size—400m from tip to toe, with mountains, seas, cities, and monuments all arranged in their proper place. Even a miniature train is on hand to take visitors up and down the boot. Due east of Bergamo, **Sotto del Monte** was the birthplace of the beloved Pope John XXIII, and is an increasingly popular pilgrimage destination.

The Bergamasque Valleys

North of Bergamo the scenery improves along the Bergamasque valleys, as they plunge into the stony heart of the **Orobie Alps**, the mighty wall of mountains that isolates the Valtellina further north. At the Bergamo tourist office pick up their booklets *Orobie Inverno* (winter) or *Orobie Estate* (summer), which, though in Italian, have lists of all hotels, refuges, winter sports, and trails.

Val Brembana

There are two main Bergamasque valleys: the western one, the Val Brembana, follows the Bremba river, and was extremely important in the Middle Ages as the main route for caravans transporting minerals from the Orobie and Valtellina to Bergamo and Venice.

Just off the main road, in **Almenno San Bartolomeo**, the tiny, round 12th-century church of **San Tomè** is a jewel of Lombard Romanesque, composed of three cylinders, one atop the other, and prettily illuminated at night; its isolation makes it especially impressive. **Zogno**, further up the valley, is the site of the **Museo della Valle Brembana** (*open 9am–12 midday Tues–Sun*), with artefacts relating to the district's life and history. Zogno is also the base for visiting **La Grotta delle Meraviglie**, with a long gallery of stalactites and stalagmites. **San Pellegrino Terme**, next up the valley, means mineral water to millions of Italians and is Lombardy's most fashionable spa, developed at the turn of the century around two Baroque/Liberty-style confections, the Grand Hotel and the Casino. Excursions include a ride up the funicular for the view, and a visit to the 'Dream Cave', the **Grotta del Sogno**.

According to legend, the humorously frescoed **Casa dell'Arlecchino** at Oneta in **San Giovanni Bianco** was the birthplace of Harlequin (*see* **Topics**, p.68); the role was invented by a *Commedia dell'Arte* actor who lived there, named Ganassa, though more likely it is just a reminder of the many men and women who, like Harlequin, chose to forsake their poor hills to become servants in Venice or Bergamo. There are any number of lovely, forgotten hamlets like Oneta in these mountains; many of them lie in a mini-region called the Val Taleggio, on the other side of the spectacular gorge of the **Torrente Enna**. The road through it, beginning at San Giovanni Bianco, was completed only recently.

The next town, medieval **Cornello dei Tasso**, may be down to only 30 inhabitants, but it preserves its appearance as a relay station on the merchants' road, with an arcaded lane to protect the caravans of mules.

In the 13th century much of the business of expediting merchandise here was in the hands of the Tasso family, whose destiny, however, was far bigger than Cornello. One branch went on to run the post between Venice and Rome, while another moved to Germany in the 1500s to organize for Emperors Maximilian I and Charles V the first European postal service. Their network of postal relay stations were in use into the 19th century, while the German spelling of their name, Taxis, went on to signify their privately licensed vehicles and from that, our modern taxis. One member of the family operating out of Sorrento was the father of the loony Renaissance poet Torquato Tasso. As well as the muleteer's arcades, you can see the ruins of the Tasso ancestral home, frescoes in the 15th-century church, and a number of fine medieval buildings.

Beyond **Piazza Brembana** the road branches out into several mountain valleys. The most important and developed resort is **Foppolo**; besides winter sports it offers an easy ascent up the **Corno Stella**, with marvellous views to the north and east. Other good ski resorts include **Piazzatorre** and **San Simone** near Branzi; **Carona** is a good base for summer excursions into the mountains and alpine lakes.

East of Piazza Brembana, a lovely road rises to **Roncobello**; from here your car can continue as far as the Baite di Mezzeno, the base for a bracing 3-hour walk up to the **Laghi Gemelli**. From here experienced mountaineers can pick up the impressive **Sentiero delle Orobie**, a 6-day trail that officially begins at Valcanale, to the east in the Valle Seriana and ends in the Passo della Presolana.

Another important village on the merchants' road, the prettily situated **Averara**, was the first station after the Passo San Marco, through which the road entered from the Valtellina. Besides the covered arcade for the caravans, there are a number of interesting 16th-century exterior frescoes.

Valle Seriana

Bergamo's eastern valley, the **Valle Seriana**, is industrial in its lower half and ruggedly alpine in the north. At the bottom of the valley, some 8km from Bergamo, **Alzano Lombardo** is worth a brief stop for one of Italy's most striking Rococo pulpits completely covered with reliefs and soaring cherubs (by Antonio Fantoni) in the **Basilica di San Martino**, along with some fine 17th-century inlaid and *intarsia* (wooden mosaic) work.

Fine old **Gandino** is another town to aim for, just off the main valley road. In the Middle Ages it was the chief producer of a heavy, inexpensive cloth called bergamasque. The finest structure in town is the **Basilica**, a 17th-century garlic-domed church, with more fine works by Fantoni and a museum housing religious art and relics of the city's medieval textile industry. **Clusone**, further up, is the capital and prettiest town of the Valle Seriana, with many frescoes, a beautiful 16th-century astronomical clock in the Piazza dell' Orologio—the most joyfully decorated building in Lombardy—and a market every Monday with many fascinating varieties of cheeses, sausages and other local produce. Near the clock, the **Oratorio del Disciplini** is adorned with an eerie 1485 fresco of the *Danse Macabre* and the *Triumph of Death*, where one skeleton mows the nobility and clergy down with arrows, while another fires a blunderbuss. There are more frescoes inside, and a *Deposition* by Fantoni. In the 1980s, more colourful paintings have been discovered and reclaimed from under the grimy stucco. Most are within a block or two of Piazza del Orologio, including one glorious, grinning Venetian lion.

Winter and summer resorts further north include the lovely **Passo della Presolana** and **Schilpàrio**, both located near dramatic Dolomite-like mountain walls.

Lake Iseo and the Val Camonica

The least visited of the larger lakes, Iseo (the Roman *Lacus Sebinus*) is the fifth in size, and a charming alternative for anyone wishing to avoid the glittering hordes that blacken the more celebrated shores. Even back in the 1750s it was the preferred resort of such eccentric Italophiles as Lady Mary Wortley Montagu, who disdained the English that 'herd together' by the larger lakes. Besides its wooded shores and backdrop of mighty mountains, Iseo bears triplet islands in its bosom, among them Monte Isola, the largest island in any European lake. Along the river Oglio, the main source of Iseo, runs the Val Camonica, a magnificent Alpine valley with nothing less than one of the world's greatest collections of prehistoric art.

Getting Around

Buses run frequently from Bergamo to the lake towns of Tavèrnola and Lovere, and there's also a direct bus from Milan to Lovere. Iseo town and the south side of the lake are best approached from the southeast—there are frequent buses from Brescia, and a **regional railway** (not an FS train) runs to Iseo and along the entire east shore of the lake from Brescia or the rail junction at Rovato, between Bergamo and Brescia. From Pisogne at the north end of the lake several trains a day continue up the Val Camonica as far as Edolo. The main **road** to Iseo is the SS510, which leaves the A4 *autostrada* not far west of Brescia. The SS42 also runs to Lovere at the north end of the lake, from Bergamo.

Steamers ply the lake between Lovere and Sarnico, calling at 15 ports; there's also a service from Sale Marasino to Monte Isola. All boats on the lake are run by **Navigazione Lago d'Iseo**, Via Nazionale 16, Bergamo, ✆ (035) 971 482, and timetables are available at all local tourist offices.

Tourist Information

The main tourist office on Lake Iseo is in **Iseo** town at Lungolago Marconi 2, ✆ (030) 980209, fax 981361. A useful tourist organization which is based in Iseo is **Co-optur**, Via Duomo 17, ✆ (030) 981154, fax 9821742, a local co-operative which has a booking service for hotels, day trips and restaurants. In the Val Camonica there are tourist offices in **Darfo-Boario Terme**, at Piazza Einaudi 2, ✆ (0364) 531609, fax 532280; **Capo di Ponte**, Via Briscioli, ✆ (0364) 42080; **Edolo**, at Piazza Martiri della Libertà 2, ✆ (0364) 71065; and in **Ponte di Legno**, at Corso Milano 41, ✆ (0364) 91122.

Franciacorta and Lake Iseo

Between Brescia and Iseo lies the charming wine-growing region known as **Franciacorta**, the 'free court', which, owing to its poverty, paid no taxes, a fact that endeared it to the villa-building patricians of Lombardy. Today, the name of the region is also synonymous with one of Italy's best-known varieties of champagne-method sparkling wine, as well as with mellowing old estates surrounded by vineyards producing a fine DOC red and Pinot Bianco. While the countryside as a whole is a prime attraction, the village of **Erbusco** is now also home to perhaps the best and certainly the most talked-about restaurant in Italy, that of Gualtiero Marchesi, **L'Albereta** (*see* p.192).

The **Villa Lana** (now Ragnoli) in Colombaro is also worth a stop for Italy's oldest cedar of Lebanon in its garden. Two other villages closer to Brescia have ancient churches—the Romanesque Olivetan abbey church at **Rodengo**, with three cloisters and frescoes by Romanino and Moretto, and **San Pietro in Lamosa**, founded by monks from Cluny in 1083, located in **Provaglio**. San Pietro overlooks an emerald peat moss called **Le Torbiere**, which blossoms into an aquatic garden of pink and white water lilies in late spring; the tourist office in Iseo rents out rowing boats to enable you to paddle through.

Iseo, between the lake and Le Torbiere, is one of the main shore resorts, with its beaches and a venerable 12th-century church, **Pieve di Sant'Andrea**, on one of its shady streets. Steamers link it with **Sarnico**, a smaller resort to the south sprinkled with Liberty-style villas, and with the real attraction of this lake, the arcadian, car-less island of **Monte Isola**. This steep rock, a fair-sized copy of Gibraltar soaking in its own bathtub, has occasionally been a resort of poets and painters; the lack of cars is not progressive

Lago Iseo

planning—there simply aren't any roads to drive them on. Several genteel decaying fishing villages dot the island's shore, connected to the mainland by tiny ferries (*see* above). Recreation is limited to walks through the olive and chestnut groves, perhaps as far as the sanctuary chapel on the top of the island—over a thousand feet above the lake. Monte Isola's people still catch fish in the lake, but their talent for making fine nets has led to a new business opportunity: now they make tennis nets for all the Italian championship tournaments.

Another steamer port, **Sale Marasino**, is one of the prettier spots on the lake, ringed by mountain terraces. From the nearby village of **Marone** you can hike up to the panoramic view point of **Monte Guglielmo** (1949m, with an alpine refuge), passing along the way **Zone** and its spiky 'erosion pyramids', similar to the pyramids of the Dolomites. A few have large boulders neatly balanced on top. On Cislano's little parish church, there is an exterior fresco of St George and the dragon. Next along the shore, the old village of **Pisogne** has the last train station on the lake shore, and bus connections to Lovere; its church of **Santa Maria della Neve** is covered with excellent frescoes by Romanino, who spent two years on the project.

Lovere, the oldest resort on Lake Iseo, has a fine church in its 15th-century frescoed **Santa Maria in Valvendra**, and a handful of good paintings in its **Galleria dell'Accademia Tadini** (*open May–Sept 2–6pm Tues–Sat*), especially a *Madonna* by Jacopo Bellini. The highlight of Iseo's west shore is **Riva di Solto** (a steamer port), with odd little bays and views across the water of the formidable Adamello mountains. **Tavèrnola Bergamasca** has a local steamer to Sarnico.

A temple of *Nuova Cucina*

For years, moneyed Milan flocked to the eponymous gourmet enclave of **Gualtiero Marchesi**, the innovative master chef and Pied Piper/founder of *la nuova cucina*. Marchesi is very much a celebrity in Italy—he has his own TV show and is author of several cookbooks, and his restaurant became more of an institution, frequented by the top politicos and industrialists of the day, than simply a place to eat. So it came as quite as surprise when in 1993 he shut up shop in Milan and moved to the country, to Erbusco, a tiny village in the heart of the Franciacorta wine region. He has opened a hotel, **L'Albereta** (*see* below, 'Where to Stay'), thus returning to his roots—his father, too, was a hotelier—and with it a new restaurant. Devotees need not have been too concerned, as the new establishment has quickly taken up its predecessor's status as one of the principal places of pilgrimage of the Italian cult of foodism. The setting, on a hill overlooking the rolling countryside, is exquisite, as is the décor, incorporating frescoes from the original villa. There are three set menus: a lunch menu at L50,000, a four-course evening meal at L80,000, and a seven-course gourmet menu at L110,000, wine not included. Marchesi usually bases his dishes on what is available at the market each day; specialities include, to begin, lightly scrambled egg with caviar, *crema di luccio*, a delicate mousse made from a lake fish, and *risotto con gamberi e seppie*, a risotto with prawns and cuttlefish. A trademark is his unusual marriages of flavours—such as pigeon and lobster ravioli, or ratatouille of sweet and sour aubergines with salted prawns. The hotel also has its own vineyard, as well as a superb selection of other wines. The seven-course meal can easily take three hours to get through, but it is meant to be savoured, rather than rushed!

Val Camonica

From Pisogne the road and railway continue northeast into the Val Camonica, one of the loveliest and most fertile of Alpine valleys. Its name is derived from a Rhaetian tribe, the Camuni, whose artistic ancestors used the smooth, glacier-seared permian sandstone of their valley as tablets to engrave solar discs and labyrinths, mysterious figures and geometric designs, animals, weapons, and people. What is especially remarkable is the unbroken length of time during which the engravings were made: the oldest are from the Neolithic era (before 2200 BC) and the latest date from the arrival of the Romans—a period spanning some 25 centuries, enabling scholars to trace intriguing prehistoric stylistic evolutions, from the random scratched symbols of the late Stone Age to the finely drawn, realistic and narrative figures of the Bronze and Iron Ages. Although it's impossible to understand the significance these etchings had for their makers, their magic must have been extraordinary: in the valley some 180,000 have been discovered so far. Some are beautiful, some ungainly and peculiar, some utterly mystifying, while a few are fuel for crackpot theories. Recently UNESCO has put the Val Camonica on its select list of sites to be protected as part of the artistic patrimony of humanity.

Some 12km from Pisogne some early rock incisions from the 3rd millennium BC may be seen in a lovely park at Luine, near the busy spa of **Boario Terme**. Unfortunately the rock here has weathered more than further north at Capo di Ponte, and the graffiti are often hard to decipher. Boario also offers the opportunity for a scenic detour up the **Valle d'Angolo** and its wild and narrow **Dezzo Ravine**.

When the Romans conquered the valley their capital was **Cividate Camuno**, and it remembers their passing with mosaics, tomb stones and other local finds in its small **Archaeological Museum** (*open 8am–2pm Tues–Sun*). It also has a fine 12th-century tower, and churches with frescoes by the excellent quattrocento painter Da Cemmo in the environs, at **Esine** and **Bienno** (Santa Maria Annunziata). **Breno**, the modern capital of the valley, lies under an imposing medieval castle; its 14th-century church of **Sant'Antonio** contains frescoes by Romanino, and its **Museo Camuno** in the town hall has an interesting ethnographic collection from the valley. From here a mountain road winds eastwards up to the Passo di Croce Domini and Lake Idro, and then down towards Brescia (*see* p.195).

Capo di Ponte

Capo di Ponte is the centre for visiting the best of the prehistoric engravings, located in the **Parco Nazionale delle Incisioni Rupestri Preistoriche** (*open 9am–1hr before sunset daily; adm; guided visits can be arranged through Capo di Ponte tourist office or the park itself, © 42140*). The main attraction is the **Naquane rock**, etched with some 900 figures during the Iron Age. Across the Oglio, in **Cemmo**, there are two other magnificent rocks, the first ones to be discovered, and a few kilometres south of Capo di Ponte, in the tiny medieval hamlet of **Foppe** (near **Niardo**); a second section of the park was opened after the discovery in 1975 of another great concentration of engravings, reached via a path from the village. In Niardo, Capo di Ponte's *Centro Camuno di Studi Preistorici* has its museum, with plans of the Camuni culture's sites among other explanatory items. Besides prehistoric art, Capo di Ponte also has two picturesque 11th-century churches: **San Siro**, with its three tall apses built on a hill directly over the river, and the Cluniac monastery church of **San Salvatore**.

Further up the valley the scenery becomes grander as the Adamello group of the Brenta Dolomites looms up to the right. Beautiful excursions into the range are possible from **Cedegolo**, into the lovely **Val di Saviore** with its mountain lakes Arno and Salarno or up Mount Adamello (3555m). From **Malonno** you can drive or walk along a scenic road through the chestnut woods of the **Valle Malga**, with more pretty lakes and easy ascents (Corno delle Granate, 3111m).

Surrounded by majestic mountains, **Edolo** stands at the crossroads of the valley and the road from Sondrio and the Valtellina to the Passo di Tonale. It is a base for a whole range of mountain excursions, and for the ski resorts of the **Valle di Corteno**, **Ponte di Legno** (the most developed) and **Passo di Tonale**. From the Passo di Tonale you can continue east into Trentino's lovely Val di Sole, while a road from Ponte di Legno cuts north through Stelvio National Park to Bormio.

Where to Stay

Erbusco

L'Albereta, © (030) 7267003, (very expensive). Italy's master chef Gualtiero Marchesi has recently decamped from Milan to open a hotel and gourmet restaurant (*see* p.190–91) in the tiny village of Erbusco in the Franciacorta. It's an old, entirely renovated villa, and the accommodation consists of 39 rooms and suites, all individual and all beautifully designed. There's every possible attention to detail, with wall paintings by Jacques Margerin, open log fires, jacuzzis in the bathrooms and a swimming pool, sauna, tennis and garage. Even so, it's still in the very expensive rather than luxury category.

Iseo

★★★★ I Due Roccoli, ℂ (030) 9821853, fax 9821877, (expensive). The top choice in Iseo and one of the best places to stay in the region, set amid its own large gardens in the hills above the town. A member of the prestigous *Relais du Silence* hotels, the hotel occupies part of an old hunting lodge. The modern suites, rooms and bathrooms are beautifully designed and equipped, some with garden views, and others with breathtaking views of the lake. There's a banqueting hall, sun terrace, pool and one of the finest restaurants in the area (*see* below).

★★★ Ambra, Piazza G. Rosa, ℂ (030) 980130, fax 9821361, (moderate). On the lake and near Iseo town centre. All its rooms have modern fittings, and most have nice bathrooms and balconies, though there's no restaurant.

★★★ Moselli, in Pilzone, just outside Iseo, ℂ (030) 980001, fax 981868, (inexpensive). A good choice as it's near the beach, in a garden; all the rooms have baths .

★★ Milano, ℂ (030) 980449, fax 9821361, (inexpensive). A short distance away along the lake shore, the Milano has smaller rooms in an old-fashioned style, many with lake views, and a small restaurant and bar.

Monte Isola

★★★ Montisola Palace, in the village of Menzino, ℂ (030) 9825138 (moderate). A pleasant, tranquil hotel on Monte Isola, with a pool and beach, tennis courts, and fine rooms, all with bath; it also has self-catering flats available (*open April–Oct*).

★★ Bellavista, in Siviano, also on Monte Isola, ℂ (030) 9886106, (inexpensive). This is a wonderful place to get away from it all—its rooms are comfortable, small and simple with, of course, outstanding views, and there's a nice little restaurant, too.

★★ Canogola, ℂ (030) 9825310, (inexpensive). Another choice in Siviano, a small hotel which offers quiet lakeside rooms, all with bath.

Sale Marasino

★★★ Rotelli, ℂ (030) 986115, fax 986241, (inexpensive). On the east side of the lake, in the small village of Sale Marasino, is this excellent bargain, with magnificent views, a pool, tennis, sauna and gym and well-sized, modern rooms at, incredibly, inexpensive-category prices of around L60,000 per night.

Sarnico

★★★★ Cantiere in Sarnico, Via Monte Grappa 2, ℂ (035) 910091, fax 912722, (moderate). One of the newer, more interesting places to stay and dine on Lake Iseo, in an old building remodelled by its new owners, with comfortable rooms.

Val Camonica

Most of the hotels in the Val Camonica are concentrated in Boario Terme or in the mountain resorts at the northern end. In Boario the plush ★★★★**Grand Hotel Boario e Delle Terme**, Via Manzoni 2, ✆ (0364) 531 061, is the duchess of valley accommodation, but at time of writing is closed for restoration.

★★★★ **Mirella**, ✆ (0364) 900500, fax 900530, (expensive). At the head of the valley in Ponte di Legno, this sleek and modern hotel is the top choice, with a pool and tennis courts among its facilities.

★★★★ **Rizzi**, ✆ (0364) 531617, (moderate). The second choice in Boario, old and slightly frayed at the edges, but having comfortable rooms all with TV, phone, safe, etc. It has its own garden, with a lovely outside verandah and a very nice restaurant featuring local dishes.

★★★ **Diana**, Via Manifattura 12, ✆/fax (0364) 531403, (moderate). A stylish modern hotel in Boario, opposite the Terme, with good-size rooms with all mod cons, large bathrooms and wonderful views of the mountains, as well as a restaurant and garden, too.

★★★ **Brescia**, Via Zanardelli 6, ✆ (0364) 531409, fax 532969, (moderate). A slightly old-fashioned hotel in Boario, but its rooms are fully equipped, and there are conference facilities, a very stylish dining room and a pub/disco downstairs.

★★★ **Dolomiti**, ✆ (0364) 900260, fax 900251, (moderate). A less glamorous but quite adequate choice located up at the Passo del Tonale. All rooms are with bath. (*Open all year.*)

★★ **Ariston**, ✆/fax (0364) 531532, (inexpensive). A good budget option in Boario Terme, in the station forecourt, which offers small, clean rooms with modern fittings, great views, and old-fashioned hospitality.

Eating Out

Clusane

Fish from the lake are, of course, a speciality, and nowhere more so than the village of Clusane, near Iseo, where the foremost speciality is *tinca al forno* (tench from the lake). The village could also lay claim to having the most restaurants per capita in the area—20, seating 4000, in a place with a population of 1500!

Erbusco

The region can now boast one of Italy's most prestigious restaurants, Gualtiero Marchesi's **L'Albereta** in Erbusco, ✆ (030) 7267003, (very expensive).

Iseo

The best place to eat in Iseo is **I Due Roccoli** hotel (expensive, *see* above), © (030) 9821853, fax 9821877, though it's outside the town, and you'll need a car to get there. The dining room is tasteful and intimate, with an open log fire, service is impeccable, and much of the food is home grown, from the small farm in the hotel grounds. Favourite dishes include an antipasto of salad and truffles, *insalata di lambetto tartufato*, a delicious green pasta with mushrooms known as *pappardelle verdi con funghi porcini*, various fish from the lake, and, for dessert, a *mousse di cioccolato bianco* that's one of the best in the country. (*Open to non-residents Thurs–Mon only.*)

In Iseo town, for a fine glass of wine (from Franciacorta and beyond) and a good plate of lake trout, among other local specialities, try **Il Volto**, Via Mirolte 33, © (030) 981462 (moderate).

Rovato

In Rovato, on the edge of the Franciacorta, there's another excellent place to feast on the freshest of fish: **Tortuga**, Via A. Angelini 10, © (030) 722980, (expensive). Specialities include wonderful seafood antipasti, and delicate scampi as a recommended choice for seconds. There's a garden for outdoor dining as well.

Sarnico

The restaurant of the **Cantiere** hotel (*see* above) features a wonderful *menu degustazione* for moderate prices, featuring dishes like risotto with oysters and prosciutto, veal cutlets with asparagus, wild mushroom soup, exquisite fish dishes, and desserts that hit the spot.

Val Camonica

In the Val Camonica most of the best restaurants are in the valley's hotels (*see* above). A good place to eat in Ponte di Legno, **Al Maniero**, © (0364) 91093, (moderate), features hearty local cuisine in a cosy, happy atmosphere.

Brescia

The second city of Lombardy, Brescia may be busy and prosperous, but it's no one's favourite art town, even though it has a full day's supply of art, architecture, and delightful corners to visit. Perhaps it's the vaguely sinister aura of having been Italy's chief manufacturer of arms for the last 400 years. Perhaps it's because the local Fascists saw fit to punch out the heart of the old city and replace it with a soulless, chilling piazza designed on the principles that might makes right. The Brescians seem to detest it, but it's hard to avoid; they would do well to raze it and the subliminal memories it evokes.

Brescia

300 metres
300 yards

N

1. Tourist Office
2. Post Office
3. Bus Station
4. Train Station
5. Duomo
6. Broletto
7. Museo Romano
8. Abbey S. Salvatore/S. Giulia /
   Civic Museum
9. S. Pietro in Oliveto
10. Castello
11. Arms Museum
12. Roman Curia
13. Pinacoteca Tosio Martinengo
14. San Clemente
15. Santa Maria del Carmine
16. San Faustino
17. Sant' Alessandro
18. SS. Nazaro e Celso
19. San Francesco
20. Madonna delle Grazie
21. San Giovanni
22. Torre Pallata
23. S. Maria dei Miracoli
24. Teatro Grande

History

Brescia was originally a Gaulish settlement, an origin remembered only in its name Brixia, from the Celtic *brik* ('hill'). Brixia was an ally of Rome early on, and in 26 BC achieved the favoured status of a *Colonia Civica Augusta*, when it was embellished with splendid monuments. By the 8th century Brescia had recovered enough from the barbarian invasions to become the seat of a Lombard duchy under King Desiderius, whose daughter Ermengarda was sought in marriage by Charlemagne as the condition for the Emperor's crown. He later repudiated her, and the forlorn Ermengarda returned to Brescia to die in the Abbey of San Salvatore, founded by her mother.

In the 11th century Brescia joined the Lombard League against the tyranny of Frederick Barbarossa and produced the great Benedictine monk, Arnold of Brescia, who went to Rome to preach against the tyranny of possessions and the worldly materialism of the Church, only to be burned at the stake for his troubles by the Pope. Brescia itself was too tempting a prize to be left in peace by the region's thugs.

Power struggles began with the unspeakable Veronese Ezzelino da Romana in 1258 and ended with the detested Visconti in 1421, when the notables, weary of the game of musical chairs in their government, invited the Venetians to adopt the city. The Venetians were grateful to get it, for strategic reasons, and for the access it gave to the area's unusually pure iron deposits. By the 16th century Brescia had become Italy's major producer of firearms, and so indispensable to Venice that the Republic imposed emigration restrictions on Brescia almost as severe as those placed on the glass-makers of Murano.

Venetian rule not only brought a great measure of peace and prosperity to the town, but initiated an artistic flowering as well. The Brescian Vincenzo Foppa (1485–1566) was a key figure in the Lombard Renaissance, whose monumental paintings were among the first to depict a single, coherent atmosphere. Towards the end of the century, Girolamo Romanino (1485–1566) synthesized Lombard and Venetian schools, while his contemporary Moretto da Brescia (1498–1554) was an ardent student of Titian and contributed the first Italian full-length portrait. His star pupil was Moroni of Bergamo. Recently, a forgotten painter, Giacomo Antonio Ceruti (1698–1767), has been the centre of interest for his realist, unromanticized genre paintings of Brescia's humble, demented and down-and-out—a rather unique subject for the place and time.

Getting Around

Brescia is the main transport hub for western Lombardy and Lake Garda, a major **road** junction as the meeting-point of the A4 Turin-Venice *autostrada* and the A21 from the south.

It is also on the main Milan-Venice **rail** line, 55 minutes from Milan, an hour from Verona, and less to Desenzano del Garda, the main station on Lake Garda. There are also frequent services to Bergamo (1 hour) and Lecco (2 hours); to Cremona (just over an hour); and to Parma via Piadena (2 hours). For FS rail information, call ✆ (030) 37961. Another, regional, railway line wends its way north along the east shore of Lake Iseo and then through the mountains to Edolo in the Val Camonica (2½ hours).

There is an even more extensive **bus** network, with frequent links to the towns of Lakes Garda and Iseo and less frequently to Idro; also to Turin and Milan, Padua and the Euganean Hills, Marostica, Bassano del Grappa, and Belluno; to Trento via Riva and to the resorts of Pinzolo and Madonna di Campiglio in Trentino, as well as to all points within the province. For information, call ✆ (030) 44061.

The **bus and railway stations** are located next to each other just south of the city centre on Viale Stazione. Bus C connects them to the centre, or you can walk there in 10 minutes up the Corso Martiri della Libertà.

Tourist information

Corso Zanardelli 38, ✆ (030) 293284, near the central Piazza del Duomo.

The Central Squares

Hurry, as the Brescians do, through the deathly pale and grim **Piazza Vittoriale**, designed in 1932 by Marcello Piacentini, a Fascist square as heavy-handed as Giorgio Terragni's **Guardia di Finanza** building in Como is as innovative and airy. Duck behind its varicoloured post office, and enter into a far more benign display of power in Brescia's Venetian-style **Piazza della Loggia**, the city's most elegant square. It has two fine loggias—one belonging to the Venetian Renaissance **Monte di Pietà Vecchia** (1489), and the other to the three-arched building known simply as the **Loggia**, an almost frilly confection designed in part by Sansovino and Palladio, the greatest Renaissance architects of the Veneto. Another remainder of the Serenissima is the **Torre dell'Orologio**, a copy of the one in St Mark's Square, complete with two bell-ringing figures on top.

Looming up behind the clock tower is the third-highest dome in Italy, the pearl-white, green-lead-roofed crown of the **Duomo**, built in 1602 by Gianbattista Lantana. From the **Piazza del Duomo** itself, however, the dome is hidden by a high, marble false front, its upper section as insubstantial as the wooden façades of a frontier town. Over the door a bust of Brescia's great Cardinal Querini 'winks mischievously, as if inviting the faithful to enter'. You should take him up on it, not so much for the few paintings by Romanino (by the bishop's throne) and Moretto that try to warm the cold interior, as to visit the adjacent **Duomo Vecchio** (*open April–Sept 9–12, 3–7.30, Wed–Mon*). Built in the 11th century over the ruins of the ancient Basilica of San Filastrio and the ancient Roman baths, the singular cathedral may well be the only one in Italy designed in the shape of a top hat, low and rotund, with a massive cylindrical tower rising from its centre, supported by eight pillars. Inside its simple form is broken only by a 15th-century raised choir. The altarpiece, an *Assumption* by Moretto, is one his greatest works. The crypt of San Falastrio, the only part of the ancient church to survive, contains a mixed bag of Roman and early medieval columns, and mosaics from the Roman baths. Several medieval bishops are entombed around the walls, most impressively Bishop Mernardo Maggi in his sarcophagus of 1308; the cathedral treasure contains two precious 11th-century relics—the *Stauroteca*, a reliquary box containing a titbit of the True Cross, and the banner once borne on the *Carroccio* (sacred ox cart) of the Brescian armies.

Just behind the new cathedral, on Via Mazzini 1, you can visit the **Biblioteca Queriniana**, containing the 18th-century collection of rare books and manuscripts compiled by Cardinal Querini (*open 8.30–12, 2–6, Tues–Fri, Sun; 8.30–12 Sun*), including the 6th-century 'Purple Evangeliary' and Eusebius' 11th-century Concordances of the Gospels; the cardinal is said to have snubbed the Vatican library in order to favour his own collection. On the other side of the Duomo, the 12th-century **Broletto** was the civic centre prior to the construction of the Loggia; its formidable tower, the **Pegol**, predates it by a century.

Roman Brixia

From behind the Broletto, take a right on to the ancient *Decumanus Maximus*, now the Via dei Musei, which soon leads to the heart of the old Roman city and the ruins of its forum in the **Piazza del Foro**. Looming above are the mighty columns of the **Capitoline Temple** (*open 9–12.30, 2–5, Tues–Sun; adm*), erected by the Emperor Vespasian in AD 73 and preserved for posterity by a medieval mud-slide that covered it until its discovery in 1823. In 1955 an earlier, Republican-era Capitoline temple was discovered beneath Vespasian's, with unusual mosaics of natural stone.

The Capitoline Temple is divided into three *cellae*, which were probably dedicated to the three principle Roman deities—Jupiter, Juno, and Minerva. They are filled with the inscriptions, tombstones and mosaics of the **Civico Museo Romano**—a considerable collection thanks to the foresight of the 1485 municipal council, which forbade the sale or transport of antiquities outside Brescia. The museum's best treasures, however, are upstairs, and include a 6-foot bronze Winged Victory, who, without the object she once held, seems to be snapping her fingers in a dance step. She, and six gilded bronze busts of emperors, were found during the excavations of the temple. There's a gilt bronze figurine of a prisoner, believed to be the great Gaulish chief Vercingetorix, a beautiful Greek amphora from the 6th century BC, and a facsimile of the fascinating 25ft-long Peutringer Map of Vienna, itself a 12th-century copy of a Roman road map.

Next to the temple is the unexcavated *cavea* of the **Roman Theatre**, while further down the Via dei Musei stands the most important complex of Lombard Brescia, the **Abbey of San Salvatore**, founded in the 8th century and disbanded at the end of the 18th. Its church of Santa Giulia, added in the 16th century, and the 8th century Basilica of San Salvatore, have been restored to house Brescia's **Museo Civico**. San Salvatore is interesting for the fragments of its lovely stucco decoration, in the same style as Cividale del Friuli's 8th-century Tempietto Lombardo. The old nunnery contains a **Museum of Modern Art**, Via Monti 9 (*open 4–7pm Thurs–Sun; adm*) while Santa Giulia houses the

Museum of Christian Art (*under restoration; for visiting times call © 44327*), a magnificent collection with two exceptional masterworks. One is the 8th-century Lombard *Cross of Desiderius*, studded with 212 gems and cameos, including one from the 4th century of a Roman woman with her two children, all peering warily into the approaching Dark Ages; the Brescians like to believe it is the great Galla Placidia of Ravenna. The other treasure is a 4th-century ivory coffer called the *Lipsanoteca*, adorned with beautiful bas-reliefs of scriptural scenes. One of the lovely 5th-century ivory diptychs originally belonged to the father of the philosopher Boethius. Lombard jewellery, medieval art and Renaissance medals round out the collection.

The Cydnean Hill

The lyric poet Catullus, who considered Brixia the mother of his native Verona, was the first to mention the Cydnean hill that rises up behind the Via dei Musei. This was the core of Gaulish and early Roman Brixia—if you take Via Piamarta from Santa Giulia you'll pass by the ruins of the city's one surviving **Roman gate**, as well as the attractive 1510 **San Pietro in Oliveto**, named after the ancient silvery olive grove that surrounds the church.

Up on top are the imposing walls of the medieval **Castello**, with its round 14th-century **Mirabella Tower**, built on a Roman foundation. There's a small children's zoo in the castle garden, a dull Risorgimento museum (*open 9–12.30, 2–5, Tues–Sun; adm*), and the recently remodelled **Luigi Marzoli Museum of Arms** (*open June–Sept 10–12.45, 2–5, Tues–Sun; Oct–Mar 9–12.45, 2–6, Tues–Sun; adm*), one of the country's most extensive collections of Brescia's bread-and-butter industry.

The Pinacoteca

From the Capitoline Temple Via F. Crispi descends to the Via Carlo Cattaneo; at No.3, in the Piazza Labus near the intersection, you can make out the columns and lintels of the ancient Roman **Curia**, imprinted like a fossil in the wall of a house.

Further down, Via Crispi opens up into the Piazza Moretto, site of the **Galleria Tosio-Martinengo** (*open 9–12.30, 2–5, Tues–Sun; adm*), Brescia's main art repository. This houses a fine collection of the local school, including paintings by Foppa, Moretto (his *Salome* is a portrait of the great Roman courtesan-poetess Tullia d'Aragona), Romanino, Moroni, and the later Ceruti, as well as a painting by Lorenzo Lotto and two early works by Raphael—a not altogether wholesome, beardless *Redeemer* and a lovely *Angel*.

From the gallery Via Moretto will take you back to the centre and the busy shops under the porticoes of Via Mazzini and Corso Zanardelli.

The West Side

In the neighbourhoods west of the Piazza della Loggia and the Corso Martiri della Libertà there are a handful of monuments worth a look if you have an hour to spare. Just west of the Via S. Faustino (which leads north from the Piazza della Loggia) there are two unusual churches—**San Faustino in Riposo**, a cylindrical, steep-roofed drum of a church from the 12th century (near the intersection with Via dei Musei), and further up, the 14th-century **Santa Maria del Carmine**, crowned with a set of Mongol-like pinnacles; it contains frescoes by Foppa and a 15th-century terracotta Deposition group.

Just off the Corso G. Mameli (the western extension of Via dei Musei) **San Giovanni** is a Renaissance church with good works by Moretto and the Bolognese painter Francia. Further along the corso stands the giant **Torre Palata**, a survivor from the rough and tumble 13th century, with a travesty of a 16th-century fountain like a bunion on its foot. From here Via della Pace heads south to the venerable 13th-century **San Francesco** with frescoes, and the nearby (at the intersection of Corso Martiri) **Santa Maria dei Miracoli** with a fine, ornate Renaissance façade. Further south, off the Corso Martiri on Via Bronzetti, the 18th-century **Santi Nazaro e Celso** houses a 1522 polyptych by Titian, portraying a *Risen Christ* in the central panel; as is often the case, Titian's care to produce the last word in emotional realism in his religious art goes overboard into a numbing vision of spiritual banality.

Brescia ✆ (030–)   ***Where to Stay***

Brescia's hotels cater mainly to business clients, and its best hotels are comfortable if not inspiring.

★★★★★ **Vittoria**, Via X Giornate 20, ✆ 280061, fax 280065, (very expensive). The city's premier hotel, which has everything one would expect— large, sumptuous rooms, palatial bathrooms of French *Rosa* marble, banqueting suites, conference facilities and liberal use of marble and chandeliers throughout. It is, though, chilly and a bit soulless, due no doubt to its severe Fascist-era architecture.

★★★★ **Master**, Via L. Apollonio 72, ✆ 399037, fax 3701331, (expensive). Near the centre by the castle, this hotel also has some of the best rooms in town, all with TV and other facilities.

★★★★ **Ambasciatori**, Via Crocifissa di Rosa 92, ✆ 308461, fax 381883, (moderate). A bit further out of the centre, this very modern hotel with a garage is a good bet for drivers; it also has very good, air-conditioned rooms, all with private bath and TV.

★★★ **Cristallo**, Via Stazione 12, ✆ 3772468, fax 3772615, (moderate). An adequate albeit nondescript place near the station.

★★ **Astron**, Via Togni 14, ✆ 48220, (inexpensive). Another very pleasant option, with clean, simple rooms at a nice price.

Brescians are not known for their cooking, and in fact are looked upon as rather stolid conservatives at the table. Kid is a popular item on the local menu, and the stews, meat on a skewer and polenta dishes the Brescians favour have been in vogue since the Renaissance. The city's most celebrated restaurant, **La Sosta**, Via San Martino della Dattaglia 20, © 295603 (expensive), is charmingly set in a 17th-century stable that has been stripped and made elegant, though a few horsey reminders may be seen in the pictures on the wall and the hitching rings on the pillars. The food, though good, is 'international' and a bit dull (*closed Mon, Aug*). In the same price range, you can have more imaginative dining but rather less atmosphere at **Alla Stretta**, Via Stretta 63, © 2002367, (expensive), with good fish and traditional Brescian meat dishes. If you're looking to fill up at the other end of the price scale, **Bersagliera**, Corso Magenta 38, near the tourist office, (inexpensive), is a good, cheap and popular pizzeria.

One of the best restaurants in the Brescia area is actually 10 kilometres away to the north, in Concesio, where the excellent **Miramonti L'Altro**, Via Crosette 34, © 2751063, (expensive), features a menu that delights both the gourmet and traditionalist, with specialities that include raw and smoked salmon, seasonal wild mushrooms, breast of duck in ginger, and kid Brescian-style. For afters, there's a fine array of cheeses, or one of Miramonti's great desserts (*closed Mon, Aug*).

Around Brescia

Besides Lakes Garda and Iseo there are a number of worthwhile excursions into the region's mountain valleys—as well as one to the south in the plain, to **Montirone** and the fine **Villa Lechi**, built in 1740 by Antonio Turbino, and little changed since the day when Mozart slept there. It has frescoes by Carlo Carloni and period furnishings, and the stables and park are equally well preserved.

To the north stretches the **Valtrompia**, a scenic agricultural valley. Its largest town, **Gardone Val Trompia**, was one of the main producers of firearms for Venice, and enjoyed the special protection of the Republic; it still makes hand-crafted sports rifles. North of Gardone the valley narrows as the road climbs to two fine summer resorts, **Bovegno** and **Collio**. The high mountains around the latter permit skiing in the winter. Beyond Collio a new road continues up to the scenic **Passo del Maniva** and over to the Passo di Croce Domini.

Long, narrow **Lake Idro** lies over the mountains from Collio, at the head of the Val Sabbia. Surrounded by rugged mountains and rural villages, it is the highest of the Lombard lakes, and one of the best for trout fishing. Named after the small resort town of **Idro**, its small sandy beaches are all low-key, family-oriented places. **Anfo** is another resort, while the most interesting lake settlement is **Bagolino**, on the trout-filled River Caffaro, with its peaceful medieval streets and the 15th-century church of **San Rocco**, frescoed in the 1400s by Da Cemmo. From Lake Idro you can continue up the Chiese river into Trentino's Val Giudicarie, towards Tione.

Lake Garda

The Italian lakes culminate in Garda, the largest (48km long, and 16km across at its widest point) and most dramatic, the Riviera of the Dolomites. With the profile of a tall-hatted witch, its wild and romantic shores have enchanted the Romans, who knew it as *Lacus Benacus.* If the waters of Lake Como are mingled with memories of the two Plinys, Garda's shores recall two of Italy's greatest poets of pure passion: ancient Rome's tragic, lovelorn Catullus and that modern fire-hazard, Gabriele D'Annunzio. For chilblained travellers from the north, its Mediterranean olives, vines and lemon groves, its slender cypress and exotic palm trees have long signalled the beginning of their dream Italy. No tourist office could concoct a more scintillating Mediterranean oasis to stimulate what the Icelanders call 'a longing for figs', that urge to go south.

Perhaps it's because Lake Garda is more 'Italian' that it seems less infected by the maiden-auntiness of its more northerly, Swissified sisters. Less stuffy and status-conscious, it is the most popular lake, attracting a wide range of visitors, from beach bums to package tourists, and sailors and windsurfers come to test their mettle on Garda's unusual winds, first mentioned by Virgil: the *sover* which blows from the north from midnight and through the morning, and the *ora*, which blows from the south in the afternoon and evening. Storms are not uncommon, but on the other hand the breezes are delightfully cool in the summer. In the winter Garda enjoys a mild climate, less oppressed by clammy fogs and mists than the other lakes. Although services are at a minimum, winter is an ideal time to visit, when the jagged peaks of its shore shimmer with snow and you can better take in the voluptuous charms that brought visitors to its shores in the first place.

Getting Around

There are two **train stations** at the southern end of Lake Garda, at Desenzano and Peschiera, both of which are also landings for the lake's **hydrofoils** (*aliscafi*) and **steamers**. **Buses** from Brescia, Trento and Verona go to their respective shores; Desenzano, the principal starting point for Lake Garda, is served by buses from Brescia, Verona and Mantua, and two exits from the *autostrada* A4. **Drivers** going to the northwest side of the lake (above Salò) and coming from the west should leave the A4 earlier, shortly after Brescia, and take the SS45.

Other local bus lines run up and down the road that winds around the lake shores—a marvel of Italian engineering, called *La Gardesana*, Occidentale (SS45) on the west and Orientale (SS249) on the east. In summer, however, their scenic splendour sometimes pales before the sheer volume of holiday traffic.

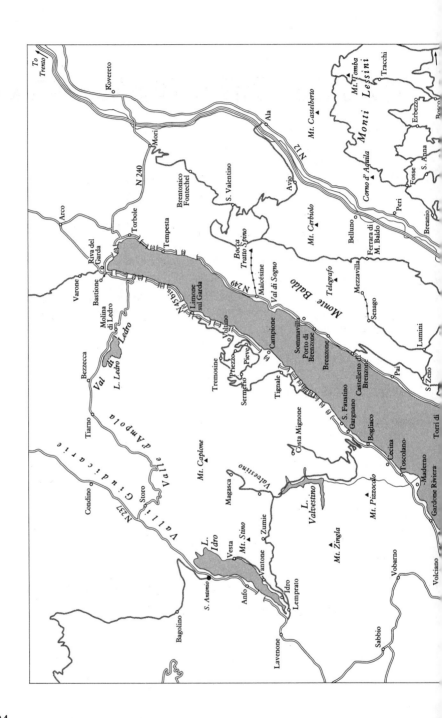

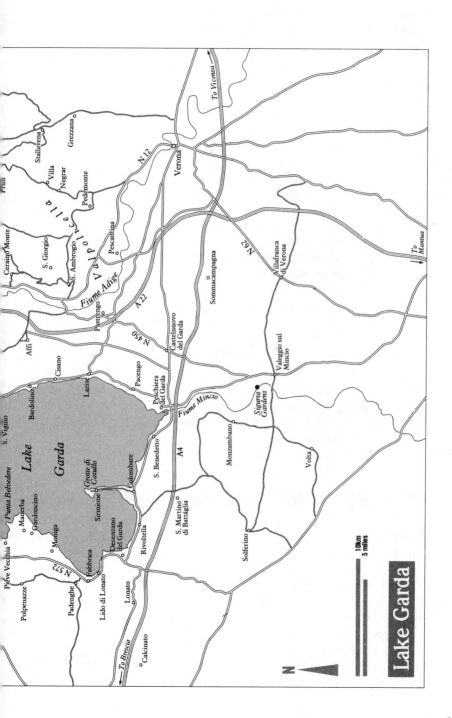

Lake Garda

10km
5 miles

N

All **boat services** on the lake are operated by *Navigazione sul Lago di Garda*, Piazza Matteotti 2, Desenzano, ✆ (030) 9141321, where you can pick up a timetable; the tourist offices have them as well. The one **car ferry** crosses from Maderno to Torri; between Desenzano and Riva there are several hydrofoils a day, calling at various ports (2 hours the full trip), as well as the more frequent and leisurely steamers (4½ hours). Services are considerably reduced in the off season, from October to March. Full fare from Desenzano to Riva on steamer is L14,200, and on the hydrofoil L19,200. There are also regular afternoon cruises from July to mid-September, calling at various different points.

Tourist Information

While Lake Garda's west shore belongs to the province of Brescia in Lombardy, its northern tip is in Trentino and its eastern shore is in Venetia, in the province of Verona. This is a product of history, not of any plan to divvy up tourist cash among regions, and each region parochially often fails to acknowledge that Lake Garda exists beyond its own boundaries; their maps often leave the opposite shores blank, if they draw them in at all. Be sure to check area codes when telephoning. However, an excellent joint publication that does cover the whole lake, and is available from any of the tourist offices around the shore, is *Garda Pocket*, which has extensive listings of museum opening times, sports facilities (riding, windsurfing, golf, tennis, and so on), discos, cinemas, boat times, and a bit of history about the area—all in English.

There are tourist offices in all the main lake resorts. Some of the more important are those in **Desenzano del Garda**, at Porto Vecchio 27, ✆ (030) 9141510, fax 9144209; **Sirmione**, at Viale Marconi 2, ✆ (030) 916114, fax 916222; **Gardone Riviera**, Corso Repubblica, ✆ (0365) 20347; **Gargnano**, at Piazza Feltrinelli 2, ✆ (0365) 71222; **Limone sul Garda**, Piazzale A. De Gaspari, ✆ (0365) 954781, fax 954355; **Riva del Garda**, Giardini di Porta Orientale 8, ✆ (0464) 554444, fax 520 308; and in **Arco**, at Via delle Palme 1, ✆ (0464) 516161, fax 532353.

Garda's South and West Shores

Desenzano and Solferino

Desenzano del Garda, on a wide gulf dotted with beaches, is the lake's largest town and its main gateway (if you arrive by train, a bus will take you to the centre). Life in Desenzano is centred around its port cafés, and a dramatic statue of Sant'Angela, foundress of the Ursuline Order. Originally a settlement of pile dwellings, Desenzano was a popular holiday resort of the Romans, and one of their **villas** has been excavated on Via Crocifisso, revealing colourful mosaics from the 4th century and a range of artefacts now kept in the small museum on the site (*villa and museum open April–Sept 9am–6.30pm Tues–Sun; Oct–Mar 9am–5pm Tues–Sun; adm*). Nearby in the parish church there's an unusual *Last Supper* by Gian Domenico Tiepolo.

As well as Lake Garda, Desenzano is also the base for visiting the low, war-scarred 'Risorgimento' hills to the south. The two most important battles occurred on the same day, 24 June 1859, when Napoleon III defeated Emperor Franz Joseph at **Solferino** and King Vittorio Emanuele defeated the Austrian right wing at **San Martino della Battaglia**, 8km away. It was the beginning of the end for the proud Habsburgs in Italy, but the Battle of Solferino had another consequence—the terrible suffering of the wounded so appalled the Swiss Henry Dunant that he formed the idea of founding the Red Cross. At San Martino you can climb the lofty **Torre Monumentale** (*open 8.30–1, 2–5, Wed–Mon*), erected in 1893, which containsmementoes from the battle. Solferino is marked by an old tower of the Scaligeri of Verona, the **Spia d'Italia**, with a collection of uniforms; there's a battle museum by the church of **San Piero**, containing 7000 graves, and a memorial to Dunant and the Red Cross, erected in 1959 (*hours same as for the San Martino tower*).

Perhaps even more important was the battle averted in these hills at the end of the Roman empire. Attila the Hun, having devastated northeast Italy, was on his way to Rome when he met Pope St Leo I here. The pope, with Saints Peter and Paul as his translators, informed Attila that if he should continue to Rome he would be stricken by a fatal nose-bleed, upon which the terrible Hun turned aside, sparing central Italy.

Sirmione

> *Sweet Sirmio! thou, the very eye*
> *Of all peninsulas and isles,*
> *That in our lakes of silver lie,*
> *Or sleep enwreathed by Neptune's smiles*

So gushed Catullus, Rome's greatest lyric poet, born in Verona in 84 BC, only to die some 30 years later in the fever of a broken heart. When he wasn't haunting the Palatine home of his fickle mistress, 'Lesbia', he is said to have visited the villa his family kept, like many well-to-do Romans, out on the narrow 4km-long peninsula of **Sirmione** which pierces Lake Garda like a pin, just over 90m across at its narrowest point.

Sirmione is the most visually striking resort on the lake, especially at the lovely **Grotte di Catullo**, entwined with ancient olive trees on the tip of the rocky promontory—romantic ruins with a capital R, not of Catullus' villa, but of a Roman bath complex (Sirmione is famous even today for its thermal spa). The views across the lakeare magnificent; there's also a small **antiquarium** on the site, with mosaics and frescoes (*open 9am–sunset Tues–Sun; adm*).

The medieval centre of Sirmione is dominated by one of the most memorable of Italian castles, the fairytale **Castello Scaligero** (*open April–Oct 9–1, 9–6; adm*), built by Mastino I della Scala of Verona in the 13th century, and surrounded almost entirely by water. There's not much to see inside, but fine views from its swallowtail battlements. Also worth a look is the ancient Romanesque church of **San Pietro in Mavino**, with 13th-century frescoes. Cars are not permitted over the bridge into the town of Sirmione, and the best swimming is off the rocks on the west side of the peninsula.

Salò

From Sirmione the steamer passes the lovely headlands of Manerba and Punta San Fermo and the **Island of Garda**, the lake's largest, where there was a monastery once visited by St Francis. Long in ruins, it provided the base for a monumental 19th-century Venetian-Gothic-style palace, now owned by the Borghese family, one of whom, Scipione, made the famous drive from Peking to Paris in the early days of the automobile.

Salò (the Roman *Salodium*) enjoys one of the most privileged locations on the lake, but is best known internationally for having given its name to *Il Duce*'s last dismal stand, the puppet 'Republic of Salò' of 1943–45. It also has, though, a number of fine buildings, including a late Gothic **Cathedral** with a Renaissance portal of 1509, and paintings within by Romanino and Moretto da Brescia, and a golden polyptych by Paolo Veneziano. There's also a small museum, the **Museo del Nastro Azzuro**, containing information on the history of the region. **L'Ateneo**, in the Renaissance Palazzo Fantoni, contains a collection of 13th-century manuscripts and early printed books. North of Salò begins the **Brescia Riviera**, famous for its exceptional climate and exotic trees and flowers.

Götterdämmerung, Italian-style

Italy's period of paralysis and confusion after the Allied landings in July 1943 was one of the tragedies of the war. The King and the Fascist Grand Council had deposed and arrested Mussolini, and not long after signed an armistice with the Allies. But they did nothing to defend Italy from the inevitable, and while the political and military leaders dithered and blundered in Rome, German divisions poured over the Alps to seize control of the country. The Italians found themselves caught in the middle, and their soldiers were faced with a choice of joining the Nazis, a risky desertion, or prison and forced labour.

Mussolini didn't proclaim the Italian Social Republic; the order to do it came from Hitler's field headquarters in East Prussia. Hitler sent an SS commando team in a tiny plane to rescue the *Duce* from the ski hotel in the Abruzzo where the Rome government had stashed him. (They might have just sent a car, so poorly was he guarded, but Hitler had just at that time decided on a major propaganda campaign to glorify the SS, and the business was built up into a heroic exploit—fooling most historians ever since.) The Nazis cleaned Mussolini up and got him a shiny new uniform; they took him up north to meet Hitler and trotted him past the newsreel cameras, and then found a nice lakeside villa for him in the sleepy resort of Salò, which they had decided upon for the capital of the new puppet republic. In the next villa over lived the German ambassador.

Salò was a place where the war seemed far away. Wealthy Milanese came whenever they could; their sons, who had somehow managed to avoid conscription, played tennis and lounged in the cafés in their white jackets. Some of the Republic's ministries were occupying other villas around the lake, but there was little work for them to do; the Germans were running everything. The SS had a strong presence around Milan and the lakes, busying themselves in earnest with the round-up of Jews that began in October '43; when there wasn't enough room on the train they simply shot those left over and threw the bodies into Lake Maggiore.

For the fortunates back in Salò, life before 5pm meant a dreary, unavoidable bit of attention to business. At one meeting, Mussolini and his men demanded aid for the thousands of Italians in the north injured or made homeless by the war; the German ambassador looked at the figures and politely noted that there were more casualties, due to the bombings, in his own city. After 5pm, all could retreat into a dream-world of pleasure; the Germans held rather noisy, drug-fuelled orgies, with car-loads of girls brought in from Milan, while the Italian officials conducted more discreet liaisons with their mistresses in their villas. Mussolini met his Clara Petacci every day at five o'clock in a room of his villa called the Sala dello Zodiaco, with constellations painted on the ceiling. The *Duce* told somebody that she was a pain, always bothering him about jobs or favours for members of her family. Occasionally there would be spectacles to relieve the routine and feed the newsreel cameras: carefully staged political rallies, or parades of German troops and Fascist die-hards, the 'Black Brigades', singing as they passed the reviewing stand the hit tune of the day, 'Auf Wiedersehen'.

Towards the end, in 1945, the atmosphere crossed over into the truly surreal. Mussolini was losing his grip, and babbled to his few confidants about the secret weapons the Nazis were getting ready—an atomic bomb, and V-rockets numbered all the way up to V-9 and V-10; Hitler had told him all about them. The Italians would do even better; Marconi had invented an electronic Death Ray before he died, Mussolini said, and he had the plans in his pocket. And if the worst happened there was the Fascists' last redoubt, up in the mountainous Valtellina, where he would lead 30,000 true believers in a fight to the death, the memory of which would live forever (such a project was actually started, but most of the men in the Valtellina eventually got tired of waiting for the *Duce* and went home). In January 1945, Mussolini gave his last public speech at the Teatro Lirico in Milan. He spoke gravely of the challenges facing the 'revolution', and at the end received tumultuous applause when he promised a steadfast determination that would surely lead to final victory. Cheering crowds thronged the streets outside to see him off.

By that time, there were some 300,000 *partigiani* operating in the north, and many rural areas were already free. On April 25, Mussolini arranged a meeting with resis-tance leaders at the archbishop's palace in Milan. He wanted to cut a deal; they offered him a fair trial. The Duce's bags were already packed, but he hesitated long enough near the Swiss border for the resistance to win over the border guards. On April 28, he wrapped himself in a discarded Luftwaffe overcoat and marched off, Clara by his side, with a column of retreating Germans on the road towards Austria; the *partigiani* caught up with him and shot him and Clara near Dongo, on Lake Como, and then took him back to Milan for his final public appearance, dangling upside-down from the roof of a petrol station on Piazzale Loreto.

Gardone Riviera has long been the most fashionable resort on the Brescia Riviera, if not in the whole of Lake Garda, ever since 1880 when a German scientist noted the almost uncanny consistency of its climate. One place that profits most from this mildness is the

Il Vittoriale

loveliest sight in Gardone, the **Giardino Botanico Hruska** (*open April–Sept 9am–6pm; adm*), with an enormous range of exotic blooms growing between imported tufa cliffs and artificial streams.

Above the garden it's a short walk to Gardone's most confounding sight, **Il Vittoriale**, the last home of Gabriele D'Annunzio (1863–1938). The house, a luxurious Liberty-style villa designed by Gian Carlo Maroni, was presented to the extravagant writer by Mussolini in 1925, ostensibly as a reward to the poet from a grateful nation for his patriotism and heroic efforts during the First World War, but also as a sop with which the *Duce* hoped to get this unpredictable figure out of the way and keep him quiet. D'Annunzio dubbed the villa, formerly owned by a German family, 'Il Vittoriale' after Italy's victory over Austria in 1918, and began to redecorate it and pull up its lovely garden, creating perhaps the world's most remarkable pile of kitsch.

More Italian than any other Italian

Gabriele D'Annunzio was a poor boy, born Gaetano Rapagnetta in the Abruzzo, who became the greatest Italian poet of his generation, but not one who was convinced that the pen was mightier than the sword; a fervent right-wing nationalist, he was one of the chief warmongers urging Italy to intervene in World War I. Later he led his 'legionaries' in the famous unauthorized invasion of Fiume, which, though promised to Italy before its entrance into the war, was to be ceded by the Allies to Yugoslavia. D'Annunzio instantly became a national hero, stirring up a diplomatic furore before coming home. For Mussolini, however, the still-popular old nationalist was a loose cannon who eventually became an acute embarrassment, and he decided to pension him off into gilded retirement on Lake Garda, correctly calculating that the gift of the villa would appeal to the great man's delusions of grandeur.

Luigi Barzini has described D'Annunzio as 'perhaps more Italian than any other Italian' for his love of gesture, spectacle, and theatrical effect—what can you say about a man who would announce that he had once dined on roast baby? Yet for the Italians of his generation, no matter what their politics, he exerted a powerful influence in thought and fashion; he seemed a breath of fresh air, a new kind of 'superman', hard and passionate yet capable of writing exquisite, intoxicating verse; the spiritual father of the futurists, ready to destroy the old bourgeois *Italia vile* of museum curators and parish priests and create in its stead a great modern power, the 'New Italy'. He lived his life of total exhibitionism, according to the old slogan of an American brewery, 'with all the gusto he could get'—extravagantly, decadently and beyond his means, at every moment the trend-setting, aristocratic aesthete, with his borzois and passionate, melodramatic affairs with the actress 'the Divine' Eleanora Duse and innumerable other loves (preferably duchesses). Apparently he thought the New Italians should all be equally eccentric and clever, and disdained the corporate state of the Fascists.

D'Annunzio made Il Vittoriale his personal egomaniacal monument, probably suspecting that one day the gaping hordes would come tramping through to marvel at his cleverness and taste. Instead, he managed to leave posterity one of the most hilarious clutter bins of all time. Unfortunately the guides only speak Italian, so the following is a summary to fill in some of the gaps if you don't.

The tour begins with what must be called a 'cool reception' room for guests D'Annunzio disliked—it's austere and formal, compared to the comfy one for favourites. When Mussolini came to call he was entertained in the former; D'Annunzio, it is said, escorted *Il Duce* over to the mirror and made him read the inscription he had placed above: 'Remember that you are of glass and I of steel.' Perhaps you can make it out if your eyes have had time to adjust to the gloom. Like Aubrey Beardsley and many of the horror-movie characters played by Vincent Price, D'Annunzio hated the daylight and had the windows painted over, preferring low electric lamps.

The ornate organs in the music room and library were played by his young American wife, who gave up a promising musical career to play for his ears alone. His bathroom, with 2000 pieces of bric-à-brac, somehow manages to have space for the tub; the whole house is packed solid with a feather-duster's nightmare of art and junk. In his spare bedroom, adorned with leopard skins, you can see the cradle-coffin he liked to lie in to think cosmic thoughts. He made the entrance to his study low so all would have to bow as they entered; here he kept a bust of Duse, but covered, to keep her memory from distracting him. The dining room, with its bright movie-palace sheen, is one of the more delightful rooms. D'Annunzio didn't care much for it, and left his guests here to dine on their own with his pet tortoise, which he had had embalmed in bronze after the creature expired of indigestion, to remind the company of the dangers of overeating.

In the adjacent auditorium hangs the biplane D'Annunzio used to fly over Vienna in the War, while out in the garden the prow of the battleship *Puglia* from the Fiume adventure juts out mast and all through a copse of cypresses. Walk above this to the **Mausoleum** on its hill, a disturbing, bizarre and alien monument to delusions of grandeur, the white travertine stone glaring on bright sunny days. Within three concentric stone circles the sarcophagi of legionary captains pay court to the plain tomb of D'A himself, raised up on columns high above the others like a pagan sun-king, closer to his dark star than anyone else, the whole in hellish contrast to the Mausoleum's enchanting setting over the lake.

The Vittoriale is *open 9–12.30, 2.30–6.30, Tues–Sun; adm exp.* There's an option of buying a ticket only for the uninteresting museum and grounds; try to arrive at 9am to avoid the crowds and tour buses. In the summer there are performances of D'Annunzio's plays in the outdoor theatre.

Toscolano-Maderno and Gargnano

The single *comune* of Toscolano-Maderno has one of the finest beaches on Lake Garda, a fine 9-hole golf course, the car ferry to Torri, and the distinction of having been the site of *Benacum*, the main Roman town on the lake. Toscolano had a famous printing press in the 15th century, and was the chief manufacturer of nails for Venice's galleys. Most of the Roman remains, however, have been incorporated into the fine 12th-century church of **Sant'Andrea** in Maderno, restored in the 16th century by St Charles Borromeo. **Gargnano** seems more of a regular town than a resort, though it was from here, in a villa owned by the publisher Feltrinelli (whose chain of bookstores are today a blessing to the English-speaking traveller in Italy), that Mussolini ruled the Republic of Salò. The main sight in town is the 13th-century Franciscan church and cloister; in the latter the columns are adorned with carvings of lemons and oranges, a reminder of the ancient tradition that the Franciscans were the first to cultivate citrus fruits in Europe.

North of Gargnano the lake narrows and the cliffs come close to the shore; here the Gardesana road pierces tunnel after tunnel like a needle as it hems through some of the most striking scenery along the lake. An equally splendid detour is to turn off at **Campione**, a tiny hamlet huddled under the cliffs, along the old military road for **Tremósine**, atop a 300m precipice that dives down sheer into the blue waters below; from the top there are views that take in the entire lake. The road from Tremósine rejoins the lake and La Gardesana at the next town along the lake, **Limone sul Garda**. Although it seems obvious that Limone was so named because of its lemon groves, prominent in their neat rows of terraced white posts and trellises, scholars sullenly insist it was derived instead from the Latin *limen*. Nor is it true that Limone was the first place to grow lemons in Europe (the Arabs introduced them into Sicily and Spain), but none of that detracts from one of the liveliest resorts on the lake, with a beach over 3km long.

Riva del Garda

After Limone the lake enters into the Trentino region and reaches the charming town of Riva, snug beneath an amphitheatre of mountains. Riva first blossomed as a resort during the days of Austrian rule (1813–1918), when it was labelled the 'Southern Pearl on the Austro-Hungarian Riviera'. It is one of the best bases for exploring both the lake and the

Trentino mountains to the north. The centre of town is the Piazza III Novembre with its plain, 13th-century **Torre Apponale**; just behind it, surrounded by a natural moat, stands the sombre grey bulk of the 12th-century castle, the **Rocca**, housing a civic museum with local archaeological finds from the prehistoric settlement at Lake Ledro and from Roman Riva (*open 9–12, 2.30–6, Tues–Sun*). The early 17th-century **Church of the Inviolata** was built by an unknown but imaginative Portuguese architect with a fine gilt and stucco Baroque interior. A funicular (or a steep path) makes the ascent to the Venetian watchtower, the 1508 **Bastione**.

A number of pleasant excursions are possible from Riva, but one of the best is the closest, the **Cascata del Varone**, a lovely 87m waterfall in a tight gorge only 3km away, by the village of Varone (*opening times variable according to season; adm*). Another fine excursion is up over the exciting Ponale Road (N240) to **Lake Ledro**, noted not only for its scenery but also the remains of a Bronze Age settlement of lake dwellings, discovered in 1929; one has been reconstructed near the ancient piles around **Molina**, where there's also a museum with pottery, axes, daggers and amber jewellery recovered from the site (*open Mar–June, Sept–Nov 9–12, 3–6, daily; July, Aug 9–12, 3–7 daily*). From here you can continue to Lake Idro, through the shadowy narrow gorge of the **Valle d'Ampola**.

There are also several attractive small and unspoilt villages around Riva, including **Arco**, a small resort town under its castle-crowned rock, the former property of the cultured Counts of Arco. Their 16th-century palace, and the botanical garden once owned by the Archduke, are Arco's other sights. **Dro**, a little to the north in the Sarca valley, is near the small lakes of Cavedine and Toblino, and on the edge of the site of an ancient glacier that left behind a vast field of boulders when it thawed. Further on lies **Drena**, and the site of another of the Counts of Arco's castles. All of these villages make good bases for walks into the surrounding countryside. Maps are, as usual, available from local tourist offices.

Where to Stay

If you come to Garda in July or August without a reservation, it can mean big disappointment. For lower prices and more chance of a vacancy, try the small towns on the east shore; also check at the tourist offices for rooms in private homes. At least half-pension will be required in season at most hotels, and despite the mild climate most close up after October or November until March.

Sirmione

★★★★★ **Villa Cortine**, Via Grotte 12, ✆ (030) 9905890, fax 916390, (very expensive). For a total immersion in the peninsula's romance, this hotel cannot be surpassed, offering its guests perhaps the rarest amenity to be found in the town—tranquillity. Its enchanting, century-old Italian garden occupies almost a third of the entire peninsula, with exotic flora, venerable trees, statues and fountains running down to the water's edge. The neoclassical villa itself was built by an Austrian general, and was converted into a hotel in 1954, conserving its frescoed ceilings and elegant furnishings. The rooms are plush, the atmosphere perhaps a bit too exclusive, but it's ideal for a break from the real world, with private beach and dock, pool and tennis courts (*open April–Oct*).

★★★★★ **Grand Hotel Terme**, Via Marconi 7, ✆ (030) 916261, fax 916568, (very expensive). Another top choice in Sirmione, without quite the same atmosphere, right beside the castle, with a private beach, pool, gym and a full health and beauty treatment programme, as well as a lovely lakeside restaurant.

★★★★ **Hotel Eden**, Piazza Carducci 18, ✆ (030) 916481, fax 916483, (moderate). A less expensive but still very comfortable place to stay in Sirmione, housed in a medieval building in the centre that has been beautifully remodelled with fine marbles, and coordinated bedrooms with princely bathrooms, TV, and air-conditioning. Unusually, it does not have a restaurant. (*Open Mar–Oct.*)

★★★ **Catullo**, ✆ (030) 916181, (moderate). Another good place to stay in Sirmione, in the heart of the old town and refurbished in 1991, with good-sized rooms and bathrooms with beautiful views and all modern amenities.

★★ **Hotel Grifone**, near the Scaliger castle on Via delle Bisse 5, ✆ (030) 916014, (inexpensive). Although it's more attractive on the outside than in the rooms, this has a great location, and some of its rooms, all of which have baths, have lovely lake views. (*Open April–Oct.*)

★★ **Speranza**, ✆ (030) 916116, fax 916403, (inexpensive). All the fittings of a three-star hotel, including air-conditioning and marble bathrooms, but at significantly lower prices.

Salò

★★★★ **Laurin**, Viale Landi 9, ✆ (0365) 22022, fax 22382, (expensive). Although less glamorous than some of its neighbours, Salò has one of Lake Garda's loveliest hotels, this enchanting Liberty-style villa converted into a hotel in the 1960s, but retaining its elegant décor. The charming grounds include a swimming pool and beach access; all rooms have bath and TV. (*Open all year.*)

★★★★ **Duomo**, ✆ (0365) 21026, fax 21028, (expensive). The first-floor rooms are the ones to request—all lead out to a huge balcony, where lake-gazing can be appreciated to its fullest. The rooms are also big and modern, and there's a fine restaurant. (*Open all year.*)

★★★ **Benaco**, ✆ (0365) 20308, fax 20724, (moderate). A pleasant choice on the lake front which has modern rooms, all with bathroom, TV, phone and lovely lakeside views, and a good restaurant. (*Open all year.*)

★★★ **Vigna**, ✆ (0365) 520510, fax 520144, (moderate). This hotel has rooms that are none too individual, but comfortable and modern, and views that really steal the show. (*Open all year.*)

Gardone Riviera

★★★★ Grand Hotel, Via Zanardelli 72, ✆ (0365) 20261, fax 2269, (expensive). Further north, Gardone Riviera and its suburb Fasano Riviera have competing Grand Hotels, both old pleasure domes. When Gardone's contender was built in 1881, its 180 rooms made it one of the largest resort hotels in Europe. It is still recognised as one of Garda's landmarks, and its countless chandeliers glitter as brightly as when Churchill stayed there in the late forties. Almost all the palatial air-conditioned rooms look on to the lake, where guests can luxuriate on the garden terraces, or swim in the heated outdoor pool or off the private sandy beach. The dining room and delicious food match the quality of the rooms. (*Open mid-April–mid-Oct.*)

★★★★ Grand Hotel Fasano, ✆ (0365) 21051, (expensive). Fasano's alternative was built in the early 19th century as a Habsburg hunting palace and converted into a hotel around 1900. Surrounded by a large park, it's furnished almost entirely in Belle Epoque style; there are tennis courts, a heated pool, and private beach, and the restaurant is one of Lake Garda's best. (*Open May–Sept.*)

★★★★ Villa del Sogno, ✆ (0365) 290181, fax 290230, (very expensive). One of the best places to stay in Fasano, just outside Gardone, is its creator's 'Dream Villa' of the 1920s—done in grand Renaissance style. Although it's not on the lake, it has a private beach 5 minutes' walk away and a pool in its flower-filled garden. (*Open April–10 Oct.*)

★★★ Villa Fiordaliso, Via Zanardelli 132, ✆ (0365) 20158, fax 290011, (expensive). A fine turn-of-the-century hotel, where the historically minded can request (for a considerable price) the suite where Mussolini and his mistress Clara Petacci spent the last few weeks of their lives. Located in a serene park, with a private beach, it has only seven rooms, all finely equipped; it also boasts an elegant restaurant, featuring classic Lombard and Garda dishes. (*Open all year.*)

★★★ Monte Baldo, ✆ (0365) 20951, (moderate). A well-aged outward appearance hides a fully refurbished and very modern interior. It now has stylish rooms, most of them with bathroom, and the hotel also boasts a swimming pool and restaurant. (*Open April–Oct.*)

★★★ Bellevue, ✆ (0365) 20235, fax 290080, (inexpensive). Above the main road overlooking the lake, with a pretty garden sheltering it from the traffic. The rooms are modern, and all have private bath. (*Open Apr–10 Oct.*)

★ Pensione Hohl, ✆ (0365) 20160, (inexpensive). Half-way up the road that leads to Il Vittoriale is another former villa in a pleasant garden. None of the rooms has a bath, but they're quiet, and a steal in Gardone at under L60,000.

Gargnano

★★★ **Giulia** in Gargnano, ✆ (0365) 71022, fax 72774, (moderate). A hotel with a pure Victorian ambience, even if the furnishings are replicas; added attractions are its fine lake views, beach, and good food. All rooms have baths. (*Open April–15 Oct.*)

★★★ **Baia d'Oro**, ✆ (0365) 71171, fax 72568, (moderate). In Villa di Gargnano, just outside the main village of Gargnano, this is a small but charming old hotel on the lake front with an artistic inn-like atmosphere. It has a private beach, and picturesque terrace; all rooms have baths. (*Open 20 Mar–Oct.*)

Limone

★★★★ **Le Palme**, ✆ (0365) 954681, fax 954120, (moderate). Prices in Limone are not as high as in other resorts, and the town's best hotel is housed in a pretty Venetian villa, preserving much of its original charm alongside modern amenities. In the old centre of Limone, and named after its two ancient palm trees, it has a fine terrace and tennis courts, though unfortunately no beach. All 28 rooms have private baths. (*Open end Mar–Oct.*)

★★★ **Sogno del Benaco**, ✆ (0365) 954026, fax 954327, (inexpensive). Many of the lakeside hotels in Limone are large and ungainly, if inexpensive by Garda standards, but this is of a more reasonable size, and has fairly standard rooms at very reasonable prices. (*Open all year.*)

Riva del Garda

★★★★ **Hotel du Lac et du Parc**, Viale Rovereto 44, ✆ (0464) 520202, fax 555200, (very expensive). When German intellectuals from Nietzsche to Günter Grass have needed a little rest and relaxation in Italy they have for many decades flocked to Riva del Garda to check in at this spacious, airy and tranquil hotel set in a large lakeside garden. There are indoor and outdoor pools, a beach, sailing school, gym, sauna, and tennis courts. (*Open April–Oct.*)

★★★★ **Grand Hotel Riva**, Piazza Garibaldi 10, ✆ (0464) 521800, fax 552293, (expensive). Turn-of-the-century hotel, majestically positioned on the main square, with eighty-seven modern rooms looking out over the lake, and a rooftop restaurant which combines fine food with incomparable views. There is also a private beach. (*Open Mar–Oct.*)

★★★ **Hotel Sole**, Piazza III Novembre, ✆ (0464) 552686, fax 552811, (expensive). Right on the port in Riva's main square, this hotel has plenty of atmosphere and a beautiful terrace; most rooms have private baths and look out over the lake, though they vary widely in size and quality. (*Open all year.*)

★★★ **Centrale**, Piazza III Novembre 27, ✆ (0464) 552344, fax 552138, (moderate). One of the best of the many hotels in this category in Riva, beside the harbour, with fully equipped, spacious rooms and bathrooms.

- ★★★ **Portici**, Piazza III Novembre 19, ✆ (0464) 555400, fax 555453, (moderate). Almost as good as the Centrale, and slightly cheaper, in a nice position on the square, competely refurbished and with modern rooms all with bathrooms.

- ★ **Villa Minerva**, Viale Roma 40, ✆ (0464) 553031, (inexpensive). A good economy choice which is not far from the centre, very pleasant, and very popular. (*Open all year.*)

Riva also has a **youth hostel**, at Piazza Cavour 10, ✆ (0464) 554911, with beds for around L12,000 per night. (*Open Mar–Oct.*)

Eating Out

Sirmione

One of Italy's finest restaurants is near the Sirmione peninsula, at Lugana di Sirmione: the classy **Vecchia Lugana**, Via Lugana Vecchia, ✆ (030) 919012, (expensive). The menu changes four times a year to adapt with the changing seasons, and the food is exquisite, prepared with a light and wise touch—try the divine mousse of lake trout.

The elegant **Ristorante Grifone di Luciano**, ✆ (030) 916097, (moderate), which shares its ancient location with the Hotel Grifone (*see* above) serves simple but delicious fish and more at moderate prices. Another fine place to dine nearby with views that rival the food is the **Piccolo Castello**, Via Dante 7, ✆ (030) 916138, (moderate) facing the Scaliger *castello*, with fish and meat specialities from the grill.

Gargnano

In Gargnano is the celebrated **La Tortuga**, Via XXIV Maggio 5 (near the harbour), ✆ (0365) 71251, (expensive), a gourmet haven on Lake Garda whose specialities are delicate dishes based on seasonal ingredients and fish from the lake, perfectly prepared; there are also delicious vegetable soufflés, innovative meat courses, mouthwatering desserts and fresh fruit sherbets, and an excellent wine and spirits cellar. (*Closed Wed, and 3 weeks in July.*)

Salò

For a good, reasonably priced and traditional meal try the **Trattoria alla Campagnola**, Via Brunati 11, ✆ (0365) 22153, (moderate). Garden-fresh vegetables are served with every dish, the pasta is homemade, and they make great use of wild mushrooms in season.

Entertainment and Nightlife

Riva enjoys quite a hectic nightlife in season, much of it geared towards the hordes of Brits and Germans that invade the town. Many can be found in the **Lord Nelson Pub**, Viale Dante 91, ✆ (0464) 55412, with its fairly authentic pub interior that becomes a disco in summer. For a more sedate evening's entertainment there are a couple of pleasant piano bars: **Bellavista**, Via Lungolago Verona, with a fairly calm atmosphere, except on Sunday evenings when karaoke takes over, and **Cantina Marchetti**, Piazza Marchetti, which stays open till 4am. The main place in town to get on down is **Tiffany** (*open all year 8pm–3am daily; adm L15–20,000*), in a lovely position in the gardens leading down to the lake. There's also live music on most Fridays.

The East Shore: Riva to Peschiera

Tourist Information

There are tourist offices along the eastern side of the lake in **Malcésine**, at Via Capitanato 6/8, © (045) 7400044, fax 7401633; **Torri del Benaco**, Via Gardesana 5, © (045) 7225120; **Garda**, Lungolago Regina Adelaide 3, © (045) 7255194, fax 7256720; **Bardolino**, at Piazza Matteotti 53, © (045) 7210078, fax 7210872; and in **Peschiera del Garda**, at Piazza Bettelloni, © (045) 7550381.

Torbole

The northern part of the east shore is dominated by the chain of **Monte Baldo**, rising up over **Torbole** at the mouth of the Sacra, the main river flowing into Lake Garda. Torbole is a pleasant resort, but it's also famous in the annals of naval history. In 1437, during a war with the Visconti, the Venetians were faced with the difficulty of getting supplies to Brescia because the Milanese controlled Peschiera and the southern reaches of Lake Garda. A Greek sailor made the suggestion that the Venetians sail a fleet of provision-packed warships up the Adige to its furthest navigable point, then transport the vessels over Monte Baldo into Lake Garda. Anyone who has seen Herzog's film *Fitzcarraldo* will appreciate the difficulties involved, and the amazing fact that, with the aid of 2000 oxen, the 26 ships were launched at Torbole only 15 days after leaving the Adige. Unfortunately, after all that trouble, the supplies never reached Brescia. The same trick, however, perhaps even suggested by the same Greek, enabled Mohammed II to bring his fleet into the upper harbour of Constantinople the following year, leading to the capture of the city.

Malcésine

South of Torbole and the forbidding sheer cliffs of the Monte di Nago hanging perilously over the lake (which nevertheless attract their share of human flies), the Gardesana Orientale passes into the Veneto at **Malcésine**, the loveliest town on the east shore. The Veronese lords have always taken care to protect this part of the coast, or the 'Riviera degli Olivi' as they dubbed it, and the town is graced by a magnificent 13th-century Scaliger castle rising up on a sheer rock over the water. The castle offers a small museum and beautiful views from its tower (*open 9am–7pm daily*). It was while sketching this castle that Goethe was suspected of spying; Malcésine has since made up by erecting a bronze bust of the poet.

As well as the Scaliger castle, there's also the 16th-century **Palace of the Captains of the Lake** of Verona, now the Municipio, in the centre of Malcésine's web of medieval streets. A cableway runs up to **Bocca Tratto Spino**, just below the highest peak of Monte Baldo, the Punta del Telegrafo (2201m); its ski slopes are very popular with the Veronese, and its views are ravishing. Malcésine is also a popular walking base—for anything from a short stroll through the woods to a full-day hike—and there are numerous *rifugi* in the hills above the town (for details ask at the tourist office).

Torri del Benaco and Garda

Further south, past a stretch of shore silvery with olives, there are two pretty resort towns on either side of the promontory of San Vigilio. The first, **Torri del Benaco**, is defended by a 1383 **Scaliger castle**, (*open 9.30–1, 4.30–7.30; adm*); in the church of **Santa Trinità** there are 14th-century Giottoesque frescoes. The ferry boat crosses over from here for Maderno; the steamer continues around the pretty **Punta di San Vigilio** with its Renaissance **Guarienti villa** by the great Venetian architect Sammicheli and old church of San Vigilio, and a 16th-century tavern.

Behind Punta di San Vigilio and the distinct souffle-shaped headland called the Rocca lies **Garda**, which gave the lake its modern name. Although Garda was founded before the Romans (prehistoric graffiti and a necropolis have been found in its outskirts), it is known by the name the Lombards gave it, *Warthe*, 'the watch'. After Charlemagne defeated the Lombards Garda became a county, and in the now-disappeared castle the wicked Count Berenguer secretly held Queen Adelaide of Italy prisoner in 960, after he murdered her husband Lotario and she refused to marry his son. After a year she was discovered by a monk, who spent another year plotting her escape. She then received the protection of King Otto I of Germany, who defeated Berenguer, married the widowed queen, and thus became Holy Roman Emperor.

Garda has many fine old palaces, villas, and narrow medieval lanes, and is the last really scenic spot on the lake.

Bardolino and Peschiera

Bardolino's most important crop is familiar to any modern Bacchus, and between the vineyards rises a fine collection of 19th-century villas. It has two important churches: the 8th-century **San Zeno** and the 12th-century **San Severo**, with frescoes. The next town, **Lazise**, was the main Venetian port, and near the harbour retains a fine ensemble of Venetian buildings, as well as another Scaliger castle.

Between here and Verona at Pescantina there's a **Dinosaur Park** for addicts of concrete brontosauri, with a zoo and reptiliarium all rolled up in one, and an autosafari if you've brought the car, replete with Tibetan oxen, jaguars, tigers and hippos, in a tropical garden setting.

Peschiera del Garda is an old military town on the railway from Verona, near the mouth of the River Michio that drains Lake Garda. Its strategic position has caused it to be fortified since Roman times, though the imposing walls that you see today are actually

Porto di Lazise

16th-century Venetian, reinforced by the Austrians when Peschiera was one of the corners of the Empire's 'Quadrilateral'. Today, like Desenzano, Peschiera is mainly a transit point to the lake, but its purifying plant still helps it to fulfil its ancient role as a defender, this time of the lake's ecology and fish population. Here, too, you can treat the children—at **Gardaland**, ✆ (045) 6410355, Italy's largest, and most massively popular, theme park (*open Mar–June, Sept–Oct 9am–6pm daily; July–mid-Sept 12 noon–12 midnight daily; adm exp*) with its Magic Mountain, Colorado boat ride, reproductuion of the Valley of the Kings, the Amazon, electronic robots, etc. for a perfect day of packaged fun.

The region south of Peschiera is known for its white wine, Custoza, and for the pretty gardens and groves that line the Mincio River between peschiera and the swampy lakes of Mantua. The greatest of these, the **Sigurtà Gardens**, were the 40-year project of 'Italy's Capability Brown'—500,000 square metres, containing 20 different Anglo-Italian gardens of flowering plants and trees, along 7km of porphyry paths. The Sigurtà Gardens are near Valeggio, an attractive town in its own right, with a castle and a bridge built by the Visconti family.

The east shore of Garda is more family-oriented, slower-paced and less expensive, than the western side.

Malcésine

★★★★ **Val di Sogno**, ✆ 7400108, fax 7401694, (expensive). An excellent hotel situated about 3 minutes out of town in a beautiful setting in its own grounds right on the lake shore. There is a pool, private beach, lakeside restaurant, and modern rooms with bathroom and balcony, and all at very reasonable prices, not far above the moderate price category.

★★★ **Vega**, Via Roma, ✆ 6570355, fax 7401604, (moderate). An inviting hotel, with big, modern rooms, all with satellite TV, minibar, safe and air-conditioning, and a private beach.

★★★ **Excelsior Bay**, ✆ 7400380, fax 7401675, (moderate). Next to the lake and not far from the centre of Malcésine, a fine resort hotel with a pool and garden, and splendid views from the balconies of its rooms. (*Open end Mar–end Oct.*)

★★★ **Malcésine**, ✆ 7400033, fax 7400173, (moderate, with some rooms at inexpensive-level rates). A hotel pleasantly situated in its garden with swimming terrace, and with pleasant rooms, all with baths.

★★ **Miralago**, Via Roma, ✆ 7400111, (inexpensive). A good budget option which has a good position, with lake views, and a restaurant.

★★ **Sirena**, Via Roma, ✆ 7400019, (inexpensive). Another good cheaper place, with some rooms with a view, and TV in most rooms, but no restaurant.

Torri del Benaco

★★★ **Gardesana**, Piazza Calderini 20, ✆ 7225411, fax 7225771, (moderate). The most comfortable hotel in the town, right on the harbour with splendid views of lake and castle. All rooms have baths, and breakfast and meals are served on the harbour patio when the weather is good. (*Open all year.*)

Garda

★★★★ **Hotel du Parc**, ✆ 7255343, fax 7256970, (expensive). Garda's best hotel, a lakeside villa that has recently been entirely refurbished and upgraded. (*Open all year.*)

★★★★ **Eurotel**, ✆ 62703333, fax 7256640, (moderate). A large, modern, quite luxurious hotel which, again, is good value compared to the west shore hotels. It has a fine garden and pool. (*Open 9 April–Oct.*)

★★★ **Flora**, Via Madrina 4, ✆/fax 7255348, (moderate). An exceptionally well-priced hotel situated slightly above the town in its own grounds, and slick and modern with pine fittings, spacious rooms, all with bathroom and balcony, and fantastic amenities—tennis, mini-golf and *two* pools.

★★★   **Continental**, Via Giorgione 6, ✆ 7255398, fax 7255927, (moderate). Next door to the Flora, also in its own grounds and well-priced, but not quite as modern or comfortable—and with only one swimming pool.

★   **Vittoria**, Lungolago Regina Adelaide, ✆ 7255065, (inexpensive). The best inexpensive hotel in Garda, at the end of the main lakefront walk. The rooms are big, with simple fittings, and service is very friendly.

Eating Out

On the landward side of Garda, almost outside the town, the **Ristorante Stafolet**, Via Poiano 12, ✆ 7255427, is worth asking directions to, for its wild duck and plump, spinach-filled *strangolopreti*, all at moderate prices. Less distinguished, but a good and very cheap place in which to find a full meal of stout local cooking is **Al Ponte Sel**, Via Monte Baldo 75.

A short way further south in Bardolino, you can dine well at **Aurora**, Via San Severo 18, ✆ 7210038, near the town's pretty Romanesque landmark, the church of San Zeno. Specialities include the produce of the lake, especially trout prepared in a variety of styles, again at moderate prices.

Atrium: entrance court of a Roman house or early church.

Badia: *abbazia*, an abbey or abbey church.

Baldacchino: baldachin, a columned stone canopy above the altar of a church.

Basilica: a rectangular building, usually divided into three aisles by rows of columns. In Rome this was the common form for law courts and other public buildings, and Roman Christians adapted it for their early churches.

Calvary chapels: a series of outdoor chapels, usually on a hillside, that commemorate the stages of the Passion of Christ.

Campanile: a bell-tower.

Campanilismo: local patriotism; the Italians' own word for their historic tendency to be more faithful to their home towns than to the abstract idea of 'Italy'.

Camposanto: a cemetery.

Cardo: transverse street of a Roman *castrum*-shaped city.

Carroccio: a wagon carrying the banners of a medieval city and an altar; it served as the rallying point in battles.

Cartoon: the preliminary sketch for a fresco or tapestry.

Caryatid: supporting pillar or column carved into a standing female form; male versions are called *telamones*.

Castrum: a Roman military camp, always neatly rectangular, with straight streets and gates at the cardinal points. Later the Romans founded or refounded cities in this form, hundreds of which survive today (Pavia, Como, Brescia are clear examples).

Cavea: the semicircle of seats in a classical theatre.

Cenacolo: fresco of the Last Supper, often on the wall of a monastery refectory.

Ciborium: a tabernacle; the word is often used for large freestanding tabernacles, or in the sense of a *baldacchino* (q.v.).

Architectural, Artistic & Historical Terms

Comune: commune, or commonwealth, referring to the governments of the free cities of the Middle Ages. Today it denotes any local government, from the Comune di Roma down to the smallest village.

Condottiere: the leader of a band of mercenaries in late medieval and Renaissance times.

Confraternity: a religious lay brotherhood, often serving as a neighbourhood mutual-aid and burial society, or following some specific charitable work (Michelangelo, for example, belonged to one that cared for condemned prisoners in Rome).

Cupola: a dome.

Decumanus: street of a Roman *castrum*-shaped city parallel to the longer axis, the central, main avenue called the Decumanus Major.

Duomo: cathedral.

Forum: the central square of a Roman town, with its most important temples and public buildings. The word means 'outside', as the original Roman Forum was outside the first city walls.

Fresco: wall painting, the most important Italian medium of art since Etruscan times. It isn't easy; first the artist draws the *sinopia* (q.v.) on the wall. This is covered with plaster, but only a little at a time, as the paint must be on the plaster before it dries. Leonardo da Vinci's endless attempts to find clever short-cuts ensured that little of his work would survive.

Ghibellines: one of the two great medieval parties, the supporters of the Holy Roman Emperors.

Gonfalon: the banner of a medieval free city; the *gonfaloniere*, or flag bearer, was often the most important public official.

Guelphs: (see *Ghibellines*). The other great political faction of medieval Italy, supporters of the Pope.

Intarsia: work in inlaid wood or marble.

Narthex: the enclosed porch of a church.

Palazzo: not just a palace, but any large, important building (though the word comes from the Imperial *palatium* on Rome's Palatine Hill).

Pantocrator: Christ 'ruler of all', a common subject for apse paintings and mosaics in areas influenced by Byzantine art.

Pietra Dura: rich inlay work using semi-precious stones, perfected in post-Renaissance Florence.

Pieve: a parish church, especially in the north.

Predella: smaller paintings on panels below the main subject of a painted altarpiece.

Presepio: a Christmas crib.

Putti: flocks of plaster cherubs with rosy cheeks and bums that infested much of Italy in the Baroque era.

Quadriga: chariot pulled by four horses.

Quattrocento: the 1400s—the Italian way of referring to centuries (*duecento, trecento, quattrocento, cinquecento*, etc.).

Sinopia: the layout of a fresco (q.v.), etched by the artist on the wall before the plaster is applied. Often these are works of art in their own right.

Stigmata: a miraculous simulation of the bleeding wounds of Christ, appearing in holy men like St Francis in the 12th century, and Padre Pio of Apulia in our own time.

Telamon: see *Caryatid.*

Thermae: Roman baths.

Tondo: round relief, painting or terracotta.

Transenna: marble screen separating the altar area from the rest of an early Christian church.

Travertine: hard, light-coloured stone, sometimes flecked or pitted with black, sometimes perfect. The most widely used material in ancient and modern Rome.

Triptych: a painting, especially an altarpiece, in three sections.

Trompe l'œil: art that uses perspective effects to deceive the eye—for example, to create the illusion of depth on a flat surface, or to make columns and arches painted on a wall seem real.

Tympanum: the semicircular space, often bearing a painting or relief, above the portal of a church.

The fathers of modern Italian were Dante, Manzoni, and television. Each had a part in creating a national language from an infinity of regional and local dialects; the Florentine Dante, the first to write in the vernacular, did much to put the Tuscan dialect in the foreground of Italian literature. Manzoni's revolutionary novel, *I Promessi Sposi*, heightened national consciousness by using an everyday language all could understand in the 19th century. Television in the last few decades is performing an even more spectacular linguistic unification; although the majority of Italians still speak a dialect at home, school, and work, their TV idols insist on proper Italian.

Perhaps because they are so busy learning their own beautiful but grammatically complex language, Italians are not especially apt at learning others. English lessons, however, have been the rage for years, and at most hotels and restaurants there will be someone who speaks some English. In small towns and out-of-the-way places, finding an Anglophone may prove more difficult. The words and phrases below should help you out in most situations, but the ideal way to come to Italy is with some Italian under your belt; your visit will be richer, and you're much more likely to make some Italian friends.

Italian words are pronounced phonetically. Every vowel and consonant is sounded. Consonants are the same as in English, except the *c* which, when followed by an 'e' or 'i', is pronounced like the English 'ch' (*cinque* thus becomes cheenquay). Italian *g* is also soft before 'i' or 'e' as in *gira*, or jee-ra. *H* is never sounded; *z* is pronounced like 'ts'. The consonants *sc* before the vowels 'i' or 'e' becomes like the English 'sh' as in *sci*, pronounced shee; *ch* is pronouced like a 'k' as in *Chianti*, kee-an-tee; *gn* as 'ny' in English (*bagno*, pronounced ban-yo; while *gli* is pronounced like the middle of the word million (*Castiglione*, pronounced Ca-stee-lyon-ay).

Vowel pronunciation is: *a* as in English father; *e* when unstressed is pronounced like 'a' in fate as in *mele*, when stressed can be the same or like the 'e' in pet (*bello*); *i* is like the 'i' in machine; *o*, like 'e', has two sounds, 'o' as in hope when unstressed (*tacchino*), and usually 'o' as in rock when stressed (*morte*); *u* is pronounced like the 'u' in June.

The accent usually (but not always!) falls on the penultimate syllable. Also note that in the big northern cities, the informal way of addressing someone as you, *tu*, is widely used; the more formal *lei* or *voi* is commonly used in provincial districts.

Useful Words and Phrases

yes/no/maybe	*sì/no/forse*
I don't know	*Non lo so*
I don't understand (Italian).	*Non capisco (italiano).*
Does someone here speak English?	*C'è qualcuno qui che parla inglese?*
Speak slowly	*Parla lentamente*
Could you assist me?	*Potrebbe aiutarmi?*
Help!	*Aiuto!*
Please	*Per favore*
Thank you (very much)	*(Molte) grazie*
You're welcome	*Prego*
It doesn't matter	*Non importa*
All right	*Va bene*
Excuse me	*Scusi*
Be careful!	*Attenzione!*
Nothing	*Niente*
It is urgent!	*È urgente!*
How are you?	*Come sta?*
Well, and you?	*Bene, e lei?*
What is your name?	*Come si chiama?*
Hello	*Salve* or *ciao* (both informal)
Good morning	*Buongiorno* (formal hello)
Good afternoon/evening	*Buona sera* (also formal hello)
Goodnight	*Buona notte*

Language

Goodbye	*Arrivederla* (formal), *arrivederci, ciao* (informal)
What do you call this in Italian?	*Come si chiama questo in italiano?*
What?	*Che?*

Who?	*Chi?*
Where?	*Dove?*
When?	*Quando?*
Why?	*Perché?*
How?	*Come?*
How much?	*Quanto?*
I am lost	*Mi sono smarrito*
I am hungry	*Ho fame*
I am thirsty	*Ho sete*
I am sorry	*Mi dispiace*
I am tired	*Sono stanco*
I am sleepy	*Ho sonno*
I am ill	*Mi sento male*
Leave me alone	*Lasciami in pace*
good	*buono/bravo*
bad	*male/cattivo*
It's all the same	*Fa lo stesso*
slow	*piano*
fast	*rapido*
big	*grande*
small	*piccolo*
hot	*caldo*
cold	*freddo*
here	*qui*
there	*lì*

Shopping, Service, Sightseeing

I would like...	*Vorrei...*
Where is/are...?	*Dov'è/Dove sono...?*
How much is it?	*Quanto viene questo?*
open	*aperto*
closed	*chiuso*
cheap/expensive	*a buon prezzo/caro*
bank	*banca*
beach	*spiaggia*

bed	*letto*
church	*chiesa*
entrance	*entrata*
exit	*uscita*
hospital	*ospedale*
money	*soldi*
museum	*museo*
newspaper (foreign)	*giornale (straniero)*
pharmacy	*farmacia*
police station	*commissariato*
policeman	*poliziotto*
post office	*ufficio postale*
sea	*mare*
shop	*negozio*
telephone	*telefono*
tobacco shop	*tabaccaio*
WC	*toilette/bagno*
men	*Signori/Uomini*
women	*Signore/Donne*

Time

What time is it?	*Che ore sono?*
month	*mese*
week	*settimana*
day	*giorno*
morning	*mattina*
afternoon	*pomeriggio*
evening	*sera*
today	*oggi*
yesterday	*ieri*
tomorrow	*domani*
soon	*presto*
later	*dopo, più tardi*
It is too early	*È troppo presto*
It is too late	*È troppo tarde*

Days

Monday	*lunedì*
Tuesday	*martedì*
Wednesday	*mercoledì*
Thursday	*giovedì*
Friday	*venerdì*
Saturday	*sabato*
Sunday	*domenica*

Numbers

one	*uno/una*
two	*due*
three	*tre*
four	*quattri*
five	*cinque*
six	*sei*
seven	*sette*
eight	*otto*
nine	*nove*
ten	*dieci*
eleven	*undici*
twelve	*dodici*
thirteen	*tredici*
fourteen	*quattordici*
fifteen	*quindici*
sixteen	*sedici*
seventeen	*diciassette*
eighteen	*diciotto*
nineteen	*diciannove*
twenty	*venti*
twenty-one	*ventuno*
twenty-two	*ventidue*
thirty	*trenta*
thirty-one	*trentuno*

forty	*quaranta*
fifty	*cinquanta*
sixty	*sessanta*
seventy	*settanta*
eighty	*ottanta*
ninety	*novanta*
hundred	*cento*
one hundred and one	*cento uno*
two hundred	*duecento*
thousand	*mille*
two thousand	*duemila*
million	*milione*
billion	*miliardo*

Transport

airport	*aeroporto*
bus stop	*fermata*
bus/coach	*autobus/pullman*
railway station	*stazione ferroviaria*
train	*treno*
track	*binario*
port	*porto*
port station	*stazione marittima*
ship	*nave*
automobile	*macchina*
taxi	*tassì*
ticket	*biglietto*
customs	*dogana*
seat (reserved)	*posto (prenotato)*

Travel Directions

I want to go to…	*Desidero andare a…*
How can I get to… ?	*Come posso andare a… ?*
Do you stop at… ?	*Ferma a… ?*
Where is… ?	*Dov'è… ?*

How far is it to... ?	*Quanto siamo lontani da... ?*
When does the... leave?	*A che ora parte ... ?*
What is the name of this station?	*Come si chiama questa stazione?*
When does the next ... leave?	*Quando parte il prossimo... ?*
From where does it leave?	*Da dove parte?*
How long does the trip take... ?	*Quanto tempo dura il viaggio?*
How much is the fare?	*Quant'è il biglietto?*
Good trip!	*Buon viaggio!*
near	*vicino*
far	*lontano*
left	*sinistra*
right	*destra*
straight ahead	*sempre diritto*
forward	*avanti*
backward	*indietro*
north	*nord/settentrione*
south	*sud/mezzogiorno*
east	*est/oriente*
west	*ovest/occidente*
around the corner	*dietro l'angolo*
crossroads	*bivio*
street/road	*strada*
square	*piazza*

Driving

car hire	*noleggio macchina*
motorbike/scooter	*motocicletta/Vespa*
bicycle	*bicicletta*
petrol/diesel	*benzina/gasolio*
garage	*garage*
This doesn't work	*Questo non funziona*
mechanic	*meccànico*
map/town plan	*carta/pianta*
Where is the road to... ?	*Dov'è la strada per... ?*
breakdown	*guasto* or *panne*

driver's licence	*patente di guida*
driver	*guidatore*
speed	*velocità*
danger	*pericolo*
parking	*parcheggio*
no parking	*sosta vietato*
narrow	*stretto*
bridge	*ponte*
toll	*pedaggio*
slow down	*rallentare*

Italian Menu Vocabulary

Antipasti

These before-meal treats can include almost anything; among the most common are:

antipasto misto	mixed antipasto
bruschetta	garlic toast
carciofi (sott'olio)	artichokes (in oil)
crostini	liver paté on toast
frutti di mare	seafood
funghi (trifolati)	mushrooms (with anchovies, garlic, and lemon)
gamberi al fagiolino	shrimp with white beans
mozzarella (in carrozza)	buffalo cheese (fried with bread in batter)
olive	olives
prosciutto (con melone)	raw ham (with melon)
salame	cured pork
salsiccia	dry sausage

Minestre e Pasta

These dishes are the principal first courses (*primi*) served throughout Italy.

agnolotti	ravioli with meat
cacciucco	spiced fish soup
cannelloni	meat and cheese rolled in pasta tubes

cappelletti	small ravioli, often in broth
crespelle	crêpes
fettuccine	long strips of pasta
frittata	omelette
gnocchi	potato dumplings
lasagne	sheets of pasta baked with meat and cheese sauce
minestra di verdura	thick vegetable soup
minestrone	soup with meat, vegetables, and pasta
orecchiette	ear-shaped pasta, usually served with turnip greens
panzerotti	ravioli filled with mozzarella, anchovies and egg
pappardelle alla lepre	flat pasta ribbons with hare sauce
pasta e fagioli	soup with beans, bacon, and tomatoes
pastina in brodo	tiny pasta in broth
penne all'arrabbiata	quill shaped pasta in hot spicy tomato sauce
polenta	cake or pudding of corn semolina, prepared with meat or tomato sauce
risotto (alla milanese)	Italian rice (with saffron and wine)
spaghetti all'amatriciana	with spicy sauce of bacon, tomatoes, onions, and hot pepper
spaghetti alla bolognese	with ground meat, ham, mushrooms, etc.
spaghetti alla carbonara	with bacon, eggs, and black pepper
spaghetti al pomodoro	with tomato sauce
spaghetti al sugo/ragù	with meat sauce
spaghetti alle vongole	with clam sauce
stracciatella	broth with eggs and cheese
tagliatelle	flat egg noodles
tortellini al pomodoro/panna/in brodo	pasta caps filled with meat and cheese, served with tomato sauce/cream, or in broth
vermicelli	very thin spaghetti

Second Courses—Carne (Meat)

abbacchio	milk-fed lamb
agnello	lamb
anatra	duck
animelle	sweetbreads
arista	pork loin
arrosto misto	mixed roat meats
bistecca alla fiorentina	Florentine beef steak
bocconcini	veal mixed with ham and cheese and fried
bollito misto	stew of boiled meats
braciola	chop
brasato di manzo	braised meat with vegetables
bresaola	dried raw meat similar to ham served with lemon, olive oil and parsley
capretto	kid
capriolo	roe deer
carne di castrato/suino	mutton/pork
carpaccio	thin slices of raw beef in piquant sauce
cassoeula	winter stew with pork and cabbage
cervello (al burro nero)	brains (in black butter sauce)
cervo	venison
cinghiale	boar
coniglio	rabbit
cotoletta (alla milanese/alla bolognese)	veal cutlet (fried in breadcrumbs/with ham and cheese)
fagiano	pheasant
faraona (alla creta)	guinea fowl (in earthenware pot)
fegato alla veneziana	liver and onions
involtini	rolled slices of veal with filling
lepre (in salmì)	hare (marinated in wine)
lombo di maiale	pork loin
lumache	snails
maiale (al latte)	pork (cooked in milk)
manzo	beef

ossobuco	braised veal knuckle with herbs
pancetta	rolled pork
pernice	partridge
petto di pollo (alla fiorentina/bolognese/sorpresa)	boned chicken breast (fried in butter/with ham and cheese/stuffed and deep fried)
piccione	pigeon
pizzaiola	beef steak with tomato and oregano sauce
pollo (alla cacciatora/alla diavola/alla Marengo)	chicken (with tomatoes and mushrooms cooked in wine/grilled/ fried with tomatoes, garlic and wine)
polpette	meatballs
quaglie	quails
rane	frogs
rognoni	kidneys
saltimbocca	veal scallop with prosciutto and sage, cooked in wine and butter
scaloppine	thin slices of veal sautéed in butter
spezzatino	pieces of beef or veal, usually stewed
spiedino	meat on a skewer or stick
stufato	beef braised in white wine with vegetables
tacchino	turkey
trippa	tripe
uccelletti	small birds on a skewer
vitello	veal

Pesce (Fish)

acciughe or *alici*	anchovies
anguilla	eel
aragosta	lobster
aringa	herring
baccalà	dried cod
bonito	small tuna
branzino	sea bass
calamari	squid

cappe sante	scallops
cefalo	grey mullet
coda di rospo	angler fish
cozze	mussels
datteri di mare	razor (or date) mussels
dentice	dentex (perch-like fish)
dorato	gilt head
fritto misto	mixed fish fry, with squid and shrimp
gamberetto	shrimp
gamberi (di fiume)	prawns (crayfish)
granchio	crab
insalata di mare	seafood salad
lamprèda	lamprey
merluzzo	cod
nasello	hake
orata	bream
ostriche	oysters
pescespada	swordfish
polipo	octopus
pesce azzuro	various types of small fish
pesce San Pietro	John Dory
rombo	turbot
sarde	sardines
seppie	cuttlefish
sgombro	mackerel
sogliola	sole
squadro	monkfish
tonno	tuna
triglia	red mullet (rouget)
trota	trout
trota salmonata	salmon trout
vongole	small clams
zuppa di pesce	mixed fish in sauce or stew

Contorni (Side Dishes, Vegetables)

asparagi (alla fiorentina)	asparagus (with fried eggs)
broccoli (calabrese, romana)	broccoli (green, spiral)
carciofi (alla giudia)	artichokes (deep fried)
cardi	cardoons, thistles
carote	carrots
cavolfiore	cauliflower
cavolo	cabbage
ceci	chickpeas
cetriolo	cucumber
cipolla	onion
fagioli	white beans
fagiolini	French (green) beans
fave	fava beans
finocchio	fennel
funghi (porcini)	mushrooms (boletus)
insalata (mista, verde)	salad (mixed, green)
lattuga	lettuce
lenticchie	lentils
melanzana (al forno)	aubergine/eggplant (filled and baked)
patate (fritte)	potatoes (fried)
peperoni	sweet peppers
peperonata	stewed peppers, onions and tomatoes etc., similar to ratatouille
piselli (al prosciutto)	peas (with ham)
pomodoro	tomato
porri	leeks
radicchio	red chicory
radice	radish
rapa	turnip
sedano	celery
spinaci	spinach
verdure	greens
zucca	pumpkin
zucchini	zucchini (courgettes)

Formaggio (Cheese)

bel paese	a soft white cow's cheese
cacio/caciocavallo	pale yellow, often sharp cheese
fontina	rich cow's milk cheese
groviera	mild cheese
gorgonzola	soft blue cheese
parmigiano	Parmesan cheese
pecorino	sharp sheep's cheese
provolone	sharp, tangy cheese; *dolce* is more mild
stracchino	soft white cheese

Frutta (Fruit, Nuts)

albicocche	apricots
ananas	pineapple
arance	oranges
banane	bananas
cachi	persimmons
ciliegie	cherries
cocomero	watermelon
composta di frutta	stewed fruit
dattero	date
fichi	figs
fragole (con panna)	strawberries (with cream)
frutta di stagione	fruit in season
lamponi	raspberries
macedonia di frutta	fruit salad
mandarino	tangerine
melagrana	pomegranate
mele	apples
melone	melon
mirtilli	bilberries
more	blackberries
nespola	medlar fruit
nocciole	hazelnuts

noci	walnuts
pera	pear
pesca	peach
pesca noce	nectarine
pignoli/pinoli	pine nuts
pompelmo	grapefruit
prugna/susina	plum
uva	grapes

Dolci (Desserts)

amaretti	macaroons
cannoli	crisp pastry tubes filled with ricotta, cream, chocolate or fruit
coppa gelato	assorted ice cream
crema caramella	caramel-topped custard
crostata	fruit flan
gelato (produzione propria)	ice cream (homemade)
granita	flavoured ice, usually lemon or coffee
Monte Bianco	chestnut pudding with whipped cream
panettone	sponge cake with candied fruit and raisins
panforte	dense cake of chocolate, almonds, and preserved fruit
Saint-Honoré	meringue cake
semifreddo	refrigerated cake
sorbetto	sherbet
spumone	a soft ice cream
tiramisù	mascarpone, coffee, chocolate and sponge fingers
torrone	nougat
torta	tart
torta millefoglie	layered custard tart
zabaglione	whipped eggs, sugar and Marsala wine, served hot
zuppa inglese	trifle

Bevande (Beverages)

acqua minerale con/senza gas	mineral water with/without fizz
aranciata	orange soda
birra (alla spina)	beer (draught)
caffè (freddo)	coffee (iced)
cioccolata (con panna)	chocolate (with cream)
gassosa	lemon-flavoured soda
latte	milk
limonata	lemon soda
succo di frutta	fruit juice
tè	tea
vino (rosso, bianco, rosato)	wine (red, white, rosé)

Cooking Terms, Miscellaneous

aceto (balsamico)	vinegar (balsamic)
affumicato	smoked
aglio	garlic
alla brace	on embers
bicchiere	glass
burro	butter
cacciagione	game
conto	bill
costoletta/cotoletta	chop
coltello	knife
cotto adagio	braised
cucchaio	spoon
filetto	fillet
forchetta	fork
forno	oven
fritto	fried
ghiaccio	ice
griglia	grill
limone	lemon
magro	lean meat/or pasta without meat

mandorle	almonds
marmellata	jam
menta	mint
miele	honey
mostarda	candied mustard sauce
olio	oil
pane (tostato)	bread (toasted)
panini	sandwiches
panna	fresh cream
pepe	pepper
peperoncini	hot chili peppers
piatto	plate
prezzemolo	parsley
ripieno	stuffed
rosmarino	rosemary
sale	salt
salmì	wine marinade
salsa	sauce
salvia	sage
senape	mustard
tartufi	truffles
tazza	cup
tavola	table
tovagliolo	napkin
tramezzini	finger sandwiches
umido	cooked in sauce
uovo	egg
zucchero	sugar

BC

80,000	Give or take a couple of 10,000 years: Paleolithic settlements along the Riviera
8000	First rock incisions in the Val Camonica
236–22	Romans conquer Po Valley from Gauls
222	Celtic Mediolanum (Milan) comes under Roman rule; Roman colony of Ticinum (Pavia) founded
219	Hannibal and his elephants cross the Alps
70	Virgil born at Mantua
87	Catullus born at Sirmione

AD

23–79	Pliny the Elder, of Como
62–120	Pliny the Younger, of Como
284–305	Diocletian divides Roman Empire in two; Milan becomes most important city in West, pop. 100,000
313	Edict of Milan: Constantine makes Christianity religion of the empire
374–97	St Ambrose, bishop of Milan
387	St Ambrose converts and baptises St Augustine in Milan
539	Goths slaughter most of male Milanese
567	Lombards overrun most of Italy, and make Pavia their capital
590s	Pope Gregory the Great converts Queen Theodolinda and the Lombards to orthodox Christianity
***c.* 730**	Desiderius, King of the Lombards, born near Brescia
778	Charlemagne defeats last Desiderius and repudiates his wife, Desiderius' daughter, and is crowned King of Italy in Pavia
888	Berengar crowned king of Italy at Pavia
1109–55	Arnold of Brescia, monk and preacher against worldly Church, only to be hanged by Pope
1127	Como destroyed by Milanese, rebuilt by Barbarossa
1154	Milan sacked by Barbarossa

Chronology

1155	Barbarossa crowned king of Italy at Pavia
1156	Barbarossa does it again
1158	Milan obliterates rival Lodi; Lodi rebuilt by Barbarossa

1176	Lombard League defeats Barbarossa at Legnano
1183	Treaty of Constance recognizes independence of Lombard cities
1252	Inquisitor St Peter Martyr axed in the head by Lake Como
1277	The Visconti overthrow the Torriani to become *signori* of Milan
1334	Azzone Visconti captures Cremona
1335	Como becomes fief of Milan
1348–9	The Black Death wipes out a third of the Italians
1386	Gian Galeazzo Visconti begins Milan cathedral
1396	Gian Galeazzo Visconti founds the Certosa of Pavia
1402	Gian Galeazzo Visconti, conqueror of northern Italy, plans to capture Florence but dies of plague
1421–35	Genoa under Filippo Maria Visconti; the Genoese fleet crushes Aragon
1428–1797	Bergamo and Brescia ruled by Venice
1441	Bianca Visconti weds Francesco Sforza, with Cremona as her dowry
1447–50	Ambrosian republic—Milan's attempt at Democracy
1450	Francesco Sforza made duke of Milan
1494	Wars of Italy begin with French invasion of Charles VIII
1495	Battle of Fornovo; Leonardo begins *Last Supper*
1500	Duke of Milan, Lodovico il Moro, captured by French at Novara
1509	Defeat of Venice at Agnadello by Louis XII of France, Pope Julius II, Emperor Maximilian, and the League of Cambrai; Venice loses new acquisition of Cremona, but soon regains Brescia and Bergamo and other *terra firma* real estate
1525	Battle of Pavia; Spaniards capture French King Francis I
1527–93	Giuseppe Arcimboldo, first surrealist, of Milan
1533	Federico Gonzaga of Mantua picks up Monferrato by marriage
1538–84	St Charles Borromeo, Archbishop of Milan
1559	Treaty of Château-Cambrésis confirms Spanish control of Italy and returns Turin to the House of Savoy
1567–1643	Claudio Monteverdi, opera composer, of Cremona
1573–1610	Michelangelo da Caravaggio
1596–1684	Nicolò Amati, violin maker, of Cremona
1620	Spanish governor of Milan orders 'Day of Holy Butchery' in the Valtellina; Catholics massacre Protestants, initiating 20 years of war
1630	Plague in Milan (described by Manzoni in *I Promessi Sposi*)

1644–1737	Stradivarius, violin-maker, of Cremona
1665	Carlo Emanuele II, with help from Louis XIV persecutes Waldensians in Piedmont; Cromwell and Milton protest
1683–1745	Giuseppe Guarneri, violin-maker, of Cremona
1700-13	War of the Spanish Succession
1713	Austrians pick up Milan
1745	Alessandro Volta, the physicist, born in Como
1778	La Scala inaugurated
1785	Alessandro Manzoni, author of *I Promessi Sposi,* born in Lecco
1790	Wordsworth lives by Lake Como
1796	Napoleon first enters Italy, defeats Austrians at Lodi, and makes Milan capital of his Cisalpine Republic
1798–1848	Gaetano Donizetti, of Bergamo
1800	Napoleon defeats the Austrians at Marengo
1805	Napoleon crowns himself with Iron Crown of Italy in Milan Cathedral
1813	Rossini composes *Tancredi* on shores of Lake Como
1814	Overthrow of French rule
1816–17	Queen Caroline of England at Lake Como
1831	Mazzini founds *Giovane Italia*; Bellini composes *Norma* on the shores of Lake Como
1848	Revolutions across Italy; Austrians defeat Piedmont at war
1849	Restoration of autocratic rule
1852	Cavour becomes Prime Minister of Piedmont
1853	Verdi composes *La Traviata* in a villa on Lake Como
1854	Piedmont enters Crimean War
1859–60	Piedmont, with the help of Napoleon III, annexes Lombardy at battle of Solferino; in return gives France Nice and Savoy; while Garibaldi's 'Thousand' conquer Sicily and Naples
1860–65	Turin is capital of Italy; in 1865 moved to Florence
1870	Italian troops enter Rome; unification completed and Rome becomes capital
1871	Mont Cenis (Frejus) railway Tunnel, first great Transalpine tunnel, opened between France and Italy
1879	Queen Victoria takes a holiday by Lake Maggiore
1881	Angelo Roncalli (Pope John XXIII) born at Sotto il Monte, nr. Bergamo
1900	King Umberto I assassinated by anarchist

1901	Verdi dies in his hotel room in Milan
1902–7	Period of industrial strikes
1905	Simplon Tunnel, the longest rail tunnel in the world, completed
1910	Peruvian Georges Chavez makes the first flight over the Alps, only to be killed in a crash near Domodossola
1915	Italy enters First World War
1925	Mussolini makes Italy a fascist dictatorship
1925–7	D. H. Lawrence at Lake Como
1938	Gabriele D'Annunzio dies at Il Vittoriale, by Lake Garda
1940	Italy enters Second World War
1943	Mussolini deposed; rescued by Germans to found puppet government of Salò in north; Milan burns for days in air raids
1944	Vittorio Emanuele III abdicates
1945	National referendum makes Italy a republic; King Umberto II exiled in Switzerland; new Italian constitution grants the Valle d'Aosta regional-land cultural autonomy
1956	Italy becomes a charter member in the Common Market
1965	Completion of Mont Blanc motorway tunnel
1980	Completion of Mont Cenis (Frejus) motorway tunnel
1983	Major landslides wreck havoc in the Valtellina
1988	More landslides and floods in the Valtellina
1990	Emergence of Umberto Bossi's Lombard League.
1994	Election of Silvio Berlusconi, Milanese media magnate, as Prime Minister at the head of Forza Italia.

Note: Page numbers in *italics* indicate maps. **Bold** references indicate main references and chapter headings.

Abbadia Lariana:
  San Giorgio 170
  Silk Industry Museum 170
Accademia dei Pugni 64
Acqua Fraggia 175
activities **33–5**, 97
Adelheid (Adelaide), Queen 47
Agilulf, King 136
Agnadello, Battle of 95
Agra 148
Agrate, Marco 83
agriturismo 40
air travel 2–3, 79
Aistulf 46–7
Alberti, Leon Battista 60, 120, 122, 125, 129
Alexander III, Pope 49, 66, 76
Allori, Alessandro 182
Almenno San Bartolomeo: San Tomè 186
alpine refuges 40
Alzano Lombardo 61
  Basilica di San Martino 188
Amadeo, Giovanni Antonio 60, 106, 108, 109, 110, 111, 115, 182
Amati family 66, 113, 116
Ambrose, St (Sant'Ambrogio) 45, 75
Ameno: Fondazione Calderara 136
Anfo 202–3
Angera: Rocca di Angera 143
Annone, Lake 172
Anselmo, St, Bishop of Lucca 119
Antronapiana 138
Aprica 176, 177
Arcimboldo, Giuseppe 61, 90, 114
Arco 213

Arianism 75
Arizzano 146
Arlecchino (Harlequin) 68–9
Arnold of Brescia 197
Arona **142–3**
  Castle 142
  San Carlone 142
  Santa Maria 143
Aronco, Raimondo D' 88
Arsago Séprio 151
  Basilica di San Vittore 151
art and architecture **57–62**
  Baroque 61–2, 67, 83, 182
  Campionesi Masters 58, 82, 156, 166, 182
  Comaschi Masters 59
  Fascist 62
  futurist 62
  Gothic 59, 83, 159
  Liberty style (Art Nouveau) 62, 87–8, 210
  Mannerist 60
  Medieval 58–9
  neoclassical 62
  prehistoric 58, 188, 191, 192, 213
  Renaissance 59–61, 67, 83, 110–11, 129, 159–60
  Roman 58, 199–200, 206
  Romanesque 58–9, 115
  Romanticism 62
  terminology 223–5
  20th century 62
art galleries: opening hours 28
Ascona 147
Attila the Hun 207
Augustine, St 75
Aurano 147
Aurogo: San Martino 175
Austria: rule by 51–3, 77–8
Automobile Club of Italy 13

Bagolino:
  festival 20
  San Rocco 203
Baldassare degli Embriachi 111
Baldo, Monte 218
Balduccio, Giovanni di 96
Balisio, Colle di 170
Balla, Giacomo 89
Ballabio Inferiore 170
banks 26–7
  opening hours 27
Bannio-Anzino 138
Barbara, St 186
Barbarossa *see* Frederick I
Bardolino:
  eating out 222
  San Severo 219
  San Zeno 219
Barzio 170
Baschenis, Evaristo 61
Basile, Ernesto 88
Baveno 141
  Santi Gervasio e Protasio 146
Bazzani, Giuseppe 62
beaches 33
Beccaria, Cesare 64–5
Bèe 146
Belgirate 143
Belisarius 46
Bellagio 158, 165
  San Giacomo 165
  Villa Melzi 165
  Villa Serbelloni 165
  where to stay 167–8
Bellano: Santi Nazaro e Celso 166
Bellini, Gentile 89, 184
Bellini, Giovanni 85, 89, 90, 110, 184
Bellini, Jacopo 89, 190
Bellini, Vincenzo 162

Index

Arcumeggia 153
Aretino, Pietro 186
Argegno 162

Averara 187
Baceno: San Gaudenzio 139
Bagni di Bormio 177

Bembo (artist) 116
Bentham, Jeremy 65
Berbenno: festival 20

Berengar (Berenguer) I 108
Berengar (Berenguer) II 47, 219
Bergagnone, Bernardino 89, 90
Bergamasque Valleys 186–8
Bergamo 35, **180–5**
  Accademia Carrara 60
  Archaeological Museum 183
  Baptistry 182
  Basilica of Santa Maria
    Maggiore 182–3
  Biblioteca Civica 181
  Carrara Academy 183–4
  Castello 183
  Città Alta 181–3
  Città Bassa 181
  Cittadella 183
  Colleoni Chapel 60, **182**
  Duomo 183
  eating out 185
  festivals 20
  getting to and from 181
  history 180–1
  Museo Donizettiano 183
  Natural History Museum 183
  Palazzo della Ragione 182
  Palazzo Scotti 183
  Piazza Matteotti 181
  Piazza Vecchia 181–2
  Pinacoteca Carrara 184
  Rocca 183
  San Bartolomeo 181
  San Bernardino 60, 184
  San Virgilio 183
  Santo Spirito 60, 184
  Teatro Donizetti 181
  Torre Civica 182
  tourist information 181
  where to stay 184–5
Bergognone, Ambrogio 60, 93,
  96, 106, 111
Berlusconi, Silvio 56
Bertini, Giuseppe 94
Besozzi, Alberto 148
Bibiena, Antonio Galli 125
bicycles: hiring 14
Bienno 191
Binago, Lorenzo 61
Bisuschio 153
  Villa Cicogna Mozzoni 156
Black Death 50

Boario Terme 191
boating 117
boats (ferries) 9, 133, 142, 158
Bocca Tratto Spino 219
Boccaccino, Boccaccio 114
Boccioni, Umberto 84, 89
Boethius 45, 110
Bonacolsi family 119, 122, 123
Bonvicino, Alessandro *see*
  Moretto da Brescia
books 26
Bordone, Paris 96
Borgia, Cesare 51, 93, 184
Borgonuovo:
  Acqua Fraggia 175
  Sant'Abbondio 175
Bormio 35
  Chiesa del Crocifisso 177
  eating out 180
  festival 20
  where to stay 179
Borromean Islands 141, **145–6**
  where to stay 146
Borromeo, St Charles 51, 61, 83,
  109, **142–3**, 147, 166, 212
Borromeo, Cardinal Federico 51,
  94
Borromeo family 141, 143, 145
Bossi, Umberto 56
Botticelli 94, 184
Bovegno 202
Bramante, Donato 59, 89, 90,
  91, 92–3, 95, 109, 113
Bramantino (Bartolomeo Suardi)
  90, 95, 147
Breno:
  Museo Camuno 192
  Sant'Antonio 192
Brescia **195–202**, *196*
  Abbey of San Salvatore 58,
    197, 199–200
  Biblioteca Queriniana 199
  Broletto 199
  Capitoline Temple 199
  Castello 200
  Civico Museo Romano 199
  Curia 200
  Duomo 198
  Duomo Vecchio 58, 60, 198–9
  eating out 202

festivals 20, 21
Galleria Tosio-Martinengo 60,
  200
getting around 197–8
history 197
Loggia 198
Luigi Marzoli Museum of Arms
  200
Mirabella Tower 200
Monte di Pietà Vecchia 198
Museo Civico 199
Museum of Christian Art 58,
  200
Museum of Modern Art 199–
  200
Pegol 199
Piazza del Duomo 198
Piazza del Foro 199
Piazza della Loggia 198
Piazza Vittoriale 62, 198
Pinacoteca 200
Roman gate 200
Roman remains 58, 199–200
Roman Theatre 199
San Faustino in Riposo 201
San Francesco 201
San Giovanni 201
San Pietro in Oliveto 200
Santa Giulia 199–200
Santa Maria dei Miracoli 201
Santa Maria del Carmine 201
Santi Nazaro e Celso 201
Torre dell'Orologio 198
Torre Palata 201
tourist information 198
where to stay 201
La Brianza 172
  eating out 173
  where to stay 173
Brissago 147
Brissago islands 147
Brixia 197, 199–200
Brueghel, Jan, the Younger 94
Brunate 160
buses 4, 11, 79, 80

Cadenabbia 163
  where to stay 164
Il Caffè (newspaper) 64
Cainallo 171

Calderara, Antonio 136–7
Caltellina: where to stay 179
Camoscio, Monte 146
Campanone della Brianza 172
Campello Monti 137
Campi, Antonio 115
Campi family 114, 156
camping 39
Campione 212
Campione d'Italia 153, 156
  Madonna dei Ghirli 156
  San Pietro 156
Campionesi Masters 58, 82, 105, 156, 166, 182
Campo dei Fiori natural park 150, 153
Campo Moro 176
Campodolcino 175
Camuni 191, 192
Candoglia 137
Cannero Riviera 147
  where to stay 149
Canneto dell'Oglio: festival 21
Cannobio 147
Canova, Antonio 62, 163
Cantù:
  Basilica di San Vicenzo 58, 160
  festival 20
Capo di Ponte:
  prehistoric art 191, 192
  San Salvatore 192
  San Siro 192
Capodiferro di Lovere 183
Capolago 157
Capriate San Gervasio: Parco Minitalia 186
car hire 13
car travel 4–5, 11–13, 78, 80, 81
Caramuel de Labkowitz, Juan 113
Carate Brianza 172
Caravaggio, Michelangelo Merisi da 61, 89, 95, 186
Caravaggio: sanctuary 186
Carloni, Carlo 202
Carlotta, Princess of the Netherlands 163
Caroline, Queen of England 162, 163

Carona 187
Carpaccio, Vittore 89
Carrà, Carlo 84
carroccio 75, 76
Casalzuigno 153
Cascata della Frua (del Toce) 139
Cascata del Troggia 171
Cascata del Varone 213
casinos 33
Caspoggio 176
Casteldidone: festival 21
Castelséprio:
  frescoes 58, 151–2
  Santa Maria Foris Portas 151
Castiglione Olona:
  Baptistry 152
  Casa dei Castiglioni 152
  Chiesa di Villa 152
  Collegiata 152
  frescoes 59, 150, 152
Castiglioni, Cardinal Branda 59, 152
Catherine of Alexandria, St 148–9
Catullus 68, 200, 203
Cavoglio Spoccia 147
Cedegolo 192
Celts 44, 180
Cemmo: prehistoric engravings 192
Ceppo Morelii 138
Cerano (Giovanni Battista Crespi) 61
Ceresa, Carlo 61
Ceresio, Lake see Lugano, Lake
Cernobbio 162
  eating out 164
  where to stay 163–4
Cerro: Palazzo Perabò 1148
Ceruti, Giacomo Antonio ('Il Pitocchetto') 61, 197, 200
Cevedale 177
Cézanne, Paul 87
Charlemagne 47, 108, 197
Charles of Anjou 49
Charles V of Spain 51, 77, 110
Charles VIII of France 50, 77
Chavez, Georges 138
Cheggio 138

chemists 26
Chiavenna:
  Crotti 174
  festival 21, 174
  Marmitte dei Giganti 175
  Paradiso 174–5
  San Lorenzo 174
Chiesa, Mario 55
Chiesa in Valmalenco: Museo Storico Etnografico 176
children 16–17
Christian I of Denmark 185
Christmas cribs 148
chronology 243–6
churches: opening hours 27–8
Cima da Conegliano, Giovanni Battista 89
Cimetta Cardada 147
Cinque Giornate revolt 52
Cisalpine Gaul 44
Cislano 190
Civate:
  San Calocero 172
  San Pietro al Monte 58
Cividate Camuno: Archaeological Museum 191
Clement XIII, Pope 166
climate 17–18
Clusane 194
Clusone:
  astronomical clock 188
  Oratorio del Disciplini 188
coaches 11
Codera 174
Cólico 167
Colle di Balisio 170
Colleoni, Bartolomeo 180–1, 182, 185–6
Collio 202
Colombaro: Villa Lana 189
Colombetti 138
Comabbio, Lake 151
Comacina 162
  eating out 164
  festival 162–3
Comaschi Masters 59
commedia dell'arte 68–9, 187
Como 159–62
  Broletto 159
  Casa del Fascio 62, 160

Como (*cont'd.*)
Duomo 59, **159–60**
eating out 161–2
Giardini Pubblici 159
Guardia di Finanza 160, 198
history 75, 159
Museo Civico 160
Piazza Cavour 159
Pinacoteca 160
Porta Vittoria 160
San Fedele 160
Sant'Abbondio 59, 160
sports and activities 160
Tempio Voltiano 159
Torre del Comune 159
where to stay 161
Como, Lake *154–5*, **157–73**
eating out 161–2, 164–5, 169
getting around 158
sports and activities 160
tourist information 158–9
Villa Carlotta 62
where to stay 161, 163–4,
167–8
Como province 35
comuni 48–9, 75–6, 108
Congress of Vienna 52
Constance, Treaty of 49, 76
Constantine the Great 45, 75
consulates 19
Corenno Plinio:
Castello Andreani 166
St Thomas à Becket 166
Cornello dei Tasso 187
Cornizzolo:
Oratorio di San Benedetto 172
San Pietro al Monte 172
Corno Stella 187
Corot, Jean-Baptiste Camille 87
Correggio, Antonio Allegri 110
Cortabbio 171
Corteno Golgi 176
Cortenova 171
Costa, Lorenzo, Il Giovane 123
Costiera dei Cèch 175
Council of Trent 142
Cranach, Lucas 86
Craxi, Bettino 56, 78
credit cards 27

Crema **118–19**
Duomo 118
history 65, 118
Museo Civico 118–19
Palazzo Terni de Gregori 119
Porta Serio 119
Santa Maria della Croce 119
Villa Ghisetti–Giavarina 119
Cremeno 170
Cremona **113–18**
activities 117
Baptistry di San Giovanni 115–
16
Cittanova 116
Duomo (cathedral) 59, 60,
113, **115**, 156
eating out 117–18
festival 113
food 113
getting to and from 114
history 113–14
International School of Violin-
making 116
Loggia dei Militi 116
Museo Civico 61, 114
Museo Stradivariano 114
Palazzo Affaitati 114
Palazzo del Comune 66, 116
Palazzo Fodri 115
Palazzo Raimondi 116
Palazzo Stanga 114
Palazzo Trecchi 116
Piazza Roma 114
Saletta dei Violini 116
San Luca 116
San Sigismondo 116
Sant'Agata 116
Sant'Agostino 116
Teatro Ponchielli 116
Torrazzo 115
tourist information 114
violin making 66–7, 113
where to stay 117
crime 18
Crivelli, Angelo 145
Crivelli, Carlo 86, 89, 184
Crodo 139
Crusades 48
Curaglia 148

Curone: Park 172
currency 5
Curtatone: festival 21
Customs 5
cycling 14
Cydnean Hill 200

Da Cemmo, Giovanni Pietro 60,
118, 191, 203
Da Cossa, Francesco 89
D'Annunzio, Gabriele 62, 203,
210–12
Dante Alighieri 110, 226
De Chirico, Giorgio 84, 89, 90
De Fondutis, Agosto 95
De Pisis, Filippo Tibertelli 84
Delio, Lake 148
Dervio 166
Desenzano del Garda 206–7
Desiderius, King 197
Dezzo Ravine 191
Diocletian 45, 75
disabled travellers 18–19
Disgrazia, Monte 175
Divizioli, Giovanni Battista 115
Domaso 158
Domodossola 138–9
Museo Civico 138
where to stay 140
Dongo 166
Donizetti, Gaetano 180, 181,
183
Drena 213
Dro 213
Duccio di Buoninsegna 89
Dumenza 148
Dunant, Henry 207
Dürer, Albrecht 184

eating out 22–4
*see also under individual
places*
Edolo 192
embassies 19
emergencies 25–6
entry formalities 5
Erba: where to stay 173
Erbusco 189, 190–1
eating out 190–1, 194
where to stay 192–3

Ermengarda 197
Esine 192
Esino Lario: Grigna Mountain
Museum 171
Este, Isabella d' 120, 124, 125
Estense, Baldassarre 94
exchange bureaux 26–7
executions: hierarchy 64

Faggeto Lario: Villa Pliniana 162
Falmenta 147
Fantoni, Antonio 61, 171, 188
farmhouses 40
Fascism 53, 62, 78, 195, 208–9,
211
Ferrari, Gaudenzio 106, 136,
160
ferries see boats
festivals 19–21
Filarete (Antonio Averlino) 59,
90
first-aid 26
fishing 33–4
Fiumelatte 165
food 21–4, 113, 127
football 34, 97
Foppa, Vincenzo 60, 86, 110,
197, 200, 201
Foppe 192
Foppolo 187
Forno 137
Fornovo, Battle of 50, 77, 120
France: rule by 50–1, 52–3
Francia, Francesco Raibolini 201
Franciacorta 189
where to eat 190–1
Francis, St 136
Francis I of France 110
Franks 46–7
Franz Joseph, Emperor 207
Frederick I (Barbarossa) 48–9,
65–6, 75–6, 96, 105, 108,
109, 197
Frederick II 49
Fugazza (architect) 110

Gaius Marius 44
Gallio, Cardinal Tolomeo 163
Gandino: Basilica 188
Ganna: Badia di San Gemolo 153

Garda 219
eating out 222
where to stay 221–2
Garda, Lake 203–22, 204–5
eating out 217, 222
entertainment and nightlife
217–18
getting around 203, 206
tourist information 206, 218
where to stay 213–17, 221–2
Gardone Riviera:
Giardino Botanico Hruska 210
Il Vittoriale (D'Annunzio's
villa) 62, 210–12
where to stay 215
Gardone Val Trompia 202
Gargnano 212
eating out 217
where to stay 216
Garibaldi, Giuseppe 53, 181
Garlate, Lake 172
Silk Museum 172
Gauguin, Paul 87
Gavirate 151
Gentile da Fabriano 89
Germans: control by 50, 51, 53
Gerosa: festival 21
getting around 8–14
see also under individual
places
getting there 2–5
see also under individual
places
Ghevio 143
Ghiaccialo dei Forno 177
Ghibellines 49, 65, 75
Ghiffa 147
Ghirla, Lake 153
Giardino Botanico Rezio 178
Gignese: Umbrella Museum 143
Giorgione, Giorgio Barbarelli 94
Giovanni da Campione 182
Golasecca 151
gold mining 138
golf 34, 97
Gonzaga, Cardinal Ercole 120
Gonzaga, Federico II 120, 1125
Gonzaga, Gianfrancesco I 120,
123
Gonzaga, Gianfrancesco II 120

Gonzaga, Guglielmo 120
Gonzaga, Ludovico 120, 124
Gonzaga, Vespasiano 60, 128–30
Gonzaga, Vicenzo I 120
Gonzaga family 49, 60, 119–20,
123–4
Goths 45–6, 75, 108
Gozzano:
Torre di Buccione 137
Villa Junker 137
graffiti rock incisions 58, 188,
191, 192
Grand Zebrù 177
Gravedona 166–7
San Vicenzo 167
Santa Maria del Tiglio 166–7
Gravellona Toce 137
Gregory I (the Great), Pope 46,
105
Gregory II, Pope 110
Gregory VII, Pope 48
Gregory XIV, Pope 172
Grigna Mountains 170
Grosio 58
festival 20
Parco delle Incisioni Rupestri
177
Grosotto 177
Casa di Cipriano Valorsa 177
San Giorgio 177
Grotta della Meraviglie 187
Grotta del Sogno 187
Grotte: Birreria Liberty Poretti
153
Guardi, Francesco 85, 90
Guarneri, Giuseppe 66, 113, 116
Guelphs 49, 65, 116
guesthouses 37–8
Guglielmo, Monte 190
Gurro 147

Habsburgs 51–2, 77, 120, 173,
207
health 25–6
hiking 34–5
Hildebrand see Gregory VII,
Pope
history 43–56
barbarians 45–6, 75
chronology 243–6

(history cont'd.)
  comuni 48–9, 75–6, 108
  Empire 44–5
  foreign rule 50–3, 77–8, 105,
    173
  Ghibellines 49, 65, 75
  Guelphs 49, 65
  Italian Enlightenment 64–5
  Middle Ages 46–50, 75–6, 83
  Napoleonic 52
  post-war 53–4, 78
  present-day 54–6
  Renaissance 49–50
  terminology 223–5
  unification 52–3, 78
  World Wars 53, 78, 208–9
hitchhiking 14
Hitler, Adolf 208, 209
holidays:
  national 28
  special-interest 6–8
hotels 37–8
houses: buying 16
hydrofoils 9, 142, 158

Idro 202
Idro, Lake 202–3
Induno Olona: where to stay 157
insurance 12, 25
Intra 146
Intragna 147
Introbio: Arrigoni Tower 170
Introzzo: San Martino 171
Iseo:
  eating out 195
  Pieve di Sant'Andrea 189
  where to stay 193
Iseo, Lake 58, 188–91
  eating out 194–5
  getting around 188–9
  tourist information 189
  where to stay 192–3
Isola Bella 145
Isola Dovarese: festival 21
Isola Madre 145
Isola dei Pescatori 145
  where to stay 146
Isola San Giovanni 145
Isola San Giulio 136
  Basilica 136

Isolino Virginia: Museo
  Preistorico di Villa Ponti 151
Italic tribes 44

Jefferson, Thomas 65
John XXIII, Pope 186
Joseph II of Austria 52, 149
Julius, St 136
Justinian, Emperor 45–6

Kauffmann, Angelica 182

Laghi Gemelli 187
Lago see name of lake
Lakes 131–222
  see also individual lakes
  getting around 133, 141–2,
    151, 153, 156, 158, 188–9,
    203, 206
Landi (artist) 184
Lanfranc, Archbishop of
  Canterbury 108, 110
Lanfranco, Giovanni 151
language 226–42
Lantana, Giambattista 198
Lanzo d'Intelvi 162, 1587
Laveno 148
  festival 21
Lazise 219
Lecco 169–70
  Monument to Manzoni 170
  Ponte Azzone Visconti 169
  San Nicolò 169
  Torre Visconti 169
  Villa Manzoni 169–70
  where to stay 171
Lecco, Lake 158, 169–71
Ledro, Lake 58, 213
Legnano:
  festival 20
  history 65, 66, 76
Lenno 163
  Baptistry 163
Leo I, Pope St 207
Leo III, Pope 47
Leonardo da Vinci 59, 77, 89,
  91, 93, 94, 95, 109, 113, 124,
  165, 169
Leoni, Leone 83
Lezzano: Grotta dei Búlberi 163

Limone sul Garda 212
  where to stay 216
Lippi, Filippo 90
Liutprand 46, 110
Locarno 147
Lodi 105–6
  history 75
  La Incoronata 106
  San Bassiano 106
Lodovico Il Moro see Sforza,
  Lodovico Il Moro
Lombard League 49, 65, 76,
  105, 197
Lombard Plain 107–30
Lombards 46, 75
Lomellina 113
Lomello:
  Baptistry 58, 113
  Basilica di Santa Maria 113
Longhi, Martino 153
Lotto, Lorenzo 60, 86, 180, 181,
  183, 184, 186, 200
Louis XII of France 77, 95
Lovere:
  Galleria dell'Accademia Tadini
    190
  Santa Maria in Valvendra 190
Lugano:
  Santa Maria degli Angioli 59,
    156
  Villa Favorita 156–7
Lugano, Lake 153–7, 154–5
  eating out 157
  getting around 153, 156
  tourist information 156
  where to stay 157
luggage 28–9
Luini, Bernardino 59, 86, 92, 93,
  94, 106, 111, 148, 156, 160,
  176
Luino:
  Oratorio di Santi Pietro e Paolo
    148
  where to stay 149–50

Maccagno 148
McEacharn, Neil 146
Macugnaga 138
  where to stay 140
Madesimo 175

Mafia 54–5, 56
Maggio 170
Maggiore, Lake *134–5*, **141–50**
  eating out 144–5, 150
  entertainment and nightlife
    145, 150
  getting around 141–2
  Santuario della Madonna del
    Sasso 147
  sports and activities 149
  tourist information 142
  where to stay 144, 149–50
Magnasco, Alessandro 62, 95
Magyars 47
Malcésine 35, 218–19
  Palace of the Captains of the
    Lake 219
  Scaliger castle 218
  where to stay 221
Malnate: Museum of Transport
  152
Malonno 192
Malpaga 185–6
Mandello del Lario: Motorcycle
  Museum 170
Manet, Edouard 87
Manfred, King of Sicily 49
Mangone, Fabio 61
Mantegna, Andrea 60, 85, 89,
  90, 122, 124, 184
Mantovano, Rinaldo 124
Mantua **119–28**, *121*
  activities 126
  Basilica di Santa Barbara 123
  Bosco della Fontana 128
  Broletto 122
  Casa di Boniforte 122
  Casa di Giulio Romano 125
  Casa di Mantegna 125
  Casa di Rigoletto 123
  Casetta dei Nani 124
  Castello 123, 124
  Duomo 123
  eating out 127–8
  festival 20
  getting to and from 120
  history 119–20
  Museo Gonzaga 125
  Palazzo d'Arco 125
  Palazzo Ducale 123–4

Palazzo della Ragione 122
Palazzo del Te 60, 120, 125
Piazza dell'Erbe 122
Piazza Mantegna 122
Piazza Sordello 122–3
Piazza Virgiliana 125
Rotonda di San Lorenzo 122
San Francesco 125
San Sebastiano 125
Sanctuary of the Madonna
  della Grazie 128
Sant'Andrea 60, **122**
Teatro Scientifico 124–5
Torre della Gabbia 123
tourist information 122
Valletta Belfiore 128
where to stay 126–7
Manzoni, Alessandro 78, 85, 90,
  169–70, 226
maps 26
Marchesi, Gualtiero 189, **190–1**,
  192
Marco d'Oggiono 172
Margerin, Jacques 193
Maria Theresa of Austria 52, 77,
  94, 109
Marone 190
Maroni, Gian Carlo 210
Masolino da Panicale 59, 150,
  152
Mastino I della Scala 207
Matilda, Countess of Canossa
  119, 122, 128
Matisse, Henri 87
Mazzarditi brothers 147
measures 37
Medici, Gian Giacomo de' (Il
  Medeghino) 166
Mediolanum 44–5, 74–5, 94, 96
Meina 143
Meinulphus, Duke 136
Menaggio:
  eating out 169
  where to stay 168
Mergozzo:
  Antiquarium of Mont'Orfano
    137
  San Giovanni 137
Mergozzo, Lake 137, 146
Mezzagra 163

Mezzola, Lake 174
Miazzina 147
Michelangelo Buonarotti 89, 116
Michelozzo, Michelozzi 96
Milan 71–106, *72–3*
  Ambrosiana 61, 93, 94–5
    Pinacoteca 94–5
  archaeological museum 58
  Archi di Porta Nuova 86
  Arco della Pace 90
  Borsa 94
  Brera 88–9
  Brera Gallery (Academy) 59,
    61, 62, 77, **88–9**
  Campanile di San Gottardo 84
  Casa Galimberti 87
  Casa degli Omenoni 85
  Casa Rustici 90
  Castello Sforzesco 61, **89–90**
    Cortile della Rocchetta 90
    Pinacoteca 90
  Cimitero Monumentale 90
  Civico Galleria d'Arte Moderna
    62, **87**
  Civico Museo Archeologico 92
  Civico Museo d'Arte Antica del
    Castello 89–90
  Civico Museo dell'Arte
    Contemporanea (CIMAC)
    62, 84
  Civico Museo di Milano 86
  Civico Museo di Storia
    Contemporanea 86
  Collegio Elvetico (Archivo di
    Stato) 61
  Colonne di San Lorenzo 96
  Corso Venezia 87
  Duomo (Cathedral) 58, 59,
    81–4
    Baptistry of St Ambrose 83
    roof 84
  eating out 100–2
  entertainment and nightlife
    102–4
  excursions from 105–6
  festivals 20–1, 75
  Galleria Vittorio Emanuele 62,
    84–5
  getting around 79, 80–1
  getting to and from 78–80

(Milan *cont'd.*)
Giardini Pubblici 87
Giardini di Villa Reale 87
history 48, 52, 53–4, 55–6,
   74–8
Leonardo da Vinci Museum of
   Science and Technology
   93–4
Monastero Maggiore 91–2
Museo della Basilica di
   Sant'Ambrogio 93
Museo del Duomo 84
Museo Manzoniano 85
Museo Poldi-Pezzoli 85–6
Museo Teatrale alla Scala 85
Museum of Musical
   Instruments 90
Museum of Science and
   Technology 93–4
Natural History Museum 87
Navigli District 96–7
Ospedale Maggiore 59, 90
Palazzo dell'Arte 90
Palazzo di Brera 61
Palazzo Castiglione 87, 88
Palazzo Fidia 87
Palazzo Marino 85
Palazzo Morando Bolognini 86
Palazzo della Ragione 94
Palazzo Reale 84
Palazzo Serbelloni 87
Parco Sempione 90
Piazza Cardusio 94
Piazza Carrobbio 96
Piazza della Repubblica 88
Piazza della Scala 85
Pirelli Building 62, 88
Porta Romana 95
Porta Ticinese 96
Pusteria di Sant'Ambrogio 92
San Alessandro 61
San Celso 96
San Giuseppe 61
San Lorenzo 76
San Lorenzo Maggiore 58, 96
   chapel of Sant'Aquilino 96
San Maurizio 59, 92
San Nazaro Maggiore 95
   Cappella Trivulzio 95

San Satiro (Santa Maria presso
   San Satiro) 59, **95**
   Baptistry 95
   Campanile 95
   Cappella della Pietà 58, 95
San Simpliciano 89
Santa Maria delle Grazie 59,
   91
Santa Maria Podone 61
Santa Maria presso San Celso
   95–6
Sant'Ambrogio 58, 59, 76, **92**,
   156
Sant'Eustorgio 60, **96**
   Cappella Portinari 59, **96**
La Scala Theatre 85, 102
shopping **30–3**
sports and activities 34, 97
Ticinese Quarter 96
tourist information 81
Via Manzoni 85
Via Montenapoleone 86
Via della Spiga 86
Villa Reale 87
War Memorial 93
where to stay 97–9
Millet, Jean François 87
Modena: cathedral 156
Modigliani, Amedeo 84
Molina 213
Moltrasio:
   Villa Passalacqua 162
   Villa Salterio 162
Monate, Lake 151
money 26–7
Monore, Domenico 123
Montague, Lady Mary Wortley
   188
Monte Baldo 218
Monte Camoscio 146
Monte Disgrazia 175
Monte Guglielmo 190
Monte Isola 188, 189–90
   where to stay 193
Monte Mottarone 143
Monte Resegone 170
Monte Rosa 138
Monteverdi, Claudio 66–7, 120,
   123

Montirone: Villa Lechi 202
Montodine: festival 21
Monza **105**
   Crown of Italy 105
   Duomo (cathedral) 58, 59,
      105, 106, 156
   festivals 20, 21
   Museo Serpero 105
   Parco di Monza 105
   San Francesco 106
Morandi, Giorgio 84
Morazzone (Pier Francesco
   Mazzucchelli) 61, 152
Morbegno 175
Morcote 156
Moretto da Brescia (Alessandro
   Bonvicino) 60, 96, 189, 197,
   198, 200, 201
Moroni, Giovanni Battista 60,
   180, 184, 197, 200
mosaics 58
motor racing 35
motorcycles: hiring 14
motorways 12
Mottarone, Monte 133, 143
mountaineering 34–5
Mozart, Wolfgang Amadeus 125,
   202
museums:
   entrance charges 28
   opening hours 28
Musso: Rocca 166
Mussolini, Benito 53, 62, 78,
   163, **208–9**, 210, 211
Muzio, Giovanni 93

Napoleon Bonaparte 52, 77–8,
   88, 90, 105, 111, 137, 138
Napoleon III 52, 207
Naquane rock 192
Narses 46
national holidays 28
Nervi, Pier Luigi 62, 88
newspapers 26, 64
Nicola da Verdun 83
Nietsche, Friedrich Wilhelm 133
Novale: Villa Suardi 186
Novate Mezzola 174

Odoacer 45, 108
Oggiono: Santa Eufemia 172
Olate 170
Omegna 137
  festival 21
  where to stay 140
Oneta 69
  Casa dell'Arlecchino 187
opening hours 27–8
Orasso 147
Orfano, Mount 137
Orobie Alps 186
Orrido di Sant'Anna 147
Orta, Lake **133–41**, *134–5*
  eating out 140–1
  festival 20
  getting around 133
  Santuario della Madonna del
    Sasso 137
  Torre di Buccione 137
  tourist information 133
  where to stay 139–40
Orta San Giulio 133–6
  eating out 140–1
  festivals 20
  Palazzotto 136
  Sacro Monte 136
  Villa Crespi 136
  where to stay 139–40
Ortanella 171
Ortles 177
Ossola valleys 137–9
Ossuccio: festival 21
Osteno 157
Otto I (the Great) 47, 219

packing 28–9
Paderno: Museo Ponchiellano
  118
Palermo 54–5, 88
Palestrina, Giovanni 142
Palladio, Andrea 198
Pallanza 146
  eating out 150
  Madonna di Campagna 146
  Museo del Paesaggio 146
  where to stay 149
Parco delle Incisioni Rupestri
  177
Parco Naturale di Campo dei
  Fiori 150, 153

Parco Nazionale delle Incisioni
  Rupestri Preistoriche 192
Parco Nazionale delle Stelvio
  177, 178
Partito Operaio Italiano 53
Passo del Maniva 202
Passo Monte Moro 138
Passo della Presolana 188
Passo di Stelvio 177
Passo di Tonale 192
passports 5
Pasturo 170
Pavia **108–12**
  Basilica di San Michele 109
  Broletto 109
  Castello Visconteo 110, 111
  Certosa di Pavia 59, 60, 76,
    96, 108, **110–11**
  Civic Museum 58
  Covered Bridge 109
  Duomo 76, **109**
  eating out 112
  getting to and from 108
  history 47, 75, 108
  Museo Civico 110
  San Francesco d'Assisi 110
  San Lanfranco 110
  San Michele, Basilica di 59,
    109
  San Pietro in Ciel d'Oro 59,
    110
  San Teodoro 109
  Santa Maria del Carmine 110
  Sant'Eusebio 110
  Studio 108, 109
  Torre Civica 109
  Torri 109
  tourist information 109
  University 108, 109
  where to stay 111–12
Pavia, Battle of 110
Perugino, Pietro Vannucci 116,
  124
Pescantina: Dinosaur Park 219
Pescarenico 170
Peschiera del Garda 219–20
  Gardaland 220
Pestarena 138
Petacci, Clara 163, 209
Peter Martyr, St (of Verona) 166
Pettenasco: where to stay 140

photography 29
Piacentini, Marcello 198
Pian di Spagna 167, 174
Piani d'Erna 170
Piani Resinelli 170
Piani del Tivano 165
Piano, Lake 157
Piazza Brembana 187
Piazzatorre 187
Piazzi, Giuseppe 176
Picasso, Pablo 87
Piero della Francesco 85, 89
Pinturicchio (Bernardino di
  Betto) 94
Piona, Abbazia di 167
Piona, Lake 167
Pisanello (Antonio Pisano) 120,
  123, 184
Pisogne: Santa Maria delle Neve
  60, 190
Piuro 175
Pius IV, Pope 142, 166
Pius V, Pope 109
Pizzighettone: festival 20
Pizzo dei Tre Signori 170–1
plague 50
Platini, G.M. 115
Pliny the Elder (Gaius Plinius
  Secundus) 67, 93, 159, 169
Pliny the Younger 68, 159, 162,
  163, 165
police 18
Polirone 128
Pollaiuolo, Antonio 85
Pollak, Leopoldo 87
Ponchielli, Amilcare 116, 118
Ponte 139
Ponte di Legno 192
  eating out 195
Ponte Tresa 156
Ponte in Valtellina: San Maurizio
  176
Ponti, Gio 62, 88
Pordenone, Giovanni Antonio de
  Sacchis 115
Porlezza 157
  where to stay 157
Porto Ceresio 156
post offices 29–30
Prealpi Varesine 150
Predis, Ambrogio de 95

Premana 171
Premano: festival 20
Premeno 146–7
    Oratorio di San Salvatore 147
presepio 148
Primaluna: San Pietro 171
Procaccini, Giulio Cesare 61
pronunciation 226
Protestants 173
Provaglio:
    San Pietro in Lamosa 189
    Torbiere 189
Punta di San Vigilio: Guarienti
    villa 219

Quarna 137
Querini, Cardinal 198, 199

rail travel 3–4, 9–11, 79, 108
    underground 80
rainfall 18
Ranco: eating out 150
Raphael 86, 88–9, 95, 184, 200
Red Cross 207
refuges 40
Rembrandt Harmensz van Rijn
    89
Renoir, Pierre Auguste 87
Resegone, Monte 170
Resistance 53
restaurants:
    prices 23–4
    types 23
Rezzonico 166
Ricchino, Francesco Maria 61
Ricengo: Villa Ghisetti–Giavarina
    119
Risorgimento 52, 65, 78, 181,
    207
Riva del Garda 35, 212–13
    Bastione 213
    Church of the Inviolata 213
    entertainment and nightlife
        217–18
    Rocca 213
    Torre Apponale 213
    where to stay 216–17
Riva di Solto 190
Rivolta d'Adda: Zoo di Preistoria
    186

road travel 4–5, 11–14, 80, 108
Roberti, Ercole de' 89
Rodari, Tommaso 160
Rodengo 189
Rodi, Faustino 119
Romana, Ezzelino da 197
Romanino, Girolamo 60, 115,
    189, 190, 192, 197, 198, 200
Romano, Giulio 60, 120, 123,
    124, 125, 128
Romans 44, 67–8, 159, 191,
    199–200, 206
Romulus Augustulus 45, 108
Roncobello 187
Rosa, Monte 138
Rossini, Gioacchino 162
Rovato: eating out 195
Rubens, Sir Peter Paul 124

Sabbioneta 60, **128–30**
    eating out 130
    Galleria degli Antichi 129–30
    Incoronata 130
    Museum of Sacred Art 130
    Palazzo Ducale 130
    Palazzo del Giardino 130
    Synagogue 130
    Teatro Olimpico 130
Sacro Monte 152–3
    Santa Maria del Monte 153
sailing 35
Sale Marasino 190
    where to stay 193
Salò 208–9
    L'Ateneo 208
    Cathedral 208
    eating out 217
    Museo del Nastro Azzurro 208
    where to stay 214
Sammicheli (architect) 219
Samnite War, Third 44
Samolaco 174
San Benedetto Po:
    Basilica 128
    Museo della Cultura Popolare
        Padana 128
    Polirone abbey 59, 128
San Giacomo valley 175
San Giorgio di Cola 174
San Giovanni Bianco 187

San Mamete 157
    where to stay 157
San Martino della Battaglia:
    Torre Monumentale 207
San Pellegrino Terme 62, 187
San Simone 187
Sansovino, Andrea 186, 198
Santa Caterina del Sasso 148–9
Santa Caterina Valfurva 177
Santa Margherita 157
Santa Maria Maggiore:
    Museo dello Spazzocamino
        139
    Scuola di belle arti 139
    where to stay 140
Sant'Antonio 153
Sant'Elia, Antonio 159
Sarnico 189
    eating out 195
    where to stay 193
Saronno 59
    Santuario della Madonna dei
        Miracoli 106
Sas Galet 148
Sasso del Ferro 148
Sasso Ramenno 175
Scamozzi, Vincenzo 129, 130,
    181
Scapigliati 62, 87
Schignano: festival 20
Schilpàrio 188
self-catering accommodation
    40–1
Sentiero dei Contrabbandieri 178
Sentiero delle Orobie 187
Sentiero Roma 175
Serodini, Giovanni 95
Severini, Gino 89
Sforza, Francesco 77, 89, 90,
    114, 118
Sforza, Galeazzo Maria 77, 118
Sforza, Lodovico (Il Moro) 59,
    77, 91, 95, 111, 113, 169
Shelley, Percy Bysshe 162
shopping **30–3**
shops: opening hours 27
Sigurtà Gardens 220
Silvera 143
Simplon Pass 138
Simplon Tunnel 138

Sirmione:
  antiquarium 207
  Castello Scaligero 207
  eating out 217
  Grotte di Catullo 207
  San Pietro in Mavino 207
  Villa of Catullus 58
  where to stay 213–14
Sixtus of Nuremberg 182
skiing 35
Socialist movement 53, 78
Solari, Cristoforo 59, 111
Solari, Guiniforte 91
Solferino:
  San Piero 207
  Spia d'Italia 207
Solferino, Battle of 207
Sommaruga, Giuseppe 88
Soncino: Castello Sforza 118
Sóndalo 177
Sondrio 175–6
  Castello Masegra 175
  Museo Valtellinese 175–6
  Palazzo Quadrio 175–6
  where to stay 179
Sondrio province **173–80**
  eating out 178–9
  getting around 174
  sports and activities 178
  tourist information 174
  where to stay 178–9
Sorico 166
Sotto del Monte 186
Spain: rule by 50–1, 173
special-interest holidays **6–8**
speed limits 12
Splügen Pass 175
Spoleto, Dukes of 47
sports **33–5**, 97
Staffa 138
  eating out 141
  where to stay 140
Stelvio National Park 177, 178
Stendhal 162, 172
Stradivarius, Antonio 66, 113,
  115, 116
Stresa 141
  eating out 144–5
  entertainment and nightlife
  145

festival 21, 143, 145
  Grand Hotel des Iles
  Borromées 143
  Villa Pallavicino 143
  where to stay 144
strikes 8
Suardi, Bartolomeo see
  Bramantino
Superiore, Lake 128
swimming 35, 97
Switzerland: rule by 50–1

Tangentopoli 54, 55, 78
Tanzio, Il (Antonio d'Enrico) 61
Tartano: where to stay 179
Tasso family 187
Tavèrnola Bergamasca 190
taxis 14, 81
Teglio 58, 176–7
  Antiquarium Tellinum 176–7
  festival 21, 176
  Palazzo Besta 176
  San Pietro 177
telephones 35–6
  emergency numbers 25
temperatures 17
Terragni, Giorgio 62, 160, 198
theatre 68–9
Theodolinda, Queen 46, 105,
  166, 172
Theodoric, Emperor 45, 110
Thorvaldsen, Bertel 62, 163
Three Parishes republic 166
Thyssen–Bronemisza, Baron
  Heinrich 156
Tibaldi, Pellegrino 152, 186
Tiepolo, Gian Domenico 206
Tiepolo, Giovanni Battista 182
time 36
Tintoretto 84, 89, 124
Tirano: Sanctuary of the
  Madonna 177
Titian 95, 124, 184, 186, 201
toilets 36
Tomba di Taino 171
Tommaso da Modena 125
Torbole 35, 218
Torno 162
Torre 171
Torrente Enna 187

Torri del Benaco:
  Santa Trinità 219
  Scaliger castle 219
  where to stay 221
Torri di Fraele 178
Toscanini, Arturo 90, 145
Toscolano-Maderno: Sant'Andrea
  212
tour operators **6–8**
  self–catering 40–1
tourist offices 28, 36
trains 3–4, 9–11, 79, 108
  hierarchy 9–10
trams 80
travel **1–14**
  insurance 25
Treménico 171
Tremezzina 163
  Villa Carlotta 163
Tremezzo 158, 163
  eating out 164–5
  where to stay 164
Tremósine 212
Treviglio: San Martino 186
Trianolo Lariano 165
Trivulzio, Giangiacomo 95
Tura, Cosmé 86
Turbino, Antonio 202

Udine, Palazzo Comunale 88
Urban IV, Pope 49

vaccinations 26
Val d'Antrona 138
Val Brandet 176
Val Brembana 186–7
Val Camonica 58, 188, **191–2**
  eating out 195
  getting around 188–9
  tourist information 189
  where to stay 194
Val Camovecchio 176
Val Cannobina 147
Val Codera 174
Val Malenco 176
Val Másino 175
Val di Mello 175
Val di Saviore 192
Val Tartano 175
  where to stay 179

Val Varrone 171
Val Veddasca 148
Val Vigezzo 138–9
Valchiavenna 173, **174–5**
  eating out 180
San Fedelino 174
  where to stay 179
Valdidentro 178
Valeggio: Sigurtà Gardens 220
Valle d'Ampola 213
Valle d'Angolo 191
Valle Anzasca 137–8
  where to stay 140
Valle di Corteno 192
Valle di Livigno 178
Valle Malga 192
Valle Seriana 188
Valli Antigorio e Formazza 139
Valli dei Bitto 175
Valorsa, Cipriano 60, 177
Valsassina 170–1
Valstrona 137
Valtellina 167, 173, **175,
  176–7**, 209
  eating out 180
Valtrompia 202
Van der Goes, Hugo 110
Van Dyck, Sir Anthony 89
Van Gogh, Vincent 87
Varenna 165–6
  Castello Vezio 166
  Oratorio do San Giovanni
    Battista 166
  San Giorgio 166
  Villa Cipressi 166
  Villa Monastero 165–6
  where to stay 168
Varese 61
  Baptistry 152

Basilica di San Vittore 152
Campanile del Bernascone 152
Castello di Masagno 152
  getting around 151
Giardino Pubblio 152
Hotel Tre Coli 88
Museo Civico 152
Palazzo Estense 152
  tourist information 151
Villa Fabio Ponti 152
Varese, Lake 151
  island in 58, 151
Varone 213
Vecchio, Palma 180
Veneziano, Paolo 208
Venice: importance 181–2, 197,
  218
Verbania 141, 146
  Villa Taranto 146
  where to stay 149
Verdi, Giuseppe 65–6, 85, 119,
  163
Verona: cathedral 156
Veronese, Paolo Caliari 89
Verri, Pietro and Alessandro 64
Vespasian, Emperor 199
Vetta Paradiso 153
Vezzo 143
Victoria, Queen 146
Viganò Brianza: eating out 173
Vigévano:
  castle 113
  Cathedral 113
  Piazza Ducale 113
Viggiù 153
  Villa Cicogna Mozzoni 156
Villa Carlotta 163
Villadossola 138
violin making 66–7

Virgil 119, 203
visas 5
Visconti, Bianca Maria 77, 114,
  116
Visconti, Gian Galeazzo 50,
  76–7, 81–3, 108, 110–11
Visconti family 49, 50, 76–7,
  81–2, 89, 113, 143, 147, 183,
  197, 220
Vitale de Bologna 85–6
Vittorino da Feltre 120
Vittorio Emanuele II 207
Vittorio Emanuele III 105
Vivarini family 89
Volta, Alessandro 159
Voltaire 64
Voltorre: San Michele monastery
  151

waterskiing 35
watersports 35
weights and measures 37
where to stay 37–41
wine 24–5, 173–4, 189
winter sports 35
women travellers 41
words and phrases 226–42
World War, Second 53, 208–9

youth hostels 38–9

Zambeletti 153
Zogno:
  Grotta della Meraviglie 187
  Museo della Valle Brambana
    186–7
Zone 190

'Most literary critics seem to agree that the guides are divine.'

The Independent

'Anecdote and the lively conveying of personal experience are what elevate a guidebook to a friend, and Cadogan's writing duo have few equals. Their humour, sensitive discussion of Italian culture and brave attempt at unravelling the country's labyrinthine history, in my opinion, places the Cadogan Guide above its rivals.'

Weekend Telegraph

'The characteristic of all these guides is a heady mix of the eminently practical, a stimulating description of the potentially already familiar, and an astonishing quantity of things we'd never thought of, let alone seen.'

The Art Quarterly

'Whether you are traveling to this area for the cultural splendors, superb cuisine or natural wonders, this exciting encyclopaedic reference is the only one you will need to consult.'

US Travel and Leisure

'*Italy* by Dana Facaros and Michael Pauls is an absolute gem of a travel book, humorous, informed, sympathetic, as irresistible as that land itself.'

The Sunday Times

'Dana Facaros and Michael Pauls...give eminently knowledgeable advice... and are not afraid...to give due warning as well as recommendations.'

The Good Book Guide

'*Tuscany, Umbria & The Marches* deserves continuing recognition as an important independent traveler's "bible" to the area.'

The Midwest Book Review

'Irreverent, unblinkered and hard-eyed, and based on a series of 15 well thought-out walks, each minutely described, the book [*Rome*] throws the city into focus with nothing spared.'

Sunday Telegraph

The Cadogan Guides Series

Italy Guides by Dana Facaros and Michael Pauls

ITALY

ITALY: NORTHWEST ITALY

ITALY: NORTHEAST ITALY

ITALY: SOUTH ITALY

THE BAY OF NAPLES &
THE AMALFI COAST

SICILY

FLORENCE, SIENA, PISA & LUCCA

ROME

TUSCANY, UMBRIA & THE MARCHES

VENICE & THE VENETO

Other Titles

Country Guides

THE CARIBBEAN

CENTRAL AMERICA

CENTRAL ASIA

ECUADOR, THE GALAPAGOS &
COLOMBIA

EGYPT

FRANCE: THE SOUTH OF FRANCE

FRANCE: SOUTHWEST FRANCE;
Dordogne, Lot & Bordeaux

GERMANY

GERMANY: BAVARIA

GUATEMALA & BELIZE

INDIA

IRELAND

JAPAN

MEXICO

MOROCCO

PORTUGAL

SCOTLAND

SCOTLAND'S HIGHLANDS & ISLANDS

SOUTH AFRICA

SPAIN

SPAIN: SOUTHERN SPAIN

TUNISIA

TURKEY

TURKEY: WESTERN TURKEY

Island Guides

BALI

THE CARIBBEAN: THE LEEWARD
ISLANDS; From Antigua to the Virgin
Islands

THE CARIBBEAN: THE WINDWARD
ISLANDS; Barbados, Martinique,
Guadeloupe

CYPRUS

GREEK ISLANDS

GREECE: THE CYCLADES

GREECE: THE DODECANESE

GREECE: THE IONIAN ISLANDS

MALTA, COMINO & GOZO

City Guides

AMSTERDAM

BERLIN

BRUSSELS, BRUGES, GHENT &
ANTWERP

MOSCOW & ST PETERSBURG

NEW YORK

PARIS

PRAGUE